G000066041

Dance and the Philosophy of Action:
A Framework for the Aesthetics of Dance

Dance and the Philosophy of Action:
A Framework for the Aesthetics of Dance

Graham McFee

DANCE BOOKS

First published in 2018
by Dance Books Ltd.,
Southwold House,
Isington Road,
Binsted,
Hampshire
GU34 4PH

ISBN: 978-1-85273-178-6

© 2018 Graham McFee

A CIP catalogue record for this book is available from the British Library

Contents

Acknowledgements

My thanks to their original publishers and editors to include the following:

- some paragraphs from McFee, 2011 ("PAD") in Chapter One.
- McFee, 2015a Chapter Seven Appendix, in Chapter Three.
- "In Remembrance of Dance Lost", *Choros: International Journal of Dance.* XXX, 2012 — in Chapter Seven.
- "Defusing Dualism: John Martin on Dance Appreciation", *Journal of Aesthetics and Art Criticism* Vol. 71 No 2 Spring, 2013 pp. 187-194 — in Chapters Nine and Ten.
- Also, Chapter Eleven began as my contribution to a panel of the Pacific Division of the American Society for Aesthetics, Asilomar, CA in April 2017 — ill-heath prevented my presenting it.

Throughout, where I could not make the point better, I have recycled some paragraphs from other works of mine (especially PAD, EKT) here.

This work was a long time in the making; and therefore a number of debts accrued to those whose contributions improved the text. I would single out:

Renee Conroy, for comments on many of the ideas here, in particular those in Chapter Eleven (and, together with Julie Van Camp, for editorial help on the paper that became Chapters Nine and Ten);

Anna Pakes, for discussion of many topics and for trying to 'set me straight' on certain key examples;

David Davies, especially for discussions relating to what became Chapter Eleven;

Bill Seeley, for disagreeing with me about much of this, and always in a charming and well-informed manner;

Leon Culbertson, for discussion of many of the key themes here, going well beyond those places where I draw on shared work;

My wife Myrene, for all her support in difficult times, as well as help with proof-reading and with the index.

Preamble: Starting places in philosophy

§1.   Introduction: sloopless in Seattle?

Although this is primarily a text for those with a developed interest in dance, to offer an elaboration of some philosophical materials on which they might draw to augment their understanding (and so it really is a book on dance, despite appearance to the contrary), it also offers something both to the general aesthetician wishing to apply familiar concepts to a less-familiar subject matter and to philosophers of action who wonder how their concerns intersect with those of the philosophical aesthetics of dance.

Like many areas of philosophy *of X*, the philosophical aesthetics of dance faces twin dangers: focus closely on the X (here, art-type dance) and one may cease to be doing philosophy; but give too much attention to the philosophy, and the interest of the cases (here, their application to the 'real world' of dance) may become obscure. For me, this has often occurred in respect of discussions of, say, dance-ontology: we know enough about examples of dances performed, choreographed, and rehearsed to know what typical dances are *like*; and if no exceptionless account meeting those conditions for identity or continuity can be found in philosophy generally, so much the worse for such general discussions. For instance, I have used a type/token contrast to describe the relation of the abstract object that is the dance-work (say *Swan Lake*) and the concrete instantiation of that work that is tonight's performance (PAD pp. 56-65 [for abbreviations, see list below]; Chapter Five §2 below). But, to my mind, its inventor (C. S. Peirce) did not clarify the type/token contrast sufficiently for us to bring it, ready-to-hand, to the familiar facts concerning multiple artworks: such facts ground both the constraints on our descriptions and any putative counter-examples. Hence, if accommodating what we recognize from our acknowledged cases of seeing *the same dance* then requires that the purified 'type/token' contrast be modified (for instance, by referring to "norm-kinds" or to "indicated types": see Levinson, 2015 p. 51), that must be our strategy, for "... at the bar of reason, always the final appeal is to cases" (as John Wisdom [1965 p. 102] reminds us). The cases or examples come first, because typically our philosophical narrative is answerable to them. On the other hand, there is a danger in sticking too closely to the cases, and especially to what is said about them by those embroiled in them — I am thinking especially of dancers and dance-makers. One enters the philosophical aesthetics of dance to bring insights from philosophy to that arena: here, from philosophy of action in particular.

Then philosophy of action cannot be entirely separated from a consideration of *persons* (as agents); and hence from philosophy of mind. At the least, as Jennifer Hornsby (1997 p. 83) acknowledged, we *cannot* "... have a credible philosophy of action until it is freed from wrong assumptions imported from the philosophy of mind". Further, as Elizabeth Anscombe ([1958] 2005 p. 170) urged, philosophy of action and mind has a connection to *normativity* (and hence to morality) such that even moral philosophy requires "... an adequate philosophy of psychology". Moreover, that commitment to normativity is crucial to the understanding of persons as *meaning-making* agents — hence as art-makers.

Two particular features from that situation initially struck me as crucial for this text: first, that meeting the demands of philosophy here could be especially revealing about philosophy, since some concepts fundamental to the elaboration of an aesthetics of dance would also be needed to permit the doing of philosophy: for philosophy is practiced by *persons* (agents and meaning-makers), who therefore can manage *normativity* to generate *responsibility*. But these were notions also crucial for dance aesthetics. In recognizing dance as a performing art, the aesthetics of dance locates at least three central roles for persons: as *dance-maker* (choreographer?); as *dance-instantiator* (dancer); and as *dance-appreciator* (audience member). And these roles in turn involve deployment of just the range of concepts mentioned: agency, responsibility, normativity. Then a discussion informative about the aesthetics of dance might also ground discussion of these preconditions for philosophy.

Second, one brings an understanding of philosophy to the discussion of dance aesthetics: some of the required philosophy can be learned *en passant*, but one cannot hope to learn it all in that way. For one cannot know — in advance of drawing the connections — what elements from philosophy will be relevant. This fact came to my attention in this case when I recognized how some abstract discussion in some fairly technical writing in Quine might bear, through intervening contributions by J. L. Austin and Kripke, on problems concerning identity-conditions and identification-conditions for danceworks, to which I shall return (see below, and Chapter Two). For, as both David Best (1974 p. xi) and Paul Grice (1986 p. 64) remark, "... philosophy is one subject, a single discipline". But, like me, Grice (1986 p. 64) grants that "... I do not know *exactly* what the thesis is that I want to maintain; and I do not know how to prove it". Still, that thesis denies the fragmentation of philosophy. In exemplification, Grice (1986 p. 64) comments:

> ... when I visit an unfamiliar university and (as occasionally happens) I am introduced to, 'Mr. Puddle, our man in Political Philosophy' (or in 'Nineteenth-century Continental Philosophy' or 'Aesthetics', as the case may be), I am immediately confident that either Mr. Puddle is being under-described and in consequence maligned, or else Mr. Puddle is not really good at his stuff. Philosophy, like virtue, is *entire*. Or, one might even dare to say, there is only one problem in philosophy, namely all of them.

In spirit, this seems exactly right (as recognized elsewhere: McFee, 2015b p. 87).

Of course, one's work can *end up* being primarily in aesthetics, as perhaps mine is (to judge by my CV), or on the philosophy of Wittgenstein (to look into my heart). Yet one's concerns cannot be circumscribed in that way: one cannot care about *philosophy* if one cares only about this or that part of it. Hence most professional philosophers, throughout their careers, teach a variety of philosophical topics, for this is as close as one gets to involvement with Grice's "... all of them". Thus, those wishing to investigate the philosophical aesthetics of dance must engage with *more* philosophy than just that. This work is designed to facilitate such an engagement, both through its level and its structure.

Further, my starting point here is our commonsense view of *persons* and *agency*: some 'rational reconstruction' may be required, to accommodate insights from philosophy. But ultimately most explanations should reflect the situation as understood by thoughtful people. Thus, Hornsby (1997 p. 228 note 12) asks of the impact of a reinterpretation, "How can people's understanding of (say) 'ring', and their ability to make reference to rings, be accounted for in the terms that the reinterpretation uses?". In particular, how could one argue *for* this reinterpretation, given that it must meet the conditions set by the pre-reinterpretation utterance? And that asks about the *place* of philosophical insight.

Returning to the more specific example, when at the American Society for Aesthetics meeting in Seattle in 2016, and pondering the framework for debates about the character of identity — but also of identification — I recalled a helpful comment by Quine ([1956] 1966): lacking a yacht, he bemoaned his state of *slooplessness*. Yet, of course (as Kripke, 2011 p. 230 noted), this situation is ambiguous between the lack of a sloop (where any sloop would do) and the lack of a specific sloop (say, the sloop *John B*). Similarly, when I discuss a particular dance, I often hope to be characterizing it univocally, as *this* object: and hence to be making an identity-claim. But, again, sometimes such remarks are simply identificatory; and sometimes, although identifying the object, they may lack the consequence — provided if one accepts Leibniz's Law — that particular identificatory properties were true of that object: thus my house can be "that white dot", as Austin (1962 p. 98 note) recognized, without being predominantly white. So not all such remarks make identity-claims! I came to this acknowledgement through being sloopless in Seattle.

§2.   Dance as a performing art

What would this recognition of the need for cases located within a broader philosophical context mean here? Asked how typical artworks differ from objects they are typically thought to resemble — say, paintings and wall-decorations, or dances and gymnastic performances — that difference is often explained by invoking *meaning* (with an associated value): thus, the painting is valued differently from the wallpaper, in just this way. Further, typical performing arts enshrine the contrast between the artwork as *performable*, and the particular performance (say, last night, by such-and-such a company). Then obviously, in typical cases, characterizing a particular dance as a *performable* recognizes the possibility that *it* (that very same dance) be performed on another occasion and by another company — even when this does not happen in practice. But the need for *performances* here also draws a connection to *agency*.

Then (to repeat), recognizing dance as a performing art locates at least three central roles for persons in the aesthetics of dance: as *dance-maker* (choreographer?); as *dance-instantiator* (dancer) — although others may be involved in dance-instantiation; and as *dance-appreciator* (audience member). Further, this last role might be sub-divided to include another 'incarnation', as *dance-critic*, were this significantly different. Therefore some discussions in the aesthetics of dance might plausibly be thought *also* discussions of the nature of persons. That strategy is adopted here: its more specific focus on *the person* inflects the discussion slightly differently from that standardly deployed in aesthetics, while still giving due weight to the dance itself. (This is perhaps to employ *Ramsey's Maxim*, such that — finding an intractable disagreement in philosophy — one should experiment with denying theses *shared* by both disputants: see Chapter One §8.)

As a result, some concerns addressed here are issues for general philosophy having implications for the aesthetics of dance, rather than issues strictly in the philosophical aesthetics of dance directly, at least as I have typically engaged with it. Spending time on these other, framework issues means this text (while difficult) might be used to introduce philosophy to relative beginners. But, since it draws on concerns in dance aesthetics, it is also reasonably seen as contributing to that area.

Two issues, in particular, provide the focus here: (i) the relation of normativity in the arts to normativity in language; and (ii) the irrelevance of causal explanation to human action viewed as action; that is, viewed normatively. This second issue exploits a conclusion explicitly drawn by Frege ([1918] 1984 p. 351): that "[e]rror and superstition have causes just as much as correct cognition". Hence this text as a whole recognizes a limitation on typical causal explanation, since much of the human world becomes inexplicable without explanation of a kind importing normativity, one that involves treating the behaviour of people as sometimes the (intentional) action of agents. In particular, allowing *only* causal explanation of events (narrowly conceived) would render unintelligible the project of philosophy — on any account.

Moreover, the interrelation of these notions (*person, meaning, action, normativity*) remains crucial here. Thus, asked, "What is missing in the cases where there is no genuine meaning?" our typical answers might stress:

- that the case lacked the *intention* to communicate;
- that it resulted from the working-out of natural, causal forces — and hence was not an example of *agency* or *action*;
- that it was not structured *normatively*.

These three explanations come together: the working out of causal forces must be contrasted with the normativity of intentional explanation for humans (see §5 below). Indeed, explanations importing normativity are best understood by contrast with those, like causal explanation: causes may be more or less effective, but cannot be better or worse — if a drop in temperature would cause a rainstorm, there either was or was not such a drop, and hence there was or was not a corresponding rainstorm. But there is no 'better or worse' here. There will also be such causal stories for a move in chess or a remark in a language: but explanations of chess, like meaningful remarks in language, import normativity — thus, the chess move can also be good or bad in that context; moreover, one might *think* a move good but be mistaken. Similarly, one's remark can misfire: for instance, the Queen's ability to name ships is not based solely on her ability to utter certain words — my uttering those words would not have the same effect. Notice too that recognizing the normativity in these cases does not relate to finding, say, what people usually do or say: so, not *norms of behaviour*. Thus, for example, a name chiselled into a wall might be mis-spelled: were these cracks from earthquake damage, no *mis*-spelling is possible, because that would attribute just the normativity this example lacks — the name is not *spelled* at all, so it can no more be spelled *wrong* than it can be spelled *right*. Such cases also highlight an aspect of agency in respect of *meaning* here: that if I utter such-and-such, and do not then excuse or attenuate what was said, then that *is* what I said — and hence what I *meant*. For we *must* mean what we say, as Stanley Cavell (1969/2002 pp. 29-31) rightly urges. That obligation has two dimensions: that what one says *is* what one means (other things being equal) just because it is what one *says*; and that one *should* mean what one says, with the major alternatives being either lying or failing to take the interchange sufficiently seriously. Further, these two aspects of 'meaning what one says' come together here. In action as in utterance, once what I 'said' is granted, then I *meant* whatever it implies, on pain of failure to meet the conditions for asserting such-and-such, either through lack of seriousness or through some distinctly moral failing, such as lying. In effect, we are recognizing what *action* was performed (even if by speech), and requiring that the agent accept *responsibility* for it.

§3.   Elaboration

This enquiry begins at the confluence of three or four factors that mark out human beings, or so it seems to me — that we are *agents* (and therefore potentially *responsible* for our actions); that we have *language*, in which we can rightly both claim such responsibility or offer excuses; that there is a *normativity* possible for our actions, such that we can do, or fail to do, 'the right thing', at least on some occasions. So my thoughts on persons, the mind, and danceworks (three interrelated phenomena that have interested me for some time) are brought together to shed light on the last of them, the philosophical aesthetics of dance. Since, as Drid Williams (2004 p. 3) notes, "[d]ancing is only one of many forms of human structured systems of action ...", these phenomena coalesce around a concern with the nature of human action. For:

> ... until we understand how movement and actions are utilized in their more complex and conscious manifestations, we are going to understand very little about the subject of movement in general. (Williams, 2004 p. 3)

And, there, the philosophy of action must be one key to unlock dancing. Further, given that we are capable of making *meaning* — crucial for language, and requiring *normativity* — we are also capable of making *art*. Hence recognizing the interrelation of these concepts can be especially clarifying for the artform of dance. So, here, I typically focus on *danceworks* that are art, combining my interest in persons and action with my concern for art. (Despite a similar focus, this *specific* justification has been lacking in previous works: UD, PAD, as well as various papers — see Bibliography.)

However, these very interconnections create a difficulty for this text. Each of our crucial ideas warrants its own exposition as well as being seen alongside the other crucial ideas, before then being appropriated for the discussion of dance. How can one recognize the interconnections and yet offer reasonable clarity on each topic, without undue repetition? Further, the intention was always to apply these ideas to dance, but that application becomes clearer if they are first elaborated without that application. As Thomas Nagel (1995 p. 3) said of a work of his, although many areas thought fundamental to philosophy are not covered in this work, "... it all belongs to the common universe of argument that defines analytic philosophy: these subjects and the methods used in treating them cannot be isolated from one another". Or so it seems to me. But how is that to be presented?

One option set aside here was writing the 'great big fat book' that attempts to meet as many of the objections as one can. Such a project inevitably contains too much that is included 'for the sake of completeness': that is, to address some arcane objection. Some professional philosophers may require this, but few others. Could a strategy target first the needs of a more general reader?

Well, this text is long enough. But, to respond structurally to this challenge, many chapters here are broadly independent discussions of loosely associated topics, each designed — as far as is consistent with literary practice — as brief, stand-alone treatments of distinct issues, aimed at those with an interest in philosophy but not necessarily a developed knowledge of it (although extensive cross-reference, both internal and to other writings, may facilitate the text's use in teaching). So, although always envisaged as a single text, this work still rewards a piece-meal reading. Perhaps the intentions in respect of both pitch and distinctness are not always fully achieved: for instance, parts of Chapter One remain more complex than one would hope of an early chapter, and Part One is less clearly focused on dance than one would like (indeed, those chiefly interested in dance might skim-read it, returning to elaborate issues as they are raised later in the text). Further, repetitions are not minimized sufficiently in general (some repetition is essential to permit discussions to be relatively self-contained). Still, even partial success here leaves the earlier segments of the book well-suited as introductory for discussions of dance in Parts Two and Three, by presenting to my colleagues clear expositions on difficult topics, without 'dumbing down'. Further, the wide range of citation generates an extensive bibliography of relevant material, with my own work also cross-referenced in the text.

The most sustained philosophical work on dance in the book occurs in Part Three. Thus, the intellectual framework the work provides reminds us of certain features fundamental to the character of philosophy, at least as I conceive it. Hence Part One is, in a certain sense, primarily a set of preliminaries to Parts Two and Three, many ideas being sketched only insofar as to meet later needs — although each discussion from those chapters should be interesting in its own right. Then, by taking seriously those ideas about persons and agency, Parts Two and Three sketch the account of dance here. Part Three also exemplifies in more detail than elsewhere one way in which philosophical positions are delineated and elaborated: namely, through criticism of others, and through responding to criticism. In this way, it exemplifies more fully the nuanced practice of philosophical debate. And, because philosophical questions are shown arising in that context too, the outcome is to discuss *in context* (namely, in the context of the aesthetics of dance) some issues identified by the philosophical literature — in line with my general contextualist concerns (see below §4). And, again, a rich if focused range of reference (with substantial cross-reference) offers readers the opportunity to expand or to substantiate what is here.

Further, our oft-repeated motto from Frege (1984 p. 351) — that "[e]rror and superstition have causes just as much as correct cognition" — warns against appeal to causal explanation of human behaviour of the kinds behind most of the mistakes identified throughout this work: the confusion of minds with brains or the introduction of causal stories for artistic appreciation; and, of course, many trends compound these errors. Thus, if looking for explanations of emotions by brain-states is somehow misguided as a task of philosophy, it will be equally misguided to then attempt to cash-out the appreciation of art, and especially dance, in such terms. No doubt dance has a very specific relationship to the body, in contrast with most other artforms — roughly, the dancers' bodies *instantiate* the dance; and typically do so in the absence of the words arguably central to drama or opera. But, insofar as dance is an artform, the perspective crucial to the appreciation of dance is necessarily that of the audience — as it is for all other arts! Yet, under the spell of the mistaken picture that takes us to have a unique privileged access to the position of our limbs, dancers may be imagined to have an access to the dance denied to others; and, since that access seems located somehow in the brains and central nervous systems of those dancers, its interrogation may require fMRI! As I argue in what follows, this picture is both pervasive and pernicious: a certain privileged position is open to the dancer, but as a product of the human forces 'around' the dancer, and in particular those typically developed through training. One necessarily looks away from such human matters if one becomes mesmerized by either the apparent power of the gadgetry or the amount of cash that seems available to pursue such inherently pointless studies: *pointless* precisely because they treat as causal what is necessarily normative (or human).

An important argument-style aligned with this concern throughout deploys an idea introduced into philosophy by Arthur Danto (1981 p. 1) in the context of artworks: that of *confusable counterparts* — that if one cannot distinguish two cases in terms of some feature (say, 'how they look'), yet recognizes them as *two cases*, their difference cannot lie in that feature. Thus, if two paintings, agreed to differ (say, in meaning), are indistinguishable in terms of 'how they look' (at least, at first glance), the difference between them cannot reside in how they look. (A fuller version appears in Chapter One §4.) Similarly, if one causal 'narrative' applies to two chess moves, normatively distinct (one good, the other bad), what distinguishes them cannot be that causal 'narrative'. Yet the opposite is assumed (mistakenly) when causal explanations of human events are offered as the final explanation. So a version of this argument highlights Frege's point (above).

Thus, despite this work having a critical or negative edge of that kind, its purpose is not wholly critical. It offers insights into some argument-forms. Moreover, in line with my view of the importance of Wittgenstein's later philosophy (see McFee, 2015a), the aim is to free us from those *pictures* that hold us captive (PI §115), where *one* way to understand the achievement might stress the absence of such pictures (or the freedom from misleading pictures). Further, locating confusion here focuses especially on unwarranted assumptions of exceptionlessness. And may not be simple. For, as Wittgenstein (PR §2 [p. 52]) points out, to untie complicated knots, one must make complicated movements with one's hands — although the desired outcome might seem simple: no knots!

§4. Thinking about philosophy

Central to this work is its philosophical character; or, if that is different, its perspective on philosophy. That perspective, pervasive throughout this text, grants a contextualism about meaning and understanding: that is, adherence to what Charles Travis (2008 esp. pp. 150–160) calls "occasion-sensitivity" (see also Chapter One §7). This idea works against the assumption of a greater determinacy than is possible: in particular, as Wittgenstein saw, against an ideal clarity only realized in some distant future (but with no sense possible of how or when). For such 'clarity' represents the entry "... into philosophy [of] a false exactitude that is the worst enemy of real exactitude" (BT p. 396). Wittgenstein rightly took this conception of exactitude as "... the sign of a totally false view" (BT p. 203). Instead, one must recognize "... the unsurveyable seething totality of our language" (VoW p. 67). Then "... what confuses us is the uniform appearance of words when we hear them in speech or see them in print. For their use is not that obvious" (PI [2009] §11): indeed, the diversity of uses reflects occasion-sensitivity. Yet, first, with the context of the utterance specified there *are*, or are usually, correct answers to questions about what is said and meant; and, second, without that specificity, no such answer is forthcoming.

Our general philosophical commitment to *occasion-sensitivity* precludes expecting a single answer (applicable everywhere) to questions of, say, the dancer's responsibilities. In particular, we should note that principles need not operate exceptionlessly (so there is no "all", no finite totality of cases or considerations); and that one cannot look for completeness here, since one cannot ensure that additional points might not arise. Such ideas flow from our contextualism, and apply most powerfully on our return to discussion of the scientism that I dread in dance-studies.

Some of the scientistic claims offered in connection with dance, especially those rooted in neuroscience, with its assumption of a complete account of events, must be contrasted with the kinds of humanistic understanding of human behaviour that follow from treating all those concerned — choreographer, dancer, audience-member — as *people*, able to recognize, to discern, and to discuss. And such scientific accounts, for dance as elsewhere, seem on the rise in philosophy. Dance-criticism as described by (and typically present in) the writings of John Martin — arguably the first critic devoted to modern dance — requires informed and sensitive perception of the kind that marks us out from creatures whose reception of the causal input (say, through perception) is at least as fine-grained as our own. In elaboration, Chapter Nine contains much of a paper on Martin (McFee, 2013) written for a special issue of the *Journal of Aesthetics and Art Criticism* (JAAC).

Related material also began life with an invitation to present to Coventry University Centre for Dance Research, in June 2013, the resulting paper being entitled "To dance is scientific: Humanistic understanding in dance studies and dance appreciation". Elaborating that discussion in Chapters Nine and Ten below builds on my responses to the contributions to that previously-mentioned special issue on dance for JAAC. When this special issue was proposed, I understood that its focus was John Martin's dance criticism (as above): certainly the context suggested concentration on the relation of Martin's practice as critic to the scientific discussion and explanation of dance. So I was surprised by the degree to which my co-symposiasts there focused on *scientism* in dance theory, especially that flowing from concerns in cognitive science. Despite mentioning the scope of scientific understanding, my contribution to that special issue lacked such a focus, since a great deal of my criticism of scientism of this kind was already included in PAD. I was equally surprised (although typically pleasantly) by the degree to which the others set out to critique ideas of mine (typically those of PAD — insofar as they attach to anything I had actually written). I saw some of those papers prior to publication, but had neither the time nor the energy to craft the response they deserved: some of that is attempted here. In summary, many of those criticisms highlight cases that I happily acknowledge, disputing only the centrality their authors implied: that is, they exemplify just that failure of *exceptionlessness* that I had elaborated. Of course, since some involved misunderstanding (for one, misreading) of what I argued, some of those *arguments* recur here, to suggest that — from my perspective, at least — rejecting a *conclusion* requires finding some reason to reject either the argument for that conclusion or its claim to be a conclusion.

Therefore, Part Three also gives considerable attention, chiefly of a negative sort, to the fruitlessness of attempting to understand dance by reference to empirical work in neuroscience (especially in Chapter Ten). This reflects long-held commitments of mine, partly in opposition to various kinds of scientism about human understanding — say, of the spatial locations of our body parts (perhaps via a spurious "kinaesthetic sense"); or to an overvaluing of the dancers' perspective, to create a "dancer's aesthetic"; and especially, in its modern form, to attempt to explain the (humanistic) appreciation of the arts via the toys of the neuroscientist (fMRI, in particular). Frege's argument, cited above, convinces me that determining the causal 'story' of some event — even some dance-event — cannot automatically offer insight into its normative complexity. And, recognizing the relation of art-making in general (dance-making in particular) to *meaning*, I would reiterate the objection to a strategy Michael Dummett (1993 p. 187) dismisses as "an outright mistake"; namely, treating the philosophy of thought as amounting to reflection on neuroscience:

> If this means a theory ... according to which a theory of meaning is really a theory of something very complicated that goes on in the brain, I think that is a completely unphilosophical way of looking at the matter. Philosophy is not concerned with what *enables* us to speak as we do, but what it is for our utterances to have the meanings that that have, and nothing that happens in the brain can explain that. (Dummett, 1993 pp. 187-188)

I do not in general agree with Dummett on 'theory of meaning'; but he is right that "[i]t is essential to treat language as a conscious activity of rational creatures" (Dummett, 1993 p. 188); and about the specifics of *meaning* here, especially as it applies to understanding artistic meaning. Further, the error he is rightly diagnosing treats philosophic concerns in terms of causal structures.

§5. Philosophy again!

These points come together when one reflects further on the nature of the philosophical enterprise. For misunderstanding what philosophy requires — easily done — can involve abandoning the project of philosophy. As Nagel (1995 p. p. 6) noted:

> [w]ithout a strong grasp of the uniquely philosophical problems, it is easy to fall prey to scientism, the idea that any *genuine* question can be handled as part of the development of a scientific worldview, and that what can't be, isn't a real question. (my emphasis)

(Opposing such scientism is a major target, as noted above.) But the project of philosophy — what makes problems *philosophical* problems — is hard to explain: here, the intention is to show the reader philosophical issues or questions in this arena so that he/she begins to recognize them when they crop up elsewhere. Further, the structure of philosophical argument should also become clearer once seen in worked-through cases here; this might illustrate why philosophical texts are usually best read through from the beginning. Responding may involving making up one's own examples or cases; and following the argument will mean explaining any omissions — one cannot simply focus on those elements one notices. For unless one recognizes that a primary method in philosophy is presenting and commenting-on *arguments*, one may miss the conceptual character of philosophy's central project.

But what does that project require of us? No doubt the fuller answer will be very complex (and I doubt there could be a *complete* answer). But a useful initial sketch deploys Dummett's recognition that, if philosophy had a 'partner' in the academy, it would probably be mathematics. The history of universities has typically located mathematics with the natural sciences. Yet, as Dummett (2010 p. 3) remarks of mathematics, "... however useful it may be to the sciences, in its intrinsic nature it is something very different from them". Why? Because, like philosophy, mathematics is primarily a conceptual enquiry: "[m]athematics ... needs no input from experience: it is the product of thought alone" (Dummett, 2010 p. 4). This is why there are "... no mathematical observations, no mathematical predictions the falsification of which will overturn a mathematical theory" (Dummett, 2010 p. 3). Hence "... the experimental method came to be seen as marking a radical difference between one mode of theoretical enquiry and another" (Dummett, 2010 p. 3). This point applies as clearly when differentiating philosophy from (natural) science — Dummett's target — as when making sense of mathematics. Further:

> ... mathematics shares with philosophy a difficulty in saying what it is *about*. Mathematicians do not concern themselves to find any general answer to this question: it is for philosophers to say not only what, in general, philosophy is about, but also what, in general mathematics is about. (Dummett, 2010 p. 5)

This may not help with an answer, but the question recognizes that philosophy is not an empirical discipline. Even those philosophers most impressed by science as a model for philosophy (Quine was one: see Chapter Eight §5) did not imagine philosophy making observations or conducting experiments of its own: at best, philosophy should "... incorporate the discoveries of the sciences to build a naturalized theory of knowledge and of the mind" (Dummett, 2010 p. 7). With Dummett, I would also reject the second part of this account of the project of science, arguing from our oft-quoted remark of Frege that causal concerns (characteristic of science) must be separated from the normative concerns generated by humans, and studied by much of philosophy.

An episode of television's *The Big Bang Theory* ("The Zazzy Substitution" [Season 4, Episode 3], first broadcast 2010) neatly exemplifies the problem: the physicist (Sheldon) says, surely rightly, that a 'theory of everything' as produced in physics would cover ... well, everything; and, in particular, the results of his colleague's neuroscientific experiments. The neuroscientist (Amy) replies that, since her results apply to all products of the human brain, they encompass his theories, like any others:

> "My colleagues and I are mapping the neurological substrates that subserve global information processing, which is required for all cognitive reasoning, including scientific enquiry, making my research ipso facto prior in the *ordo cognoscendi*."

Their mistakes here, of course, reside in each assuming models of explanatory completeness drawn from causality in natural science; and hence searching for a spurious *priority* to the version drawing on the concerns of his/her preferred science. Each misses the *erotetic* character of research, and hence of scientific research: that its claims function as the answers to particular questions. Thus, as might be expected, the physicist's responses address or answer questions raised by physics!

Most importantly, I see no possibility of a *philosophy* that made its own observations, or conducted its own experiments: in part, the reason lies in the character of our concern with language — for philosophy is not typically concerned with what people *do* say, but with what they *should*. To understand what people *do* say, even in respect of some normative matter such as morality, might at best count as the sociology of moral life. Yet projects of that sort *are* conducted, under the title 'empirical philosophy'. For instance, broadly empirical methods are used to investigate whether a meta-ethical commitment to kinds of moral realism might alter both one's moral judgements and one's degree of commitment to them (for instance, Young & Durwin, 2013; Goodwin & Darley, 2008). These are investigations of what people *think* or *believe*, including the impact on their degree of conviction, such that "... priming a belief in moral realism improved moral behavior" (Abstract to Young & Durwin, 2013). While perhaps legitimate as sociology, could it have a place in philosophy? If 'most people' agreed on a certain mathematical result, that alone would not make it right. And my concern in philosophy is only with what one *ought* to think (that is, with the truth) — and that *is* what others too ought to think, since the alternative is being deceived or deluded (as, say, in the case of the Yeti, if there are no Yetis). After all, if (say) moral realism is false, any 'believers' have found a new way to delude themselves — or others.

One of the mentioned papers explicitly considers whether I would behave *better* if I accepted moral realism, and draws on survey results to conclude that I would indeed then behave better — that most people do. If correct, this offers a practical reason (resembling Plato's myth of the metals) to trick people into being moral realists. But if moral realism is true, no trick is needed: people should be moral realists (in the correct version) *because* moral realism is true; and not if it is not. That people might behave better if misguided cannot have a bearing. Indeed, I am also unhappy about the way their 'result' is arrived at: truth is too important to knowingly permit delusion. (Perhaps this is an issue with, say, religious belief: grant for a moment that the claims of religion are false, and then it cannot matter if believing them helped one live better or behave better. And if these claims *are* true, that cannot be *because* the beliefs helped one live better — assuming they did!)

Roughly, the study of those patterns of commitment (call it "belief" if you like) that people *do* adopt is a topic for sociology: discerning that, in such-and-such a region, 42% of people think there is a Yeti, we then look at the origins of such a belief. This is, of course, a perfectly legitimate area of study; and could be conducted for truths rather than (as here) falsehoods. Yet that case is more complicated only because, then, the fact that an assertion reflects the truth offers one a good *reason* to believe it.

Here, a concern with the conceptual (in philosophy) contrasts with such a concern with people's *views* or their *practice*: yes, they do say such-and-such ... but are they right so to do? Philosophy should not be turned into a game of *Family Feud* (USA)/*Family Fortunes* (UK) by trying to match our answer to what 'most people' think. To decide on the rightness of their claims, one must address what precisely they say (looking at its implications, and such like), not merely reiterate their words. So asked, 'Why do people say this?', my answer has been, 'because they think it true'. And *only* that answer offers a rational *justification* here — at best, false beliefs offer explanations of *why* they are believed: that is, of how believers *became* deluded. Further, if views *are* false, one explanation for our interest in them disappears.

Moreover, one cannot realistically urge that there is no *truth* here: that, for instance, The Truth must be independent of human conceptualizations. Such an absolutist conception of truth misses our starting point in the practices of agents. Faced with my claim to have forty dollars in my bank account, one cannot just object that money is a human invention — rather, there is a uncontentious truth of the matter here, whether we know it. And such claims can to fail to be true *only* by being false: that is, on the scale of *possible* truth. Truths need be no more profound than this.

So there are, as it were, two 'levels' of objection to the mistake of importing causal explanation into philosophy. Then philosophical investigation into the centrality of *normativity* is required to combat the error of imagining that the causal story of my behaviour precludes my being responsible for my actions. By contrast, imagining that survey results could *answer* philosophical questions (as opposed to merely *posing* them) involves *giving up* on philosophy as I recognize it, as a conceptual enquiry.

Abbreviations for references, used throughout

(a) Standard Abbreviations for works of Ludwig Wittgenstein
PI — Wittgenstein, 1953/2009
BB — Wittgenstein, 1958
Z — Wittgenstein, 1967
OC — Wittgenstein, 1969
PG— Wittgenstein, 1974
PR— Wittgenstein, 1975
WWK — Wittgenstein, 1979
CV — Wittgenstein, 1980/1988
PO — Wittgenstein, 1993
VoW — Wittgenstein, 2003
BT — Wittgenstein, 2005
PPF — Previously PI part Two; new name in PI, 2009
[References to the unpublished 'Legacy' (or *Nachlass*) use the listing from PO pp. 480-510.]

(b) Abbreviations for works of Graham McFee
UD — McFee, 1992
FW — McFee, 2000
EKT — McFee, 2010b
PAD — McFee, 2011a
AJ — McFee, 2011b

Chapter One

Action, language, and persons in dance-aesthetics

§1. Introduction

One of the hardest questions for philosophy is, roughly, "What can justifiably be taken for granted?" or "What can one use as a starting place?". For, as Wittgenstein (OC §471) put it, " ... it is difficult to begin at the beginning. And not try to go further back". Moreover, the attentive, at least, will recognize this issue in Descartes: that his project in his *Meditations* concerned "what can be *called* into doubt" (CSM II p. 17: my emphasis), rather than simply to doubt everything. So his starting place is what *cannot* be "*called* into doubt". Those of his critics who note (correctly) that Descartes did not doubt the power of reason, or logic, are just making *his* point — these cannot be *called* into doubt, since doing so requires reasons for doubting; and hence presupposes the power of reason.

A similar strategy might realistically be adopted here: what, if one denied it, would make nonsense of any project in philosophy? My three-fold answer to that question stresses the possibility of our engaging with the world, in an attempt to understand some aspect of it (here the aesthetics of art-type dance). At its heart, this answer recognizes *agency*: that there are *actions* in the world — the actions required to do philosophy. Or, to put that another way, some events in the world must be explained in ways emphasizing a *normativity*; hence they cannot be explained purely causally. But which events are these? For me, it is fundamental that these events are genuinely meaning-bearing — with linguistic events the most obvious exemplars. Thus, the wall cracked by the earthquake is not a message for my beloved, even if it seems to be spelling her name: it cannot be! And not everything that sounds like language (linguistic utterance) *is*; and for a similar reason. In recognizing some sound-sequence as an utterance in a language, one grants both that (at least typically) *something* is being said, and that this utterance might *fail* to be saying that: that is, utterances in a language import *normativity*. Many examples suggest this point: in chess, for example, moves exploiting the rules of the game should be distinguished from regularities in the movements of pieces, the kinds of regularity that might be captured causally. Many legal moves are not made because they are obviously bad; and yet other moves that would in fact be good are overlooked — either by these players or by players more generally. For rule-following provides a normativity (here) that those regularities do not display: they cannot describe (nor attempt to describe) what one *should* do in these circumstances, but only the working out of causal forces — as one predicts the weather.

Similarly, sequences of sounds are not automatically words or sentences; and the sounds made by tape-recorders or parrots are not, by themselves, genuine linguistic interventions unless they exhibit the possibility of being *misused*, or used *incorrectly*. Thus, the tape-recorded words used by Arnold Schwarzenegger's character in the film *True Lies* (1994) are only appropriate to the context, at least mostly, because he previously selected them for the purpose (when having the tape made); and even then this goes wrong in one place — the distance between the tape-recording and a genuine utterance is apparent. Moreover, if captured by Italians during the Second World War (to use an example from Searle, 1969 pp. 44-45), I may hope for release by convincing them I am German; and doing so by uttering — in my most 'master-race' accent — the one piece of German I know. When, as is likely, that turns out to be words from a Marlene Dietrich song, I will have said that I am head-over-heels in love with my captors (translated), even though they do not take that from my utterance. For when addressing language-based expression, the issue is not how a term *is* used, but how it *should be* used (how it is used *when used correctly*). To see this, one need only consider a word regularly *misused*. No doubt the term "refute" is often used (say, by journalists) as though it meant nothing more than *reject*; hence that some claim could be refuted merely by saying that one had done so, rather than providing an actual refutation. As Ossie Hanfling (2000 p. 70) puts it:

> ... if the word 'refute' came in due course to mean nothing more than 'reject', it would not mean that to refute a proposition would have become easier than it is now.

For, of course, what one *then* did would not be what *now* counts as a refutation. So, for philosophical purposes, not everything that 'we ordinarily say' should be tolerated: we sometimes speak unacceptably loosely. But one must discover which utterances to dispute in this way, by looking at what follows from them: that is why I can 'say what I choose' (PI §79) here, as long as I respect the distinctions thereby drawn.

For, of course, my intention is not to regulate what people do say. Rather, as Philippa Foot (2001 p. 49 note) puts it:

> I am not wanting to run an everyday expression out of town: only to give it its proper place in the whole of a conceptual scheme. As an architect must distinguish a pillar that merely holds up an internal arch from one that is weight-bearing in relation to the building itself, so a philosopher must be careful not to exaggerate the structural importance of some common form of words.

For philosophical purposes, though, that may involve some 'rational reconstruction' of what is said, so that tendencies towards (say) misplaced dualism are neither suggested nor encouraged.

Further, these linguistic (or language-using) practices are regulated by what Hanfling (2000 p. 54) calls their *participatory* character: because we join together in speaking the language, "... each participant is constantly kept on the rails by sanctions coming from the others" (Hanfling, 2000 p. 54). Of course, granting this recognizes again *persons* acting as *agents* — that is, normatively. Moreover, the 'rails' mentioned above operate contextually here: one only insists on a level of accuracy *appropriate* for this question or topic, rather than imagining some abstract level of perfect or complete accuracy. Hence, the normativity of language-use (that is, of meaning) connects with the normativity implicit in recognizing the actions of persons. Moreover, the normativity required for meaningful language-use is precisely that required for the possibility of moral judgement. As Cavell (1969/2002 pp. 29-31) rightly urges, we *must* mean what we say: recognizing that obligation has two related dimensions — that what one says *is* what one means (other things being equal) just because it is what one *says*; and that one *should* mean what one says, since the major alternatives are either lying or failing to take the interchange sufficiently seriously.

Drawing explicitly on the contention that "[e]rror and superstition have causes just as much as correct cognition" (Frege, [1918] 1984 p. 351) might have led directly to our recognizing a limitation on causal explanation: that much of the human world becomes inexplicable without the kind of explanation that imports normativity. Then the behaviour of people must often be treated as the (intentional) action of agents. In particular, the project of philosophy — on any account — fails to be intelligible if *only* causal explanation of events is permitted.

§2.   Meaning, intending and acting

The key fact here is the interrelation of these notions (*person, action, meaning*). Thus, to repeat from "Preamble", asked what is missing in cases where there is not genuine meaning, one might reply:

- that the case lacked the *intention* to communicate;

- that it resulted from the working-out of natural, causal forces — and hence was not an example of *agency* or *action*;

- that it was not structured *normatively*.

These three explanations come together: the working out of causal forces must be contrasted with the normativity of intentional explanation for humans. Hence, when thinking about meaning, cases where some intention to mean is operative (like meaning in language) must be distinguished from other, similar-ish cases. Thus, David Best (1978 pp. 139-140) rightly contrasted my catching your eye at some boring departmental meeting, and extravagantly yawning, with the case where — bored at the meeting — I am unable to stifle the yawn. For these yawns are importantly different: the first is intentional in a way that the second is not; in the first, I *mean* something (and, ideally, you understand it) while, in the second case, my departmental head might have learned how boring I found the meeting — the very last thing I wanted! That yawn did not really *mean* anything, even though someone (my department head!) might learn something about me from it. In a similar case, above, the cracks in the wall may seem to spell out the name of my loved one. But, insofar as they are genuinely cracks in the wall (caused by earthquake or subsidence, say, rather than chiselled), they do not spell out her name: they *could* not since, lacking the relevant intention, they are not candidates for meaning-bearing of the right sort. And that despite the fact that someone might urge that the cracks *did* mean something: say, that another earthquake was due. For that is precisely to use the term "mean" as a synonym for, say, "indicate"; where what is indicated here is the kind of causal explanation that precludes genuine meaning. (These cases were used on PAD p. 130; p. 190.)

Of course, the connection to normativity is also clear. As we noted previously, the name chiselled into the wall, for example, might have been misspelled: in our case, where the cracks reflect earthquake damage, there cannot be *mis*spelling, because that attributes to the example just the normativity it lacks — since the name is not *spelled* at all, it can no more be spelled *wrong* than it can be spelled *right*. Such cases also highlight the other aspect of agency in respect of *meaning* here: that if I say such-and-such, and do not go on to excuse or attenuate what was said, then that *is* what I said — and hence what I *meant*. As noted above, the two aspects of 'meaning what one says' come together here. For once I recognize that this is what I said, then I *meant* whatever it implies: my alternatives are to have failed to meet the conditions for assertion of such-and-such, either through lack of seriousness or through some distinctly moral failing, such as lying. In effect, in discussing how to characterize the behaviour accurately, we recognize what *action* was performed; and require that the agent accept *responsibility* for it. These options are obvious when we criticize the person for saying something he or she was not committed to — one line of excuse would be accepting frivolity ('it was just a joke'), while the other amounts to confessing ('it was a lie' — perhaps with the partial mitigation of '... a white lie'). Perhaps, like Euripides's Hippolytus (see Austin, 1975 pp. 9-10), one can say that " ... 'my tongue swore to, but my heart (or mind or other backstage artist) did not' ...". But, as Austin (1975 p. 10) continues, doing so "... puts on record my spiritual assumption of a spiritual shackle". Moreover, the places where our word is our bond (say, in various kinds of promising or oath-giving) build on precisely this aspect of our responsibility for our actions, but now recognizing the actions as linguistic. Further, the cases under consideration do not require some complex speech-act theory to deliver these results: for asserting is the simplest of cases here, followed by promising. Then our special concern here is with the actions that constitute art-type dances; and our understanding of them.

§3.   Thinking about art

Having laid out my view of dance-aesthetics with some care in PAD (prefigured in UD), the arguments are not generally repeated here. As a starting point, though, the variety of kinds of art include at least:

1. Particular object artworks — paintings, cut-sculpture: if you are not in *that* place, you cannot see *that* thing.

2. Multiple artworks (of at least three sorts):

   • particular-object-type multiples (cast sculptures, prints);

   • performing arts (maintaining the distinction between performer and work, even if performed by the maker);

   • literature, film.

Danceworks, our primary interest here, are typically works of performing art: these contrast revealingly with other cases within the class of multiple artworks. Thus films, while multiples, are not *performing* arts (there is no performance/work contrast); but what should we make of the recording of music? Literary works are multiples too, although we read them — and "read" is a peculiar verb of perception. Moreover, the poem can be read aloud, and still be *that* poem. (Other complications — set aside here — include translations, and our making sense of, for instance, literary works in languages other than our own.)

Similarly, the distinctive place of dance among performing arts explains why the philosophical aesthetics of dance-the-artform perhaps differs from other areas of philosophical aesthetics.[1] Like other performing arts, typical artworks (here, danceworks) are *performables*: that is, the very same dance can be re-performed on another occasion, despite the inevitable differences between such performances; and despite the dances themselves being concrete only at the "perpetual vanishing point" (Siegel, 1972 p. 1) of such performances. So the central ontology (ugh!) is of *danceworks* viewed as *performables*. But, for me, *dancerly* or *artistic* matters have priority over the claims of the very abstract metaphysics of abstract objects such as types (see Chapter Five §5). And this emphasis on beginning from dance *practice* is crucial to my methodological commitments. As we will see, the precise role of *the dancer* makes a big part of the difference, consonant with another theme in this work: namely, stressing the normative capacities of persons, capacities operative both in making dances and in making sense of dance.

But a distinctiveness to the artform of dance resides in its drawing more concretely on the specific physicality of the performers in two ways, as compared with other performing arts. First, dancers differ here from musicians. For musicians *make* or *cause* the sounds that instantiate the musical work: they bring about "... those things ... of which the witnessable work consists" (Urmson, 1976 p. 243). By contrast, in typical cases dancers *are* the dance — their movements instantiate the artwork, rather than merely *causing* it.

Then, second, dancers also differ from typical practitioners in other performing arts, such as theatre and opera, which have commonalities: perhaps "[o]pera is ... *drama per musica*" (Sharpe, 1983 p. 26), despite the stress Jim Hamilton (2007 pp. 58-59) rightly places on the variety within what might, in everyday speech, be called *acting*. Both opera and theatre should recognize the place of language, or language-like understanding — both typically involve language (which must therefore be given a role in their artistic meaning). Further, in those other arts, the typical behaviour of practitioners is in certain ways similar to the rest of human life: words are involved. (On the idea that our everyday lives are circumscribed by talk, see EKT pp. 49-52.) Hence the movements of those practitioners can be understood in relation to those words, as with everyday conversations. If the relationship is not always complimentary, that too is an everyday experience: people's postures and gestures can conflict with their utterances. For dance, though, that meaning or intending is centrally bodily: that begins to distinguish danceworks from performance involving *linguistic* meaning ... setting aside, of course, any critical commentary they develop. And that is problematic for those seeking to make understanding dance more like understanding the linguistic. Certainly, something distinctive should be said about dancework-*meaning* (AJ pp. 54-55).

Further, in practice, danceworks have additional connections to the *specific* bodies of specific dancers. For many dances today are made on the bodies of particular dancers, with particular skills and mastery (to whatever degree) of particular techniques; that fact has *some* bearing here — although perhaps less that is sometimes imagined, since those danceworks (being performables) could *in principle* be performed by different dancers.

Moreover, it is a commonplace that dance performances are, in some sense, ephemeral, only available to us as we watch them: that they "... exist at a perpetual vanishing point" (Siegel, 1972 p. 1). Yet is this limitation merely practical? Is it even a *limitation*? Perhaps, instead, at least from the dancer's perspective, the ephemerality of dances should be celebrated, in ways Renee Conroy (2011) has suggested. Certainly, too much *professional* ontology looks unhelpful. As Drid Williams (2004 p. 72) points out:

> It is as though we are being asked, '*where* is, e.g. *Swan Lake*, when no one is performing it?' Otherwise sensible, rational people who would hoot at the question, 'where is spoken language when it is not being spoken?' ... do not hesitate to ask this question about dancing.

But perhaps they should. For language is typically not ephemeral: perhaps the case of dance is different. Still, the question as she raises it should reinforce my decision to stress aspects of dance *practice* as a starting point.

§4.　　Recognizing dance as art: 'confusable counterparts'

Our discussion of persons above urged the centrality and interrelation of three concepts: *language*, *action*, and *persons*, recognizing the *normativity* that the persons-based perspective offered to the others. As elsewhere, the dances that concern me here are artworks. And, in the context of dance (from among the arts), the phenomenon paralleling "language" should be considered first; namely, artistic *meaning* — its application to dance is almost exactly like other arts.

Then thinking philosophically about *dance* requires acknowledgement that making art involves making artistic meaning; that, as Arthur Danto (1997 p. 195) saw, "[t]o be a work of art is to be (i) *about* something and (ii) to *embody its meaning*". Yet, for many, the most puzzling element when thinking about artworks remains the possibility of generating the *normativity* required so that the putatively 'meaningful' becomes understandable (as well as permitting failures of understanding). But danceworks, being *performables*, are realized in performance. So our perspective on understanding of dance begins from the *fact* of performability; from the *agency* involved (in ways this might suggest). In dance, then, such meaning is typically embodied in *actions*.

Do such actions *constitute the dance?* This is not quite right, since bodily movements must undergo *transfiguration* into dance. Hence one must not only identify the requisite movements of the body but also reflect on them *as dance*. Thus Yvonne Rainer's "Room Service" (1963) includes a sequence where "... two dancers [are] carrying a mattress up an aisle of the theatre. Out one exit, and back through another", where:

> [t]he point of the dance is to make ordinary movement qua ordinary movement perceptible. The audience observes the performers navigating a cumbersome object, noting how the working bodies adjust their muscles, weights and angles. (Carroll & Banes, 1992; in Banes, 1994 p. 11)

The possibility of 'confusable counterparts' reminds us that *more* than just those movements are required — they must be rightly seen *as dance*. Yet might the dancers provide *only* the bodily movement, such that the notationality offered by a potential score (real or imagined) really constrains only those bodily movements, on a parallel with music? No, for performances can misfire in other ways: for instance, by generating *rehearsals* of those danceworks (with all the movements performed), rather than the works themselves.

Understanding the judgement and appreciation of art here begins from Danto's argument concerning 'confusable counterparts', where (with pairs of indistinguishable objects) one mistaken for its counterpart is misperceived. There are two versions with pairs of indistinguishable objects, one of the pair an artwork, where different properties are truly applicable to each. First, the *naturally-occurring* contrasts with the *made* or constructed: thus, a meteorite might be indistinguishable from a sculpture (Ground, 1989 p. 4). To recognize the differences here, notice which of the following terms, from Ground's list, apply to only one:

> Elegant, Dainty, Graceful, Poised, Clumsy, Dumpy, Natural, Balanced, Heavy, Smooth, Bland, Interesting, Boring, Controlled, Courageous, Responsible, Insightful, Intelligent, Childish, Vulgar, Crass, Glib, Absurd, Heavy-handed, Witty, Lifelike, Romantic, Overnice, Dramatic, Classical, Moving.

Some terms apply only to the sculpture, some to both sculpture and meteorite: one class recognizes the intention, and hence the detail of planned decisions, reflecting the concern with art. The other, picking out a naturally-occurring object, necessarily lacks these. Then, for clarity, the appreciation and judgement of artworks ("artistic appreciation", "artistic judgement") differs in important ways from (other) aesthetic appreciation. Here, a stringent version of the contrast is adopted, focusing only on artistic appreciation and judgement. (In reality, I hold a yet more a stringent version, on which artworks lack aesthetic properties: see AJ pp. 5-17).

The second kind of 'confusable counterpart' yet more strongly exemplifies those concerns, with cases reflecting the enfranchisement of the ordinary/ everyday: here *both* objects are designed. But the art-type painting is rightly regarded differently from wallpaper on the wall on which it hangs; again, that difference is clear in what could truly be said of each. For dance, cases also typically involve "transfiguration of the commonplace", understood to generate 'confusable counterparts' (Danto, 1981 p. 139), objects that can be mistaken either for a specific dance or for a dancework at all. And, here, our slogan from Frege ([1918] 1984 p. 351) should again be recalled: that "[e]rror and superstition have causes just as much as correct cognition". Thus, the transfigured actions — those comprising the dance — require explanations different from the pre-transfigured version, despite the causal story (the sorts of thing neuroscientific study of the brains of dancers, or even audience, might provide) being necessarily the same.

Consider here three brief points about 'confusable counterpart' cases: first, as Ground's list above illustrates, when one object is art, and the other not, whatever they *share* cannot be what makes the one *art*. Second, "confusable" here cannot require indistinguishability. Thus, with Warhol's "Brillo Boxes", that one 'can't tell them apart at a glance' is enough (Danto, 2000 p. 132), even though some philosophical discussion appears to require more.[2] Third, distinguishing the objects is already being able to recognize *artworks* (and sometimes distinguish between artworks); and hence has a *theoretical* component once analyzed, even if it is acquired as a recognitional ability.

Then, when considering danceworks, three kinds of confusable counterpart should be addressed: (i) with our dancework indistinguishable from the actions of a roadsweeper (PAD p. 16) — even were the dance choreographed from observation of the sweeping, the dance is not that sweeping, nor vice versa, despite the performance area ending up cleaner. Or (ii) consider the fate of the Archie Gemmill goal (against the Netherlands) in the 1978 FIFA World Cup: recorded using the movement notation system Labanotation, its score was 'translated' into a dance by Andy Howitt — and performed on at least three occasions, including once at Sadlers Wells theatre. But how exactly does dance relate to goal? If one constraint on successfully performing *that* dance was, say, to follow the Labanotation score, Gemmill's own dribbling run and goal would have the wrong 'direction of fit', since the Labanotation score was made from what Gemmill *actually* did. In his case, any mismatch between notated score and behaviour would be a criticism of the score, not the movement. Yet then, at the least, the elegance of that sequence of movements — as captured through the dance, perhaps, and then transfigured into art — has really nothing to do with football: anymore than choreography based on the expressive movements of a roadsweeper (above) would mean that the resulting dance *was* the road sweeping; or even that it was 'about' roadsweeping. So Gemmill's movement pattern is elegant *as a goal*: that means as part of the match, with the concomitant connection to the aspiration to win. So, watching the dance *is not* really watching that goal.[3] In abstracting from that context, the dance loses any connection to football (as though, if it were performed tomorrow, a new player might succeed in tackling the Gemmill figure!).

Finally, the case already introduced, (iii) Yvonne Rainier's *Room Service* (1963) included "… two dancers carrying a mattress up an aisle in the theatre, out one exit, and back in through another" (Carroll & Banes, 1992; in Banes, 1994 p. 11), an activity at first sight indistinguishable from ordinary, everyday moving-men, but which is nevertheless a dancework. Avoiding misperception of the dance requires recognizing that fact — one can get it wrong, but could then be corrected. As these cases show, mistaking an artwork for a non-art object, or even an artwork in one genre for a work in another, is misperceiving it: to engage with art, it must be regarded *as art*. So one goal here must be to avoid misperception.

§5.   Dances as performables

Since dance is a performing art, typical cases involve two 'objects': the dance itself, and various performances of it. (Works not, in this way, performable on another occasion, I have called "happenings": PAD p. 160.[4]) And these two 'objects' generate two active roles in respect of dance: as maker of dances and as performer of dances. Both roles are crucial, even when one person fulfills both; but that of the maker, understood as the artist (as for other arts), is more easily characterized (see below; and Chapter Five §1).

Then specifying *what* dance is performed, faced with a candidate artwork, typically requires discussion of identity-conditions for the particular dancework: what movements *should* be performed, in what order, to instantiate such-&-such a dance (say, *Swan Lake*)? This is a *numerical-identity* question. Comparison with cases from music suggests one variety of answer: identity-conditions for musical works typically begin from a specification via a notated score, typically in terms of what tones to produce, of what duration, and in what order. A parallel strategy might be offered for dances. But, unlike typical music, many danceworks are not notated; further, no widely-agreed notation system exists for dances; and, even when works are notated, the notated score at best only specifies bodily movement[5] — it is a *movement* score, not a dance-score; moreover, many works are specified by sets of instructions *other than* those using a formalized notational system, such as Labanotation.[6]

Still, my response, in two parts, accepts this idea, framed as *notationality* — the possibility of a score — *and* then builds-in the art-status of the work, to set aside at least one kind of putative confusable counterpart. For a pattern of movement is thereby sketched that, if instantiated, *is* that particular dance – at least, if it is a dance *at all* (and setting aside the possibility of 'confusable counterparts'). This further allows that the adequacy of the score, and its mode of realization by dancers, is partly in the gift of the dance-maker. The *notationality* of (typical) dance provides one criterion for correctness of movement, located in the fulfilled intentions of the dance-maker, as embodied.

The idea of notationality offers a constraint on the bodily movements: so, do the dancers provide only the bodily movement, as robots might? No, for *dancers* are required to generate performances; at the least to turn the 'recipe' provided by the choreographer into a performance. Here, an additional normativity connects with *action* or *agency* (above): as dancer, how do I know

I did it *right?* This is not some puzzle-question in epistemology: rather, the answer is well-known — I learned to do it. Then some sophisticated account is required to avoid dancers being viewed simply as automata, obeying the whims of the choreographer. To make sense of the performer's role, I suggest drawing on the literature on *craft-mastery* (see Chapter Six §6), so that this is thought *craft-knowledge*. Further, as with actions generally, I also know how to excuse or extenuate my failures, if what I hoped to do (or what the choreographer instructed me to do) is not what then occurred.

What will a focus on agency bring? Three distinct agential roles — or four if criticism is taken as a distinct action — must be recognized and distinguished, not least because recognition of dance as a performing art automatically contrasts the role of dance-maker with that of performer, with each role bringing its own responsibilities. These three 'hats' (or roles) for agents here are:

- choreographer (or dance-maker);

- dancer (or performer, who may be the same person as above);

- audience-member — but these are not really agents here, except that their appreciation is a prerequisite of successful performance.

Finding the way to *explain* the operation of these roles exposes a number of difficulties for dance-aesthetics. But crucially the *dance itself* remains our focus (especially since legitimate critical commentary, from dancers as from audience-members, must be answerable to the dance). Therefore retaining this focus will avoid dismissing a concern with the dancework itself as though it were, say, just about the dance-maker (the artist) and her aims, or about the dancer (the performer) and his. For reducing, say, the purpose and direction of the artworks to the plans or purposes of the individuals involved would be a big mistake here. Works in performing arts embody the artist's fulfilled intentions; but, especially for an hypothetical intentionalist (see PAD pp. 135-150), those intentions are logically tied to the *artistic* aim and purpose of a work from that time, in that category or genre, at that time — not to the specific aims of the artist. Here, though, I simply sketch that position, as crucial to any artistic theory attending to the responsibility of (in our case) the dance-maker for the work. Then one way to ask about the dancework involves addressing what the choreographer must do to bring about the *abstract* object (for me, the type: see §8 below) that is the dancework *itself*.

§6.   Back to action!

As we saw, a basic idea here is that I am an agent: that I can *do* various things.[7] (Not, of course, that I can do just anything.) Further, we must recognize that behaviour that rightly counts as conscious and intentional may nonetheless not be explicitly thought through. Thus Dummett (2010 pp. 88-89) reports Wittgenstein's example of a person writing with a pencil who breaks off to look at its point, shrugs and then resumes work. Here, the writer's thoughts need not be embodied in words, only in actions. Yet that person clearly thought something like: "The pencil is blunt; oh, well, it will do". Nor need explicit thought of what to do next precede actions. Here, calling the behaviours "intentional" may be no more than denying that they occur as reflexes, or came about by accident. Indeed, walking down the garden path, say, would not usually be described as *intentional* unless we had some contrast in mind: as Austin (1979 p. 189) urged, one should avoid modification without aberration. And here, to recognize our capacity to initiate *action*, one of Wittgenstein's favourite slogans (quoting Goethe) could be invoked: "in the beginning was the deed".

Yet how should such a capacity of mine be understood? Early in his career, Danto (1965 p. 45) espoused a theory of *basic action*, such that:

> If *a* is an action performed by *M*, then either *a* is a basic action of *M*, or else it is the effect of a chain of causes the originating member of which is a basic action of *M*.

Here, basic actions are identified as a class unrelated to their contexts of occurrence; whereas the actions of concern here occur precisely only in the relevant dances. And, as we will see, the explanation of action should be treated contextually, such that what counts as a basic action in this context, or relative to that question, need not do so in some other context, or faced with a different question. Such a contextualism, integral to other positions of mine (PAD pp. xii-xiv; AJ pp. 29-57), also bears on uses of the idea of *basic action* when discussing dance: namely, as answers to the question, "How did you do that?" Further, at this time Danto's account was explicitly causal: it suggests that when action *a* is not a *basic action* of the agent (*M*), it is the causal outcome of such a basic action. But are *all* the connections here *necessarily* causal? After all, insofar as dance involves transfiguration of the commonplace of human action, visible in the 'confusable counterpart' cases exemplified by Rainer's "Room Service" (1963) above, the transfigured action requires explanation *different* from the pre-transfigured version, even when the causal story of the movements was the same; for, as Frege ([1918] 1984 p. 351) noted, "[e]rror and superstition have causes just as much as correct cognition".

More recently, Danto (1989 p. 221) presented a slimmed-down, less formal account, with no direct mention of causality and without necessarily denying our contextualism:

A pilot turns the ship by turning the wheel, and he turns the wheel by moving his arms. But he does not do anything of the same order to move his arms — he *just* moves them, immediately and directly, performing what I have spoken of elsewhere as basic actions. An action is basic when it is done, but not done through doing anything other than it.

And, in explanation, Danto (1989 p. 221) gives some examples:

> I lift a finger, or shut an eye, directly. But I have to move my hair by moving my hands against it, and unless I have a special gift, I cannot move my ears unless I do it with my fingers.

So we should be broadly sympathetic to the idea that, at some level, there are things one can just *do*; a feeling reinforced by reminding ourselves of a logical point here:

> There is a traditional theory that in order to move my arm I must, somehow, execute a volition — an act of will. But ... this raises the problem all over again; namely, how do I form a volition? Do I form it directly? Or do I need another volition — and how do I form *it*? So there is either an infinite regress, or some volitions can be formed directly. (Danto, 1989 p. 221)

Since the regress must be avoided, should we concede that "... some volitions can be formed directly"? No, for the whole idea of a volition is just a place-holder for our being able to *do* certain things. We should grant these as powers and capacities of persons, at least in favoured cases: we can just behave in these ways without doing anything else. For, as Danto (1989 p. 221) continues, "... if I can form a volition directly, why cannot I in the same sense lift a finger directly?" Here, the answer must be that I can! Then the temptation always to require such a psychological prerequisite there exemplifies Wittgenstein's comment (OC §471) that, "... the difficulty is to begin at the beginning. And not try to go further back". Nor need a particular action (or level of action) *always* be taken, or explained, as basic: rather what action is *basic* depends on the context. So what is basic for the experienced performer might not be so for the novice who — having not yet become habituated — must pay more attention to, say, how one changes gears, rather than simply doing it. So the novice-driver of a car with a stick shift might count as experienced when driving an automatic transmission. (Dummett, quoted below, makes this point for punting.) Likewise, the need to concentrate on accurately performing this particular aspect of a *pirouette*, once becoming habituated, may no longer seem *basic*. Yet, as we shall see, answers to such 'back beyond the beginning' questions are still regularly requested. For, of course, asking, "How did you do that?" can be crucial for dance, although our strategy *here* is primarily to show how that question cannot be answered in the context where many of its contemporary inquisitors find it.

As Wittgenstein recognized (PI §281[8]), the normativity of human action, such that the move in chess can be good or bad (as well as legitimate or not), cannot be completely explained causally. For example, regularities in the movements of chess pieces might be captured causally; but such regularities should be distinguished from moves in line with the rules of the game. For those regularities cannot display the normativity that (here) rule-following provides: they do not describe (nor attempt to describe) what one *should* do in these circumstances, but only the working out of causal forces — as one predicts the weather. Yet many moves that might be legal in chess are not made because they are obviously bad; and other moves that would in fact be good are overlooked— either by these players or by players more generally. And *chess* cannot be understood in another way. Hence the human, and the normative, must not disappear from our explanations. Thus, as Elizabeth Anscombe (1957 p. 83) notes, if I close my eyes and write, "I am a fool" on a chalkboard but, because the board is damp, no words actually appear, my failure to *know what I was achieving* is the result of bad performance, not well described as reflecting some mistaken *belief* of mine. Further, our human capacity to initiate action is just something about us: in typical cases, we do not do anything (or at least anything additional) to achieve it; and nor is there a causal explanation of *how* we do it, as distinct from the account describing that we do so.

Sometimes, the point here reflects that actions, explicitly thought through initially, can become 'automatic'. Dummett (2010 pp. 37-38) gives the example of learning to punt:

> When you first try to punt, for example, you have no idea how to control the direction of the boat, which will probably go in a circle. You are then shown the angle at which to throw down the punt pole in order to send the boat in this direction or that, and how to correct any error. You practice, bearing these instructions in mind. After sufficient practice, the proper use of the punt pole becomes "second nature". Now you think, "I must avoid this oncoming canoe", and steer skillfully to keep out of its way, without the least conscious thought of the movements of the pole by which you accomplish this.

In such a case, we may no longer think through what we are doing; indeed, we may have no need to do so. But, if the context changes, we can return to that explicit concern. Thus, as Dummett (2010 p. 38) continues, although the explicit punting techniques are not typically 'before one's mind':

> [y]ou can still bring them to mind if you have to instruct a beginner; but

when you are simply punting for pleasure, the technique has been buried at a level below consciousness.

So, here, as an agent, I can *do* various things. Of course, there will be limitations, both practical and conceptual, to what I can do, and also what I can intend — I may lack the relevant concept, for instance; or the contacts to make this an intention for me (as opposed to a vague aspiration). But if I am asked how I did such-and-such, I can sometimes reply by breaking the action down into smaller actions (see also the discussion of 'basic action' above). Here, compare Schwarzenegger in *True Lies* (1994):

> *Samir*: Is there anything you'd like to tell me before we start?
> *Harry*: Yeah. I'm going to kill you pretty soon.
> *Samir*: I see. How, exactly?
> Harry: First I'm going to use you as a human shield. Then I'm going to kill that guard over there with the Patterson trocar on the table. And then I'm thinking about breaking your neck.
> *Samir*: And what makes you think you can do all that?
> *Harry*: You know my handcuffs?
> *Samir*: Mmm-hmm..
> *Harry*: I picked them.

This is just a sequence of actions which amount to his escaping.

Thus, in the cricket match, I play a forward defensive stroke. How did I do it? I did it by stepping towards the pitch of the ball, with the bat angled in such-and-such a manner. I brought the bat through, ensuring that it was so angled that the ball would be played down. The problem here, of course, is that each of these (say, ensuring that the bat was angled just-so) is itself another action. Hence, given a *general* question about how one performs actions, such comments do not help. Rather, the right answer is just that one does — that one is an agent. Or, if the question is about my ability ("How were you able to play that stroke?"), I can reply by reference to my being taught the stroke at school, and (once having mastered it) not forgotten how. And, again, this is description at the level of action.

Another explanatory story for the behaviour, the story of the causal changes, might seem forthcoming. But, in typical cases, *I* cannot tell this story. How did I decide that the forward defensive stroke was appropriate? Well, I just *decided* — although my decision was influenced by the speed of the bowler, the condition of the wicket, and the fact that I only just came in to bat (that I hadn't "got my eye in"). But I did not *do* anything to decide: that is the force of "In the beginning was the deed". No doubt my deciding might be characterized in terms of changing states of my brain and body. But those states *compose* my thinking this or doing that — I do not, somehow, bring them about.[9]

In typical cases, I know what I am intending to do, or trying to do, or meaning to do: but not necessarily what I have achieved. To highlight the difference, Anscombe (1957 §32 [p. 56]) contrasted the list compiled by the detective, noting all the items I bought in the department store, with *my* list (assuming I bought all and only the items on that list). The lists match; but with a different *direction of fit* — he draws up his list from what I *did* buy, while my list reflects my plans. Are the two lists the same? Well, they contain the same words; but contextual considerations make their difference clear. In particular, errors in the detective's lists are just that — errors in what he saw: for me, the most likely divergencies result from changes of mind, Moreover, one does not have 'privileged access' here to what one *did* buy, but only to one's plans. Now, those trained in placing their limbs and body exactly may be better at recognizing the position than the rest of us — as a result of their training, then, dancers may typically be more accurate here than most of us. But they have no 'privileged access', as the presence of mirrors in dance studios attests; to be *sure* of the position of her limbs, the dancer (like the rest of us) must look.

But how many such steps might be considered? Obviously, there is no limit: we need mention only those steps as we take to be informative. But is there always a first step? Davidson, who mistakenly thinks reasons operate causally, imagines that there must be — after all, chains of causes have a beginning, although we might not know it. Thus Davidson (1980 p. 83) imagines a kind of 'pure intention' of which the agent might not be aware; and which, since it might not issue in behaviour, cannot be inferred from what one does:

> Someone may intend to build a squirrel house without having decided to do it, deliberated about it, formed an intention to do it, or reasoned about it. And despite his intention, he may never build a squirrel house, or do anything whatever with the intention of getting the squirrel house built.

This seems to reflect what Anscombe (1957 §27 [p. 47]) calls "an interior act of intention". Two things seems clear: first, such an act of intention is not necessary once we grant that *persons*, as agents, can initiate actions; second, this looks like a case where the most plausible course would be to deny that this person genuinely intends to build the squirrel house — the burden of proof would be on him/her!

Sometimes, then, what I do will be explained in terms of reasons of mine; or intentions that I have — although, of course, much of what I do has no specific reason, and nor did I think about it prior to doing it. So, insofar as intending requires prior planning, what I do will sometimes not be intended. That is not the same as saying that it is, somehow, unintentional or (worse) accidental. But, in the simplest case, we have no reason to introduce a modifier of that sort (see, as above: "no modification without aberration":

Austin, 1979 p. 189). We are confident that my walking across the room was neither an accident nor, specifically, unintended — we have no basis for thinking it *unintentional*. And we do not doubt that it was an action, as we might if it resulted from post-hypnotic suggestion or the taking of some drug. But is it *intentional*? Here, we should be asking: what are our choices? If my choice is just between intentional and unintentional, or between intentional and accidental, I make my choice by denying that it is unintentional, or accidental, as the case may be. But I need say no more. Only once the 'either-or' (in each case) has been foisted on me will I conclude that *therefore* it was intentional. Further, the content of calling the action "intentional" in such a case is just that it isn't unintentional or accidental, as the case may be.

Moreover, here is where Austin's panoply of excuses fits in: these include "[i]nattention, carelessness, errors of judgement, tactlessness, clumsiness ..." (Austin, 1979 p. 193). For these are all excuses in relation to one's actions. Additionally, Austin (1979 p. 194) recognizes the importance of cases where "... a plan of action leads to disaster ... through failure at the stage of *appreciation* of the situation ...". For *how we see the situation* can be crucial to what we do; and hence to the success or failure of our projects to which those actions lead. As Austin (1979 p. 194) remarks: "A course of E. M. Forster and we see things differently: yet perhaps we know no more and are no cleverer". So that, "... even thoughtlessness, inconsiderateness, lack of imagination, are perhaps less matters of failure of intelligence or planning than might be supposed ..." (Austin, 1979 p. 194). Still, the key point is that all these discussions are of actions — of humans as agents, who can (among other things) decide and act on those decisions.

Further, *doing* something (say, washing the dishes) *thoughtlessly* may mean neither that one is not thinking — some thoughtless action arises for thinking of something *other* than one is doing — nor even that one is not thinking about washing the dishes: perhaps, I am paying attention to hot water, soap and grease-removal right enough, but not to the delicate condition of these particular dishes; or perhaps those concerns lead me to pay insufficient attention to the drying or stacking of the clean dishes. So what may seem a brief digression actually offers a profitable area for the philosophy of mind to pursue: but, again, as an investigation into *action*, not into any causal substate of that action — if my grip is insufficient to hold heavy plates, my washing them will need an excuse different from thoughtlessness! Why ever did I agree to do so? And if the problem that led to some plates being broken were an unexpected muscular spasm, perhaps the failure is not well-characterized as a failure in dish-washing at all. Certainly, I wasn't clumsy or inept. So this case reinforces the sense in which discussion of action may be fundamental here. (At the least, stressing its legitimacy as a strategy for *some* philosophy of mind.)

§7.   The occasion-sensitivity of understanding

Moreover, it will important to recognize that meaning cannot be psychological: one cannot *mean* by an utterance just whatever one likes. Our bulwark is Frege's treatment of the meanings of utterances as including what he calls "thoughts" (Frege, 1984 p. 253; see Chapter Eight §4 for discussion), such that "[a]n utterance is meaningful just in case it can be understood, which means: understood as *saying* something. ... Frege called what is expressed by a sentence a 'thought' ..." (Dummett, 1993 p. 59). This account generates a difficulty here, in providing a reason why, as Frege (1984 p. 360 note) says, "I cannot put a thought in the hands of my readers ...". Yet why is that? The answer is in two parts: first, in Frege's use of the term, "... a thought is something impersonal" (Frege, 1979 p. 134), rather than something merely psychological (what Frege calls "ideas"). Second, to be understood by others, any thought must be expressed; and he recognizes that, since "... a sentence *expresses* a thought" (Frege, 1984 p. 354[10]), that expression can vary on different occasions — it would be *occasion-sensitive*. Further, as Frege (1979 p. 135) notes:

> It is no objection [to his position] that a sentence can acquire a different sense in the course of time; for what changes is of course the language, not the thought.

Of course, we might offer the same expression to, say, our readers, hoping they take a particular expression of the thought the same way, but that cannot be guaranteed. So when Frege said, "I cannot put a thought in the hands of my readers ...", he might have said: "I cannot put an occasion (or a context) in the hands of my readers" — better, he cannot do that reliably.

But why not? The answer is that he cannot offer *just* the thought; that any thought must be expressed via a sentence (roughly). And then the appropriate expression for that thought would vary on different occasions — as we said before, it would be *occasion-sensitive*. Moreover, it follows that "... we do not, properly speaking, ascribe truth to the series of sounds that constitute a sentence, but to its sense ..." (Frege, 1979 p. 129). Then, as Dummett (2006 p. 38) urges, "[t]ruth is an attribute of what is said, of utterances"; but he continues, "... so regarded, it is a notion applicable to linguistic terms". Dummett's first claim seems uncontentious (one reason Frege speaks here of "thoughts", and some other philosophers mention "propositions"): but does Dummett's second claim follow? Utterances do not seem linguistic items, at least straightforwardly: of course, one might regard this as purely a *verbal* matter. But it is agreed on all sides that *sentences* (alone) cannot be true or false — that is the point that weighs heavily with me here. And what is lacking, in line with occasion-sensitivity, is "... certain conditions accompanying the utterance" (Frege, 1984 p. 358).

So, basically, Frege sometimes recognized a version of what we have called "occasion-sensitivity",[11] such that:

> ... the same sentence does not always express the same thought, because the words need to be supplemented in order to get a complete sense, and how this can be done can vary according to circumstances. (Frege, 1979 p. 135)

Thus, my relatively straightforward claim that the door of my house is blue tolerates quite a number of correct answers, reflecting different situations with respect to that door, such that the very same door might count as blue on this occasion but not blue on some other occasion, without its pigmentation changing in the meantime. For instance, the doors in the street were all painted either red, green or blue — this was one of the blue ones, although the paint itself can have faded to the point where some observers might doubt my claim about the door's colour; or, again, might dispute my claim ('that the door is blue') given how much of the paint has peeled. Still, its being blue can be used to identify a meeting place, whatever its current state of deterioration, while denying that it was blue for a colour-chart. So the claim that the door was blue now counts as true, while previously it counted as false, need not reflect simply a change in the world crudely conceived. Perhaps, in a more extreme case, all the houses in the street have glass doors, with a small coloured edge — now my house is indeed the one with a blue door, even though the majority of the door's surface is not blue. The point here is that, once the context of the question is understood, there is a determinate answer — here, to the question of the door's blueness — but not otherwise. So there is *answerability*. Yet the very same situation of the door that correctly gave the answer "Blue!" on *this* occasion might not do so on some other occasion.[12]

Moreover, on any particular occasion, the requirement would only be for the kinds of answerability appropriate on that occasion, not to all kinds — indeed, the idea of a finite totality of such difficulties should be rightly set aside: there could be no "all" here; and hence no approaching such an "all". Instead, one should enquire when descriptions of events answer to the ways things are. Then, as Travis (2011 p. 105) notes, "[t]here are various standards that *might* apply to settle that; one might hold *that* description to any of the various conditions on its truth". For the issue addressed depends on the circumstance in ways the words typically will not capture alone. As Austin (1979 p. 130) put it:

> The statements fit the facts always more or less loosely, in different ways on different occasions for different intents and purposes. What may score full marks in a general knowledge test may in other circumstances get a gamma [a fail mark]. And even the most adroit of languages may fail to 'work' in an abnormal situation.

So one cannot assume that what is meant (say, in uttering, "My house-door is blue") has a single *fixed* meaning, across all the occasions of its utterance. Rather, we must see what those words, said on this occasion, amount to. For, as Travis (2008 p. 152) puts it, "[a]ny of many different things may thus be said of a given item in saying it to be that way". And, notice, this is not a recipe for vagueness or ambiguity: select an occasion, and typically saying such-and-such amounts to something particular. One way to illustrate this point, and also to argue for it, is to imagine a pair of utterances of the form of words such that, in different contexts or on different occasions, "... one member of the pair says something true, the other something false" (Travis, 2008 p. 153). Consider asking:

> 'When *would* something be coloured blue? How about Lac Leman? It has a blue appearance on a sunny day. But its water is not blue in the way Lake Louise's water is green. Is it blue? We find that we *can* understand (a lake's) being blue such that Lac Leman is that way, but also such that Lac Leman is not.' Neither understanding is ... either required or excluded by what being blue is *per se*. So neither is required or excluded by 'is blue' meaning what it does. (Travis, 2008 p. 154)

Notice, too, that this is both a general claim about understanding and a specific claim about understanding utterances (understanding language). And that again reflects our commitment to the interconnections between meaning, saying and understanding.[13]

§8.   Making sense of intention (for action and for art)

We will return to the impact of context. But first we must recognize how the impact of the context might operate slightly differently. In the context of sport, consider in particular those team sports such as soccer (football), rugby, or grid-iron (American) football, whether the actions that comprise the sport are, one might think, directed to the winning and losing in that sport. Against those who thought that sports-spectating in such sports might be understood as an aesthetic activity, David Best (1978 p. 104) urged that "... an activity ... could not count as football if no one ever tried to score a goal" — here we see the *purpose* implicit in football, by reference to which any other attainment (such as defensive ones) will be considered. As a result, for Best (1978 p. 106), "[h]owever successful a sportsman may be in achieving the principal aim of his particular activity, our *aesthetic* acclaim is reserved for him who achieves it with maximum economy and efficiency of effort". His critics, though, saw (as they thought) a mistaken assumption in Best's account. Thus, Stephen Mumford (2012 p. 41) offers a counter-argument that runs as follows:

While beauty is certainly to be found in sport, can we not see that it is merely incidental? It is a kind of by-product of good sport, but it is not the goal for which it aims. In sport, the aim is to win; it is not to be beautiful. Similarly, the sports fan wants to see a win ... not to see beauty. It is alleged that there is a contrast with the arts here. The primary aim in art is to produce beauty, by which I mean something with positive aesthetic value. This is intrinsic to the practice of art. The intrinsic aim or goal of sport is winning.

Whatever one thinks of Mumford's claims about the "primary aim of art", its relevance here is that he proposes to investigate what he takes to be the location of any such 'primary aim' in specific acts in the psychology of the sports' players. Yet, in talking of "purpose" here, Best was not referring to the purpose a particular person might have in doing such-and-such; instead, he referred to the purpose inherent in the action. Thus, once we see that this is sport-playing, it follows that the actions have what Best is calling a specific *purpose* — equally, we might have said a specific intention *behind* them. But this would not suggest, nor require, specific acts of intending on the part of, say, the players. Appeal to the rules and their impact on (especially) rule-related behaviour is not addressing the psychology of specific individuals. So here we have a model for a human practice that has a purpose, here provided by winning and losing, where that purpose (in providing a set of intentions to its participants, intention embodied in the practice) offers us ways of explaining their behaviour. Yet, while such explanation may seem to appeal to the thoughts and feelings of the participants, they *need not*; and typically *do not*. For the psychology of the participants only becomes relevant when there is a mismatch between that psychology and the intentions embodied in the practice: then, the agents might note that, *here*, their behaviour deviated from that indicated (embodied) in the practice.

Two points are fundamental: first, no exceptionless account of intention will be possible, since other factors might always be raised or mentioned (as occasion-sensitivity guarantees, as — in other circumstances — other factors might be crucial); second, even supposing that one's account turned out (serendipitously) to be *complete*, determining that fact would also be impossible. As Wittgenstein (VoW p. 43) notes, saying "and so on" is unhelpful here unless one can both complete the list and demonstrate that it is complete.

Thinking of appeal to the artist's intention in respect of making sense of artworks readily reinforces these points about intention in general. My strategy for dealing with the so-called "intentional fallacy" begins from Ramsey's Maxim: "... whenever there is a violent and persistent philosophical dispute there is likely to be a false assumption shared by both parties" (Bambrough, 1969 p. 10). And, for the role of the artist's intention, it makes sense to identify the shared assumption(s), and then experiment with denying those shared assumptions. [Having written extensively on this topic in AJ & PAD, I will abbreviate my remarks here: but it is worth stressing explicitly that using Ramsey's Maxim denies part of what each view asserts; and hence is *not* 'a middle way'.]

Here, two such assumptions are shared by both anti-intentionalists (such as Wimsatt and Beardsley, 1978) and most of their intentionalist critics:

- the matter is "all-or-nothing", in that intention is either always relevant or it never is — hence the strategy here is to hunt for counter-cases; only a plausible strategy on that assumption;

- intentions are just prior planning, 'in the head of artist', at best causally connected to the resultant artworks.

Having given these up, an artist's intelligence must still be seen behind the artwork: that artwork was not accidental — in that sense, it *is* intentional. That artworks are, broadly, meaning-bearing objects could equally have been stressed; that too would make us recognise these artworks as intentional. Our focus is on the *artwork*: and hence on the intentions it embodies. Thus, with Wollheim (1973 p. 112):

> If we wanted to say something about art that we could be quite certain is true, we might settle for the assertion that art is intentional. And by this we would mean that art is something we do, that works of art are something we make.

So the usual case for artworks will resemble other cases of human action: the artist's intentions may be expected to cohere with the understanding of his/her work. As Wollheim (1987 p. 37) notes:

> ... the burden of proof would seem to fall upon those who think that the perspective of the artist, which in effect means seeing the art and the artist's activity in the light of his intentions, is not the proper starting point in any attempt to understand painting [or any other artform]. For it is they who break with the standard pattern of explanation in which understanding is preserved.

This is rightly regarded as just a "starting point"; further, its impact involves not separating the artist and work: as above, the relevant intention is the (satisfied) intention embodied in the work. It will be an exception (and itself open to explanation) when the artist's perspective differs from that of his audience — perhaps the audience has missed his originality or his irony; perhaps he failed to achieve his aim. Either way, as Wollheim notes, the artist's responsibility for the work must be granted — his normative role here, in typical cases. That is, to recognize that " ... the part of the work that came about through design did indeed come about through design and not through accident or error" (Wollheim, 1980 p. 190), because this coheres with our ordinary way of understanding human action, especially in relation to responsibility.

But the *claims* of the artist are not necessarily authoritative here. Thus Dr. Johnson rightly disputed the author's claim about the meaning of the word "slow" in his poem:

> Goldsmith said it meant 'tardiness of locomotion' until contradicted by Johnson. 'No, sir. You do not mean tardiness of locomotion. You mean that sluggishness of mind that comes upon a man in solitude'. (Cioffi, 1965 pp. 175-176)

So, when the claims of the audience and those of the artist diverge, the claims of the artist need not always be preferred. Again, this replicates the general cases: what I aim to do is typically what I do, but I may fail. Yet, equally, I may be misunderstood.

§9.   The rejection of causal explanation for human beings

Treating human agency primarily in terms of the explanation offered by reasons flowing from agents' intentions (albeit in contexts) sets our faces against the kind of explanation for human beings given to most of the world around us; and that our doctors offer for us. That is explanation in terms of the working out of causal forces. Now, a fuller discussion must wait until Chapter Two. But broadly psychologistic explanations commit this error because such explanations would be constrained by the ways people *do*, as a matter of fact, think rather than how they *should*. Yet there will be causal stories for mistakes, too. That is the insight from our oft-repeated slogan from Frege (1984 p. 351): that "[e]rror and superstition have causes just as much as correct cognition". Hence the causal story is insufficiently "normative" (Frege, 1979 p. 128). It highlights the irrelevance of causal explanation to *action* rightly understood, by displaying the normative indifference of causal explanation.

But this error now emerges as a major philosophical tradition, importing results from (say) results from neuroscience, as we shall see. As Frege (1984 p. 365) comments:

> We believe that the thing independent of us stimulates a nerve and by this means produces a sense-impression; but strictly we experience only the end of this process which impinges on our consciousness.

Such 'beliefs' might seem to support the psychologistic position just dismissed.

But it must not. In his response, Frege (1984 p. 351) in effect deploys our slogan (above) to make two points. First, one cannot appeal to the causal story to insist on the veridical character of our 'experiences' of the world. Second, and more crucially, our normative process cannot be reduced to such causal explanation: just "[a]s I do not create a tree by looking at it, ... neither do I create a thought by thinking. And still less does the brain secrete thoughts, as the liver does gall" (Frege, 1979 p. 137). Urging otherwise risks "... blurring the boundary between logic and psychology" (Frege, 1984 p. 352), a boundary (with natural scientific explanation) fundamental to elaborating a province for philosophy.

Frege's natural description of a legitimate knowledge-seeking explanation (using the German word *Wissenschaft*) clouds his target for us. For *Wissenschaft* is often rendered in English as "science". This precisely misses Frege's point — that in key respects logic (and therefore philosophy) are unlike, say, the natural sciences. Indeed, Frege would have been sympathetic to Wittgenstein's point that:

> Philosophers constantly see the method of science before their eyes, and are irresistibly tempted to ask and answer questions in the way science does. This tendency is the real source of metaphysics, and leads the philosopher into complete darkness. (BB p. 18)

For the danger lies in the presumptuousness of natural science, a point Frege (1979 p. 130) recognized in saying that, were the claims of logic interpreted as about ideas (rather than thoughts) "... we should obtain a quite different science; this new science would be a part of psychology". But Frege rightly regards this as a mistake.

§10.   Conclusion

This chapter develops an integrated picture of the person as agent, capable of making meaning (particularly through language), with the *normativity* that implies. Then the possibilities of my *language*-using are connected to both my *agency* (I can utter the words, typically as I chose) and to the *normative* context: what I say and do can misfire as well as fail to occur. As we saw, recognizing that I can be *right* (operating normatively) or can explain my errors, and perhaps excuse them, are all aspects of my capacity to *mean what I say*, and my obligation (in most circumstances) to do so (see Cavell, 1969/2000 pp. 24-28). And my being understood, as well as my meaning anything, is a contextual matter: it exhibits the *occasion-sensitivity* crucial to all understanding.

Part One

Persons as Agents

Chapter Two

Personal identity, and identity more generally

§1.   Introduction to numerical identity

At the least, the notion of numerical identity is crucial to our discussion of danceworks but also to discussion of persons.[1] For our knowledge of objects — of shoes and ships and sealing wax — typically requires that we be able to identify such objects, distinguishing them from objects of other kinds, that we know where one object begins and another ends, and that we be able to re-identify particular objects. And, for these purposes, both danceworks and persons seem *objects* in this sense. So, initially, this chapter elaborates questions of identity more generally partly by posing the philosophical problem of *personal identity*, even though not all uses of the term "identity" (and its cognates) applied to persons need consideration; and partly because our issues do, after all, relate to persons! However, the conception of numerical identity that applies to danceworks will differ from that for *individuals* (substances), as we recognize (see §2 below). Some issues concerning identification, and constitution, can also be profitably introduced in this way.

For substances, then, consider *the very same person*, understood as that idea applies in simple cases of inheritance: in order to inherit my grandfather's fortune, I must be the genuine grandson. As we might say, "he wouldn't be *my* grandfather *unless ...*", where that "*unless*" highlights factors to be determined here, factors distinguishing me (the genuine grandson) from others who resemble me, since the will leaves the fortune to the *grandson*; and I am his only grandson (*ex hypothesi*). As here, personal identity problems typically arise across time:

> Is the person identified this way at **this** time the very same person as that one, identified that way, at **that later** time?

In standard cases, there being such *identity* here is compatible with my now being very different from, say, when my grandfather last saw me: so personal identity should not be confused with (nor taken to require) similarity. Not only is my appearance very different (I was seven years old when last we met) but also my *views* — I now have some — and my *memories*. His will makes clear, let us suppose, that only I (the legitimate grandson) can inherit, because only I am the very same person as the curly-haired cherub that he saw all those years ago, the very same person that will picks out. (Of course, that only means that I *should* inherit, not that I actually do so.) Notice, too, that here expressions applying only *at a time* (or in a *tensed* way) still genuinely apply; and are *true* of (here) the person.

In English, the terms "identity", "identical" are used at least in two further ways. The first, typically as "identical", is sometimes called "qualitative identity": roughly, two objects one cannot tell apart are identical. In this case, *two* objects are compared (with numerical identity, the question is typically whether a single 'object' was identified at different times or in different places); and objects are (qualitatively) *identical* to the degree that they share properties. Thus, two chairs from a mass-produced set are *qualitatively identical*: they share the same properties, and so cannot be distinguished. But, since there are *two* chairs here, this is not numerical identity. (If I sat on a particular chair on Friday, and chairs were moved on Saturday, I might sit on a *different* chair on Monday, although one qualitatively identical.)

In a second use of the term, referring to our *identities* somehow picks out what is important to us: thus, when I return shell-shocked from the war, my friends say that I am not the same person; asked to elaborate, someone might speak of a *change of identity*. But this case is unlike the other, for here numerical identity is not at issue. To give such changes a name, let us say instead that *my personality* has changed.

Compare that case with one that *would* concern numerical identity: the film *Sommersby* [1993] raises real *identity* questions about whether the Richard Gere character is who he claims to be — relating to whose husband he is, what he can inherit, and such like. By contrast, what I am calling "my *changed* personality" just means that I am not behaving as you expected. (Similar changes might, of course, have been deliberate: I have found religion, or become more charitable, or less.)

While perhaps not quite the usual deployment of the term "personality" in English, this is not without precedent. Thus, to diagnose and identify a person with Multiple-Personality Disorder involves accepting that there is only one person here (numerical identity), despite differences in personality. Of course, meeting such a person under appropriate circumstances, one might mistakenly *think* that one had encountered different people on the two occasions, because 'they' acted so differently. These might provide interesting cases for any account of personal (numerical) identity for, although *not* examples of numerical identity, they may indicate that numerical identity — while a logically fundamental notion — might be less important than our focus on it suggests. Still, (numerical) identity has a clear role in inheritance; and in responsibility, of course, since I cannot be praised or blamed for some action unless I was the *agent* in respect of that action.

Similar responses handle neatly those occasions when we say that someone does not understand himself/herself: this does not claim some *self* here as the non-comprehending subject (compare Wiggins, 2016 pp. xx-xxi). Rather, the confusion resembles that engendered when, hearing that, "It is snowing", one asks, "What is the *it*?". Talking of selves typically involves recognizing that one's current thoughts or actions seem at odds with how one usually thinks or feels — all of these are remarks about the only person in that story; namely, that person puzzled about how his/her thoughts and feeling cohere with those in the past (hence, at best, about changes in *personality*). But focusing on one's thoughts and feelings relates them to one's actions; and hence invokes responsibility, as above.

No doubt there are complications here when, say, I pay another to do some act; also cases where, although *I* am the agent (numerical identity), the passage of time has had a bearing on whether responsibility will be enforced or enacted: thus, the shell-shocked person above might not be held responsible for his pre-war doings. Still, these cases are predicated on our recognizing the numerically-identical person in the case.

Connections to inheritance (and similar) mentioned above show this *philosophical* problem has more than mere intellectual interest: it connects with my getting *my* just desserts (not someone else's); with what I am responsible for, or can (genuinely) remember. Moreover, this background from understanding personal identity is brought to identity questions for danceworks. And that background assumes that there are continuants: this is the 'common-sense' view here.

Thus, overall, this chapter serves five purposes: in addition to (a) introducing philosophical investigations of identity-conditions, and (b) sketching key features of such investigations as they apply to *persons* — and hence to agents — to advance our explorations in the philosophy of action, it also (c) discusses and deploys some key methodological issues for philosophy (in particular, the use of thought-experiments to consider logical possibilities); and introduces (d) some other philosophical issues best understood as *contrasting* with those concerning identity; before (e) offering some comments on dance-related themes.

§2.   Identity, persistence, and danceworks

In various works, David Wiggins has argued for the logical centrality of numerical identity in this sense when characterizing *substances*,[2] explaining it via Leibniz Law, such that two characterizations of one object must share all their properties: that is what it means for there to be a single individual in the story. Moreover, this requires re-identification of that individual (recognizing it as *the same* again) as well as its identification: we must know where this one starts and that one ends. Certainly, one danger is that one treats a " ... world in which nothing really persists through change *as if* some of the things in that world did persist through change — a sort of make-believe" (Wiggins, 1980 p. 3): instead, any analysis here must reflect our common sense idea that " ...

there is persistence through change" (Wiggins, 1980 p. 3). Thus Wiggins (1967 p. vii) begins from "... persisting material substances". Then, if one takes the issue, for numerical identity, as one of "coincidence as a substance" (Wiggins, 1980 p. 4), that raises the question of what (in our world) can *count* as substances.[3]

Hence, while "[i]t is not an option for philosophy to reject the four-dimensional conception of the world urged upon us by philosophers and metaphysicians of science", Wiggins (2016 p. 17) recognizes that it remains an open question how such a conception applies (if at all) in our cases. Then, while exploring some of the complexities of four-dimensional talk, Wiggins (1980 p. 196; also note 16; p. 70) highlights " ... some of the introductory explanations needing to lean on the crutch of the three-dimensional language ...". As he comments, "... it is simply a mistake to suppose that we *must* ... identify the persisting entities articulated by the three-dimensional world view with those articulated by the four-dimensional" (Wiggins, 1980 p. 196). And he had already urged that, "[n]o human being is any stage of a human being, or an 18-year-old cross-section of a larger 70-year-long space-time worm" (Wiggins, 1980 p. 27). For, as Wiggins (2016 p. 17) rightly remarks, "[t]he four-dimensional conception need not favour either side in the logico-metaphysical dispute in which we have been engaged". Indeed, the non-continuant wing of this debate — in referring to constructs such as, say, "... this-horse-at-t, that-river-at-t, or David-Lewis-at-t" (Wiggins, 2016 p. 17) — will "... lean shamelessly upon the ordinary understanding of substances when we come to specify that from which these constructs are to be seen or assembled" (Wiggins, 2016 p. 17). At the least, it seems improbable that dancers *must* deny that persons are continuants (or treat them as though they were not). Indeed, with Reid ([1815] 2002 p. 577), this is a further place where "[p]hilosophers should be very cautious in opposing the common sense of mankind; for, when they do, they rarely miss going wrong"; although here too we should recognize how often "a picture held us captive" (PI §115) — and hence that the pursuit of truth requires rational reconstruction.

Of course, dances are clearly not continuants in the sense in which persons are, since danceworks are multiples: the very same dance can be performed on Monday evening in London and in New York; similarly, the very same dance can be performed on Monday evening and on Tuesday evening, despite differences between the performances. Such claims explain what it means to be a *performable* in a performing art; and are not hugely contentious: rather, they apply to any danceworks that are such performables (PAD pp. 31-39). Still, saying that we saw *the same dance* again seems to offer numerical identity judgements in respect of them — without meaning either that the same company performed the work or that the second performance was indistinguishable from the first. So works in the performing arts seem a special case here, not reducible to mere qualitative identities, but not persisting in the way that persons (and other substances) do. At the least, dances are artefacts, if of a distinctive kind.[4]

Hence, danceworks provide a case for later discussion: there, one's concern is with identifying (if only in principle) the *very same dance* — perhaps despite differences in performances. However, since dances are not substances in this sense[5] (although dancers are), what we learn about *numerical identity* here will need some modification.

One might wonder if, say, *The Nutcracker* does indeed persist:[6] but, at the least, it makes sense to ask how many one has seen during a particular Christmas season, without meaning that one has re-seen a particular company's performances; and where this would be contrasted with seeing Mark Morris's *The Hard Nut* (1991). Further, it seems odd to imagine that the work only *exists* when being performed: after all, the work could be discussed ('in the abstract'), and extracts could be rehearsed or performed, without being strictly extracts from, or rehearsals of, any particular performance. These characteristics, and especially their similarity to claims for *words*, suggest to me treating such danceworks as abstract objects (see §10 below; and Chapter Seven §1).

§3.   Examples; and some properties of numerical identity for substances

Our immediate concern is for some methodological issues: what do we take for granted? How do we move forward? Clearly, we bring to such debates a range of concepts, and sets of cases — clear to us — of identity: for instance, of garages that *should* return our car to us, the very same car we delivered, despite the new parts; of watchmakers with a similar injunction. Our practice shows that such cases do not leave us 'in the dark'; and therefore we can learn from them. So the cases are important both because they reflect the contours of the relevant concepts and because they can be used in arguments here (as part of a case-by-case procedure: Wisdom, 1991 pp. 104-107), trading on consistency; or, as Wisdom used to put it,[7] "twitting the other with inconsistency" — that is, urging, "you *think* this, so to be consistent you should agree to *that*".

One aim here, especially for dance aesthetics, will involve staying as close as possible to danceworld practices: roughly, to what dancers, choreographers, dance critics, dance theorists, and the audience for dance *say* about danceworks. So that the concepts are broadly those of commonsense, which after all, As Austin (1979 p. 182) noted, embodies "... all the distinctions ... [people] have found worth drawing, and the connections they have found worth marking, in the lifetime of many generations". Hence our everyday concepts embody:

> ... something better than the metaphysics of the Stone Age [although perhaps not much better] namely, ... the inherited experience of many generations of men. ... if a distinction works well for practical purposes in ordinary life (no mean feat, for even ordinary life is full of hard cases), then there is sure to be something in it, it will not mark nothing .... (Austin, 1979 p. 185)

Thus Austin (1979 p. 195) rightly reminds us that ordinary language "... embodies ... the inherited experience and acumen of many generations of men (and women)". Yet that may leave us at a loss with cases well outside that compass.

For instance, what should one make of a goldfinch that suddenly quotes Virginia Woolf (Austin, 1979 p. 88)? Presently, we do not know what to make of it. If such creatures became widespread, we might grant that there were two kinds of goldfinch, the one with a partiality for Bloomsbury literature, and ... With a proliferation of the first kind of creature, we might *even* come to regard non-Woolfian goldfinches as somehow defective or deviant examples of the genus. So one does not so much *begin* from fixed categories as come to them.

But, to explore such concepts, we must turn to *examples*, relatively uncontentious cases where we grasp what should occur. So one moves forward here from a test-bed of cases of *identity* (say, about watches, or cars, or statues: see §2 above) since any arguments for identity-conclusions draw on such parallels. Reflection on such simple cases, beginning from numerical identity for material objects, offers an informal presentation of five related points.

First, chopping the end from my walking stick (say, to make it more comfortable) may still leave *my stick*, the very same stick, and so on (numerical identity). But if the stick is broken in half, neither half is uncontentiously the original stick. Similarly, the 'mother' amoeba that splits is (one might think) not *the very same amoeba* as either of the 'descendent' amoebae. So there may not be *identity* solutions in every case.

Relatedly, and second, one reason that the stick broken in half does not fit our identity-relation is that each half has as good a claim as the other to being *the very same one*. But the identity-relation is one-to-one. Since *both* cannot be (numerically) identical with the one 'predecessor' (after all, there was one; now there are two), our conclusion must be that neither is.

Third, as recognized above, our topic is not the continuity of properties or attributes: the seven-year-old my grandfather last saw was pink, chubby, monoglot, and so on — now I am tall, handsome, etc. ... well, perhaps still monoglot, but otherwise different. But that is irrelevant to the identity conclusion. In the simplest case, the seven-year-old had brown hair while I have grey hair (now). This 'difference' does not preclude identity. Indeed, such differences are to be expected: we would not know what to make of a case where they were absent. In the jargon, one does not begin from indistinguishability; although, of course, there will be *a way* — perhaps by taking the properties, and such like, to be *tensed*— where what *was* true of me (then) and what *is* true of me (now) just count as true of me.

Fourth, in a suitable resolution of the case as discussed, I am *the very same person*; and genuine identity judgements always have some such covering concept 'in the offing'. Hence, identity-claims are importantly connected to covering concepts. As Wiggins (1980 pp. 15-18 & ff.) has shown, this need not be explained by seeing identity as *relative* to such covering concepts — better, its impact is recognized by noting that the covering concept is missing when I ask if, say, this is the same *thing* as that: unless the context clarifies what *kind* of thing is under discussion, the question is not even well-formed! And a useful idea here is that, roughly, whatever could be a covering concept here would be *countable*: if we can reidentify, say, the chairs in a particular area (for instance, a room), we could ask *how many* of them are there (but contrast Wiggins, 2016 pp. 218-219).

Relatedly, and fifth, the watch is composed of its spring, face, hands, cogs, and so on, but the watch-repairer can change those cogs — at least, if he does not change too many — and return to me the very same watch, but now with a slightly different composition. (And, of course, the way the cells comprising our bodies are replaced over time might best be seen as *serial part-replacement*, on this model.) Thus identity-judgements must not be confused with those relating to *composition*. (We return below to crucial questions about composition or constitution in §8.)

This collection of features may suggest a method for exploring the personal identity conditions that Wiggins (1967 & 1980) applies to identity in general: namely, subjecting candidate identity-conditions for persons to 'trial by problem-case' or 'inquisition by counter-example' (see Perry, 2002 p. xi: also §8 below). These examples also display three crucial features concerning determinacy. First, many key properties here are context-relative: "I asked him for a bread knife and he gives me a razor because it's sharper" (Wittgenstein: Ms 121: 9th April, 1938) — not that sharpness *is not* a virtue of knives, or that the razor is not sharper than the bread knife. But, in this context, the sharpness needed is of the kind the bread knife offers. Although the issue indeed turns on what sharpness amounts to in the context, the person here has misunderstood the relevant *standards* of (here) sharpness. So, second, our view of what is true here recognizes *occasion-sensitivity* (see Chapter One §7), acknowledging such contextualism. Here, we must draw, in context, on our fund of knowledge of *persons*, and of (say) responsibility, because "... there is a definite result as to truth only if the circumstances of the describing, or those of its evaluation as to truth, somehow make one standard or another the right one for the purposes in hand" (Travis, 2011 p. 106). For a person might not be master of the conditions (what Travis calls "the standards") for what counts in *these* circumstances as, say, the drapes being red — for example, in knowing what to make of the stains on those drapes. This means that a person not only:

> ... could not grasp a thought that the drapes were red if he lacked the concept red ... [but also] one may know all there is to know as to what being coloured red would be as such — and for all that, ... not yet be in a position to see whether a given judging, or stating, say, that the drapes were red is to count as having answered to the way things are. (Travis, 2011 p. 106)

That is to say, "[p]arochial human responsiveness" (Travis, 2011 p. 108) must be recognized to understand the application of, say, colour concepts. Yet, third, there may still be such standards *in a particular case*, for:

> [t]he statements fit the facts always more or less loosely, in different ways on different occasions for different intents and purposes ... [although] even the most adroit of languages may fail to 'work' in an abnormal situation . (Austin, 1979 p. 130: quoted Chapter One §7)

But not all questions admit answers of the kind offered. In fact, most words in ordinary use are explained ostensively. So, in summary, one cannot safely import the assumption that, in every case, the concepts to hand will be adequate. On the other hand, these concepts — *person, responsibility* — are central to much that we do and say. And all that is required is sufficient determinacy *in any specific context*, rather than a context-free determinacy.

§4. Finding the covering concepts

Thus the concepts to deal with *all* the cases may not be ready at hand, especially for the problem cases potentially offered. But what concepts concern us centrally here? One debate is whether X (identified at one time, say) is the *very same person* as Y (identified at another time): does that concept (*person*) bring with it a unique set of identity-conditions, timelessly applicable? Must it?

As Austin (1962 p. 76) points out, in respect of what is or is not a *real* X, "... the criteria we employ at a given time can't be taken as final, not liable to change". The same is true of our concepts more generally, including the 'covering-concepts' for our identity-judgements: centrally *person*. By way of explanation of (and argument for) this point about concepts:

Suppose that one day a creature of the kind we now call a cat takes to talking. Well, we say to begin with, I suppose, 'This cat can talk.' But then other cats, not all, take to talking as well; we now have to say that some cats talk, we distinguish between talking and non-talking cats. But again we may, if talking becomes prevalent and not talking seems to us to be really important, come to insist that a *real* cat be a creature that can talk. And this will give us a new case of being 'not a real cat': that is, being a creature just like a cat except for not talking. (Austin, 1962 pp. 76-77)

This example may indicate how some concepts might change; hence how what *being a cat* requires might become different. But, regarding the situation from *our* current perspective[8] (as, say, art critics must, in their field), we would correctly deny that the talking creatures were cats (where "cat" meant what we now mean by it). On the other hand, the longer view offered by the philosophers' perspective on this matter suggests that one recognize incommensurable changes: one cannot know exactly what some future people will say — certainly, "talking cat" does not capture its full nuance.

Yet, first, our concern here is not 'what we *do* say', but 'what we *should* say' (see Chapter One §1). That, in turn, alerts us to the need for care in who counts as this "we". Then second, and consonant with that thought, we recognize that our everyday concepts are not sacrosanct: that there must be occasions for 'rational reconstruction' of, for instance, 'what we say' as it applies to danceworks. Further, philosophy offers one basis for such 'rational reconstruction' (and compare Chapter Nine §§4-6). To take the simplest example, suppose (as I would urge) that dualism of mind and body offers a misguided picture of persons, such that we can mislead ourselves by thinking (and talking) of persons as 'mind-plus-body' (or mind-plus-body-plus-something else; or body-minds). Then any of our commonsense remarks about dance that are readily interpreted dualistically — or which might be so interpreted, if one is not careful — should be set aside *once they begin to mislead*. And, as David Best (1999 p. 133) recognized, such dualist tendencies are easily located in many dance theorists, almost since the beginnings of such theory. For instance, suppose we read that, "[t]he dance breaks down the distinctions of body and soul ..." (Sachs, 1937 p. 3) — implying that there are such distinctions — or that:

Every emotion has an appropriate and peculiar movement. There is a movement of joy, rage, excitement, peace, fear, devotion, and so on through the list of feeling states. (H'Doubler, 1940 pp. 88-89)

We might well take the claim to be that such movements *stand for* the emotions or feeling: parallel issues arise with the suggestion that movements symbolize thoughts or feeling (in terms reminiscent of Eleanor Metheny, 1968: for discussion, see Best, 1978 pp. 124-142) — this is sometimes true, but rarely for dance. Similar 'modifications' will be required for contemporary talk of *kinaesthesis*, on some readings (see Montero, 2013 p. 173: for discussion, Chapter Nine §3; §9, and note 15).

Equally, other kinds of mistaken claims about the nature of dance must be set aside. Since our concern is with art-type dance, what limits does that set to the concept "dance" for our enquiry? What should be set aside? Mere *similarities* to the behaviour of birds or animals clearly have no place here, despite claims about "... the well-known dances of the higher animals" (Sachs, 1937 p. 9): they are *not* (part of) artworks; and we recognize — in acknowledging the possibility of confusable counterparts (see Chapter One §4) — that even sophisticated behaviours can be *mistaken* for dance. For, as Adrienne Kaeppler (1985 p. 92) noted, "[i]n many societies ... there is no indigenous concept that could be adequately translated 'dance' ...": in such societies, indigenous *dance*-making would be impossible (although members of such societies could, of course, learn to choreograph ballets). Further, even using the word "dance" (or something translated as "dance") does not make the activity *dance* in our sense (as I noted for the Native American "Ghost Dance": UD p. 286). Any of these activities might provide inspirations for dances, or movement sequences for them — as the Archie Gemmill goal for Scotland against the Netherlands in the 1978 FIFA World Cup provided material (actually, *all* the material) for a dance by Andy Howitt. But that does not make the actual *goal* into dance: nor are we watching *dance* (in our sense) when watching it, even if the movement sequences are indistinguishable from those of Howitt's dance.

These examples make clear both the need for, and character of, what I have called the "rational reconstruction" of commonsense conceptions, as they might apply both for "person" and for "dance", and their derivatives.

§5. Psychological discontinuity; and Wiggins (1980) 'solution'

So what contours has the concept "person" in this context? What is it for a person to *survive*; or, more generally, *persist*? Of course, in this context, thinking of *survival* to involve imagining survival through our children (or our children's children), or through our literary accomplishments, or charitable works, would not reflect *personal identity* concerns. So what personal survival *involves* clearly bears directly on questions of personal identity; what is it that *survives*? When the result is not personal survival, the hope (or whatever) that *I* survive will be vain.

Yet psychological accounts for personal continuity are typically more complex than physically-based ones: say, ones rooted in the brain or body or some such. For tracing physical continuity is relatively straightforward (although not unproblematic): at least, a conceptual model for the simplest case (say, the body — or whatever — constantly followed by a television camera, with no splitting, and so on) seems easy. Nothing comparably simple exists for psychological accounts: after all, having graduated from the same university on the same day, you and I might both remember that graduation (from a participant-perspective); we might both love the same woman (so that our love, characterized in terms of what/who it was *love of*, seems the same); again, we might both be depressed at having been 'dumped' by the same woman. In all such cases, it is tempting to say that you and I feel or recall the same thing: cases where my psychological state appears the same as yours seem easily multiplied. Yet, of course, that alone cannot make us *the same person.*

In response, Locke ([1689] 1975 p. 346: Essay II. xxvii. 25) asked rhetorically, "Could we suppose any spirit wholly stripped of all its memory or consciousness of past actions?" In modern terms, Locke's position is roughly that a particular person (X) at a particular time is *the very same person* as one identified as "Y" at an earlier time if and only if both are persons; and X remembers at the later time his doing what Y did at the earlier time. So if John (now aged 40) genuinely *remembers* falling from the apple tree (when aged 8), it follows that John is *indeed* the person (the boy, Johnny) who fell from the tree — only he can genuinely *remember* his doing this. (If, say, John recounted that fall to his brother Tom, then, while Tom could remember being *told*, he could not remember *the fall* — he did not *have* the fall!) Further, this view models all accounts explaining personal identity (or personal continuity) as *psychological continuity* (of some kind — here in terms of memory). For, in all, the requirement (as here) is that I *was* the person who felt this or thought that or remembered such-and-such; and so that I *still* am.

The Locke-type account requires that the person genuinely *remember doing the thing*: that I remember my brother joining the army does not mean that I am my brother. He would remember the ceremony (say), while I just remember *that* he joined; or, were I at the ceremony, remember from the audience-perspective what he remembered from the participant-perspective. But this appeal to memory is problematic. For I can honestly *think* I remember doing such-and-such because I was told about it (in a particularly vivid way) when I was young (or some such). Were the account under consideration correct, my honestly *claiming* that I remember doing such-and-such seems to make me the person who did it: and that is at least wrong — for instance, I might claim to remember doing something done before my birth. (Such cases, called *paramnesia*, are less rare than one might think: thus, in his later years, King George IV supposedly 'remembered' leading troops at the Battle of Waterloo, a hundred years previously!) More importantly, surely my *forgetting* does not make me a different person.

Yet does the problem for such a position derive from its focus on memory? Might some other psychological capacity provide the psychological continuity taken (on this account) to ground, or be a criterion of, personal identity? Two good reasons suggest answering "no" (always assuming that a single psychological capacity must be invoked): first, the others fare no better, faced with objections parallel to those just raised (for instance, a 'stream of consciousness' must be identified *as mine* before it can be used as a criterion of *my* identity); then, second, memory seemed (at first glance) especially well-suited to the task here — after all, numerical identity-judgements for persons relate a person identified at an earlier time to one identified at a later time; and memory is a temporally-related capacity. But parallels for the problems of amnesia and paramnesia beset other possible accounts. So, even modifying the key terms of Locke-style accounts, one arrives at an untenable position.

The discussion of psychological continuity makes clear that an account of *personal identity* cannot reduce to the psychological *only* — say, to memory-continuity — because, roughly, a *material basis* for that continuity is presupposed in such continuity. Yet our common-sense concerns with responsibility (say, in the form of inheritance) suggest that something positive should be said here. Perhaps our (present) understanding of persons cannot deal with every case; but it surely deals with most, even if its explication is not uncontentious, or even when it cannot be applied exceptionlessly.

Indeed, the determinacy needed here is only contextual (see §4 above). Read one way, Wiggins (1980) incorporates this requirement into his account of persons by recognizing that, although the sorts of properties (especially psychological properties) appropriate for persons can be *indicated*, these do not form a *finite totality*. Hence, one cannot specify them *all*; nor rule out (in principle) a candidate person on the basis that this or that is *absent*. Further, such properties are rooted in the physical. Hence, Wiggins (1980 p. 188) transforms the famous claim from Locke ([1689] 1975 p. 335 — quoted above) to read:

> ... a person is any animal the physical make-up of whose species constitutes [that is, makes] the species' typical members thinking intelligent beings, with reason and reflection, and typically enables them to consider themselves as themselves, the same thinking things, in different times and places ... (Wiggins, 1980 p. 188)

This remark must be augmented, Wiggins (1980 p. 171) insists, by expanding our account of reason and reflection and the like. He speaks of the need for persons to:

> ... perceive, feel, remember, imagine, desire, make projects, acquire a character as they age, [be] happy or miserable, [be] susceptible to concern

for members of their own or like species ... conceive of themselves as perceiving, feeling, remembering, imagining, desiring, making projects, speaking ... have and perceive of themselves as having, a past accessible in experience-memory and a future accessible in intention ... etc.

But, even so, this account is clearly incomplete. Hence we must:

> ... supply the lacunae, which we marked there [above] by dots, by drawing upon the indefinite and extensible fund of our knowledge of men, *knowing* that we shall never close off the enumeration or evaluate once and for all the relative importance of the various differentia. (Wiggins, 1980 p. 188)

Here Wiggins recognizes, and surely rightly, the *impossibility* of ever finding a list of properties or behaviours that provide a genuine test for personhood (understood as conditions individually necessary and jointly sufficient) *just because* any such enumeration cannot be completed. But this does *not* lead to the pessimistic conclusion that we cannot *know* that what is around us are people — we can, because their biological origins can be taken for granted. So our 'unit' for persons will be an organized parcel of matter to which is appropriately ascribed the relevant (open-ended) set of properties. Since this reflects what we know about ourselves, such an account of persons should cover most cases. After all, Austin (1979 p. 182) is surely right to take the everyday understanding of persons as adequate for most of what is asked of it.

§6.   Hunting logical possibility

What of some more difficult cases? We have seen (above: §5) that attempts to use only psychological building-blocks in explaining psychological continuity will always be problematic. In this context, one set of cases (at least *seemingly* relevant here) are rightly described as Multiple Personality Cases. So, asked how best to characterize the 'Three Faces of Eve' case (Thigpen & Cleckley, 1957), or the 'Sybil' case (Schreiber, 1973), the right answer begins by recognizing that, for our key concern (say, with inheritance), there is unquestionably only one *person* here, despite multiple personalities.

Multiple personality cases, as well as bizarre cases of transplantation, and fission, all seemed to put pressure on any account of personal identity. Yet now multiple personality cases can be put aside: whatever their interest in other ways, they clearly involve just *one* person. Moreover, a typical human being viewed across time will change her views, sometimes dramatically. Comparison of what she said or thought at this time, and then at that one, and so on, produces just the sorts of differences (diachronically) that our cases of Multiple-Personality Disorder display synchronously: that is, within the same time-frame. So such extreme cases, in permitting recognition precisely that one person may have numerous personalities, allow us to put aside cases built on acknowledgement of differences of personality.

In general, some consensus exists not only for such cases (one person, lots of personalities) but also for some cases of, say, transplantation of organs, a consensus arrived at by considering part-replacement of material objects such as automobiles or watches: more importantly, most cases combine bodily continuity with psychological continuity. Only when these familiar continuities come apart do we turn to thought-experiments: cases where we are asked to consider what *would* happen in some presently impossible, but still logically possible, situation. Of course, our intuitions over such things may not be reliable. But appeal to parallels can reinforce them, as here; say, to numerical identity for animals or machines.

Such cases (see §3 above) are typically constructed with whatever features makes them most likely ("best case scenarios"); further, simple cases are needed; and, where possible, clear cases (hence cases from identity-questions for objects are often helpful); moreover, the issue always concerns what is *logically possible*, not what is practically possible (nor what is likely); additionally, consistency is of great importance ("If you are saying this here, you must be saying that there — the cases are the same."); again, the importance of *relevant* differences must be stressed — and so the need to *argue* the relevance: thus, if someone urges, "cars do not have brains" ... well, that is true, but so what? What is its relevance? If the thought were that, "When we talk about brain removal/transplantation for persons, we take the brain to have certain causal powers: so the brain, viewed that way, is an *essential* part of a person's body — cars do not have *essential* parts in this way". Well, now we understand the point! That leaves us free to consider contesting it. Finally, the whole procedure depends on the thought-experiments reflecting only what is *logically possible*. Too often, though, the idea becomes that 'what we can imagine is logically possible!' — but perhaps there are more constraints than we first thought on what we can *imagine*.

When such thought-experiments provide the most extreme of apparent counter-cases to candidate theses in respect of personal identity, are our concepts equipped to deal with them? One might think not (see §§3-4 above). Moreover, even cases apparently available at first can prove problematic on investigation. In perhaps the most well-known, from Shoemaker (1963 pp. 23-24), the brain of one person (Brown) is transplanted into the body of another (Robinson) with the usual assumptions about the causal capacities generated by the brain. Hence, the resulting person ("Brownson") "... recognizes Brown's wife and family ... and is able to describe in detail events in Brown's life ... of Robinson's life he evinces no knowledge" (Shoemaker, 1963 pp. 23-24). Can we extract from such a case some minimally controversial claims about who should inherit Brown's money?

A consensus over the Shoemaker case is that Brownson is Brown; yet, in part, that surely derives from our *description* of the case: that it is a body-swap! And it benefits from both candidates being men. But is it really so compelling? Would Angelina Jolie really have swapped Brad Pitt's body for a husband who looked like ... (insert the name of someone less than attractive — say, Donald Trump!) if she thought this creature was Pitt *really*? So perhaps the consensus is really less than at first appeared: then that will be a way to critique the methodology.

The potential power of such cases, when that power is not abused, cannot be doubted. In effect, though, sketches of two or three familiar difficulties mentioned above problematize the characteristic deployment of problem-case thought-experiments in such discussions. First, guaranteeing that the putative counter-case is indeed *logically possible* is often more difficult than the creators of such problem cases assume: what this required, of course, is that the case be assertable without self-contradiction. Yet, on mature reflection, this requirement is more problematic than it might appear — a difficulty rarely addressed directly! Thus, the drawings of M. C. Escher, say, might *seem* to represent logically possible (although physically impossible) situations – say, for staircases – when in fact the drawings contravene the 'logic' of pictorial representation (see Hacker, 1976). In a not dissimilar way, imagining such-and-such may well require far more detail than is typically given; and may prove impossible once one tries to supply that detail.

A second point concerns the procedures for generating counter-cases — that problem cases build in the assumption of a determinate *answer* to whether there *is*, or *is not*, numerical identity: that is, whether the person involved in this complex business the *very same person* as the one identified initially. But, for the assumption of a determinate answer to be plausible, the relevant concepts must be fully determinate in these cases. This seems contentious. Certainly, our commonsense account of persons may reasonably be expected to apply for most cases of, say, inheritance. But it is less clear that such an account *must* be able to accommodate, say, complicated duplication cases deploying something like the *Star Trek* transporter, not least because it seems ill-equipped to deal with any case where there are candidates of equal standing: thus, as Wiggins (1980 p. 72 note) recognizes, we have no good way to describe the relation of a 'mother' amoeba to its resulting [post-split] 'children', our usual kinds of descriptions being misleading, or otherwise problematic.

Thus, with Austin (1979 p. 88), we might wonder whether our concepts are sufficiently well-elaborated to resolve the extreme cases, such as those developed in the thought-experiments of philosophical problem-cases; faced with what we took to be a goldfinch, but which subsequently exploded or quoted Virginia Woolf, we might be left literally speechless — words (or, better, concepts) might fail us: we might not know what to say, because there is nothing that we *must* say in that context. As Austin (1979 p. 195) rightly reminded us (see §3), ordinary language "... embodies ... the inherited experience and acumen of many generations of men (and women)". But that cannot cover cases hugely outside its compass. This point is regularly raised generally to indicate how easily that method of 'problem cases through thought experiments' can be abused (see Wilkes, 1988). For instance, consider:

> ... a man whose memories on the even days of his life comprise the events of all those days, skipping entirely what happened on the odd days ... without a feeling of discontinuity ... Are we bound to say here that two persons are inhabiting the same body? (BB p. 62)

The "Three Faces of Eve" case offered alternative ways to regard such a case; say, in terms of multiple personalities. As Wittgenstein (BB p. 62) asks, rhetorically, given these alternatives:

> ... is it right to say that there are, and wrong to say that there aren't [two persons], or vice versa? Neither. For the *ordinary* use of the word 'person' is what one might call a composite use suitable under ordinary circumstances. If I assume, as I do, that these circumstances are changed, the application of the term person or personality has thereby changed ...

Once the details of the case are agreed, nothing may remain for dispute: so here, we might readily treat "Eve" as multiple personalities of the same person. As Wittgenstein (BB p. 62) continues:

> ... and if I wish to preserve this term and give it a use analogous to its former use, I am at liberty to choose between many uses, that is, between many different kinds of analogy. One might say in such a case the term 'personality' hasn't got one legitimate heir only.

Certainly it would be wrong to think that one or other answer here was *obviously* right: to urge, "persons are substances, so this must be a feature of personality (only)" is simply to *decide* the matter one way. Yet, as Wiggins (1980 p. 3) notes, "there is persistence through change". For numerical identity, the issue typically concerns "coincidence as a substance" (Wiggins, 1980 p. 4). But what (in our world) can *count* as substances? That question need not be problematic: our work-a-day world is full of continuants through change — of cars and watches to be returned after mending, for example.

Of course, the concept of a *person* might also be problematic, since (after all) "person" is not *obviously* a natural kind (for instance). Hence a fuller account of the difficulties of 'social objects' would indeed have something special to say about persons. Similarly, we must decide how best to characterize continuity for danceworks through their performances.

§7.   Determinacy for sortals?

Wiggins accepts that at least some concepts, such as those identifying substances (say, *person*), must be completely bounded; hence there would indeed be cases with determinate answers as to whether a particular instance does, or does not, fall under that concept. We might differ. In part, Wiggins's restriction of his discussion here means he addresses only what he calls "sortal-concepts": but what are sortals? Certainly the counting question ("How many Xs are there in the room?") will typically be answerable for sortals; and gives a useable sketch for them.[9] But even those who accept Wiggins's picture for *sortals* might worry about generalizing it. And, of course, even when our attention is restricted to those artworks that are particular objects (for instance, painting and cut-sculptures), it is not self-evident that the key concepts for identifying the very same ("numerically identical") artworks do indeed count as *sortals* (even for Wiggins: 1980 p. 125). So what should one say of artworks and their 'essences'? For Wiggins (1980 p. 125), the requirement was for a "... theory of individual natures": he comments that, "... easel pictures, carved sculptures and frescoes come as close as anything can come to meeting this requirement" (Wiggins, 1980 p. 125). But will that be close enough? And where does it leave artworks in performing arts, such as dances?

In addition, when the problem-cases for *persons* (for use as models) invoke very elaborate accounts of persons, ones very far from our usual situations, it is less likely *both* that our current concepts will be adequate to deal with them (our second criticism, above) *and* that a useful model for discussion in aesthetics will be provided. So that I, for one, have no idea how to address the question of whether persons are four-dimensional entities: but I am fairly sure that the usual view of persons (say, as parcels of matter with certain psychological properties, or some such) cannot accommodate that conception; or, at least, that there is no reason for confidence that it can.

The issue is broadly methodological: one cannot just assume that the concepts employed in describing artworks (those that *are* particular objects) will be able to deal with extreme problem cases. That returns us to the claims about artworks elaborated above. Looking to the future (and our consideration of dance), the discussion of numerical identity for persons can clarify what *is* at issue for dance (still numerical identity but for danceworks, a kind of multiple: see §10 below); as setting aside indistinguishability as a condition for such identity; and as reinforcing the question of what *kinds* of thing are dances.

Asking 'What kinds of thing are dances?', where typical danceworks are recognized as multiple objects, broadly abstract objects actualized in performance, might be called a focus on the 'ontological'. But a theme throughout has been that ontological debate is problematic (see especially

Chapter Five §5). Here, though, we are just reporting some common-sense distinctions. Quite a lot of what we know of art-type *dance* provides a solid basis for our investigation; and we know quite a lot. The relevant concepts do not yet seem especially problematic. Hence we grant that two performances are of the very same dance (say, *Swan Lake*) although we recognize that there will be differences between performances. More centrally, artworks that are multiples (and especially those that are performances) do not fit well with the concern Wiggins (1967 p. vii) evinced with "... persisting material substances". So, since dances will not typically count as "material substances", less may transfer here than might be imagined — the idea that artworks might resemble persons in some relevant respects (see Wiggins, 1980 pp. 124-126) holds at best for some artworks; and not the kind we are addressing (see PAD pp. 33-39; pp. 289-306).

Now three problematic assumptions behind typical procedures in such cases should be noted: the first, mentioned already, is that our current concepts are adequate to deal with problem cases — we have little reason to assume this; second, and relatedly, will there always be a *determinate* solution? One might wonder whether a particular situation is resolvable as *definitely* identity or *definitely* non-identity; and, of course, this might reflect back on both the use of our current concepts and our ability to recognize the logically possible — crucial for the construction of genuine thought-experiments. Finally, one wonders about the impact of presentation of issues from a first-person perspective: does that import the idea of *"the* real me", and hence dispose to an identity-solution? All three here might suggest limitations to the usefulness of focusing on identity-investigations, at the expense of others.[10]

§8. Identity and composition

In at least two further situations, one says truthfully, "A *is* B", without asserting identity between A and B. The "is" of composition (Wiggins, 1980 p. 31 note; see also Wiggins, [1968] 2016 p. 35) provides one (discussed here: for the other, see §9), whereby saying that this woolly hat *is* (or was) a scarf does not assert identity between the two, but simply acknowledges that the second was unpicked and its material re-knitted to make the first. This idea, arguably fruitful in some discussions of personal identity, becomes crucial when considering the relation of thoughts or feelings to brain-states (see Chapter Four §5).

With the "is" of composition, although the wool *composes* the scarf, it is not *identical* with the scarf. They share material, but that is all. There is nothing to the scarf other then the wool, so that all of the properties of the scarf depend on properties of the wool, including properties emergent from that base and rooted in the interrelations of properties of the wool. (To remind ourselves, although the water is liquid, water-molecules are not: but the liquidity of the water, although 'emergent', can be explained by detailed discussion of the properties of those molecules.[11]) Similarly, the scarf has stripes of red and yellow on a black ground: this comes about because *this* section of the wool comprising the scarf is red, *that* section is yellow, and other sections are black. And the scarf really is striped, even though it is not true of any of the wool. In that sense, "being striped" is a higher-level property — a property of scarves not wool, even though the scarf *is* (that is, is *composed of*) the wool. So the broadly causal relationship here is quite complex; and not explicable at the 'lowest common denominator' of causation. Such uncontentious facts about composition often escape our notice.

Further, by its colours, this is the Students' Union scarf of the University of Keele (in the UK). That fact imports a normative element taking us completely outside the realm of causality. For only a particular combination of stripes amounts to the Keele University Students' Union scarf — although perhaps one with stripes approaching that combination would count as approximating that scarf, at least for some purposes. But (a) it is true of the scarf that it is the Keele University Students' Union scarf; (b) nothing *external* to the scarf makes it true (viewed one way) — the properties depend on the scarf; and (c) the relationship of wool to this fact is certainly not causal.

One difficulty here (see also Chapter Four) reflects the relationship between mind and brain. Thus, suppose that one set of causes of my behaviour in, for example, a chess game relates to states of my brain — say, to changes in my biochemistry. Then, as Frege ([1918] 1984 p. 351) reminds us, "[e]rror and superstition have causes just as much as correct cognition". So simply addressing the causal story here — how my judgements and actions *came about* — does not yet approach the *normative* question of whether this is, say, a good move in chess. A *good* move in chess will have *one* causal story in these terms; but so will a bad move. Further, the problem here has nothing to do with complexity, since the bad move and the good one are on a par in this respect. To apply, there seems no straightforward way, drawing solely on the resources from causality, to account for this normativity.

But we are materialists: clearly the brain offers (part of) the *material composition* of the mind. However, approaching that point requires recognizing that the "is" of composition is not centrally causal: the scarf is not *caused* by the wool; and few of the scarf's properties are the direct low-level causal consequences of the wool. In the same way, the mind is not *caused* by the brain. The best that might be said is that the brain (as I am calling it) *composed* the mind: that is not necessarily too far from the truth, at least for the purposes of our discussion. For, minimally, certain brain-states (and hence the brain-functioning to permit them) seem required in typical cases if certain mental states are to occur. And, since we *are* all materialists here, mind-states certainly have *some* (physical) 'incarnation', however understood. This means, though, just that my specific mind-state has some specific 'incarnation' in me: that offers nothing yet to take us beyond what follows in any single case — although, of course, Wittgenstein (PI §281: see also Robinson, 2007 p. 19ff.) rightly insists that mind-properties are really only applicable *strictly* to persons (or something very like human persons); for only *persons* could actually perform the mind-functions at issue, like perception, memory and intention.

§9. Identity and recognition: is my house a white dot?

Recognizing *composition*, and thereby acknowledging statements readily mistaken for identity-claims but in fact having different uses, allows for productive comment on the second set of such cases noted above: the "is" of *identification*. As Collingwood (1938 p. 265 note) says, Oxford philosophy Professor John Cook Wilson:

> ... used to point out in his lectures that the written sentence, 'That building is the Bodleian' represents two different propositions, '*That* building is the Bodleian' (answering the question, 'Which of these is the Bodleian?") and, 'That building is the *Bodleian*' (answering the question 'What is that building?').

Here our occasion-sensitivity allows us to recognize these as, in effect, two different claims, their difference being apparent once one considers (roughly) what question each answers — a strategy in line with noting that these utterances amount to something different, in answering different questions.

Here the term "is" will be deployed in *identification*: that is, identifying either *that* building (as the Bodleian) from among other buildings, or *the Bodleian* from other candidates for the Oxford University library — such that one might continue (also pointing) "... and that is the Sheldonian Theatre". So here is another dispute, apparently about identity ("the identity of the building"); but, as my initial clarifications reflect, many uses of the term "identity" are irrelevant to philosophical concerns with (numerical) identity, even when they intersect with such a project.

Identity-issues occur naturally in philosophy where one has some interest in deciding, of two object-describing descriptions, if they are in fact of the same object: if there is really only one such object in the story. Thus, in the classic case for inheritance (see §1 above), is this old man the very same person as the young boy mentioned in the will? Or is a particular mountain identified when seen from the south the very same mountain as that seen from the north (Ateb/ Aphla: Frege, 1980 p. 80)? Or when is a particular heavenly body, identified in the morning, the very same heavenly body as one identified in the evening (Hesperus/Phosphorus: compare Frege: 1984 p. 145; p. 162)? To understand the "yes" answer in all these cases, one must understand that (some of?) the properties of each apply timelessly, or something similar. Thus, Jim Jones (the boy) was short, hairy and ill-tempered while James Jones (the man) is tall, bald and even-tempered. Recognizing the *tensed*-character of the applications of these expressions avoids saying that the same man is both tall and short, and so on. (Moreover, this result coheres with commonsense: we expect people to change with time; but that cannot alter our numerical identity conclusion, at least if the changes are within limits.)

Moreover, other trivial issues can be set aside: if one description means *seen from the south* that will not sit happily with the application to the mountain of "seen from the north"; or if one description means *seen in the morning* it will cohere badly with the application of "seen in the evening". But this connection to their meanings will not undermine the identifying uses of the expressions.

In this vein, the claim by Austin (1962 p. 98 note) was that, although his house was the white dot on the horizon, he did not live in a white dot! Similarly, Warnock (1971) asks how the English magazine *Country Life* might advertise that house for sale: certainly not as "white dot for sale"! (see Kripke, 2013 p. 96[12]). Here too the issue concerns, not a genuine identity-judgement, but one reflecting identification. For it is true that the white dot on the horizon is Austin's house, and yet false that Austin lives in a white dot.

The cases Austin mentions might be treated as *like* the tensed case for identity, so that the properties do apply but not in a contradictory fashion. This option does indeed look unpromising. One cannot be invoking Leibniz's Law, since one is deliberately characterizing the (my) house in terms one knows are not true of it, when it is conceptualized under a different description – that is Warnock's point about how to describe the house for sale; or the fact that the white dot gets bigger as one approaches it, while the house does not. For my house is *not* a white dot, despite my using that expression to pick it out. This strategy would conflict with our explanation of identity via Leibniz's Law above (following Wiggins).

If that option is set aside, what is the alternative? Perhaps more promisingly (and attempted here), these might be treated not as highlighting properties at all but just identifying descriptions, akin to pointing, in line with the idea above from Cook Wilson (via Collingwood). Certainly, *identity-claims* are helpfully distinguished from the use of other classes of statements which — given their linguistic form — might be mistaken for identity-claims. And, of course, these are *uses* of expressions (and hence utterances) rather than statements as such: we are not addressing linguistic expressions. Then, for some cases, where the point is to acknowledge that a single object is given two different "modes of designation" (Frege, 1984 p. 156) — where the object has been "determined in different ways" (Frege, 1980 p. 80) — one is *aiming at* (and hence dealing with) an identity-claim: in insisting that there is only one object (say, mountain) 'in the story', despite the two characterizations ("Ateb", Aphla"[13]).

But that is not Austin's purpose in characterizing his house as "that white dot": rather, this is simply an *identifying* expression. With *identifying expressions*, one is *only* offered a way to identify the object, not (or not necessarily) any property of it.[14] As Kripke (2013 p. 4) points out:

> If you call a man 'the man who corrupted Hadleyburg', you have referred to him by virtue of describing him as the (unique) man who corrupted Hadleyburg. But if you simply call him 'Sam', you have simply called him that and have attributed no properties to him.

So this last is merely identifying. Thus, for identification purposes, Austin's house is a white dot on the horizon; say, in contrast to the grey dot that is his neighbour's house. The point is not simply that — as Austin recognizes — it does not *follow* that he lives in a white dot, but further that one cannot even infer that his house is, or is not, (predominantly) white. So that even the one *substantial* property seemingly ascribed in the identifying expression is not (automatically) true *of the object thereby identified*, but without this counting against the identification. Hence the *content* of such identifying-expressions need not be among the properties that — for an identity-conclusion — apply to the object, if in some tensed way. This *seems* the case of the petitioner who, asking to see the same official as on her previous visit, "... sees the *same official* but not the *same man*" (Wiggins, 1980 p. 29; p. 36[15]), this is predication rather than identity. It is not intrinsically true of the man, although there is a sense in which it could identify that person at that time; and hence is (timelessly) true of him at that time of speaking since, at the time, he has that role! And some things might rightly follow from this role.

Perhaps that is one reason why proper names regularly function so effortlessly as such *identifying-expressions*, for there we are not tempted to ascribe any content from the name to its bearer. (Someone called "Tiny" need not be, and usually is not, *at all* tiny.)

Given his interest in identity-claims, Kripke (2013 p. 93ff) seems keen to determine whether Austin was, or was not, asserting identity here (or making an identity-claim). Or, at least, he seems to assume uniform answers across the cases discussed. So that finding one case where Austin was (or might plausibly be thought to have been) asserting identity should settle all the other cases. And, in the text, here are places (perhaps many places) where Austin does discuss one object characterized in two ways ("Hitler"/"man with black trousers": Austin, 1962 p. 99).

But this worry misses Austin's characteristic contextualism — his commitment to occasion-sensitivity. So that, *sometimes*, to speak of so-and-so being such-and-such will be an identity-claim: as with the man who inherits under his grandfather's will just because he is the very same person as the young boy initially identified by the grandfather's will. But such a claim need not be taken as asserting (an) identity (complex gender-reassignment cases, for example, might make the remark simply identificational); and one cannot always tell by scrutinizing the words used. Further, since the remark need not be an identity claim, no argument here can *require* that an identity-reading be offered globally or across the board.

Notice that there is *identification* presupposed even here: that the man is the very same person as a particular young boy — so that, asked, 'Which young boy?', the grandfather might plausibly have pointed across the room. Hence Austin's remark might be seen as purpose-specific – it allows for identification only: it is used to contrast the white dot on the horizon (*my* house) with the grey dot (my neighbour's), addressing the question, 'Which house is yours?'. For the one piece of *apparent* information imparted about my house —that it is white — extends only so far: my house, as the white dot, is the whiter of the two dots.

Of course, if a part of our project involved how to *formalize* the claims Austin is making, then it would be important to understand whether or not to use the identity-symbol to express this particular "is"; and, with a limited number of alternative formulations, the decision might be tough. As one strategy, identity could be characterized in an abstract way, as Wiggins (1980 p. 3) does; then ask to what extent the relations between, say, the two descriptions here ("White dot", "my house") accord with that characterization of identity — dismissing, as not identity, any instances where they part company. But this is not our problem, and hence need not be our position. (Sometimes, with McDowell (2009 p. 155), "... I am not sure I understand the problem to which this is supposed to be a solution".)

Consider an example from fiction: in Alexander McCall Smith's novel *The Minor Adjustment Beauty Parlor* (New York: Pantheon Books, 2013), one character has an incestuous relationship with his sister, which results in a son — although the character does not know that. Some years later, the son is introduced to his father on the pretext of being a nephew: the two become friendly, and — on the father's death — his will directs that the so-called "nephew" inherit his father's farm. From the perspective of the law, of course, there is no nephew — and hence no heir. But, for me at least (and in the novel), moral concerns operate differently: the young man *is* the person who was supposed to inherit; he is the one *meant* in the making of the will, and he performed the actions that fostered his father's love, and so on. So, if the expression "my nephew Liso" is viewed simply as an *identifying-expression*, picking out which person was meant, but no more, the young man's inheriting is clearly in line with his father's wishes. And justice is thereby done.

The moral from this tale, of course, is that, on some occasions, philosophical concern with the truth (or otherwise) of the *content* of such identifying expressions is beside the point. (In this way, Leibniz's Law is set aside.)

§10.   Dance-identity and notationality — an adequate score?

We recognized (above) that, in typical cases, a particular dance could be performed with a different cast; that performances of the very same dance will differ on at least these occasions. This is guaranteed by the fact that *performables* are necessarily re-performable; therefore, in principle, with a different cast — indeed, there *will* be such differences (tired performers, different performers). How might, say, the thinking of a dance company accommodate that situation? How can these performances being of *one* dancework be made sense of, given that they obviously *are* of one work? An elementary idea would be: *same movements (plus music, costume, etc.?) equals same dance*. But that is not, or need not be, satisfied by either of the main cases implicitly raised here: we can have 'confusable counterparts' for the movements that are not that dancework; and performances with different movements (as well as differences in costume, and such like) can be uncontentiously of that work. So this suggestion does not fit what we know of danceworld (with danceworld practice, as it were).

Raising an identity-question for dance asks in effect, 'Is performance B a performance of the very same artwork as performance C?', *not* 'are they indistinguishable?', as we *know* they won't be! At least three cases must be distinguished:

(a) *Central case of performance in traditional style*:
    What you want from your first *Swan Lake* is a production that doesn't mess with the music, the story or the flock of identical swan-maidens in white tutus. Once you know the conventions, the madder caprices of directors and designers can be indulged or deplored to your heart's content. (Parry, 2002 p. 14)

(b) *Borderline case* — as far from traditional as possible, but still the same dance [although, as above, not necessarily with same artistic value]: for instance, the Matthew Bourne *Swan Lake*, with all-male cast.

(c) *'Over-the-border' case* — no longer the same dance (same artwork) despite similarities — of music, etc.: for example, the Mats Ek *Swan Lake*.

How might such cases be discussed? (If the categories are accepted, the examples are not important — although the choices must be explicable. See also Chapter Five §2.)

Further, since works in the performing arts are encountered only in *performance*, *identity* here is not 'identity of *performance*', but identity of *artwork*. What is 'the dance itself' for these purposes, given that it is experienced only through performance? Typically, both identity-conditions *and* also identifying remarks will require discussion. Thus, Austin (1962 p. 98 note) pointed out that "the white dot" (on the horizon) was a perfectly good identifying-remark for his house, without suggesting that he lived in a white dot (see §9 above). That is to say, the remark was not an identity-claim, despite any similarities of form. Then, referring to two performances as both of *Swan Lake* need, as yet, have no further content — the context for the remark has not been provided. In particular, it is not automatically an identity-claim.

Under what conditions is a dance performance an *authentic* performance of, say, *Swan Lake*? Elsewhere (PAD pp. 62-64), I stressed that notated scores could make explicit constraints from the *type* (treating danceworks as type/token objects). The notation becomes important just because it allows one to describe (even if only in principle) whether or not the object in question is a token of a particular type. But this is of limited help in 'the real world': most cases lack either *any* score or (at least) any *adequate* score. Still it represents a useful *insight*, by:

• treating dances as type/token objects (in Peirce's sense);

• seeing the notated score as offering the constraints from the type — that is, as making public and accessible what is, in principle, unavailable to us *directly*; namely, the abstract object;

• offering the possibility of notating primarily what is *important* for that dance.[16]

On some occasions, then, such a comment will imply that performances are tokens of the same type; on others, it need not. When one needs to speak exactly, a performance can be identified as, say, the Mats Ek *Swan Lake*, thereby contrasting it with both the Matthew Bourne and Ivanov & Petipa versions. Moreover, features used to identify particular performances need not be features of the work: this is obvious for, say, "performed last Wednesday"; but equally true, if less obvious, of references to the performers; and even reference to roles may be contentious — perhaps we cannot have *Hamlet* without the Prince of Denmark, but some minor characters might not be essential for work-identity. The same would apply to dances.

Further, a parallel with music suggests an answer when/if there is a notated score for a dance: as with music, a dance-performance in accordance with that score is a performance of that work. The mere possibility of notation is all one needs to give performances answerability to the movements performed. Thus, my 'Thesis of Notationality' (PAD p. 62) urged that a dancework satisfying the score for work X in a notation-style agreed by the knowledgeable to be an adequate notation for dances of that sort was in fact dancework X; further, this both requires that the performance be a *dance* — not guaranteed by compliance with the score — and roots the judgement in those "knowledgeable in the artform"; so the notation must be suitable for that dancework.

However, some contrasts with music should be noted (for further discussion in Chapter Five §3):

(a) for dance/movement, there is not just one notation system, but three; also, an adequate score need not be inscribed in one of these three — other things count;

(b) these systems (such as Labanotation) offer movement notation, not dance notation — which is a benefit for anthropologists, etc., who are often interested in movement patterns, rather than patterns of *actions*;

(c) Notation systems are not familiar to dancers and choreographers in the way music notation is for (most) musicians.

Moreover, most musical works in the canon *will* have scores, unlike dances. Even where a dance-score exists, it is often constructed 'after the fact', thereby reflecting a particular performance (as arguably with the Stepanov score for *Swan Lake*: see below). So scores are not necessarily available in practice; and, at best, identify only bodily movement even in favoured cases of formalized notation systems, such as Labanotation (see PAD p. 97: Williams, 2004 pp. 197-198). That repeats the question: *but is it a dance?* (We return to the potential for 'confusable counterparts'.) For dance scores are not like play-scripts (PAD pp. 55-56), not least because the notation-systems are for movement-notation: there is no guarantee one is seeing a *dance*.

In reality, the danceworld sets aside (say) the Stepanov score for *Swan Lake* as not adequate: here, this means that performing in line with that score *will* generate *Swan Lake*, but also that performances which do not follow it — or go against it — may also generate *Swan Lake* (these would make some features of the dance concrete in ways other than those specified by the Stepanov score). Clearly this score fails to uniquely identify *Swan Lake*; it does not mirror the constraints from the type. Moreover, the adequacy or otherwise of a score might itself be open to debate: in some contexts, quite ordinary scores might count as adequate, seen in this light — and that would be a judgement of the Republic of Dance (or some sub-set of it: see AJ pp. 166-170). In practice, such a debate is quite possible, so the 'adequacy' of scores is not fixed; further, other claims to revise the 'official' version (or to reconstruct a dance with no 'official version') draw on the same resources.

Moreover, in practical cases, the notation need only be *appropriate* — it need not be comprehensive in describing *all* that every dancer does. Thus, compliance with the score for Elaine Summers' *Instant Chance* (see PAD p. 148 [there mistitled]) yields the work: what is not specified is thereby left flexible! As an example, consider Trisha Brown's *Accumulation* (1971), a task-dance where one problem is "... keeping the movement clear in the face of endless repetition" (Banes, 1987 p. 82). Here, the dance:

> ... starts with a movement — the rotation of the right fist with the thumb extended — that is repeated seven or eight times. The next movement, a gesture with the left thumb, is added, and the two are repeated in sequence several times. As the piece progresses, succinct gestures — a twist of the pelvis, a bend of the knee, a turn of the head, a step back, a lift of the leg — are strung onto the end of the accumulation. (Banes, 1987 p. 82)

Moreover, as Banes (1987 p. 82) notes:

> [o]riginally, *Accumulation* was four and a half minutes long and performed to the Grateful Dead's "Uncle John's Band". The second version (1972) was fifty-five minutes long, done in silence.

So that no particular music or duration is specified for the work: but *Accumulation* can be performed when the movements as set are combined in an order acceptable to Trisha Brown, where the "several times" noted above might also reflect the duration of the performance. Hence the 'rules' here constitute an adequate score. Indeed, no other criteria for completeness make sense.

§11.   Audience

Encountering *that* dance — say, *Swan Lake* — requires a *performance* of it; but also that there is an *audience* for it, at least in principle. In elaboration here, Cavell (1969/2002 p. xxxviii) rightly urges that:

> It is tautological that art has, is made to have, an audience, however small and special. The ways in which it sometimes hides from its audience, or baffles it, only confirms this.

At its simplest, this thought reminds us that art is made to be *appreciated*, so that a third role for people is indeed provided here, when one thinks about danceworks: not just as art-maker or as dancer, but also as audience member — even when these roles are shared by the same person. So one cannot *require* that the same person share those roles: just as granting that dance-maker and performer (dancer) are two roles guarantees that, in theory or in principle, a dance could be performed by some dancer other than its creator, so the role of audience-member cannot require that one be the dance-maker or the performer. Then the requirement for an audience is earned by artworks in general, danceworks in particular, along with the right to be taken seriously — to fail here is to fail to be art (or, at the least, to contest the judgement of that segment of the Artworld: AJ pp. 164-170). Further, the requirement for an audience in this sense is fragile; and more fragile in the case of dance than in some other arts just because its realization requires a suitable performance, but also an audience sufficiently informed and sensitive to make sense of this work, as performed. Yet that audience can disappear (see Chapter Seven §5), especially if the performance no longer captures the imagination: perhaps what was once new is now such a commonplace that the audience misses its fundamental originality; or perhaps the reverence *this* performance shows to past performances makes it stale. There are other possibilities, but many suggest either that the dancers have not grasped how to present *this* work or that the audience has lost it understanding of the traditions of performance appropriate to the work.

Many artworks are fairly mundane: the moment they seemed revolutionary has past. But, still, finding something worthwhile in them may be sufficient to keep them vivid *enough*. One potential weakness here follows from the need for the dancer of today to manage a variety of techniques. For that can lead (again) to the "hired body" with its "... rubbery flexibility coated with impervious glossiness" (Foster, 1997 p. 255) characteristic of many modern dancers (quoted PAD p. 266); and hence to difficulties in performing some techniques expressively. A revealing comparison arises when, having dismissed one pianist as merely technical, in contrast to the expressiveness of another, the suggestion is made that the difference here is *imperceptible*. For, of course, the claimed difference (once granted) has been *perceived*: it depends on the differential pressure on the piano keys, or some such. What is missing is a good way to describe or characterize it! The same applies to our dancers: they simply do not seem expressive in certain works — Twyla Tharp (2003 p. 173) characterizes this as an absence of *passion*, claiming that, "[w]ithout passion, all the skill in the world won't lift you above craft. Without skill all the passion in the world will leave you eager but floundering" (see Chapter Six §3). That makes it sound like a kind of commitment — which describes the effect: the dancer looks detached from the emotional content of the movement. But a suitably informed audience can *see* this in the performance, reflecting subtle defects of technique in respect of such roles.

Here, comment on the relation of the *audience* for dance to dance-criticism is appropriate. Like other arts, the audience (or at least its sophisticated version — call him the critic) needs the work to be in its category, genre, etc.; thereby minimizing the risk of *misperception* (see Chapter Eight). In effect, this discussion identifies the potential force of critical judgement: namely, of critics operating as a taste-makers, hoping (or aiming) "... to shape the taste of their readers" (Carroll, 2008 p. 193) by pointing out what they see as valuable in the artworks they discuss. In this way, an audience for art of a certain kind can be developed. For one can *learn* to see a dance, by having the features the critic values pointed out to you, with the implicit suggestion that you should value these features too — that they are *worthy* to be valued. In this way, one can learn to see and to value, thereby filling the need for informed and sensitive understanding. We can learn, and hence develop our critical powers: indeed, John Martin offers a positive account of dance criticism in the shaping of taste (see Chapter Nine §§4-7) — he saw his role, through his critical writings, as teacher both of dance understanding and, ultimately, of dance criticism.

§12.   Conclusion

In this chapter, we have considered the notion of identity typically discussed in philosophy, focusing on the case for persons. Doing so allowed us to set aside two other cases: first, when one might say that the scarf *is* wool (the "is' of composition: see §8); and second, when one might say that my house is the white dot on the horizon (the "is" of identification: see §9) — although recognizing that these do not exhaust the occasions when apparent-identity claims turn out to be doing something else; and that these are elaborated in terms of, say, the questions to which they provide answers. Thus, the "is" of composition explains what the woollen scarf and the woollen hat might share: they were the same wool — the scarf having been unpicked and the resultant wool knitted into the hat. Such cases are important when we look at other issues, since — on some occasions — apparent-identity claims ('The electrical discharge *is* the lightning') have been mistakenly treated as genuine identity-statements, rather than simply designating composition. This error, widespread in the philosophy of mind, has a bearing both when we look to understand artificial intelligence and when our interest turns to how thoughts are instantiated in (roughly) the brain. Moreover, the "is" of identification, too, suggests one way of setting aside, as not urging *identity*, claims not designed to permit the standard inferences concerning properties such that, at least in a tensed way, what is true of an object under one designation is true of it under all other designations. As such, it combines with our general commitment to the occasion sensitivity of utterance, or of understanding. The questions here would be like either/both of those that Collingwood relays from Cook Wilson: 'Which of these buildings is the

Bodleian?', and 'What is this building?'.

Addressing personal identity, we have followed Wiggins (1980) in stressing the role of persons as a *kind* necessarily embodied and necessarily having powers and capacities from an open-ended list ... one not in principle open to completion.[17] Such a view offers a reply to most puzzles raised by philosophers over whether a person described at one time is the very same person as one described at some later time (if only slightly later). These might well include:

(a) *Multiple-personality cases*, where there are a series of different 'phases' (Ansel Bourne/Brown, in James [1890] 1950 pp. 391-392; or Phineas Gage before and after his accident: Tallis, 2011 p. 23; p. 35). (Note that if these are cases of 'same person' continuity, our model has a physical dimension.);

(b) *Brain-transplantation* (Shoemaker, 1961 pp. 23-24), especially if we switch the brains, so that two people survive. Which is the real continuant? On what assumptions?;

(c) *Split-brain brain-transplantation* (Wiggins, 1967 p. 50; Parfit, 1984 p. 256) — here, as with a stick broken in half, identity may lapse in the face of two equally convincing candidates;

(d) *'Star-Trek-type transporter replication'* (Parfit, 1984 pp. 199-201) — might something less than identity be crucial? Might 'survival' as one 'descendent' be enough?

We see, too, how discussion here draws usefully on consideration of numerical identity for, say, material objects like cars and watches; or even animals like amoebas.

So, although having no responses yet, the issues are clarified in central cases. For instance, Wiggins's position allows a plausible response in many cases, especially those where *identity* is at issue: but there is not *always* an answer. For, first, our concepts may not be robust enough to deal with all the imaginary cases that might be projected; second, the need to give *all* the details may be rendered impossible by there being *no such finite totality*, in line with our occasion-sensitivity. But, as well as pointing to solutions to standard issues in personal identity, a background conception of persons is provided, arguably suitable to consider the claims of artificial intelligence and the possibility of androids.[18] Moreover, we have begun to reflect on a technique standardly used in philosophical debate: the deployment of thought-experiments.

Further, some issues for dancework-identity are clarified: describing typical danceworks as *performables* emphasizes how concerns with 'confusable counterparts' in other human behaviours help recognize distinctive roles for dancer and dance-maker (choreographer). In particular, granting the strengths of *recipes* of dances (capturing their notationality), as against recordings of particular performances (compare PAD pp. 76-78), allows one to assign both dancer and dance-maker clear roles in the identity-conditions for dances (as well as their identification conditions), incorporating a sketchy account of the intention embodied in the work.

Some limitations of such a 'recipe-based' account of work-identity were recognized, given that typical danceworks are *abstract objects* (indicated types, perhaps) only realized in performances: thus, tokens of those types. The need for an audience was acknowledged, with its details and roles remaining under-explored.

Chapter Three

The inexorability of (scientific) causality

§1.   Why might the possibility of agency be doubted?

Thus far, we have stressed the centrality of agency to our conception of persons as engaging normatively with a world structured in part by their ability to use language. And we have identified a moral dimension within such an ability: we *must* mean what we say — where the major alternatives are lying, self-deception or frivolousness. In this way, then, the place of responsibility has been emphasized. Further, when turning to dance, we again recognize roles for agents as dance-makers, dancers, and dance audiences; and the responsibilities such roles imply.

Why might such a conception of persons be doubted or disputed? The confluence of two factors might motivate such a doubt or dispute: (a) the success of science; and (b) moderate materialism — we are made of the same stuff that science explains (or seems to explain), give or take some comments on complexity. So, if scientific descriptions and explanations work so thoroughly elsewhere, to predict outcomes as the working out of causal forces, why not in our case too?

Of course, our default position must involve humans (us) who think ourselves able to attend to this presentation, perhaps to read it (which involves turning the pages), to understand it (to whatever degree), and to evaluate its argumentative potential. Thus, it invokes our *responsibility*. For, if all events were, in this way, completely explicable causally, there seems no room for that normativity that grounds human life as it is ordinarily understood — on the face of it, not just responsibility for one's actions (and hence morality) would disappear, but also the difference between *saying something* (which can misfire) and merely making sounds. Meaning too depends on the possibility of a normativity created by humans, as we have seen, but is nonetheless real for that.

The problem is pressing because, if 'the world' is indeed explicable without remainder through the causal accounts in natural science, it becomes hard to locate the intellectual virtues philosophy stresses or the affective (and intellectual) ones realized through an artform such as dance. The mind or consciousness has no obvious place in such an account; and, while *panpsychism* ("the view that the basic physical constituents of the universe have mental properties, whether or not they are parts of living organisms": Nagel, 1979 p. 181) may be no worse than other accounts of the relation of the physical to consciousness, as Nagel (1979 p. 193[1]) seems to urge, it cannot be an attractive option. At the least, it would make difficult assigning any importance to dances, to dancers or to dance-making: they would all, in effect, be relegated to (say) the 'dancing' of stilt-birds (Curt Sachs, 1937 p. 9; see UD p. 293; Williams, 2004 p. 80). Moreover, just this point has been recognized in the dance-literature. For instance, when William Powers (1983), reviewing Judith Hanna's (1979) book, *To Dance is Human*, suggests that *To Dance is Scientific* would be a more accurate title since (as he puts it), in that book, "... all humanism has disappeared" (Powers, 1983 p. 51[2]).

Yet what are the constraints on any considerations here? The problem lies in giving *due* weight to the achievement of science, and to the scope of scientific explanation of sublunary events (events here and now), without that achievement automatically swamping the *possibility* of human agency; and, with it, human responsibility. Any discussion of human agency must respect the explanatory power of science: laws of science seem to operate exceptionlessly over objects and events whose material construction is the same as our own (give or take some comments about complexity). Denying these powers to science seems frankly unrealistic; yet, if science explains *so much*, how is there *logical space* for explanation in terms of intentions, reasons and choices? For nothing sublunary seems to escape the explanatory power of science. And any answer to this range of questions cannot *escape* scientific explanation by denying our physicality through appeal to some "backstage artiste", as Austin (1975 p. 10) puts it. But neither must a picture of causality from (say) neuroscience hold us captive when discussing action (compare Chapter Four).

§2.   Some preliminary contrasts: the 'free will' debate

When considered within philosophy, such issues are standardly approached as part of debates concerning the possibility of free will or genuine action. In those terms, our commitment to agency means that we become some kind of 'free-will defenders', since we must be predisposed to accounts that permit the *truth* of claims about agency (such as the ones given above).[3] To repeat: this means that our topic will be the possibility of genuine agency. This is the real topic when considering 'free will'; and is both unconnected — at least directly — with what can be *willed* (or wanted), and recognizes from the start that circumstances can affect what one can realistically choose to do: hence, is not completely open or *free*.

Standard responses to this problem in philosophy are of two major types: the first urges that such freedom is *incompatible* with accepting universal causation, the second searches for some manner in which such freedom is *compatible* with such causation. The first position yields both those (typically called "libertarians") who urge that, since there *is* the kind of freedom compatible with genuine agency for humans (they claim), it must somehow be counter-causal and those (here called "determinists": see below) who argue from universal causality to the impossibility of the freedom of action, and hence of responsibility, rejecting the very idea of the counter-causal. Then debates around this first position turn on whether there are counter-causal events (that could count as genuine actions) or, again, whether the account of causality offered can avoid the determinist consequences.

By contrast, the second position yields compatabilist or reconciliationist accounts. They begin by granting what (they take it) the project of natural science assumes; namely, that every event has a cause. (Call this "the causalist assumption".) Then debates typically concern whether granting the freedom of action urged thereby achieves *enough*, since universal causality is implicit in, say, the project of natural science: if bodily movements all result from the electrochemical changes in the brain, Central Nervous System, musculature, and such like, is there any room for *action* — with its associated responsibility? For success, then, the positive view here must distinguish what the causalist assumption implies from what responsibility requires.

If this description is even roughly accurate, a straightforward resolution is unlikely, given the twin pillars upon which the debate stands. There seems little prospect of denying the causalist insight behind the project of natural science, with its recognition that humans too are composed of just that *matter* to which the laws of science apply — that must be granted even were human responsibility conceded. Equally, the freewill-defender's insight that much of our lives would be nonsensical without responsibility seems equally secure: indeed, the positions sketched cannot be asserted, or urged, unless humans are agents (capable of asserting, and of meaning what they say). So throughout this work, *agency* (with its connections to *meaning* and to *normativity*) is taken as a prerequisite for artistic production as well as philosophical investigation. There seems no plausible 'middle way'. Hence, producing a 'resolution' here requires that the *problem* be rejected somehow.

With this in mind, my alternative strategy recognizes the contrasts just mentioned as posed starkly by the *picture* of causality often drawn from the causalist assumption. Giving up this picture of causality need not undermine natural science (even if it makes us re-think how we present its project); and will permit us just the conclusion needed — namely, that the successes of science cannot suggest a logical bar to free action. Then the *problem* as classically conceived (and hence the classically-conceived alternatives, listed above) could dissolve, thereby returning us to a common-sense commitment to ourselves as agents, at least in typical cases.

Elsewhere (FW pp. 139-143; McFee, 2015a pp. 315-317), two related thoughts were stressed. The first amounts to asking for whom this 'free will' issue is really an issue. Borrowing an expression from Kant ([1787] 1996

B xl: p. 36 note 144), I claimed that it is only a scandal *for philosophy*, not more generally. That is, the issue does not really apply to the activities of, for instance, lawyers or psychologists, and perhaps yet more generally, although it is regularly introduced to (say) students as though it did. And this thought connects with a distinctive problem for (consistent) free-will deniers, apparent when one considers *from a first-person perspective* the *scope* of worries about the freedom of action: how to apply such conclusions to oneself, and how to justify one's adoption of them — given that the description in terms of *reasons* is precluded. Certainly it would be problematic for (say) a lawyer like Clarence Darrow to argue that his clients are not free agents in the *philosophical sense* (that is, denying the possibility of action) while not applying such thoughts *to himself*. Perhaps Darrow genuinely thinks that, in the peculiar situations that mark the lives of his clients in the Leopold and Loeb case (the basis for Hitchcock's film *Rope* [1948]), *nothing but* their behaviour was a possible outcome; perhaps they could not have behaved other than they did, given those circumstances (see FW p. 142). In considering his own behaviour, though, Darrow surely sees himself as uncontentiously *choosing* to do this or that; say, organizing his defence of them, and constructing speeches in that direction. Certainly, he regards such choices as within his gift. Yet Darrow cannot consistently *both* endorse some general thesis of free-will-denial and take praise and payment for his achievements, achievements for which (consistently) he could have no responsibility.

Yet why should this be just an issue for philosophers? My reply has been that the discipline requires philosophers to follow arguments where those arguments lead. Thus the issue arises *for philosophers* because, faced with the determinist *argument*, philosophy must address both such arguments and their supposed consequences. That response focuses our strategy on rejecting that argument itself, since the issue depends *directly* on that argument. But, in fact, that issue derives, at least *indirectly*, from the picture of causality that argument employs. Here, then, we focus more directly on that picture.

One further clarification: throughout, the term "determinist" is used to describe the person who concludes, on the basis of philosophical argument, that genuine *agency* or *action* is impossible. This purely terminological decision explicitly recognizes such theorists' position as indeed philosophical. By contrast, simply accepting that *every event has a cause*, and drawing no conclusion from that claim, as yet involves no move in philosophy. Such players are only committed to universal causation; they might, as above, be termed "causalists".

§3.   The exceptionlessness of (some) causal explanations

A simple example offers three plausible 'intuitions' about causality here. Suppose that, on Monday, one snooker ball (the cue ball) on the snooker table strikes another, and the second ball (the object ball) falls into the pocket. Now (first thought: *same situation, same outcome*) if, on Tuesday, the balls are in *precisely* the same configuration, with the cue ball moving as on Monday, and the object ball positioned as it was, then the object ball will again fall into the pocket. But (second thought: *different situation, uncertain outcome*), that confidence in our prediction about the behaviour of the object ball disappears when the situation changes, so that it is no longer *obviously* the same as Monday — say, the snooker table was re-built overnight. Perhaps, in re-building, the engineers gave the table a slope; or perhaps corrected a slope from the previous day. Either would defeat our claim. Without knowing that these things have *not* happened, assent to the claim that the same thing will happen on Tuesday as happened on Monday would rightly be withheld — we suspect that the situation is different (although, to anticipate, not yet whether it is *relevantly* different). Moreover, regaining our confidence here involves checking that *all* the important features of the situation are unchanged (checking *all* defeaters). Thus, the baize is now blue instead of green; but, were its other characteristics the same, our prediction remains unaltered. Yet which features are important? Full confidence depends on checking *every* feature of the initial situation (Monday) and finding it unchanged, or not relevantly changed. (But what exactly *are* the features of that situation; and how does one check on them *all*?) Then (third thought: *different outcome, different situation*) when the object ball does not fall into the pocket, we know that something is different — or some number of things are. (Of course, a slight deviation in the situation leads ... we know not where. At the least, our confidence in a repeat of the previous outcome would be weakened.)

Furthermore, what *would* happen, in certain circumstances, cannot be an *open question*; and especially when what happened previously in relevantly similar circumstances is known. Urging that it was an *open question* is both counter to a modern commitment to science, and plainly absurd:[4] the working-out of causal forces fixes whether, on a particular occasion, my car will start when I turn the ignition key — that question cannot be *open*, even when its answer is not known. So what is urged as *causal necessity* is actually the claim that the antecedent state of the world is *causally sufficient* for the outcome: that, given the exact state of the world, one (and only one) outcome was possible.

Our simplified picture depicts exceptionless causality: or, as one might put it, *causal necessity* in operation. Confidence in the outcome is justified only if *all* the factors — or, anyway, all the *relevant* factors — are the same: so a finite totality of factors for consideration is implicitly assumed. And *all* the factors must be addressed to ascertain which are relevant.

This assumption forms the basis for an objection to this picture of causality, and so to the generalized claims of *causal necessity*. For the assumption is that *all* the considerations relevant in any particular case could be addressed (in principle), and therefore that such considerations constitute a finite totality; hence, that *some* of them can be considered directly, setting the rest aside with a *ceteris paribus* clause. In "every event has a cause", that "every" (and any corresponding "all") implies a finite totality: that we could arrive at "every-minus-two", and then "every-minus-one", and finally "every". By the same token, there will be parallel processes for "all".

But now we can ask about the kinds of exceptionlessness in natural science characteristic of its exceptionless causation: as we have seen, that exceptionlessness is guaranteed just by assuming a finite totality of relevant factors, and then granting the applicability of *ceteris paribus* clauses. In effect, we *specify* that the causation is exceptionless.[5] So *exceptionless* causation of the kind characteristic of natural science is possible *only* when the *ceteris paribus* clause is granted. For the 'things' that need to be equal cannot be listed (or otherwise articulated): there is no finite totality of them. Hence one could *not*, say, be almost there with two to go; and then one to go; and then success! Yet this conception of *causal necessity* belongs to the assumptions of a certain picture of natural science, such that causal regularities here cannot be completely elaborated without appeal to *ceteris paribus*.

One might follow Mumford and Anjum (2011 p. vii) such that, although "[t]he world is a messy place", the theory to deal with it should not be messy. Then the familiar phenomenon of salt (sodium chloride) only dissolving in water *ceteris paribus* is taken to show that:

> ... the attribution [of causality] is dispositional: salt disposes towards dissolving in those circumstances but it is not necessary that it does so. (Mumford & Anjum, 2011 p. 167)

For, of course, various other factors, such as temperature and pressure, as well as the proportion of salt already dissolved in the water, will affect the salt's dissolving, or not. So it will not be true of every teaspoonful of salt, added to a glass of water, that the salt will dissolve in the water. Now we see what is meant by a "messy world": a world in which inanimate objects, such as heaps of salt, have dispositions to behave in certain ways. And then, for Mumford & Anjum at least, 'theory' should be comparatively straightforward: salt's dissolving is just such a disposition. Or, more generally, they identify "... the dispositional character of causes" (Mumford & Anjum, 2011 p. 167). In particular, there is no suggestion of necessity here.

In effect, this 'theory' simply re-describes the event to accommodate the details of the case: the salt sometimes dissolves; and when it does not, the sorts of factors that precluded its doing so in this case can typically be located. Moreover, those factors will themselves operate causally. So that there is no suggestion here that, say, a variety of outcomes is possible in that particular circumstance: no, in *that* circumstance one and only one outcome is possible. So there is a certain inexorability here. But the dispositional theory of causes reminds us, in effect, that there is no exceptionless uniformity here: the thought that 'salt dissolves in water' cannot be used as though it read "every teaspoonful of salt will always dissolve when immersed in any glassful of water". And the explanation offered lies with the messiness of the world.

Instead, I locate the centre of the issue in our explanatory powers: there are occasions when the right way to regard causation is as *exceptionless* — and then one has a kind of causal necessity. [And, *pace* Mumford & Anjum (2011 p. 166), acting in this way does not treat induction as though it were deduction: Strawson (1952 pp. 248-260) rightly set aside expecting inductive inferences to behave like deductive ones.] Thus, when I turn the ignition key in my car on a particular morning, I expect that the engine will start — and that expectation builds, in particular, both on my inductive evidence of its having done so in the past (when nothing seems to have changed) and on my conviction that in a particular circumstance — like the one the previous morning — *that*, and *only* that, could be the outcome. Hence, if there is another outcome (the car does not start), something must be different.

Of course, my version is only achieved by introducing *ceteris paribus* clauses since, as Geach (1961 p. 102[6]) recognized, and Mumford & Anjum (2011 p. 167) repeat, "... a causal relation can be prevented". That form of words is revealing when we *say* what caused the failure of the causal relation ("water under the distributor cap") — thereby showing the causal story for the failure of the causal account originally projected. But, equally, that form of words can mislead in seeming to suggest that any 'preventers' or 'interferers' might have been checked for, if only we had been more scrupulous. And hence that there is some finite totality of such potential 'preventers' or 'interferers' for any causal interaction, such that the possibility of such preventing or interfering could have been excluded. Yet that generates the difficulty with the understanding of *ceteris paribus* clauses: unlike alchemy,[7] natural science requires exceptionless causality, such that finding a different outcome to an experiment on the second occasion, one is entitled to infer that *something* — or some set of *somethings* — was different on that second occasion, as against the first. Here, the world is not really *messy*: if we could find the one or more factors that made the difference here, functioning as preventers or interferers in this case, there would be reliable causation. Then, with *all* the preventers identified, and excluded, one's causal relations could be stated in something approximating a law-like form. So, as expressions like "preventer", "interferer" suggest, this model is rightly operating smoothly *unless* ... even when we do not know the specific interferers. Moreover, natural science — and especially in an applied version, such as engineering — requires a kind of exceptionlessness. From the perspective of such science, the world cannot really be messy: and rightly so. Then, if we do not know these preventing or interfering factors, or cannot know them, excluding them via a *ceteris paribus* clause is one way forward.

One problem arises, though, when one's target is regarded as 'some set of preventers': we saw that, having identified *all* the preventers, one's causal relations could approximate a law-likeness. But, as above, there is simply no finite totality of such features to be our candidate preventers — often the crucial one can be identified, the one making the difference *in this case*. Yet we do not (typically) expect to tell the *whole story* of the causal nexus — perhaps because we concede that there is no *whole story* — but only to identify the crucial part of this case. So, in the previous example, the water under the distributor cap was the cause of the breakdown of the usual causal regularity whereby my turning the ignition key in my car caused the engine to start: this water *made the difference*. Hence the evocative characterization of causes as *difference makers*[8] — although the whole context is crucial, why is the case today simply not the same as that yesterday? What has *made the difference* here? (Answer, for this case: the water under the distributor cap.) In any case, we are sure that whatever outcome there is will be an inevitable one, given the nature and proportions of the various constituents of any particular event. It is all a matter of the components and their quantities, of the physics and chemistry, and such like. The thought, then, is that — in the situation that occurred — *this*, and only this, is a possible outcome (as noted above). Hence, were exactly those constituents placed in that same situation again (*per impossibile*), the same outcome would also recur. This is the inexorability that one refers to here when speaking of "causal necessity".

Natural science, then, behaves as though there were a finite totality of relevant preventers or interferers (even while granting there are not: FW pp. 121-123). And the behaviour of much of our causal world (say, our cars) is rightly seen in terms drawn from natural science. Thus, however much we curse the behaviour of our computers, our behaviour there resembles cursing the dog: we do not regard the dog's behaviour as suitable for normative critique — rather, it is just being a dog. Similarly, the computer suffers from faulty parts, soft-wear glitches, or operator error.

Notice that none of this suggests the world is messy, although it does suggest circumstances in which different questions, and hence different answers, are appropriate. To recycle an example, viewing my car as a hot-rod may invite one set of questions, viewing it as a custom car might invite another (FW pp. 119-20). Then, giving 'hot-rod' answers to 'custom-car' questions will be inappropriate — but will it be false? Our best answer would echo Austin (1975 p. 143):

> In real life, as opposed to the simple situations envisaged in logical theory, one cannot always answer in a simple manner whether it is true or false.

And, as Austin recognizes, the difficulty arises because one finds oneself in a new situation, such that what is true is "... only a general dimension of being a right or proper thing to say as opposed to a wrong thing, in these circumstances, to this audience, for these purposes and with these intentions" (Austin, 1975 p. 145). Still, once the appropriate context is located, thereby identifying the question at issue, determinate answers can typically be expected. And the sharpest case here involves erotetic contexts where *ceteris paribus* clauses are assumed or invoked; as with those provided by natural science.

Before continuing though, an objection to our procedures that might seem to be rooted in science must be put aside: it urges that we have misunderstood, or misrepresented, the nature of science by stressing its (apparent) inexorability. Thus, someone unduly impressed with quantum physics might urge that uncertainty considerations here are sufficient to set aside such a picture of causal sufficiency. This is a red herring: thus, in explanation of his claim that the idea of free action "... cannot be made conceptually coherent", Harris (2012 p. 5) urges, "[e]ither our wills are determined by prior causes and [therefore] we are not responsible for them, or they are the product of chance and [therefore] we are not responsible for them" (*my inserts*). Thus, if our desired outcome is *responsibility*, with its implicitly causal contribution to what occurred, the determinist *causal sufficiency* cannot be replaced by probabilistic or chance-based models: they could not save what is required — I am not responsible for what happens by chance! Thus, while finding that causality in scientific explanation was not exceptionless (because chance-based) might remove a motivation to discuss the possibility of action in a world of science, it could not offer what is needed here — it simply offers a different defeat for the responsibility required to make sense of (say) dancing or dance-making.

So, we have recognized that *causal necessity* (of the kind required for the determinist argument) only follows when such a *ceteris paribus* structure could be deployed. Yet even in the natural scientific case, there will be the required finite totality of factors only when we make it so — that is the force here of the *ceteris paribus* clause! It permits our imagining that *all* relevant factors either have been considered or remain unchanged by setting aside any not addressed. That assumes both some finite totality of such features (such that *all* had been considered) and a clear sense of what is or is not relevant. In natural science, our *ceteris paribus* clause guarantees the first of these (compare Dummett, 2006 pp. 86-87), while theory (or our complete enumeration) might provide the second. Such a picture gives a (false) impression both that what is and is not of relevance (and why) is understood, and that some finite list of features should be considered. Such assumptions are only plausible if one adheres to the *ceteris paribus* idea here. Then science does provide *causal necessity*, but only for science.

§4. Causality and agency

Turning to human action, three features should be recognized. First, those persons for whom causal explanation seems most pertinent — such as the kleptomaniac (FW p. 8 [and *passim*]) — should be treated as *importantly different* (from the rest of us) on this account: *ex hypothesi*, they lack our capacity for choices. Yet that allows recognition of the explanatory power of science (as before): in its domain, with causal necessity assumed and *ceteris paribus* clauses deployed, it operates exceptionlessly.

Second, since this power for science depends on assuming both some finite totality of such features (such that *all* had been considered), as guaranteed by *ceteris paribus* clause, and a clear sense of what is or is not relevant, provided in natural science by theory (or our complete enumeration), neither assumption is *safe* (in the legal sense) applied to human action: to repeat, one does not even know what *cetera* are required to be *paria*. More specifically, we have been warned against *always* treating human behaviour in causal terms, since "[e]rror and superstition have causes just as much as correct cognition" (Frege [1918] 1984 p. 351). Its normativity is one feature of human action incompatible with exceptionless causality, because causal accounts of the genesis of my chess move (say, in terms of states of my brain, Central Nervous System, and musculature) cannot explain why this move is *good* (when it is) since — as Frege urges — poor moves too have causal explanations of the same kind. Similarly, that Queen Elizabeth of England can name ships, and I cannot, is not explained by her greater capacity to hold and release champagne bottles, nor our relative abilities at certain vocalizations. Our differences are contextual. Hence any account that *could* do justice to normativity (or to misfires of this sort) cannot be solely causal — especially on the account of exceptionless causality sketched here to characterize determinism. So this case differs radically from that in (natural) science. Then claiming (truly) that "A causes B" is not exceptionless just because there are always cases that (if they occurred) upset the claimed or urged outcome. Hence this cannot be a 'law'. But one cannot check for such cases since, among other things, the (potentially) relevant factors cannot be enumerated — there is no finite totality. And if they cannot be enumerated, one obviously cannot check them *all*. So "A causes B" cannot mean that in *every* circumstance A will be followed by B — unless it is *made* to mean that (as happens in natural science)[9].

Third, context-sensitive reasons and choices were important for *characterizing* human action (as well as making sense of it); what action is in fact performed will depend in part on what *was* intended as well as what *could be* intended in that context. An example from an interface between aesthetics and the philosophy of sport may prove helpful (compare Culbertson & McFee, 2015); for philosophical aesthetics has surely included one of the fullest discussions of the kind of non-psychological conception of intention required here. Thus, to characterize accurately the actions that take place in a sporting event (say, a cricket match) requires that one recognize them as cricket (typically visible in their description using the technical vocabulary of cricket). This might be expressed in terms of the *intentions* of players, spectators and the like; but that would not be a request to interrogate their psychologies. Equally, asked what Shakespeare *meant* or *intended* in some passage, aestheticians have long realized that this was not typically a request to unpack Shakespeare's mental states, the kind of prior planning he engaged in before writing the relevant passage. Moreover, we recognize that what is not accidental is *thereby* intentional, or meant. And that this requirement cannot typically be over-ridden by specific acts of intending: one cannot typically make one's words amount to something new and distinctive merely by planning or intending that they will. As Stanley Cavell (1969/2002 p. 36) put it:

> ... an individual's intentions or wishes can no more produce horses for beggars, or home runs from pop flies, or successful poems out of unsuccessful poems.

Even Richard Wollheim (1987 p. 37: see Chapter One §8), whose account of intention has a psychological dimension, recognizes both that a non-psychological view of intention underlines the responsibility inherent in action and that such a view operates as well inside art as out of it: for "...the standard pattern of explanation in which understanding is preserved ... [will be maintained when one adopts the] ... perspective of the artist, which in effect means seeing the art and the artist's activity in the light of his intentions" (my order). To ask what has occurred will be to hunt for the correct description in that context: how was the action conceptualized? And that, in the end, will relate to (roughly) the purpose, or set of purposes, implicit in performing such actions. Then, a particular sport offers a clear example, where speaking of *purpose* typically amounts to a recognition of such a purpose (or intention) implicit in the project of — here — the sport, the sort of thing that is implicitly adopted by those undertaking to play that sport. So that the reference to intention or purpose here does not commit us to the mistaken conception of intention whereby, to determine the intention implicit in this practice or rule-system, one interrogates its practitioners. Thinking otherwise is slipping back towards a generalization of the kind of broadly Gricean conception of linguistic meaning (see Grice, 1989 esp. p. 25) that Charles Travis (2008 pp. 9-11; 19-64; 65-93) has repeatedly demonstrated to be unsatisfactory. For, *pace* Grice and his tradition, *intention* should not be interpreted simply in psychological terms: that is, in terms of specific intentions or claims of specific individuals. Instead, there is something positive to be said here, roughly parallel to discussions of the artist's fulfilled intentions as they are embodied in the artwork, while recognizing this intention-as-embodied in recognizing the artwork's meaning, by granting that the artwork necessarily flows from human decisions and intelligence. Further, the context will provide a powerful constraint: as Gilbert Ryle (1954 p. 32) noted, a player "... cannot keep wicket in a game of tennis. He can switch from one set of sporting functions to another, but one of his functions cannot be switched to the other game". Then, if we ask what he is doing, these are facts that must be taken account of; and got right. So that what one can do — what can be done then and there — will differ with the context.

But such considerations undermine the very commitment to *ceteris paribus* clauses built into this picture of *causal necessity*, by rejecting the thought that explanatory factors here constitute a *finite totality* (see below). Recognizing the lack of exceptionlessness in cases where human action is central speaks against claiming *causality* in much social research; or precludes our taking as exceptionless any 'causality' identified. That merely repeats the assumption (or model) of causation in natural science as exceptionless; thereby granting the applicability, in that domain, of *ceteris paribus*.

Now consider the problematic character of the idea of *exactly the same situation* for human beings in social settings. As the second element of the sketch of causality above (§3) suggests, our warrant in predicting the future on the basis of the past (and present) runs only to the *degree* that the future *resembles* the past (and present). For when we know there is a difference, we must gauge anew its impact. But the difficulty in *claiming* (much less, in *knowing*) whether the future would be like the past was already apparent: in what features or respects should the past (and present) resemble the future? Our first two answers might be: "in relevant respects" (for then we have *relevantly* the same situation); or, "in all respects" (for then we have *exactly the same situation*). But both answers are unhelpful. For *which* respects are relevant? Relevant in what way? And how is such relevance to be determined? (Typical cases in natural science can give answers to these questions.) Or, if we refer to *all* respects, how can we be sure we have got them *all*?

For natural science, with the cue ball from a snooker game (snooker is pool for grown-ups) travelling at exactly the same speed and in the same direction on Tuesday as it was on Monday, and with the other balls in the same position with nothing else changed, then the same thing will happen on Tuesday as happened on Monday — say, the object ball will be pocketed. Should this not happen, there *must be* some difference after all (contrary to my assertion). We specify, on the basis of *theory*, that certain factors can be ignored; we control for the factors that we can, 'handling' the rest by the *ceteris paribus* assumption. Notice that this device does not involve *checking* which 'things' are 'equal'. Instead, we specify that *any* differences can be put aside as irrelevant.

The human world lacks precisely this kind of specificity.[10] Suppose our picture includes the shot in question being played on Monday by former World Snooker Champion John Higgins. The shot on Tuesday will be too, since — in the example — the situation is to be replicated. Further, Higgins has neither been injured nor damaged his snooker cue in the meantime. But, while it made sense to think of *exactly the same things* being in place on the table, and so on, it makes no sense with a person, John Higgins, in the story. First, he cannot be in exactly the situation on Tuesday that he was on Monday — if for no other reason than that, on Monday, he had not potted *that* ball! He cannot return to his previous state. In fact, we cannot even know where to start looking. Has he had exactly the same meals? Well, even if he sampled the same menu-items from his favourite Chinese restaurant on both occasions (which is unlikely), he has not eaten *the very same* food. Or perhaps a vital conversation with someone on the Monday evening changes his motivation, say. And so on for every feature of his life. But, if the involvement of just one *person* precludes clear replication, with a set of relatively closed skills (moreover, skills of which he is a master), how much less likely is it when more persons, more situations, and the like are involved? So causality with persons must be differently conceived: the assumption of a finite totality of factors must be given up; and, with it, the picture that produces (or permits) *causal necessity*.

Of course, there is no such finite totality in natural science, either: there, the 'gap' is *legislated away* with the (real or implied) *ceteris paribus* clause. Yet that seems plausible because — while we do not know *all* of the things relevant in science (there being no *all*: no finite totality) — the *kinds* of scientific investigation that we engage in at least localizes the factors relevantly considered. So, the position of the moon is relevant in investigating tides, but not in analyzing some runner's gait. The moon's gravitational effect is granted even in that case — as not exactly irrelevant perhaps, but not significant either. Similarly, some experiments require a Faraday cage to isolate the experimenters from the earth's electro-magnetic field; but others can simply ignore such effects, without compromising their results. These inclusions or exclusions are guided by *theory*; and all are weighed for relevance as factors within that branch of science.

A similar point should be recognized for human actions. No doubt Harris (2012 p. 4) is right when — referring to a notorious killer — he comments:

> I cannot take credit for the fact that I do not have the soul of a psychopath. If I had truly been in Komisarjevsky's shoes on July 23, 2007 — That is, if I had his genes and life experience and an identical brain (or soul) in an identical state — I would have acted as he did.

But that conclusion is guaranteed by the strong reading given to *identical* (and other such ideas) here. For, as above, if some other behaviour then occurred, one would infer that — after all, and despite all appearance to the contrary — there *must* be some differences. So of course Harris (2012 p. 4) is right to continue that "[t]here is simply no intellectually responsible position from which to deny this", so long as one's account of causality is the exceptionless one sketched above (§3).

It is revealing here to find J. R. Lucas (1970 p. 12) characterizing the position of (some) philosophers as follows:

> We use the word 'free' ... to say of [certain] actions that no complete causal account can be given of them.

For what is required for such *completeness* here? We have recognized its connection to the sorts of exceptionlessness achieved by *ceteris paribus* assumptions. Then the determinist argument (mentioned in §2 above) cannot go through without qualification because its picture of causality incorporates an assumption (namely, a *ceteris paribus* assumption, or something similar) required for the *causal necessity* operative in a key premise of that argument, an assumption justified *only* when one is doing natural science. That assumption is not sustainable where consideration of (human) action or choice is acknowledged: where, indeed, talk of 'free will' more typically reflects lack of compulsion, rather than the absence of (complete) causal explanation. Hence the determinist thesis — in appealing to such a picture (and only powerful with such an appeal) — should be rejected because (roughly) it assumes two contrasting sets of background conditions: those of natural science for its introduction, and deployment, of *causal necessity*; and those of human action for its conclusion. These two background conceptions cannot be conjoined, since they depend on competing presuppositions. My terminological decision helps make this plain: to be a *determinist* is, for me, to argue *from* universal causation *to* the impossibility both of genuine action and (hence) of genuine responsibility.

In a sense, then, the picture just described, while *true* for natural science, is implicitly *made* true (or specified as true) through the use of the idea of controlling for variables (say, in an experiment) and, ultimately, by the use of *ceteris paribus* clauses, such that any area of variation not covered through the process of controlling for variables is thereby *specified* as irrelevant. This explains what the determinist position gets right, thereby granting the force of the conclusions of science: no counter-causal account will be plausible. That also explains why *general* contextual matters need not be considered in natural science: in effect, a simplifying assumption is introduced to constrain the scope or sense of *pertinent* questions in the context of natural-scientific investigations.

Here, discussing what counts as causal, Anscombe (1957 §47 [p. 86]) contrasts two list of descriptions, identifying one as those " ... which go beyond physics" — we might add "... and biology". In exemplification, Anscombe ([1983] 2005 p. 100) offers as "a causal history" that:

> Henry VIII longed for a son; the death of many children made him believe he had sinned in marrying Queen Catherine; he formed the intention of marrying Anne Boleyn. All this led to, helped to produce, the Act of Supremacy, to his decision to break with Rome.

Moreover, she notes that the physiological history, though of "a different type", intersects with this one:

> ... but only at certain points. Henry signed something ... and this was an episode in the above history. Ink got onto the page in a certain pattern. It was deposited on the paper by a pen pushed by the royal hand. At the other end of the chain perhaps there was a noise — a courtier saying, 'Here, Sire' and messages up the afferent nerves ... (Anscombe, [1983] 2005 pp. 100-101)

While Anscombe ([1983] 2005 p. 101) writes that, "[t]he causal histories of the two types [of what?] aren't rival accounts", someone might with justice think they *were* rivals, having noticed that the second was *deterministic*, and the first was not. At the least, the inexorable, exceptionless, scientific causality is clearly distinguishable.

§5.   Is it worth learning to swim?

An example may help. On my understanding, many sailors on large sailing ships in the eighteenth century did not learn to swim. Their reasoning was that, since there was no hope of turning the ship to rescue them if they fell overboard, and even less of them being picked up if the ship sank, it was better to die *then* than to swim for some time before, overcome by fatigue and/or cold, they drowned *later*. Such an attitude might strike us as fatalistic in some way; but, of course, is not strictly fatalism that this example offers (compare FW p. 15-17). Instead, the sailors' thought (if correctly described) retains a certain logic; in *their* context, it seems reasonable. By contrast, Gilbert Ryle (1954 p.

25) raises the question of whether it is worth learning to swim, since:

> ... some drownings ... would not have happened had their victims learned to swim ... We can say that a particular person would not have drowned had he been able to swim. But we cannot quite say that his lamented drowning would have been averted by swimming lessons. For had he taken those lessons, he would not have drowned, and then we would not have had for a topic of discussion just that lamented drowning of which we want to say that *it* would have been prevented. We are bereft of any 'it' at all. Averted fatalities are not fatalities.

The point here is that, here, only 'after the fact' of his drowning do we have a drowning to discuss; without the event, there is nothing in need of explanation and justification. Then of course — whatever the causal story for what *did* happen — a certain kind of 'defeater' is difficult to invoke, although it *would* defeat our prediction of (say) the drowning. Yes, recognizing that So-and-so would not have drowned if he had taken the swimming lessons defeats my claim that, given certain factors, his death was *inevitable* once he fell into the water (assume this to be the only defeater in the case). Further, we know that the defeating condition *did not* apply since, lamentably, he *did* drown. But what should be made of this? Clearly, the relevance here of the swimming lessons is granted — had he taken these lessons, he *would have* survived (*ex hypothesi*). But until we have the drowning as an *event* to discuss, the relevance of potential lessons is not discernable; hence, it is only discernable 'after the fact'. But, as Ryle (1954 p. 25) continues, this is not the same as saying that "... it is logically impossible to avert any fatalities". Rather, there are two points here: (a) one cannot predict exceptionlessly what *would* be relevant to predicting (say) a fatality, if that amounts to listing all potential defeaters; and (b) if we look to a disaster that *almost* happened (he fell in but, fortuitously, had taken swimming lessons, and so survived), we can seize on that feature as the decisive defeater *in this case* only because it was causally efficacious *in this case*. A rough parallel might be with the water under the distributor-cap that prevents my car starting: I might mention *that*, and get it fixed — but focusing there is setting aside all the other conditions causally-required for the car's starting, any of which might have also made the difference.

Of course, in learning certain skills, there is a clear sense in which I am changing my capabilities, changing the options open to me (the sorts of changes not open, in *sui-generis* ways, to chemical reactions) as well as changing the potential defeaters of predictions; for instance, of my drowning. We might say that I am changing myself, although not in ways relevant to Chapter Two. So what is available to me, or available to thwart some prediction, is not fixed in some permanent fashion; although, for any event, it is fixed by the 'totality' of its actual precursive events — although not, of course, by its potential ones.

Here, as Ryle (1954 p. 22) notes, there is something right in saying, 'What is, always was to be'. Given that So-and-so *did* drown, there was no time, prior to his death, when it was false that he *would* drown. Yet that sounds as though his death was inevitable; and that, of course, is what we *are* denying. Rather, we have built into the story his death by drowning: that generates the appearance of inevitability here. Things could have gone differently previously, where this might have a bearing on his situation when in fact he drowned. For instance, he might have learned to swim; and this might have saved him from that fate. Yet here, too, one must not urge too much: for the time spent learning to swim might have had other effects on where he was and when. Roughly, if he had been someone else (in the sense noted above), perhaps this lamentable death by drowning would not have occurred.

While one might guess at the details of such an alternative future — as we might have guessed at this one (and even been right) — that is not the sort of things we could have known: even the most well-grounded guess at the future is still a guess at what will be. Ryle (1954 p. 22) right recognizes that:

> The questions, what makes things happen, what prevents them from happening, and whether we can help them or not, are entirely unaffected by the logical truism that a statement to the effect that something happens, is correct if and only if it happens. Lots of things could have prevented Eclipse from winning the race; lots of other things would have made his lead a longer one. But one things had no influence on the race at all, namely the fact that if someone guessed that we would win, he guessed correctly.

The relevant factors concerning what did or did not happen may be largely causal: the correctness or otherwise of the guess was causally inert — except of course that, someone else (knowing the guesser's good luck) might have been prompted to do something. And of course, this too is not a causal outcome of the correctness of the guess.

§6.   On Davidson's anomalous monism

To some, the view just presented might resemble Davidson's *anomalous monism*, the view that, although "all events are physical", it is *not* true "... that mental phenomena can be given purely physical explanations" (Davidson, 1980 p. 214). Given its widespread interest, it seems worth drawing the contrast between our view and this view, which purported to follow from three further "principles" (Davidson, 1980 p. 208):

- "... that all mental events ultimately, perhaps through causal relations with other mental events, have causal intercourse with physical events."

- "... that where there is causality, there must be a law: events related as cause and effect fall under strict deterministic laws."

- "... that there are no strict deterministic laws on the basis of which mental events can be predicted and explained."

At one time, he took these to generate his conclusion. Thus, when introducing *anomalous monism*, Davidson (1980 p. 231) referred to "first premise", "second premise", and "third premise"; and, more recently, Davidson (2005 p. 185) stated those premises as:

(1) that mental events are causally related to physical events, (2) that singular causal relations are backed by strict laws, and (3) that there can be no strict psychophysical laws.

Davidson (2005 p. 186) has also urged that, although the thesis of anomalous monism is "... weaker than the premises", those premises are still thought to be part of any elaboration of anomalous monism; and when repeating these "premises" now, Davidson (2005 p. 185) presents them as detachable in some way which he offers diagrammatically, as "(AM + P)" (Davidson, 2005 p. 187). Further, since the newer version "... will involve some clarification, and perhaps modification, of the original thesis" (Davidson, 2005 pp. 185-186), I will concentrate on his exposition there.

Davidson aims to avoid that 'reductionism' that treats mental phenomena as *nothing but* physical phenomena, but without sliding into any kind of dualism. In part, this monism is defended by appeal to that *supervenience* (explained Davidson, 2005 p. 187) that implies monism but "... does not imply either definitional or nomological reduction" (Davidson, 2005 p. 187). Although the notion of *supervenience* is not unproblematic, none of my difficulties here turns on it; so I shall set it aside — although one should recognize that, for Davidson (2005 p. 188), anomalous monism really amounts to "(AM + P + S)".

It helps to see just why the presence of ("strict") physical laws is not necessarily reductive. Here, consider an example from Baldwin (2001 p. 199):

If a hurricane is described at the top of page one of today's *Times* and the damage caused by the same hurricane is described at the top of page ten of the same newspaper, then the event described at the top of page one of today's *Times* caused the event described at the top of page ten; but this truth brings no commitment to the existence of a strict law that events described at the top of page one of the *Times* have effects described on the top of page ten. It suffices that there is a physical law which connects the forces inherent in the hurricane with the physical description of the damage thereby caused.

So, in one way, Davidson is not committed to the idea that the operation of causal relations depends on the description offered of the events. Indeed, "[r]edescribing an event cannot change what it causes, or change the event's causal efficacy" (Davidson, 2005 p. 189). But it seems to make a difference when one characterizes the event in what Davidson calls "mental terms": for now the law-likeness disappears: or, more exactly, "... mental concepts are not reducible by definition or by strict 'bridging' laws to physical concepts" (Davidson, 2005 p. 194).

Central to Davidson's defence of this position is the thought that, while physics would be a "closed science" (Davidson, 1980 p. 241) or a "closed system" (Davidson, 2005 p. 193), the same cannot be true of psychology: and that such closure would be required if there were to be "*strict* psychophysical laws" (Davidson, 1980 p. 240: my emphasis). Further, Davidson (2005 p. 192) sees at least some of those who differ from him as failing to recognize "... the distinction between strict laws and other sorts of regularities".

Moreover, for Davidson (2005 p. 193[11]), it is important that such physical laws really are the laws of physics viewed as "... genuinely strict, exceptionless laws, since physics, being the fundamental science of the universe, applies absolutely to all events and processes" (Baldwin, 2001 p. 200) — what Davidson (2005 p. 193) speaks of as "the laws of an ideal physics". For, as Baldwin (2001 p. 200) goes on to explain:

> Whereas sciences like biology have to allow for interventions in biological processes that are not themselves susceptible of explanation in biological terms (such as changes in the Earth's climate) there cannot be interventions in physical systems which do not admit, in principle, of a physical explanation, even if we do not presently possess it.

Then Davidson's point might be put as urging that "... there are no strict laws at all on the basis of which we can predict and explain mental phenomena" (Davidson, 1980 p. 224[12]): again, the contrast is with those cases, typified (at least) by physics in Davidson's view, where in principle strict laws hold. As above, Davidson insists that his account is not reductive; and discusses the form(s) of supervenience. Neither of these points need concern us, for my aim here is simply to elucidate where my view differs from Davidson's.

I agree with Davidson that psychophysical laws cannot be elaborated, and for roughly the reasons he gives: that such laws would depend on how the psychological events were characterized, where many such characterizations would be possible in principle, all equally acceptable (in their contexts). We differ on the possibility of those strict laws operating in the "closed systems" that, as Davidson imagines it, are found in an idealized physics. My objection might be put in three ways. First, as an objection to the idea of a "closed system": closure is only achieved in physics through the introduction of *ceteris paribus* clauses, as there is no finite totality of features to be considered (see below). Second, as an objection to the "idealized physics": *of course*, if physics is explained so that there *must* be exceptionless laws, the problem will lie in finding them, and in confirming that one has done so — perhaps there *must be* a single ultimate explanation of an event, given that set of assumptions. But, if we can never know for sure when (or if) that ultimate explanation is found, we can never be sure that there are not other features that might function here as "defeaters", "preventers" or "interferers" (Geach, 1961 p. 102[13]), in respect of any explanation offered. Or, to put that another way, there is no basis for getting beyond the idealization. Then, third, like the closed-ness of the system, the *strictness* of the laws is only achieved by importing *ceteris paribus* clauses when we have no idea of what 'other things' (what *cetera*) should be 'equal' (*paria*).

So I differ from Davidson primarily in what to say about natural science: that there, where (in principle) he finds *strict*, exceptionless laws — at least in physics — I see the tactical deployment of *ceteris paribus* (or something very like it) so that, thereby suitably idealized, there will be *apparently* exceptionless laws. But in reality such strict laws are an illusion introduced to allow us to practice (at least) physics. They import a conception of the natural world meeting three conditions (see §3 above):

- with the same initial conditions, there will be the same outcome (only one outcome is possible, given those conditions);

- with differences in initial conditions, there is no guarantee of what will occur (in different conditions, no particular outcome is guaranteed);

- when, in what seemed like the same initial situation, a different result obtained, there must have been a difference in the original conditions.

For, as we saw, this is broadly what is meant by *causal necessity*. And such a conception makes sense only in a closed system, the sort providing *strict laws* by allowing that *all* the relevant factors might be considered — if sometimes obliquely, via the *ceteris paribus* clause.

In this way, the possibility of the 'regularity' or 'uniformity' (as identified by the covering law) being defeated by some as yet unconsidered factor is granted. Geach (1961 p. 102) rightly imagines that "... any alleged uniformity is defeasible by something's interfering and preventing the effect", so that setting aside such possibilities requires that the system was closed, with a finite totality of possibilities (so that *all* might be considered, in principle); and such closure is achieved in natural science (especially in physics) by the *ceteris paribus* assumption.

With events involving human beings, two related factors are crucial: first, it matters how the event is characterized, since it will only be intentional under some (true) descriptions, not all; and, second, the human world incorporates what Friedrich Waismann (1968 p. 43) characterized as the "... *essential incompleteness*" of description, whereby "... it is always possible to extend some description by adding some detail or another. Every description ... stretches into a horizon of open possibilities" (Waismann, 1968 p. 44). But one must here part company with Waismann, who took such openness to apply to *most* empirical propositions. For us, by contrast, the situation centrally applies only for human events, not for those others where the aim (or perhaps the ideal) involves offering explanations of the kinds typified by the natural sciences, deploying *ceteris paribus* clauses. Still, our view of such cases coheres with Waismann's view of the alternative to openness: in these situations — as in mathematics — "... one could construct ... a thought model which anticipates and settles once for all every possible question of usage" (Waismann, 1968 p. 44). That is just the condition Davidson envisages for a closed system.

Thus the anomalousness comes from the fact that one cannot really even *approximate* strict laws for human action, as one can for physical events. Moreover, is Davidson right to insist that what are anomalous are, speaking exactly, *mental events*? No; they are really *personal* events — occasions where persons are *agents*, importing the normativity associated with agency. Then, of course, Davidson is correct that one element thereby lost in regarding these events from the perspective of physics (or even perhaps of biology) is their connection to human psychology — to what permits there to be *mental* events. Yet the crucial characteristics of such events are the ones that fit least well with the conception of strict covering laws. For they will precisely be the cases where what I intend or mean to do bears on the success of what I actually do — hence, on what *action* is performed. But, to repeat, that will be more than merely psychological; and hence may seem badly described as "mental". Indeed, one might agree with John McDowell (2009 p. 256) that:

> ... we need a way of thinking about the mental in which involvement in worldly facts is not just a point about describability in (roughly speaking) relational terms (like someone's being an uncle), but gets at the essence of the mental.

Or, better, reject any such *essence* but reflect "... an availability, to the judging subjects, of facts themselves, which she may incorporate into her world view ..." (McDowell, 2009 p. 255). For instance, in perception our visual experiences bring our surroundings into view (compare Travis, 2013 p.

30). For perceptual judgements too might seem to count as 'mental', and hence as 'mental events';[14] and what is central to the human world includes judgement, with its associated normativity: that is what must be taken here from our capacities as rational agents.

Further, to elaborate the situation for human behaviour, we can turn to a discussion of (broadly) determinism found in Gilbert Ryle (1954 p. 27[15]), who rightly notes that:

> ... before 1815 ... there could not be true or false statements giving individual mention to the Battle of Waterloo ... The prediction of the event can, in principle, be as specific as you please ... If gifted with a lively imagination ... [the forecaster] could freely concoct a story in the future tense with all sorts of minutiae in it and this elaborate story might happen to come true. But one thing he cannot do – logically and not merely epistemologically could not do. He could not get the future events themselves for the heroes and heroines of his story, since while *it is still an askable question* whether or not a battle will be fought at Waterloo in 1815, he cannot use with their normal force the phrase 'the Battle of Waterloo' or the pronoun 'it'. [my emphasis, identifying a key notion]

In our language, we recognize that the question remains *askable* at this point just because the situation is not *closed* in this respect: there might always be *defeaters* for any inference from, say, the placing of troops by Wellington or Napoleon, the state of mind of each, the needs of each country, and so on ... to a conclusion about the inevitability of the Battle of Waterloo — perhaps one might urge that some battle was inevitable but, even though Wellington had picked 'his ground', it does not follow absolutely that there would be such a battle nor that it would be fought there. 'Defeaters' here are recognized in two easy ways. The first involves recognizing other specific factors that, had they occurred, would have militated against there being, in 1815, the battle we now call 'the Battle of Waterloo'. For example, had Blücher's Prussians been yet closer to the French army, Napoleon might well have preferred to retreat; or instead to again attack the Prussians directly, to prevent the two forces combining against him. And such a strategy might well have been successful: we have Wellington's word for the actual outcome having been "... a close run thing".

A second, more abstract way acknowledges the place of defeaters by noting the use, above, of the expression "and so on" (combined, perhaps, with dots of omission): there was no specific list of candidate 'defeaters' here — the "and so on" is just a way to recognize that fact. But there is an additional insight to be gleaned here. For, of course, if the claim for events occurred in the natural sciences, the outcome could indeed taken as inevitable; but doing so would assume, if implicitly, the use of the *ceteris paribus* clause to set aside precisely those 'defeaters' (known and unknown). In this way, the sciences (or, at least, physics) do constitute a closed system, permitting strict necessities, in just the way Davidson approves. But such closure does not mark the physical from the psychological: rather, it is ensured by our commitment to *ceteris paribus*, in those cases where we are so committed. And, as Ryle suggests, that will not be any case where the outcome is "... still an askable question". This, in turn, will be all cases where the presence of human beings, with their motives and intentions, precludes the kind of closed system where the 'answerability' of such questions is settled. But it would also be any case in the natural world where *ceteris paribus* was not deployed or assumed.

§7.   Conclusion

This chapter has presented an elaboration of the conception of causal inexorability widely assumed, not without justice, as characteristic of natural science. Faced with the claims of natural science and its practical achievements, and a commitment to that minimal materialism on which we humans just are (composed of) this anatomy and physiology, one cannot deny that such explanations will apply to our doings and saying, insofar as those doings and sayings are regarded in terms of the physical structures that produce or instantiate them. But what place can that explanatory structure offer to *responsibility*? For responsibility is also too central to our self-understanding to be readily given up.

As Bernard Williams (2014 p. 264) noted:

> The problem of free will has two parts. One part is the question ... whether there can be genuine, intentional, chosen action if the agent's doings are located in a causal network that reaches beyond him. The second part concerns the relations of all that to certain moral notion — in particular, responsibility and blame. Do these notions make sense in the light of our understanding of people and their actions?

Unlike most philosophical discussions, we were, of course, here concerned directly with both parts, since our attention to dance (and hence to dancers and dance-makers) requires adjudication on their responsibilities in respect of the actions constituting the dancework. Hence, our discussion assumed that such notions do make sense; and explored how. We saw that the standard argument for determinism in effect urges a "No" answer in respect of the question from the first part: and, further, how that argument is unsound — how its conclusions do not follow from its premises. Further, the insight that undermined the determinist argument (namely, recognizing its unwarranted assumption of completeness of action-based descriptions on the basis of a completeness only achieved for causal accounts in science by the introduction of *ceteris paribus* clauses) also allowed us to offer a "Yes" answer for the first part: the notion of a "causal network" applied to humans does not function as our determinist assumed.

Thus, the strategy here urges that the exceptionless picture of causality typically ascribed to science poses starkly the contrasts between the causal and the normative: it also imports the two-fold assumption (manifest in its deployment of *ceteris paribus* clauses) that some finite totality of such features is relevant to the explanation or description of any event (such that *all* had been considered) and that a clear sense of what is or is not relevant can be achieved. But such an assumption is not plausible outside natural science; and especially not when human action is at issue. Giving up this view of causality need not undermine natural science (even if it makes us re-think how to present its project); and will permit just the conclusion needed: namely (as we put it before), that the successes of science cannot suggest a logical bar to free action. There is, of course, a study of dance that focuses on the anatomy, physiology, and nutrition of dancers: perhaps some of it will involve studying the neurophysiology of those involved as dancers, dance-makers and dance-audience. But there is a limit on what such causal description can achieve if our interest is in art. We have seen here that one cannot reduce the descriptions of humans, much less of dancers, to their purely causal descriptions. Later chapters will draw out some of the consequences of this realization.

Now, a segment of our discussion has defended, in part, commonsense claims concerning human agency and responsibility: here, as Reid ([1815] 2002 p. 577) remarked, "[p]hilosophers should be very cautious in opposing the common sense of mankind; for, when they do, they rarely miss going wrong". And in few places is that more true than when locating our starting points for both dance-making and its philosophical investigation in the powers and capacities of humans. But, in this way, we are actually following Kant's *Second Critique* on the pre-eminence of practical reason. So that, like him, we begin from "the fact of reason" (Kant [1788], 1956 p. 31), which "... reveals itself in decision, not in contemplation" (as Nagel, 1997 p. 117 puts it). For the normativity of such decisions is typically clear. This will have relevance, of course, when we turn to dance appreciation and dance-criticism (see Chapter Nine), as well as to the (practical) decisions of dancer and dance-maker. But it also highlights a moral (both for action and for art): that one's powers and capacities are often reflected in what one *should* do as much as what one actually does. From the normativity implicit in granting that I *ought to* refuse to do such-and-such, it follows that I am free to do so, even when I am (say) too cowardly to actually refuse (see Kant [1788], 1956 p. 155). In this way, we in effect return to the claims made earlier, implicitly following Wisdom (1965 p. 102: see Preamble §1), in recognizing the fundamental role of cases or examples in our discussion.

Chapter Four

Causality and the brain

§1.   Introduction

A number of issues for agency, and thence for dance, remain even given acceptance of my dissolution of the problem of the freedom (or, better, possibility) of genuine agency: see Chapter Three above. Here, elaborating my account of causality pays special attention to some misconceptions that follow from attempts to locate the causality for human action uncontentiously in the brain; as when Colin Blakemore (1999 p. 270) writes:

> The human brain is a machine which alone accounts for all our actions, our most private thoughts, or beliefs ... All our actions are products of the activity of our brains. It makes no sense (in scientific terms) to distinguish sharply between acts that result from conscious attention and those that result from our reflexes or damage to the brain.

Accepting this view would deny the reality of actions, as we have discussed, explicitly contradicting our oft-repeated slogan from Frege, in offering the same (causal) explanations of actions as of other movements. Moreover, much of the confidence views such as Blakemore's manifest derives from having a 'gadget' to study the brain, functional Magnetic Resonance Imaging (fMRI); a 'gadget' that "... more than anything else, ... has taken the analysis of brain function beyond the laboratory and into the wider world of popular science" (Tallis, 2011 p. 37). But:

> ... fMRI scanning does not directly tap into brain activity ... fMRI registers it only indirectly by detecting the increases in blood flow needed to deliver additional oxygen to busy neurons ... (Tallis, 2011 p. 76)

Further, this indirect evidence takes place against a background where, since:

> [m]uch more of the brain is already active ...., all that can be observed is the *additional* activity associated with the stimulus. Minor changes noted diffusely are regularly overlooked. (Tallis, 2011 p. 77)

Acknowledging this limitation, then, would speak against our *knowing* the full causal story. But surely there *is* a complete causal story in respect of any action that actually occurred. After all, (a) every event has a cause; and (b) the action that was this event *did* occur: in that sense, the state of the world was causally sufficient for the event that comprised that action.

§2.   The causal story of past behaviour: causal sufficiency

Discussions of causality regularly presuppose, for genuinely causal relations, the *inevitability* of outcomes — such that only a difference in initial conditions could preclude the same outcome in a second case. This must be correct, as far as it goes; but it assumes replication of *all* the initial conditions. In a sense, then, this assumption mistakenly requires the *completeness* of the account of initial conditions: that they too comprise a finite totality. For if, at some time, some finite totality of initial conditions, in conjunction with some finite totality of relevant factors, meant that only a particular outcome was inevitable (*"causal necessity"*), that outcome would be knowable, in principle if not in practice. But, since there *is* no such finite totality of initial conditions, any aspiration, even in principle, to exceptionless prediction of the future — say, my future states or actions — on the basis of the past and/or present is always misplaced. With no such finite totality of conditions or features in fact relevant to even a single causal interaction, no set of causal factors can ever guarantee a particular (causal) outcome. Of course, the deployment of *ceteris paribus* clauses in natural science can conceal that fact: that is how the illusion of *causal necessity* is introduced [see Chapter Three; also FW]; and how *ceteris paribus* assumptions secure the sufficiency of sublunary causal interactions, as viewed scientifically[1] — say, the starting of my car when the ignition key is turned. Recognizing the nature of genuine *causal* relations here removes the connection of causality to inevitability, at least for human actions. Instead, what was, in fact, the outcome of a particular causal interaction might have been different, since (in reality) one cannot rule out *all* the potential counter-possibilities that, if actualized, would have precluded that outcome. This is especially true when agents, with their differential conceptions of particular events, are involved.

So there is a clear reason for the illusion of causal sufficiency: *whatever* was causally sufficient for X was in place (and operative) when — or perhaps just prior to — the occurrence of X. For X occurred. So it might seem that *therefore* an account of the factors causally sufficient could be given, at least in principle — the illusion is just that *therefore* such sufficiency could be completely described. But this illusion is achieved by a piece of sleight of hand: for adding another feature could always undermine this *sufficiency* to the specification of what is previously taken as causally sufficient. With this granted, the sleight of hand is obvious: a *ceteris paribus* clause was imported. Having such a clause in place conceals the failure to specify the conditions causally sufficient in the case.

This point also bears directly on any discussion cast in terms of the causal sufficiency of neural events. Thus, according to John Searle (2007 p. 110), his opponents, Maxwell Bennett and Peter Hacker:

... say that the neural processes are causally *necessary* ('need to occur') for a mental process to occur. But we need to know, in that context, what is causally *sufficient*, what made it happen that I 'went through' a mental process?

The references here to "causal sufficiency" seem justified because all sides agree that the relevant 'mental process' did occur: that I *did* think such-and-such or decide so-and-so. But, as we have just seen, no set of conditions at time T1, when my brain is in state A, is sufficient to guarantee that, by time T2, my next brain-state will be state B, because there are always potential 'defeaters', counter-possibilities that — were they realized — would preclude brain-state A *causing* brain-state B. And they cannot *all* be ruled out, since there is no *all* here; no finite totality of such possibilities. (This standard argument for scepticism shares its presuppositions with the conception of causation it undermines.) So granting the earlier causality cannot imply that a recurrence of *roughly* those neural factors will be sufficient in another case for my thinking that same thing, or intending that same behaviour.

Of course, another sleight of hand here specifies that *exactly* those past conditions — if recreated — would have the same outcome. The term "exactly" does the work here for, were there some *other* outcome, one could conclude that the situation was not in fact replicated *exactly*. Yet that makes no sense when, as here, no finite totality of factors or conditions is open to consideration. So we cannot (say) list the factors; nor conclude that this situation mirrors that *exactly*.

But this conception fuels determinism (as Chapter Three demonstrated[2]): that causal forces lead inexorably from one event to the next — or they would not be genuinely causal. Having set aside the inexorability of causation, our account of brain-states connects with our discussion of the possibility of genuine action in a world of universal causation through the elaboration of four points. First, my brain eventually arriving at brain-state B is indeed a causal transition. But the illusion of *sufficiency* here is achieved partly because, after all, I *in fact* arrived at that brain-state (hence the actual conditions in total *must* have been sufficient); and partly through the implicit appeal to a *ceteris paribus* clause. Then while no such account can alone identify a causal chain sufficient for the transition to brain-state B, faced with potential 'defeaters', any other requirements for such sufficiency are accommodate through this *ceteris paribus* clause. And, of course, my brain does end up in state B. It provides the illusion of causal sufficiency (as urged by Searle, 2007 p. 110: quoted above): but, strictly, it *is* an illusion.[3]

Second, the conceptual moves from this case (after the fact) cannot be used predictively for human action, because — with no finite totality of the sorts of counter-possibilities potentially relevant here — *ceteris paribus* clauses cannot be deployed in those future-directed or predictive cases. The feature permitting the use of *ceteris paribus* in that other case (namely, that the transition *had* occurred) is now absent. So that *this* causal transition being sufficient (*ceteris paribus*) does not generate the kind of causal necessity fundamental to the determinist argument. Hence, from claiming (a) that the transition from brain-state A to brain-state B is causal, and (b) that brain-state A is such-and-such a thought, one cannot reliably infer (c) that this thought *causes* another thought, namely that instantiated by brain-state B. Now, separate — or, anyway, separable — issues concerning the relation of brain-states to psychological states are not addressed here (See the discussion of Nicole in §6 below). Yet, even within those constraints, descriptions relating thoughts to one another — that is, in the language of human action — cannot be substituted seamlessly for description in the (bodily) language of causation.

A third point follows from Wittgenstein's insight (PI §308[4]): that one cannot simply set aside *sine die* the character of such states — for, insofar as one is concerned with the relationship operative here, that concern involves clarifying the appropriate *relata* in the context at issue ("are they facts, material objects, conceptual terms, events, conditions?": Robinson, 2007 p. 177), as well as determining the character of the relation. (The remarks above highlight the inadequacies of the answer "causation": for what are the features of causation?) And of course, and fourth, a further insight from Wittgenstein (PI §281) must also be accommodated:

> Only of a human being and what resembles (behaves like) a human being can one say: it has sensations; it sees, is blind; hears, is deaf; is conscious or unconscious.

[We will return to this topic below.]

To some, the action-story here might still seem defective: but, in effect, their objections have been put aside elsewhere, along with the determinist argument (see Chapter Three; FW). The causal universalism of *Every event has a cause* sustains no logical bar on genuine action, although conditions genuinely causally sufficient for that action cannot be completely specified in advance to exclude 'defeaters' (once one excludes the use *ceteris paribus* clauses, as deployed in natural science).

To other objectors, the account offered here may seem inadequate in failing to capture the *causal* story: in particular, that story here might seem defective in not bringing out why exactly you did what you did; say, ran away from the tiger. For a part of that explanation here, at the level of persons, involves your seeing the tiger *as dangerous*. Without that, your flight seems unmotivated. And this seeing or recognizing (we can grant) is centrally intentional: the causal story will not reflect it. Or so it seems.

But, since we are materialists, your *seeing the tiger as dangerous* is still comprised by some bodily state broadly conceived (to include brain-states) — a state different from that you would have been in had you not recognized the *danger* of that tiger. And, to reiterate, both must be states of your body (broadly conceived) once our materialist commitments are maintained. Further, the realm of action — governed for us by "in the beginning was the deed" — is differentiated from the realm of causality precisely because some kinds of explanation offer no purchase on action-accounts (and vice versa).[5] Here, it may appear that such causal accounts cannot (*ex hypothesi*) reflect intentional features, at least directly — a key omission. Yet, in reality, granting this view of action-description excludes nothing genuinely causal.

As a simpler example, consider the causal story of: *I shoot you with my catapult*: and, in particular, how little *you* actually feature in that story. For, although I aim at *you*, that causal story involves my aiming it only insofar as doing so alters the state of *my* musculature, including the musculature of my eyes. After that, *you* are in the causal story only when the pellet hits you — if it does, for a mainly similar story would have me *missing* when I shoot at you with my catapult. Moreover, such a story does capture the causality here, but without catching what (for the agents) is crucial. Indeed, we cannot move seamlessly, in every case, from our knowledge of that causal story to an understanding of the action performed. Yet that is just a way to reaffirm the need for *both* kinds of description and explanation.

§3.   Brain-states and behaviour

This seems, then, a kind of *terminus ante quem* for the explanation of the causal structure 'behind' action. No doubt much here cannot currently be done: some rational reconstruction (or science fiction) will be involved. But Searle (2008 p. 143) accurately identifies the stages of one project here — not ours! — that he rightly calls the search for the Neuronal Correlate of Consciousness (NCC[6]).

> [1] The idea is this: in order to solve the problem of consciousness, we should find out first what is going on at the neurobiological level at a time when the subject is conscious.[7] ... [2] The first step is to find a neuronal[8] correlate of conscious states. This would be the NCC. [3] The second stage is to investigate whether the NCC is actually a *causal* correlation ... [*my numbers*]

So Searle [1] presents the problem in terms of what occurs in the brain during consciousness, and then interprets the path forward as, first, [2] the building up of correlations and then, second, [3] determining any causality. But problems arise even in respect of the relation to correlations: must such correlations be exceptionless? And how exactly could these correlations be built up? Moreover, can the correlation really be just with *consciousness*, in all its variety, rather than with, say, *thought*? Yet, with *thought*, surely the focus must be on specific thoughts. But now the details become important: does a particular thought (of mine or yours) really correlate exceptionlessly with some particular neurobiological event? We will return to these matters.

How should the previous questions be resolved? In explanation, the quotation from Searle (2008 p. 143) above concludes:

> The second stage is to investigate whether the NCC is actually a *causal* correlation, and we do this by the usual tests.

But what are "the usual tests"? As Searle (2008 pp. 143-144) continues:

> [4] In an otherwise unconscious subject, can you produce consciousness by producing the NCC? [5] In an otherwise conscious subject, can you shut off consciousness by shutting off the NCC? If you have affirmative answers to these questions, then it is *a reasonable supposition* that the correlation is more than accidental; it is, *in all likelihood*, a causal correlation. [my numbers, and emphasis]

Here, Searle *is* clearly thinking of an exceptionless relation, at least as far as causality is concerned. For the relevant "producing" and "shutting off" provides evidence only if exceptionless — or so it appears. At the least, if Searle simply wants the matter treated statistically, he does not say so. But, even were he to do so, the issue is not straightforward. Moreover, as described by Searle, "the usual tests" seem quite inadequate for the job, in two ways: (a) they cannot guarantee the move from correlation to causation. Thus, a statistically well-founded (that is, statistically significant) relation between the occurrence of red rays of the setting sun and kitchen fires in Chicago guarantees that this could not have come about by chance — it is "more than accidental". But we rightly reject this as a causal explanation: the causality here is, of course, not the one sought. For the correlation is, say, between the time of day when the red rays of the setting sun occur and people's use of the kitchen to prepare the evening meal. And that causation draws on mechanical conditions of the kitchens, or human carelessness, or some such. So correlations, however well-founded, cannot guarantee causation. Then (b) Searle seems at first to accept this, in calling the move to causality just "a reasonable supposition" and simply "in all likelihood". But this cannot be what was sought to move beyond the NCC, always supposing one can get that far.

Finally, Searle (2008 p. 144) identifies, as the next stage, the theorization of one's observations in an explanatory way. Thus, this third stage is:

> ... to get a general theory, a general statement of the laws or principles by

which the correlation functions causally in the life of the organism.

Ideally, this theory would be integrated into some more general theoretical picture, as a fourth and final stage. While Searle (2008 p. 144) concedes that, even for the third stage, "... we are a long way from reaching this stage", he expresses himself "... quite optimistic about its long term prospects". But such optimism is unwarranted, given the present state of the earlier parts of the project Searle here articulates.

Re Searle's [1] above: it seems right that there is some physical substrate here — we are materialists in just this limited sense that each of us amounts to a particular anatomy and physiology with its 'associated' psychology, although one should not assume or claim too much. Here Freud offers some good advice; like us, he was a materialist. And, as he puts it:

> We know two kinds of things about what we call our psyche (or mental life): firstly, its bodily organ and scene of action, the brain (or nervous system), and, on the other hand, our acts of consciousness, which are immediate data and cannot be further explained by any kind of description. Everything that lies between is unknown to us and the data do not include any direct relation between these two terminal points of our knowledge. If it existed, it would at the most afford an exact localisation of the processes of consciousness and would give us no help towards understanding them. (Freud [1940], Vol. 23 1966 pp. 144-145)

One obvious problem faced by any stripe of materialist (that is, anyone who accepts that persons are composed of this anatomy and physiology) is how one's psychological states (one's thoughts, intentions, dreams, and so on) relate to states of one's body, broadly conceived; and especially to states of one's brain and central nervous system — or whatever else gets included (hereafter, I shall just say "brain" for short).

What does Searle (2008 p. 144) mean in urging that "... the correlation functions causally in the life of the organism"? In particular, the term "causally" seem puzzling. Searle (2008 p. 144) asks "[h]ow exactly do brain processes cause our conscious states in all their enormous richness and variety?". Must events in the neurobiological substrate *cause* events at the human level — events in the mind, say, such as thoughts? If A causes B, then they are separately identifiable. Hence talking of mind-brain causality sounds like dualism, which cannot be Searle's view.

In effect, Searle's discussion identifies five or six fundamental although related problems here, treated in the succeeding sections:

- the problem of neural plasticity — can mental or psychological functions be ascribed uniquely to any particular brain architecture?

- the problem of identity; or, better, how to replace identity with composition;

- the problem of identification of psychological events, in a world of neural events;

- the problem of the mereological fallacy in psychological explanation;

- the problem of the persistence of scientific explanation.

Attempting to answer these problems will generate some others, all challenging the plausibility of the programme Searle discusses.

§4.   The problem of neural plasticity

What exactly would be required to locate the neuronal correlate of a conscious state, in line with Searle's hope? What is it hoped such *locating* would achieve? First, once that is achieved for a particular state, one should be able to identify recurrences of that state in the brain (for, otherwise, why is it useful?). Second, the ability to do so presupposes this neuronal correlate's realization in a particular place in the neural architecture — it will be more or less the same place in any realization, at least in the brain initially considered. (Note, in passing, that many ascriptions of particular brain-functions to particular parts of the architecture assume that this has been achieved: Searle, more modestly, only assumes this as a possibility, although one required by this project.)

Of course, "... history of science is littered with the debris of theories that were not just factually mistaken, but conceptually awry" (Bennett & Hacker, 2003 p. 4). Still that is not our issue here. Rather, our interest lies in what can be inferred from what we know; moreover, the scientists must draw on the best *science* they can muster.

Then the key issue here is: are the powers and capacities of humans instantiated in a unique neural/cortical architecture? Thus, pursuing a "yes" answer, neuroscientists presented themselves as "... discovering which parts of the cortex are causally implicated in human beings' thinking, recollecting, deciding ..." (Bennett & Hacker, 2007 p. 142). And, more importantly, even philosophically-oriented writers such as Bennett & Hacker (2003) do not typically dispute this. Thus, Searle (2007 p. 110) is committed to "saying exactly where [in the brain, such-&-such] ... occurred". Now, determining whether there is a unique cortical or neural location for any psychological event, such as "... thinking, recollecting, deciding ...", is a task for neuroscience: "[e]mpirical questions about the nervous system are the province of neuroscience" (Bennett & Hacker, 2003 p. 2). But it is incumbent on those working on *that* topic to draw on results from their colleagues.

Neuroscientists should be familiar with two related difficulties here: the first concerns "... the biological complexity of the synaptic network systems" (Bennett, 2007 p. 59); indeed, one should conclude that "... [t]he brain is not entirely hard wired: it is 'plastic'" (Tallis, 2011 p. 26). The second acknowledges the relation of plasticity to "... remedial treatment" (Bennett, 2007 p. 58), as for example the author Sherman Alexie, who functions within normal ranges despite his hydrocephalus; or hydroencephalopathy.

Thus, when Bennett & Hacker (2007 note 26 p. 213) sketch the project of cognitive neuroscience as, in part, aiming to identify "... as yet unknown neural processes, the locus of which can be roughly identified by inductive correlation using fMRI", the evidence sought is "inductive correlation" at best; and the "roughly" here acknowledges our earlier point: that the architecture cannot be inferred exceptionlessly.

By way of summary, then, the "... reorganization at the level of individual synapses, and at the microscopic level of brain maps, is central to our understanding of what is happening in the developing, learning and healing brain" (Tallis, 2011 p. 27). These are not philosophical objections; instead, by the neuroscientist's own lights, such *plasticity* should rule out this conception of location, architecture, and such like, since it implies that one cannot infer a single, inevitable architecture in *all* cases (even if granting it in most).

§5.   Deploying the "is" of composition

One set of responses to the second of the problems above comes from central-state materialism (or "The Australian Heresy" as it is sometimes called) or from eliminative materialism.[9] Yet many of the flaws in such views[10] arise from the difficulty in saying how the mind *is* related to the brain, once that "is" cannot readily amount to identity, even contingently. Of course, we do not wish to become eliminative materialists in claiming identity between brain-state and mental state — as the lightning just *is* the discharge of electricity. Searle has been notably cagey about the relationship required here: speaking of a "correlate" (as in the NCC) might leave open the possibility of exceptions while aiming at "causal sufficiency" (Searle, 2007 p. 110) seems to preclude it. But, granting that there can only be brain-brain causality, one alternative might still allow recognition that (roughly) the mental event *is* the brain event: deploying the "is" of composition such that mind events are *composed of* (or constituted by) brain events.

Uncontentious facts about composition often escape our notice. As Wiggins's elaborates the "is" of composition (see Chapter Two §8), the wool is not *identical* with the scarf, but the wool *composes* the scarf. Since the scarf is nothing other then the wool, all of the properties of the scarf depend on properties of the wool, including properties emergent from that base and rooted in the interrelations of properties of the wool. As we saw, "being striped" is a property of scarves not wool, even though the scarf *is* (that is, is *composed of*) the wool. So the relationship here, of a broadly causal kind, is quite complex; and not explicable at the 'lowest common denominator' of causation. Could this notion, arguably fruitful in some discussions of personal identity, offer anything here? A consideration of that topic will lead to further issues concerning the specificity of the relations posited — especially the causal relations. To introduce them (in §6), six cases are presented as a stimulus for further discussions.

The difficulty here reflects the relationship between mind and brain: clearly the brain offers the *material composition* of the mind — although, of course, as Wittgenstein (PI §281) rightly insisted (see Chapter One §6), mind-properties are really only applicable strictly to persons (or something very like human persons); for only they could actually perform the mind-functions at issue, like perception, memory and intention. However, the "is" of composition is not centrally causal: the scarf is not caused by the wool; and few of the scarf's properties are *direct* low-level causal consequences of the wool. In the same way, the mind is not *caused* by the brain. At best, the brain (as I am calling it) composes the mind: that is not necessarily too far from the truth, at least for the purposes of our discussion here. For, at the least, certain brain-states (and hence the brain-functioning to permit them) seem required in typical cases for certain mental states to occur. As materialists, we grant to mind-states *some* (physical) 'incarnation', however understood; that means just that my specific mind-state has some specific 'incarnation' in me — it offers nothing yet that takes us beyond what follows in any single case.

Introducing some neuro-physiological data might help when considering the relation of mind-states to brain-states: thus, reportedly (Jabr, 2011) London taxi-drivers typically have an enlarged hippocampus. On the plausible assumption (granted here) that the hippocampus has some connection to a relevant kind of memory, our fact from science might be explained by the need to master 'the knowledge' — a comprehensive grasp of the arrangement of streets of London. Suppose this is so: what exactly does that tell us?

First, our scientific 'fact' is clearly not necessarily exceptionless — there may be London taxi-drivers for whom this was not true; and perhaps by now they have been found. At the least, too many taxi-drivers (past, present and perhaps future) remain unexamined for us to place much confidence in the generalization viewed as exceptionless. And, if it is not exceptionless, what is really being granted about *memory*, say (rather than just about the memory of the individuals examined)? Still, these worries can also be set aside, for the sake of the argument (at least).

Now, what is to be said in this case? A tempting misconception would be that the mental or psychological activity of learning or acquiring 'the knowledge' *causes* this development of one's hippocampus. But a moment's thought highlights the error. For the 'mental state' of having mastered 'the knowledge' — at least in typical cases — is composed by this enlarged hippocampus. Nor can we think that the activity of a mind involved in acquiring 'the knowledge' is (on a parallel with 'working out' in relation to muscular development) the causal mechanism for the development of the hippocampus. Or, more exactly, there must be a sense in which the *fact* that one learns 'the knowledge' explains (when it does) this comparatively enlarged hippocampus. Indeed, that has been an assumption here. But that need do no more than reiterate our general mechanist commitments. The hope was that it would prove more informative. Yet any causal relations cannot be between the learning and the changes in brain-states (however generously understood) for, on this view, the learning *comprises* just those changes in brain-states. That is, acquiring knowledge or understanding is just for one's brain to arrive at that state. Further, nothing is yet specific to 'the knowledge' (for taxi-drivers). Hence there may well be a causal story about how one set of brain-states leads to another: in any particular case (say, mine), there must be such a causal history. But, since mental states are not mentioned, this cannot be an account of causation by mental states, such as learning 'the knowledge' (nor, of course, of mental states) if that is regarded directly.

All this means, of course, that taking seriously the "is" of composition is accepting that brain-states (or whatever) *comprise* mental states without taking the relations between them to be *causal* relations. Indeed, deploying the "is" of composition here required this conclusion. For it concedes material composition; but it does not suggest, at least so far, the sorts of generalizability that would suggest causal laws here. No doubt your mental states have a physical substrate, as do mine. But nothing yet requires nor allows us to understand one case in terms of the other. So where does this leave us — and, in particular, our materialism? What would be the chief difficulties in taking our brain-states to compose mental states?

§6.   Reducing thoughts to brain states?: six cases of Nicole

The upshot of the discussion so far is, of course, that — while knowledge of some mental states may be explanatory of later mental states in particular individuals — the same cannot be said of the relationship of such mental states to the causality of the brain. Neither is the reverse position defensible: since the relation between one thought and the next is not (in typical cases) straightforwardly causal, knowing the first mental state (and even knowing its causal substrate or compositional brain-state) cannot lead us inexorably to the next mental state (or even its compositional brain-state). Further, presenting such changes as *actions* of the brain is misleading. Especially given the idea of neural plasticity (§4 above), it may make a kind of sense for me to speak of 'exercising my brain', *roughly* as I might my biceps: but this is not something my *brain* could do. A point Flew (1984 p. 119) made eloquently for genes applies to brains — that they:

> ... do not and cannot necessitate our conduct. Nor are they capable of the calculation and understanding required to plot a course of either ruthless selfishness or sacrificial compassion.

For, at best, our plans and intentions are instantiated in our brains (see §5 above).

In part, the difficulty here is typically obscured by introducing so-called 'information' about thoughts with, at best, the wrong degree of generality. For identifying, say, parts of the brain typically associated with moods or with pains might *seem* like progress, a step towards a similar move for individual thoughts. But it is quite likely a step forward only in the sense in which climbing a tall tree gets you nearer to the moon — it does so, but not in a manner that might get you all the way. Psychology's barrenness (as Wittgenstein observed: PI p. 197 [PFF §371]) follows in exactly this sense from the conceptual confusion that it can bring to its empirical methods, rather than from the need for *time* to elaborate its conclusions or to develop further its technical notions. Those methods have become associated with issues they *could not* address. So, when trying to explain the detail of the transition of one thought to the next, or the reoccurrence of a particular thought, in the context of claims about brain-states, the specificity of the one cannot be matched by the universality of the other, at least if the target is exceptionless laws of the kind science employs (or rightly favours). Thus, the specificity of my partly-lustful thought about Nicole Kidman wearing a thong cannot be matched with any degree of specificity about the states and relations of my brain, if the hope was either to be able to describe, in terms of your brain-states (and such like), your having similar thoughts about Nicole, or to predict (on the basis of my brain-states and such like) when I am having those thoughts again. Or so I shall urge, by considering some cases. Of course, there *is* some state of my brain that is my having that thought — this is our commitment to materialism. Yet that need not tempt us to regard my thoughts of Nicole as also a state or process *on the same model* (see §11 below).

In effect, my claim here is two-fold. First, that my thoughts are heavily contextual, in ways difficult to reflect in even the most detailed consideration of brain-states — hence, small differences in thought as they affect *me* will be hard to plot at a neural level (say, of voxels) against similar small differences of thought for you (a point that we will return to). Second, that my brain-states (and similar) are too particular to me (and my context) to permit reliable generalizations, either for my own case or — worse — for yours. And, if this is right, the prospect of *laws* for such mind-brain connections seem bleak.

Here, in all of the five or six cases considered, the assumption is that brain-states (and similar) are known with the highest degree of specificity. So that nothing turns on failures to *know* the state of brains, bodies or central-nervous-systems: that is, straightforwardly epistemological questions of *that* sort are all set aside.

Case 1: On Tuesday, I am thinking longingly about Nicole Kidman in the thong. (Make this more specific, as appropriate, to indicate the curliness of her hair, and such like.) Since we are materialists, this thought is somehow instantiated in my brain. Let us call that state of my brain, and whatever else is considered relevant, "State A": my brain being in this state composes my having that thought. (A good question: if I imagine Nicole, rather than thinking longingly, am I still in State A, or not?)

Case 2: On the same Tuesday, I am thinking longingly about Nicole — she is otherwise the same, as is the rest of the context, but now she wears a camisole. How does my brain-state in this case relate to State A? It would be odd if there were no relation, given the overlapping content of the thoughts; equally, it must differ from State A, since it comprises a different thought. So call it "State B".

Case 3: That Tuesday again, and I am thinking longingly of Nicole, but now (being bilingual) I would report my thought by saying, "Elle porte une petite camisole". Here, two questions: first, how far are we from State B? After all, my thoughts seem to express the same proposition. But, equally, the differences in my *presentation* of that thought must still be instantiated in differences in the state of my brain. So this is State C. Second, is my being bilingual really relevant when it comes to my brain-states here? Would altering that assumption produce yet more, still marginally different, cases to consider? It seems so.

Case 4: On that Tuesday, *you* are thinking longingly about Nicole in that thong. For ease of exposition, imagine that your thoughts are not related to mine — I haven't, for instance, mentioned my obsessions. (Of course, yet another case might be generated by considering how my mention of Nicole, should it occur, would be manifest in your brain-state comprising that thought about her.) Still, your brain-state here must obviously *resemble* State A in some way or to some degree (or there are no generalizations to be found). Further, we are members of the same species, and such like. But even regarding this simply as though my exact thought is instantiated in your brain, you cannot just *be* in State A. Your brain clearly differs from mine to some degree. Moreover, this is *your* thought, connecting to other thoughts of yours in ways different to any connections of my original thought to my other thoughts. So at neither the brain-level nor the human level can one move seamlessly between these cases. Since it will recur, call this "State D" — but remember that, unlike the others so far, it is a state of *your* brain.

Case 5: On the next day, the Wednesday, I think longingly of Nicole in the thong — as far as the thought goes, everything else is the same. But, of course, this cannot be simply the recurrence of State A. For things have 'moved on' in my brain since Tuesday. In that sense, the passage of time has altered my brain. One way to characterize these changes refers to what I have learned, or forgotten, or argued (and so on) since Tuesday. Another way, not necessarily a competitor, would focus on the causal or structural changes in my brain: indeed, the material of my brain is at least partly redistributed since Tuesday. But, however described, it will be difficult to arrive at the specificity of my thinking *again* of Nicole: I insist that this is *the very same thought* (incorporating the same longing, and so on). Yet in this case, I am thinking of her *again*. It seems that my brain *must* be in State A — it is the very same thought! Equally, it cannot be State A. Of course, Functionalism in the philosophy of mind offered a way forward: that my brain-states instantiated the same functional relations — but, of course, this is precisely where Hilary Putnam's own critique of Functionalism has most bite (Putnam, 1988 esp. pp. 77-78; Putnam, 1994 pp. 441-45). So I shall set that line of response aside.

Case 6: Although it is Wednesday, you are once again thinking about Nicole in the thong: how does your current brain-state relate either to State A (of my brain) or to State D (of your brain)? The considerations raised above (case 5) in respect of my brain apply here: you cannot be in exactly State D, since the passage of time has altered your brain. So your brain-state cannot amount to exactly State D. On the other hand, it should be similar to State D if broadly causal laws operate over brain-states as they comprise mind-states. And that broad similarity must be sufficient to relate your State D to my State A (and, indeed, to States B and C). If they are not, any explanatory scheme here seems distinctly unlikely. (We might lapse into an anomalous monism: see Davidson, discussed Chapter Three §6.)

Yet how can the minor differences in the thought be instantiated in the brain? To be clear, the issue raised does not dispute the instantiation of the thoughts. As materialists, that is granted from the beginning. No, the question is whether what could be known about my brain now (assuming one knew everything) offers something useful about either my brain for the future or — an additional step — your brain either present or future.

The difficulties here could be brought out by recognizing a crucial difference here between brain-states and mind-states: that one's brain-states — no matter how complex, and especially when relational states are considered — are finite, while there is no such finite totality to one's thoughts. So that we can keep 'looking' more and more closely at Nicole, her thong, the background, and such like. And adding new descriptions. Hence there is no final or ultimate level of analysis (although there will typically be one where the question raised are satisfactorily addressed). For whenever one seems to arrive at something ultimate here, another contextualization is always possible. The same cannot be true of any physical system *viewed as a physical system*: that is, through the eyes of physics. For physics, like the other sciences, 'cheats' here by introducing a *ceteris paribus* clause. By claiming in that way that 'other things are equal', it removes those 'other things' from consideration; and so becomes a 'closed system'. Hence, for such physical systems, perhaps *all* of the features and relations could be articulated in principle, even if that is impossible in practice. Thus, seen through the 'spectacles' of scientific practice, there *is* a finite totality here (contrast Chapter Three §6). For the contextually varied world of thought, though, the impossibility here is conceptual: more detail as to what *exactly* was thought on any occasion could always be requested — as if some determinate answer here were possible in *all* cases. But now reporting past thoughts must be contrasted with thinking anew. And, for past thoughts, the sort of determinacy implicit in the science cannot be assumed. So that one cannot come to *all*-minus-two of the objects and relations thought, and then *all*-minus-one, and finally *all*! For there is no *all*, no finite totality of possibilities. Yet that is what is assumed when one imagines (or asserts, or assumes) that a *complete* description is possible. (And what science achieves by setting various matters aside with a *ceteris paribus* clause.)

The computer whose screen on Wednesday has exactly the same image as it had on Tuesday cannot be our model here both because changes to our brain-states are organic rather than simply chemical and because changes to the computer build in the necessary compartmentalization, whereby changes *here* have no bearing on other changes. For (*ex hypothesi*) in the computer, the expectation is that any changes to the computer as a whole (say, the down-loading of additional programmes) can be isolated from the specific programmes (or their running) under consideration. In this sense, the 'original position' is reproduced, but only via a set of assumptions drawn from a picture of natural science as applied to computing. For this assumption of independence is of a piece with the general *ceteris paribus* assumptions that natural science employs. So the elements of the computer's running are conceived as compartmentalized to produce exactly this effect — and, when the compartmentalization breaks down (say, the impact of a programme newly-installed since Tuesday precludes this outcome) the computer is taken to have failed in this respect.

So, do all my Nicole cases reflect slight differences in brain-states? Of course, there is a sense in which they do — or, for materialists, they would not constitute different thoughts. But do they offer us hope for *laws* or *principles* that allow understanding of the mind through understanding the brain? Perhaps some broad concepts (such as, say, the identification of certain neural firing as composing *pain*) might fit into a mould of that thought. And perhaps optimism might be generated by focus only on a brain fully described, like mine imagined here (although still with no explanation of how that was derived from fMRI). By contrast, the real thoughts of people seem too Procrustean for this sort of analysis to capture them all. Here, my cases offer enough about the specificity of thoughts and brain-states to encourage resistance to the forcing of them into that particular 'bed'.

Indeed, this whole discussion simply makes vivid the idea (from Wilkes, 1988 pp. 41-42) that:

> ... to sort out which sets and patterns of [neural] firings and inhibitions are engaged in realizing *this* thought about cameras rather than *that* thought about cuckoo clocks would presuppose that some of the brain's functioning go along with the former rather than the latter, and vice versa.

But, instead, Wilkes (1988 p. 41) stresses our inability "... to isolate the individual contents of individual mental states (beliefs that p, desires for x, expectations that q, and so forth) in A's brain, let alone recreate them in B's". And explains that inability by recognizing:

> The billion cells of the brain are in incessant flux — firing, resting, inhibited — and synaptic connections change over time; every cell will be implicated in dozens of different patterns, but may be replaced by another cell or set of cells if it is resting or if it decays; although cells do decay, axons sprout and dendrites grow to form new connections; changes in the amounts of the various neurotransmitters make great differences to cellular activity ... and so on. (Wilkes, 1988 p. 41)

If so, there seems little hope for the project of localization. So *that* conception of the project needs to be challenged. As a partial analogy, think of those television sets where the picture was generated by an electron gun, operating in a vacuum tube; and ask, "Where is the picture?" We understand the sense in which there is no picture: that the lines tracked by the electron gun illuminate points from colour fields, and – when viewed with the human eye — Brad Pitt is visible. So writers might suggest that the picture is nowhere; or even that it does not exist. But philosophers saw through such talk, at least since the time physicists asserted that tables did not exist (for critique, see Stebbing, 1937[11]) — that they were just clouds of molecules! No, the picture is real, just as the table is. And the causal narrative sustaining it can be provided. But the hope of localizing that picture, beyond offering its causal story, is unpromising.

Of course, Searle's defence here returns us to his search for something more unified: rather than the matching of thoughts/feelings and brain-states, as here, he aims to answer the question, "How does the brain produce the unified, subjective conscious field?" (Searle, 2008 p. 13). But, at one level, granting *that* brains achieve this raises again specific questions about what that would mean for the neurobiology of specific thoughts and feelings.

§7.   Contemporary science and the permanence of explanation

At issue here is the connection of the science — and especially the claims of the science presented in popularized versions — to the philosophy. That is why great care is needed when articulating the claims of the science for general audiences: to avoid misleading metaphors, and forms of words that (while appropriate in one context) are not appropriate if transposed into another. Thus, it is important to avoid any purposive language applied to brains: say, appearing to warrant purposive language in the sense of the operation of thermostats in air-conditioning systems — the thermostat itself is just a mechanical device, built with our purposes and intentions in mind. And then merely using the word "cause" (or the word "because") cannot imply that causality is at work.

The philosophy of mind cannot depend on a particular working-out of the science (especially the neuroscience). So that, if later discoveries prove that the amygdala plays no role ... that shouldn't matter to the philosophy — we know what we as persons do ... Indeed, Charles Travis (2011 p. 110) pointed out that that one species of psychologism "... would be specialized scientism — a mistaken insistence as to how empirical investigation *must* turn out". For the shape of empirical investigation cannot be determined *a priori*: hence we cannot insist that future enquiries take the form of *present* empirical investigations, except in the very broadest terms.

There may be no (reliable, exceptionless) way to move from the discussion of *thought* to the discussion of brain-states: in particular, the Nicole cases above provide one account of the difficulties; and a related one can be derived from thinking-through the way *intention* works — such that:

[t]he agent can possess knowledge of his future actions, but this knowledge will be of a non-inductive kind and is most succinctly expressed in an assertion of the form 'I intend to do such-and-such a thing'. (Wollheim, 1973 p. 12)

So I doubt that the specificity of thought can be realized in differences in brain-states. In particular, my interest in dreaming (see McFee, 1993/4) reflects a set of reservations about how *temporally specific* causal relations can reflect the intentional relations, even though they compose them — the causal states and the 'experiences' have a very complex relationship. Thus, the causal story of dreaming certainly relates in some way (if not exceptionlessly) to the brain states associated with REM sleep in some way: but certainly not in any straightforward way.

Some other details may require special attention. As materialists, we accept that the person just *is* this anatomy and physiology; so careful consideration of the "is" of composition is required (see §5 above). Since some terms appropriate to the person (intentional terms with normative outcomes) cannot be applied to causal structures, and since such terms are certainly needed to describe the actions of persons, some kind of "two-language" or "dual-aspect" theory is required (its details are not crucial here). For only then can we do justice to the oft-quoted slogan from Frege ([1918] 1984 p. 351) — that "[e]rror and superstition have causes just as much as correct cognition". Then a *good* move in the chess game will have *one* causal story (say, relating to states of my brain, or to changes in my biochemistry); but so will a bad move — the move that gets me checkmated! So simply talking about the causal story here — how my judgements and actions came about — does not yet address the *normative* question of whether this is, say, a good move in chess: the need for *both* stories is highlighted.

But, if right, this also identifies two problems: the first concerns the difficulty in elaborating explanations across the "two-language" gap; for the intentional language is context-specific in ways the other is not. Hence some inferences cannot be drawn across that gap. Thus, as materialists, we accept that, in favoured conditions, one brain-state is caused by a preceding one: this is standard electro-chemical causation. But that prior state *was* a particular thought (it comprised that thought, using the "is" of composition) and the succeeding state *was* a particular thought, in the same sense. Can we now say that the first thought caused the second? Clearly, while there is no guarantee here, in the abstract our answer must be "no": thoughts are typically caused, if at all, by other thoughts — although smells and such like are also commonly involved.

The second difficulty occurs whenever philosophy puts undue weight on natural science: then, modifying the science would require modifying the philosophy. But the science one depends on will always be *contemporary* science: its content changing as and when theory changes (Chapter Ten §8). In that sense, the application to philosophy requires that one get the science right. For sometimes (exceptionally!) changing the *content* of the science bears on the content of the philosophy. That, in itself, is a peculiar situation: for the possibility of revision in the light of new experiment or new theory is widely held, with justice, to be characteristic of science — this is one way to articulate the empirical character of science. And that need not make one's philosophy of science Popperian: one need not proceed from mere conjecture to mere conjecture. For instance, our science was empirical in just the required way if the outcome of new observations generates anomalies of the sort that, for a Kuhnian, might lead eventually to a new period of crisis, and thence to a new *normal science* (Kuhn, 1970 p. 53ff.; EKT pp. 91-97) — even when, prior to the new crisis, the scientific claims were regarded as true. For, after the crisis as before, the scientific practice was "... firmly based on one or more scientific achievements, achievements that some particular scientific community acknowledges for a time as supplying the foundation for its future practice" (Kuhn, 1970 p. 10: notice "for a time"), with practitioners who have "... assimilated a time-tested and group-licenced way of seeing" (Kuhn, 1970 p. 189). So the claims of science will be open to falsification; and science *answerable* to the state of the world.

For this reason, the truth of scientific claims can never be absolutely *guaranteed*, especially when looking to the newer reaches of enquiry. But, whenever the scientific claims are modified, one must ask what that means for the philosophy. Contrast a very different kind of case: suppose that, at one time, causal powers and capacities of the sorts currently associated with the brain were thought to derive from the heart: the impact in some places in one's philosophy might be profound. Yet in respect of a view of personal identity stressing a unified material parcel as the seat of certain causal powers, nothing (much) need have changed — in this sense, that view of personal identity did not draw on the *mechanics* of personal powers and capacities.

§8.   The body's role?

Surely, though, there are causal relations between, roughly, the body and the person: the alcohol I ingest has an effect (or set of them) on the whole person. But the causal direction seems somehow *from* the body. Still, in this case, there is personal action too — I ingest this alcohol. Might that aspect disappear?

Here, the metaphor of the 'drug rush' may seem very tempting, faced with some of the claims made by scientists about the effects of brain chemistry on behaviour: in particular, that — like the 'drug rush' — such effects seem overwhelming but of a fixed duration. To move forward, we must first recognize a distinction between those things we *do* (and for which we are therefore responsible) and those things that *happen* to us. Thus, my opening the door allowed the leaves to blow into the house: I should sweep them up — I did it (although not all the forces at work began from me). But if a falling tree smashes the door, I am not responsible: I did not do it.

Although not hard-and-fast, this distinction is suggestive applied to the case of drug-taking: the male Olympic athlete, whose blood is tested for anabolic steroids, is expected to have some level of testosterone. As such, its presence is not evidence of drug-taking, or drug-use: he is not regarded as having a drug in his body — although, were this testosterone extracted and ingested or injected by another, that would constitute drug-taking. Since this testosterone is normal, nothing here needs explanation. Hence there is nothing for which the athlete might be censured or penalized. Moreover, no particular level of testosterone is taken as the norm: it is recognized to differ from case to case. The same goes for other substances that, in different contexts, might count as drugs. This is a recognition that testosterone-levels in typical cases need not be something the athlete *does*, but rather something that happens to him in the working-out of typical body chemistry.

Four further features should be noted immediately. First, suppose there is some mileage in knowing that certain kinds of moods have a broadly fixed duration (such that it might be useful knowledge for the person in that mood, or other emotional state, to recognize this fact): that information can be conveyed in the human language of moods, without recourse to the biology of the moods. Second, the same goes for the idea that, if I am to 'buck up' such that taking a different view of my situation will change my mood, it must be done quickly — before the mood takes hold. For here too the language of moods is in part the language of humans *doing* certain things. Third, many changes brought about by humans — many things they do — should be thought *intentional* changes, rather than causal ones: they depend on how the event is characterized by, especially, its agents in ways causal changes do not — I get the cardio-vascular advantages of the work-out however I conceptualize the activity. But here there may be areas of dispute as to what is or is not causal. Still, that leads to our fourth point: namely, that 'chemical rushes' are not typically under intentional control of this sort. Perhaps some practices (maybe meditation) offer some level of control here; certainly that is not the usual situation.

Suppose, with a clear case of meditation, a change in brain waves is noticed. In that sense "I am meditating" might roughly equal "I am changing my brain waves" — it might not matter (in line with PI §79: "Say what you please"). But, as Austin warned Cavell (2010 p. 324), it *matters* what one says: both *morally* (are you lying or just being frivolous?), and because, if one says such-and-such, one can be offered a set of apparent 'consequences'. Thus talk of "sunrise" might seem to suggest a pre-Copernican cosmology on which the sun (normally) moved, and hence of the possibility of God making the sun stand still. If such consequences are excluded, expressions concerning *sunrise* will not be misunderstood: hence, will not be misleading.

Yet this tells us little. If I can learn to control my angry responses by thinking of them in terms of, say, a dragon inside me, and this really helps me to control those responses, we have achieved what is wanted. (You might want to add that thought that your story of the amygdala is true of the brain ... but, of course, the person can't change that story ...) Hence you *cannot* then say, "But I got the science right" since (a) that confuses conceptual and empirical *and* (b) seems to conflict with a certain provisional character fundamental to science.

So how the person manages to achieve things is mostly not explained causally at all; but, instead, in terms of motives, intentions, reasons (as well as things done for no reason) ... and these have no straightforward 'translation' into the causality of brain-events.[12]

Why, in this specific context, does this combination of brain-conditions constitute my deciding to do X? (This only seems a problem if we think of the causality of these conditions in the determinist-type way — the best account that can be given is *never* exceptionless, and only 'after the fact' — where my doing X just is my brain/body moving from state P to state Q. But *I* don't *cause* the change: since I am the whole structure, my doing X is composed of the change from one brain/body state to another. And, in typical cases, no explanation will be equivalent to how I did it — I just did it! ("In the beginning was the deed": OC §402.)

§9.   The 'mereological fallacy', from Bennett & Hacker?

This emphasis on the *person* as agent returns us to a key insight from Wittgenstein (PI §281[13]):

> Only of a human being and what resembles (behaves like) a human being can one say: it has sensations; it sees, is blind; hears, is deaf; is conscious or unconscious.

An aspect of what Wittgenstein proscribes here has been identified by Bennett and Hacker (2003 p. 72) as the *mereological fallacy*: that the explanation of most psychological states can be approached only by treating them as states of *persons* (rather than, say, of parts of persons — such as brains); that "[i]t makes no sense to ascribe psychological predicates (or their negations) to the brain, save metaphorically or metonymically". As they ask:

> ... do we know what it is for a *brain* to see or hear, for a *brain* to have

experiences, to know or to believe something? Do we have any conception of what it would be for a *brain* to make a decision? (Bennett & Hacker, 2003 p. 72)

Clearly, these suppositions make no sense: it is people, not eyes (or, worse, brains), that see. And so on. Further, we noted above that, while it makes a kind of sense for me to speak of 'exercising my brain', *roughly* as I might my biceps, this is not something my *brain* could do. Moreover, as Bennett and Hacker urge above, the suggestion here is that ascription of these capacities to eyes or brains makes no sense — they are not simply urging its falsity. Additionally, causal explanation here cannot provide a reductive or eliminative analysis of the normativity of human judgement. Saying that harnesses (once again) our slogan from Frege ([1918] 1984 p. 351) — that "[e]rror and superstition have causes just as much as correct cognition". As we saw, simply talking about the causal story here — how my judgements and actions came about — does not yet address the *normative* question of whether this is, say, a good move in chess. And the problem here has nothing to do with complexity: the bad move and the good one are on a par in this respect.

So, while I am happy to call myself a *materialist* (in the sense that I *am* just this anatomy and physiology), this materialism is neither eliminative nor reductive. In this context, that means that my decisions to do such-and-such amounts to the transition from one brain-state to another; but there is no strictly causal account sufficient for that transition (although, of course, after the fact there will be the appearance of one). And there will be no clear way to characterize that decision at the level of causality: in particular, discussions of its duration are not confounded if one turns to, say, work by Benjamin Libet (2005[14]) to suggest some uniform structure of temporal relations between decisions and actions. For, first, there are lots of cases where we just do something — walk across a room say, and only explain it later. So such cases are not under consideration. Yet, since our walking was clearly not accidental, we might want to say we decided to take the walk, but couldn't say when. Second, we know that decisions can take various amounts of time. So, for instance, we know — if we watch the play — that it takes Hamlet about four hours to make up his mind; sometimes we 'sleep on a decision', and wake up having made it; we might even dream the decision. These are facts about decision-making (among others) the philosophy of mind should be exploring.

In reality, this means that granting causal continuity here cannot entail that the causal story instantiating my actions would permit the prediction of those actions. For those actions are not causally necessitated by a finite totality of antecedent conditions, if that means they could be reliably predicted if only one knew enough (if only one were Carnap's Logically Omniscient Jones, or LOJ for short): that is the mistake the determinist makes, and which the picture of action shared with determinism imports. Rather, in at least some cases, the fact that I *decided* to do such-and-such is crucial here. That fact can only be constituted by one brain-state becoming another: that is, instantiated via the change from one brain-state to another. But there is no threat to consciousness, or intentionality, or decision-making in that account. For, to repeat, that instantiation of psychological states (even when granted — which it is not here!) can never amount to the causal necessity required for determinism.

§10. Exceptionlessness in correlation?: the return of 'other minds'

Now we can return to a consideration of the claims Searle introduced, in sketching the NCC project (§3 above).

Re Searle's [2]: Searle stresses building-up correlations here, but such correlations depend on independent identification of the two facts or states to be correlated: one needs access both to the moving of the windmill's sails and the blowing of the wind to begin drawing up a correlation between them. So, in this case, independent access to the neurobiological process and to 'the conscious process' is required in order to correlate one with the other.

This replicates the classic 'Other Minds' problem: how do you, as researcher, have reliable access to my mental states? You can observe me, of course, but I might be a stoic (expressing few, or no, psychological states) or an actor (expressing states I did not feel[15]). And, of course, if you ask me, my truthfulness becomes an issue. Moreover, it will surely be insufficient to say that, because I am walking around, I am conscious. After all, androids or zombies can readily be imagined of whom this was not true. Or so it seems. So it is very unclear how to achieve reliable, direct access to both the events you wish to correlate.[16]

Suppose that, deciding that I am trustworthy, you accept my word as to my psychological state or event: further suppose your sophisticated information about my neurobiological states. Yet perhaps I am unusual (on a parallel with colour-blindness perhaps): then you must set aside my 'data' when building up the correlation about *people* and their psychological states. Or starting with a few such deviant cases might explain finding no such correlation being built up. (A real parallel here:[17] Allan Hobson (1988 p. 290) talks about "... an impressive correlation" between dreaming and the occurrence of rapid-eye-movement (REM) sleep; but even Patricia Churchland (1986 p. 206) acknowledges that some people dream without such sleep occurring — she calls this "dream-like mentation". Researchers starting with the facts Churchland acknowledges might never have found the "impressive correlation".) At the very least, one must be much more guarded when discussing this topic.

Note here, in passing, Freud's sage advice about the impact of popularization on his own work, where:

> ... qualifications and exact particularisation are of little use with the general public; there is very little room in the memory of the multitude; it retains only the bare gist of any thesis and fabricates an extreme version which is easy to remember. (Freud, [1905] 1966 p. 267)

Freud's point is that something inexact is *taken* from his theoretically-precise accounts of human beings, with that inexactness following from how his works are presented to a general audience. For, of course, anything even approaching correlation (or the NCC) might find itself inflated in this process.

Further, as we saw, exceptionlessness really raises two different issues here — first, are there exceptionless correlations between some psychological activity of mine on Monday, and some brain-state of mine, as the psychological state (say) recurs on Tuesday? Then, second, how are questions about my psychological states related to the states of *your* brain? For a correlation must involve roughly activity in the same part of the brain in your case as (we are supposing) was discovered in mine. On the one hand, the fact of our being the same species might speak in favour of such a correlation, at least in typical cases; and the thought of a *science* here (with law-like generalizations, at least) more or less requires it. But, on the other hand (see §4 above), well-documented cases speak against any such symmetry through the relation of plasticity to "... remedial treatment" (Bennett, 2007 p. 58), where a person, such as the author Sherman Alexie, functions within normal ranges despite his hydroencephalopathy; but also in any cases where people function normally despite abnormal brain conditions; or even the relation between one's life and the development of one's brain, known or not known. (And see here the taxi-drivers, mentioned §5 above.)

Re Searle's [3]: We have already recognized the gap between correlation and causation: even well-entrenched correlations offer no guarantee of causal relations. So that even if the NCC were found (*per impossibile*), the next step in the process would be inherently problematic — since one might well take for difficult what is actually impossible!

§11. Wittgenstein's question about states and processes
Moreover, we seem drawn to the causality of, say, mind-states by brain-states, or psychological processes by neural ones. As Wittgenstein saw, the language

of 'states and processes', which seems so natural here, has the potential to mislead:

> The first step is the one that altogether escapes notice. We talk of processes and states and leave their nature undecided. Sometime perhaps we'll know more about them — we think. But that's just what commits us to a particular way of looking at the matter. For we have a certain conception of what it means to learn to know a process better. ... (PI §308 [4th ed.])

So that the innocent language of 'states and processes', which seemed merely a place-holder awaiting further investigation, takes on a life of its own. That explains some of the puzzles posed by the six cases of thinking about Nicole (above): in them, the assumed similarity across all the brain-processes was imported into our discussion of the thinking — so that it too appeared a unitary state or process. In effect, two difficulties overlap here. First, as Wittgenstein (VoW pp. 415-417) noted:

> So we come up once again against the old problem: How can a process be an expectation, a fear or a belief? I think the mistake lies in one's speaking here of a 'process'. Certainly there occur in me various psychological processes, but these *are* not the expectation.

Further (PG pp. 74-75):

> We say that understanding is a 'psychological process', and this label is misleading, in this as in countless other cases. It compares understanding to a particular *process* like translation from one language to another, and it suggests the same conception of thinking, knowing, wishing, intending, etc

This amounts to a misrepresentation of certain psychological phenomena as 'processes': but then, second, such processes are taken as unitary or uniform:

> Well, 'Understanding' is not the name of a single process accompanying reading or hearing, but of more or less interrelated processes against a background, or in a context, of facts of a particular kind ... (PG p. 74).

Indeed, Gordon Baker (2004 p. 144) recognized that "... a recurrent theme in the *Blue Book* (a kind of refrain) and ... in [Wittgenstein's] dictations to Waismann in the early 1930s" was partly "... advice to discard the label 'a mental process'" (Baker, 2004 p. 144); and partly aimed "... to persuade someone puzzled by the nature of thinking to acknowledge certain *grammatical prejudices* in himself that generate his conceptual confusion" (Baker, 2004 p. 145). In that sense, our strategy (like Wittgenstein's) is to point out the misleading analogy, even when it was merely implicit: as Wittgenstein (BT p. 302e) said, "... I must always point out an analogy according to which one has been thinking, but which one did not recognize as an analogy". For Wittgenstein, one mistaken analogy here took thought to be somehow behind expressions of thought: but "its sense is not located behind it" (BT p. 65e). Instead, Wittgenstein urged that we should regard the thought as *in* its expression. Not, of course, that he took thoughts to be expressible only in language (as the case of the 'dull pencil' shows: see Chapter One §6). But he saw that the possibility of a *concrete* expression of the thought would show that, "for our purposes" (VoW p. 49), thinking need be nothing occult: that, for example, treating one's knowing something in terms of the injunction "to keep a piece of paper on which it was written" (PG p. 49). Here, Wittgenstein aims "... to exhibit an unfamiliar *form* of the use of all these expressions" (Baker, 2004 p. 167) — "thinking", "knowing", understanding", "wishing", "expecting", and so on — where a part of his point is that the "and so on" would not exhibit 'more of the same'. As Wittgenstein (PG p. 48) noted:

> If knowledge is called a 'state' it must be in the sense in which we speak of the state of a body or of a physical model. So it must be in a physiological sense or a sense used in psychology that talks about unconscious states of a mind-model. Certainly no one would object to that; but in that case one still has to be clear that we have moved from the grammatical realm of 'conscious states' into a different grammatical realm.

The 'process' analogy suggests that, just as there are distinctive mental processes, there must be distinctive brain processes — and then we search for them (say, in different structures within the brain). But perhaps that method, importing the psychological concepts as presently deployed into our investigations of neurophysiology, is inherently misleading. If so, it will not be because we are offering only rough-and-ready 'folk psychology', but rather because the understanding of the psychology of persons and their actions — which generally works pretty well, and is intentional — is an inappropriate starting point for a causal investigation of the kind neuroscience would require.

Part Two

Persons in Dance-Making

Chapter Five

Responsibility — The need for two 'hats'

§1.   Introduction

As far as I know, only its choreographer, William Louther, ever performed the dance *Vesalii Icones* (1969); and, on those occasions, its music (composed by Peter Maxwell Davies) was performed live by Davies's own music ensemble, "The Fires Of London"[1] with the addition of a cellist (Jennifer Ward Clarke, at its first performance at the Queen Elizabeth Hall, in London). Certainly, Davies specified that the dance draw on images inspired by the anatomical drawings of Vesalius, a perfect vehicle for Louther who "... possessed not only a sensational, impeccable athleticism, but also a fine-drawn beauty and athleticism" (Meisner, 1998). I first saw this dance performed, at Sadlers Wells Theatre in London, with a proscenium arch; in Queen Elizabeth Hall, in 1975, its performance was more or less in the round. Each performance was powerful; and clearly a performance of the same dancework, despite differences — most obviously the one just mentioned.

From the later 1970s, beset by arthritis, Louther largely ceased performing, since "... he preferred not to sabotage the memories of his sensational virtuosity" (Meisner, 1998[2]). No doubt, performing *Vesalii Icones* requires a comparable virtuosity, even of (for example) someone taught it by Louther. So, in reality, performer and work seem inexorably connected in such a case. Of course, that merely reflects the practicalities: for Louther had two roles in respect of *Vesalii Icones* — as its choreographer and also its dancer. Moreover, it is crucial to distinguish these two roles, as two 'hats' that might be worn, even if (as in this case) *in practice* worn jointly by one person. For Louther's responsibility for this dance *as choreographer* clearly differs from his role as dancer: inherent in the idea of a work in the performing arts is the conceptual possibility that someone else might have been taught the dance, although this did not happen. Hence, as a work then potentially to be performed on different occasions.[3]

So what will a focus on *agency* bring to the study of dance? Three distinct agential roles operate here — or four if criticism is taken as a distinct action: as dance-maker, dancer, audience-member, and dance-critic — even when just one person inhabits all these roles! Crucially the *dance itself* remains our focus (especially since legitimate critical commentary, from dancers as from audience-members, must be answerable to the dance). Retaining this focus avoids dismissing concerns with the dancework itself as though they concerned, say, just the dance-maker (the artist) and her aims, or the dancer (the performer) and his. For reducing the purpose and direction of the artworks to the plans or purposes of the individuals involves a big mistake here. Works in performing arts embody the artist's fulfilled intentions; but, especially for hypothetical intentionalists (see PAD pp. 135-150), those intentions are logically tied to the *artistic* aim and purpose of a work from that time, in that category or genre, at that time — not (necessarily) to specific aims voiced by artist. Here, though, I simply assume that position, as crucial to any artistic theory attending to the responsibility for the work of (in our case) the dance-maker.

My discussion focuses on typical dances: the kinds of *performable* that, in principle, might find their place in the repertoire of a dance group; and might be rehearsed and discussed — the 'untypical' will amount to different sets of occasions. Here, it is informative to remind ourselves (see PAD p. 170) of the claim by Collingwood (1938 p. 321) that "[e]very performer is co-author of the work he performs". Insofar as our concern is with dance as a performing art — and hence with danceworks as *performables* — this idea is clearly mistaken. For such performing arts embody the maker/performer contrast: in principle, they can typically be performed by some other dancer or dancers, even when (as with Louther) this does not happen in practice. And so the possibility of the dancework not being known, or of other dancers lacking the requisite technical mastery, can be set aside as conceptually irrelevant. Then Collingwood's view would have the counter-intuitive consequence that performance by a different performer automatically instantiated a different work — a work with a different co-author! For the identity of that work depends, at least in part, on its authors: when work A and work B have different authors, we should rightly conclude that they were different works, at least typically. Rather, my aim was to clarify why, in typical cases, dancework-identity did not depend on the identities of performers — where this was a liberation in our understanding of the role of the dancers. Notice, too, that I am not *retreating* from a bold position here, towards some middle way: my position here is not one where there is "... the bit where I say it, and the bit where I take it back" (Austin, 1962 p. 2). Instead, my view recognizes typical danceworks as performables; and, in denying that dancers were artists (in the sense in which dancemakers are: see PAD Chapter Seven), I was urging only that point. Moreover, I was not advancing that view exceptionlessly.

So it would be sufficient if my view were clear enough for standard cases (sometimes called "the received canon": see Banes, 1998 p. 11). Now, Sally Banes (1998 p. 11) is rightly suspicious of any "received canon" for dance, recognizing that "... it necessarily leaves out many valuable works and authors"; in particular, like any 'Test of Time'-type account, it fares less well in correctly assigning value to contemporary works — or, anyway, explaining that value.

But, as Banes (1998 p. 11) notes, one's purpose "... in analyzing the high art canon cannot be to reinscribe it". Hence, to operate *critically* here, one must invoke the context within which projected works can be seen as dance; or, if this is different, within which the dance-maker's fulfilled intention make sense: for *what* can the artist intend? In illustration here, Noël Carroll (2001 p. 91) imagines someone confronting the achievement of Isadora Duncan who denies that Duncan's "... barefoot prancing and posing" is art. In reply, Carroll (2001 p. 91) suggests the beginnings of a *narrative*[4] to show that:

> ... Duncan was able to solve the problem of the stagnation of theatrical dance by repudiating the central features of the dominant ballet and by reimagining an earlier ideal of dance.

Such a narrative still draws heavily on established features of past works, thereby granting both some art-status and some value to those past works. And, as Carroll illustrates, that narrative also shows what advantages Duncan saw in (and hence what values she brought to) this revitalized dance: both her pronouncements and her actions constitute an 'argument' for a modification of practices of art-making and art-understanding. That this 'argument' succeeded in changing taste (to the degree that it did) also reflects the state of the art-minded community at the time: in that artworld, Isadora's strategies were appropriate — we know that because we know they worked. But we can infer that other strategies would have been less successful although, typically, we cannot readily give examples here, since any counter-argument (once granted) would remove Isadora's work from the tradition of art-making and art-understanding: it would *then* have had no place in the narrative. So accounting for the artist's activities (rendering them intelligible) is in part looking at the values challenged, in part considering what Carroll (2001 p. 91) called "the lay of the artworld". Thus an artwork — and even the artform that sustains it, since *But is it art?* "... cannot be asked of isolated objects" (Danto, 1987 p. 60) — must be understood as part of a complex tradition of art-making and art-understanding.

If a particular putative dancework cannot be seen *as dance*, attracting a knowledgeable audience able to bring to bear the concepts required to recognize it as dance, it cannot contribute — as Duncan's came to — to the future development of the artform: that is, to future answers to the question, 'Is this dance?'. Hence it would become detached from the project of dance, as history will record it. The need to build in recognition of that possibility amounts, in part, to locating the artwork in question in its appropriate history or tradition; as part of "the lay of the artworld".

As a concrete illustration, consider its operation when relating Mark Morris's *The Hard Nut* (1991) to a work certainly *included* in such a 'received canon' (if without great enthusiasm): namely, *The Nutcracker* (1892). In contrast to other 'reworkings' of traditional ballets, Joan Acocella (1993 pp. 187-188) writes of Morris here as:

> [a] young artist taking on an old, idealistic form, classical ballet, and de-idealizing it with a flood of modern junk ... *The Hard Nut* also has a political edginess of its period, and not just in its fiddling about with gender. ... To some extent *The Hard Nut*, like so much other art of its time, seems to be saying that the Old World is dead.

Although Acocella (1993 p. 188) then qualifies this claim ("... to a very large extent it is saying the exact opposite: that the ideal meanings of old art ... is still very much alive"), her commentary makes sense of the modern work by comparisons, and contrasts, with the traditional version. And such 'arguments' always involve comparison of one concrete case with another: as John Wisdom (1965 p. 102) put it, "... at the bar of reason, always the final appeal is to cases".

But, even when this mode of argument connects a (then) new work to the 'received canon', it does so from the perspective of the audience: how do dancers come to understand this work? In particular, how do they come to understand its unity?

The answer, of course, is that they are taught it; partly in learning this dance (or their parts in it) they come to see this work as a whole; and partly they have learned, through their training, ways that danceworks can be unities — even when this is not evident. Thus, Twyla Tharp (2003 p. 199) reports that:

> ... in devising *The Fugue* [1971] ... I discovered I had given myself a completely new way of handling movement. Reversal, inversion, retrograde, retrograded inversion, stuffing, canon, and so on.

But these are just the sorts of devices used in explaining the structure of modern music, another case where the perception of unity by performers might seem problematic!

§2. Identifying dances: the role of the choreographer

The role of the dance-maker draws expressly on the three features of our understanding of persons: (a) as agents, they make the dances, and are therefore responsible for them; (b) as makers of *meaning*, whose intention-as-embodied shapes the meaning of the work; and (c) as those whose fulfilled intentions set the conditions for locating the work's meaning in its features, since that meaning functions normatively.

When is the dancework performed on Tuesday the *very same dancework* as the one seen performed on Monday? This issue, concerning what might be called "the identity-conditions for danceworks", also bears on the relevant identification-conditions (Chapter Two §9). In PAD, danceworks were certainly identified primarily in terms of the *choreography*, by stressing the role of choreographer as creative artist in respect of danceworks: that is, the *responsibility* for the dance was assigned to the choreographer, in two senses of the term "responsible" that go together — as bringing that work into being, and as recipient of any praise or blame due to the work. But I also granted that danceworks were only confronted through their performances (give or take some hand-waving about recordings); and hence the dancers in particular had a key role in what one *saw*, in seeing that dance. Further, I acknowledged the contribution of music, costume, lighting, and staging of all kinds. All this still seems to me broadly right. And if I had to say just one thing, it would still be this.

Moreover, my thought was roughly that embodied in the claims of the Screen Directors' Guild against other uses of the term "director" in relation to films: yes, there is a key role in films for casting — but calling the person(s) who do this "the casting *director*" does not give appropriate weight to the degree to which the final decisions here rest with the members of that Guild; the ones usually credited as "Director" (*punkt*). Of course, the final 'say' in film-making does not lie so smoothly with the director: we have "director's cuts" of films (for instance, of *Blade Runner* [1993, from 1983] or *Pat Garrett and Billy the Kid* [1988, from 1973]) just because the film originally released to movie theatres left something to be desired, from the director's point of view. Equally, the *producer* (not the director) collects the Oscar when the movie wins one — he or she is thereby presented as *responsible* for that film in at least the second of the two senses noted earlier. Reflection on this case might induce more caution in ascribing authorial rights (and responsibilities) for danceworks *to the choreographer*.

A more taxing argument, raised especially by Anna Pakes, urges that dependence on the choreographer — and hence on work-identity explained via choreography — is a relatively recent phenomenon in the history of dance. So that, for example, perhaps there are better accounts of what amounts to *the very same dance* when: if choreography did not provide dances with their unifying factor, what (if anything) did? Here, a conception of what provides that identity is needed; and of what one is trying to maintain. The relevant condition for other artforms has typically related to the identity of the creator: poems or paintings are typically identified partly via the poet or painter. Perhaps the diversity of those having a claim to author-hood here is one complexity: but the same difficulties arguably arise for opera and film (as above, for the facts of the resolution for film). The dance case may reflect the historical facts about the recognition of dance as a (fine) art: that, for some time, it was not recognized as the sort of activity where authorship was *important* (as, perhaps, it was not for medieval architecture). But, at least for danceworks acknowledged as artworks, it makes sense for the artworld — in this case, the danceworld — to decide this matter. If (say) huge differences can be justified independently of choreographic intervention, dance-historians may doubt that past practice would be best reflected by a focus on choreographers. When that is true (as it might have been in the past if not the present), perhaps some other method of identifying dancework-identity might be applied. Yet such debates seem within dance history.

Now I am an institutionalist about art (AJ pp. 147-150): that is, my account of art in general, dance in particular, gives due weight to how its practitioners treat relevant cases — although sometimes theory must override practice in some cases (basically, those where the practice generates unnecessary philosophical perplexity). On that basis, my account in practice should match closely the appeals of the practitioners. So that if, at a certain time, something *other than* choreographic intention 'defines' dance-identity for those practitioners, and does so unproblematically in practice, I have nothing to add. Perhaps such practitioners should be asked *whose* dance it is; who has the *responsibility* for it. But the answer should not be any more complicated than, say, that for the movie: often, the responsibility is clearly the director's; sometimes (in some cases, or perhaps for some purposes) it is clearly the producer's; and sometimes it is a matter for debate.

However, danceworks resemble musical works and plays in three important respects: first, they are *abstract objects* in the sense that one cannot destroy the dance, the symphony, or the play by destroying all instances of that dance, symphony or play — new performances are possible if ... But *if* what? For plays and symphonies, the feature most usually mentioned would be the score: roughly, finding the text for Jack B. Yates's play "The Deathly Terrace" would allow one to perform it, at least once some conventions of performance are built in. Second, the performances — the concrete objects, as it were — can differ in some ways without becoming performances of different artworks. And each is equally that artwork: none are more so. Now, these two features seem shared with, say, flags: destroying all the instances does not destroy the Stars and Stripes or the Union Flag ("Union Jack"); and all instances of a flag are equally instances, even if one is faded by the sun, another shredded by gunfire, and so on. So some theorists (including the author of PAD pp. 56-68) had suggested using a distinction drawn from C. S. Peirce[5] to present this situation, such that the works themselves are *types* (the abstract objects) and the performances (the concrete objects) are *tokens* of those types. Moreover and third, performing artworks — like flags — are designed at some time, by some person or group of persons. In these respects, then, the type/token structure seems to offer a useful way to characterize the relation of dance-performance to dancework.

For some,[6] one objection to such a view is that abstract objects cannot be made: that they are eternal objects. If so, of course this would be an unsuitable model here. But surely one can (with Levinson, 2015 p. 51-53) postulate *indicated types* (or initiated types) as otherwise types, but lacking that feature (compare Thomasson, 1999 p. 41): after all, flags too have a beginning in time and a historical-cultural aspect. (And someone giving up the type/token language must replace it with something similar.) Ideally, any revision should maintain a crucial three-part contrast: we can refer to *central cases* (where the performance is somehow paradigmatic of the dancework), to *peripheral cases*, which differ as far as possible from those central cases while still being the same dancework, and to cases which are as similar to uncontentious works as possible, while being a *different dancework* (see Chapter Two §10 where, for *Swan Lake*, candidate examples were the Ivanov and Petipa 'original', the Matthew Bourne and Mats Ek *Swan Lakes* respectively[7]).

The second kind of case (the different-as-possible performance) might be thought to arise from the interpretations that particular stagers or companies produce. And the differences from the central case have led some writers to suggest that these are different artworks. Now, here one must not simply be disputing the examples: but, if one begins from the type/token contrast, it might seem that another object can be postulated, standing roughly as *type* to the performed token, and yet as *token* to the dancework type. This arrangement is incompatible with using the type-token framework, since the new object would both *be and not be* an abstract object — and, equally, *be and not be* a concrete object. But such a move is unnecessary: the stagings can simply be regarded as the route from the (abstract) type to the (concrete) token. Moreover, such a strategy has the advantage of place the responsibility for dance-making squarely on the dance-maker: it is a *Martha Graham* dance, say. But it allows us to assign the special role in generating these sets of performances to someone other than a further dance-maker. And this seems to me to accord with danceworld practice.[8]

§3.   Making dances

Yet how does one make dances? Wollheim (1973 p. 256) rightly distinguishes two ways to make artworks that are multiples: by making an exemplar — an object that is the artwork — or by writing a recipe (or score) from that work. My idea of *notationality* for dance effectively runs these two ideas together in a productive way, so that in reality most choreographers create their works primarily by moving dancers' bodies (in ways that regularly draws on ideas from those dancers). Of course, often it is not so simple: compare Twyla Tharp's use of video: see Chapter Six §3. On my view, then, the choreographer develops for those sessions — if only in his mind — a set of instructions for dancers: of course, this is just an idealization (for some complexity, see Twyla Tharp's comments: Chapter Six).

Then *our* target — constructing an *abstract* object (the dance itself) — is most easily conceptualized as following the other route: that is, construction of a recipe. So the choreographer is imagined as putting the instructions envisaged above into a score, insofar as he formalizes them at all. Of course, no specific *kind* of score would be required here (not necessarily, say, one using Labanotation): if a set of instructions specifies whatever sequences of movement are needed, in the context of performing dances, to perform *this* dance, those instructions fix the dancework. Further, if one did not need the dancers to do X or Y, the specification would not be specific in that respect.

Moreover, this 'score' is best conceptualized as just an instructional device to explain how the choreographer's intentions — embodied in his action — create the dance: that is, the 'recipe' here can be regarded as *sets of constraints on what dancers must do to perform that dancework*. Importantly, the decisions rest with the dance-maker: as Wollheim (1980 p. 190) recognized, that "... the part of the work that came about through design did indeed come about through design and not through accident or error". Of course, what movements are 'set' does not determine completely what occurs in any particular performance: the limits to what counts as an acceptable performance, succeeding in instantiating the work appropriately, varies with the style of dance — some classical ballet, for instance, may give less leeway for difference than other dance. In practice, the dancers may deviate from a score: our model here is the performance of musical works from a score where some 'wrong notes' can typically be tolerated in an authentic performance of the work. And, notice, this is not improvisation, but thoughtful realization.

Indeed, variety in performance is both possible and part of the interest of performing arts (in contrast to movies, which are the same each time, give or take the release of a director's cut: compare Chapter Eleven §2) — in any performing art, this is permitted by the role of performers (here, the role of dancers). For the differences that each dancer brings to different roles, and to the same role on different occasions, explain why one can with benefit see the same ballet danced by the same cast on two occasions — the performances will differ. Moreover, it explains why there is typically something different to be seen, more to be learned, even in the same performance; since it too will have differences worth thinking about.

Throughout, a central issue with dance-making is *responsibility*. At one point, the Alvin Ailey company elected to assign the whole company as the dance-maker for their new works (note: only the dancers, not those responsible for costume, lighting, and so on – so there was a hierarchy here): the thought was probably egalitarian (with perhaps a financial dimension). No doubt a certain amount of altruism is required to maintain this attitude when other dancers present 'your' role. But what happens when a dancer leaves the company permanently? Surely the work cannot now be performed without the say-so of the departed dancer (since that work is partly *his*). And surely he cannot take that work with him, to be performed by his new company, even if he was (in fact) the major contributor to its choreography. So what follows when the whole of the then-company is taken as the dance-maker? In practice, these are serious, not trivial, questions. Thus, a similar situation arose in December 2005 (see PAD p. 90), when Pilobolus Dance Theatre parted company with Alison Chase, a founder member who had choreographed many of the works in the group's repertoire, and Chase claimed "... they don't have clear title to my work" (Pasles, 2006 p. E35). But, conceptually, these issues are simple: dancing the role does not *give* you control over that role, however much you put into it by way of suggestion.

So granting that, in typical cases, a particular dance could be performed with a different cast recognizes performances of the very same dance differing on at least these occasions. In fact, there can be differences *just* between performances by that company of same work (tired performers, different performers) — indeed, there *will* be such differences. For performables are necessarily re-performable; therefore, in principle, with a different cast. And there can be differences explicable by something else — staging, 'version', etc. (even 'So-and-so's version': see later for extreme versions). Yet, in both cases, there is one dance here; both performances are of that same work, despite the differences. Then the issues become:

- When do we have the same dance (or artwork) on two occasions?

- When do we have *performances* of the same work on two occasions?

These will be equivalent questions across the performing arts, since encountering the same work twice requires encountering two performances (although, of course, not necessarily performances having the same artistic *value* — one version can be preferable to another!).

A parallel with music suggests one obvious answer: the dance itself could be identified via its score. But four main differences in the situations make this problematic (see Chapter Two §10). First, given the possibility of confusable counterparts, just knowing the movements cannot alone guarantee that their performance leads to an instantiation of the dancework; this exploits a strength of notation systems sometimes used for dance (such as Labanotation) — they can be used to record *any* human movement; hence are of use to anthropologists. By contrast, musical scores are rarely produced except for music! Second, scores in such notation systems are both difficult to write[9] and difficult to read: the conceptual decisions involved in translating the four dimensions of dance onto a two-dimensional score are huge. Then, third, while mastery of musical notation seems a prerequisite for many engaged with music as performers or composers, the same is not true of dance — perhaps because there are three (or more) notation systems in use; and because most danceworks are not notated. Therefore, most works for which scores exist were notated 'after the fact', from performances. Goodman (1968 p. 217) imagined a time when (say) Labanotation "... becomes standard enough [that] its underlying analysis of movement into factors and particles will prevail: arbitrary decisions will bloom into absolute truth ..." just because that analysis would then be ubiquitous, as is almost true for music. But that time is not here (nor, I suspect, will it be). Finally, the power of some notation systems generates problems of its own: one must make choices about what it is *important* to notate; and different decisions might be reached. Further, we recognize the power of the training: it might have been more difficult for Tricia Brown to 'set' the movement she wanted in her *Accumulation* (1971) — described as "... the rotation of the right fist with the thumb extended" (Banes, 1987 p. 82: Chapter Two §10) — had a similar but conflicting movement been taught to most dancers; a *port de pouce*, as it were. Thus, at least sometimes, the notator may score the movement the dancers *will* perform, given the training of those dancers, rather than what they should. So, while a conception of notationality may capture a constraint here (see below), one cannot hope that it will be of much practical help in uniquely identifying the movement component of danceworks.

But, in asking, 'what are the conceptual constraints on correctly identifying a performance as of (say) *Vesalii Icones?*', we might be aiming at *identificatory features* (see Chapter Two §9). What might candidates be? What Louther choreographed, and what he was thereby taking responsibility for, was a solo (at least as far as the dancer was concerned). So it seems right that any performance of the work must also be a solo — although it would be hard to predict what might be made of, say, a suitably organized duet. Also, here, the music seems fixed, especially given the acknowledged contribution of the composer, Peter Maxwell Davies, to the images behind the dance. So any performance must involve his composition of the same title.

Suppose, in reality, every performance was by Louther himself, and was accompanied by Maxwell Davies' ensemble, "The Fires of London": now, what about the music? Is the *live* music an essential feature of this work, or would a suitable recording be adequate? Equally, if the music must be live, need its players be "The Fires of London"? Well, differences in the membership of "The Fires of London" surely cannot preclude a performance being of this work. Hence there need be no simple answer.

The overall look of the piece seems important: yet what is recognized, as what is recorded, is a particular performance: so, is *Vesalii Icones* 'in the round' or not? Agreeing that it can genuinely be performed in either context

— and the history of the work requires this, since Louther himself performed it in both situations — is granting that these cannot be among that work's identity-generating features.

Further, in respect of *Vesalii Icones*, Louther had roles both as its choreographer and also its dancer. But, when we ask about his responsibilities, the first of these roles is, as it were, *used-up*: the dance-making has occurred. The responsibilities of the dancer are on-going. So Louther's responsibility for this dance *as choreographer* clearly differs from his role as dancer. As before, then, these two roles must be distinguished, even if (as in this case) *in practice* both 'hats' were worn only by the one person.

However, had Louther been alive, performances without his blessing might be thought at least doubtfully *of that work*. If so, that suggests that some of his responsibility *as author* could remain for *identification* of the work as the one he choreographed. And this idea is familiar from cases where choreographers make modifications to extant works — roughly, we accept them as the same work if the choreographer says so, as long as the changes are not too great. (Compare Braques's paintings!)

Equally, turning to the performer — and assuming just one — must it be William Louther? That this dancework always actually had the same performer, and moreover that the performer was also its choreographer, are *contingencies*: they *were* true in practice, but need not have been. Louther might have taught the dance to someone else: although this did not happen, its conceptual possibility is inherent in the idea of a work in the performing arts, because in principle the work is a *performable*. That is, a work that might be performed on different occasions. So all that precludes (say) my performing the work is the need to have learned the work — where this may already implicate kinds of virtuosity that most of us may lack, as well as the right kinds of technical training.

Now, that Louther largely ceased performing so as "... not to sabotage the memories of his sensational virtuosity" (Meisner, 1998), if indeed he did, might well suggest that performing *Vesalii Icones* requires a comparable virtuosity. Then, although performer and work can *seem* inexorably connected, any apparent connection merely reflects the practicalities. For, of course, these requirements are perfectly general: similarly, Martha Graham had difficulty finding dancers with the distinctive talents needed to perform the roles she had choreographed for herself once she no longer could.[10] And, if Bob Fosse's choreography for himself reflects problems with his physique (as he claims: see UD p. 321 note 5), suitable performers might need to replicate these. So Louther's case, like these others, requires a very particular virtuosity of a replacement-dancer.

Are other characteristics of Louther important here? For example, must the performer be African-American? Obviously, a British Afro-Caribbean might have learned the technique; so this seems unnecessary, even though we are used to *Othello* played in 'blackface' by virtuoso actors, such as Lawrence Olivier (for Shakespeare) and virtuoso opera singers, such as Placido Domingo (for *Otello*, by Verdi or Rossini): here, at least, there is some justification *in the play* or *in the opera*. (My feeling is that this practice is dying out.) Still, there anyway seems no obvious reason to require a particular ethnicity of this dancer. Here, what started as a *identifying condition* might, now, be set aside if viewed as an *identity-condition*!

Moreover, these conditions, and any others, function at best (a) defeasibly — we see how identification would be ruled out if something were amiss in one or more of these ways; and, even then, (b) as only the *beginning* of a discussion. Additionally, all conditions must be seen in the light of making sense of the work as a whole — one's 'reading' or account of it. For the appeal to the art-maker here aligns with our hypothetical intentionalism.[11] Thus, in summary (see PAD pp. 151-152):

- there is no obvious and decisive limit as to what might be brought to bear in justifying one's account of the meaning of a dancework;

- any account must be constrained by the need to offer (roughly) evidence for one's reading, especially in the face of competing 'readings' or interpretations;

- accounts operate *defeasibly* with the idealization, or fiction, of total evidence, in line with Carnap's *principle of total evidence* (Carnap, 1950 p. 211) — such that the evidence one has is all the relevant evidence;

- justifications take place in contexts: one answers (or addresses) *the question asked*, not some exceptionless demand.

The upshot of this discussion is just to stress the place of the *debate*, within the artworld of dance (and especially among informed observers — including both dancers and choreographers): as contextualists, we do not expect a single resolution, and especially not one holding exceptionlessly for all time.

§4.   Dancers are not robots

Above, distinguishing the role of dance-maker from that of dancer acknowledges that both roles are crucial; but that of the maker, understood as the artist (as for other arts), is easier to characterize — so what to say about performer? First, the centrality of that role must be restated: one could not have a performance without performers. In this sense, as Williams (2004 p. 73) puts it:

... dancers are logically prior to dances — to the *act of* dancing or the notion of *the dance* —just as speakers are logically prior to speeches — to the act of speaking or the notion of language.

At the least, they cannot be logically secondary, since — without dancers — there could be no dances. (To count as speech, sounds must have 'understanders'.)

Then, having recognized the need for two roles (maker and performer), the importance of the performer's role was stressed. Since it was *crucial*, it should not be undervalued — last of all by dancers! Thus, one aim central to much of my work (including PAD) was giving due weight to the importance of dancers. As I imagined it, a dancer might say with pride: "No, I am not an artist — that is because I have spent my time, energy and creativity on being one hell of a dancer!" (PAD p. 175). But what might this mean?

Certainly, not enough philosophical work has been done on dancers: the idea of a dancer combines many roles.[12] As with other performers, such as opera singers, a new research agenda is required; but it will not be aided if the model for such performers remains painters, poets, and novelists — that is, artists in the fine arts. But, for the key role, perhaps we can ask: *What is really needed to be a performer in a performable?*

Within that new research agenda, the *craft-mastery* of being a dancer[13] must be acknowledged; this in turn connects with the sorts of training required to perform danceworks that are art. So part of the answer here must elaborate the character of the dancer, reflecting the need for strong, mobile bodies capable of performing danceworks of an appropriate difficulty as well as having knowledge of the relevant technique(s), and mastery of the manner of performing appropriate to danceworks (that is, artworks) of that kind, because that body has been trained in certain techniques; for instance, Graham technique — and such techiques bring with them a range of expressive possibilities; as one might say, what they do *well*.[14] In mastering the technique, to whatever degree, the dancers 'acquire' mastery of these expressive resources, in that they can bring them to bear in performances, if required. So that, for many dancers, the artistic ideas embodied in the technique (the "technique-as-aesthetic": Siegel, 1972, p. 107; UD p. 202) become second nature. Then, second, there are the specific resources from *this* company or *this* dance technique: the sorts of habits of mind and body (that is, behaviour) built up in daily *class*. Next, third, there is what our dancer has learned of *dances* – both in general and specifically in respect of the dances this choreographer makes. Knowing this is *knowing how* to present the dance (say, to the audience) in line with it. Hence it amounts to what I call "performance traditions" for dance: one knows how dancers behave in this context — what flows naturally from the technical resources of the dancer in this technique. (In Chapter Six (§4-5), this is characterized as the dancer's mastery of *practice traditions*, there sketching such traditions within both ballet and modern dance. In this way one develops a vocabulary to describe many cases, including aiming to explain some of the craft knowledge of dancers by contrasting the dancers' training in *performance traditions* with the understanding of *traditions of performance* as a requirement for an audience). In particular, dancers' craft-mastery might be accommodated through the idea of a "reflective practitioner" — on its attributive use, such that it cannot be 'split' into 'reflective + practitioner', but rather is 'practitioner in a reflective manner' (considered briefly in Chapter Six §6).

Further, one's work must be (or at least become) accessible to an audience, to permit one to perform — without which there would be no actual performances of the performable (again, this requirement operating only in principle). As above, this last is here called a *tradition of the practice*, such that the audience (or, anyway, some select part of it) knows what to expect when going to art-dance. Moreover, both traditions are mutable under the impact of general changes in what I have called "the artworld"; or, better, the *various* artworlds for different artforms, and sub-classes of these forms.

Relatedly, the fragility of performances of particular works, which depend on dancers, as well as audiences, must be acknowledged. In particular, the relation of dancers to the choreography they can instantiate is important. One way of failing to meet these requirements — an explicable one, given the economic hardship borne patiently by many professional dancers — is elegantly captured when Susan Leigh Foster (1997 p. 255: quoted PAD p. 266) characterizes modern dancers in terms of the "hired body" with its "... rubbery flexibility coated with impervious glossiness". Such a body would meet to the highest degree the first of the conditions in an earlier paragraph. And its attractions can explain the appeal of star dancers (for example, Baryshnikov as discussed in Chapter Six §5). Further, this characterization no doubt reflects the need for today's dancer to work in many different styles in order to secure and maintain employment. But that very availability to *all* or *most* dance-styles will impact negatively on the expressiveness of at least some kinds of dancing. For, in reality, such a dancer cannot be relied on for mastery of the relevant dancers' *practice traditions* in such a way as to engage reliably with the *traditions of practice* built into the expectations of the audience. Still, the requirement here for appropriate dancers is clear, even if the 'conditions for adequacy' are not.

§5.   Questions of authorship and ontology

Sensitivity is needed "... to capture ... the role of the performer even in notated, non-improvised music [or dance]" (Levinson & Alperson, in Levinson, 2015 p. 164). For one aspect of the dancer's role, even in typical cases, is to instantiate the dance that the choreographer makes (roughly: to follow the dance-maker's recipe). But dancers are not robots: so this cannot simply be conceptualized as though it were puppetry (an accusation sometimes levelled against me). For that is not all that is involved: as well as the need for technique adequate to perform this dancework, the dancer may well need to 'join up the dots' tonight, when other dancers may be tired, or injured or some such.... In effect, two key thoughts here pull in opposite directions: that the dancers should do the same thing each night, to instantiate the very same dance; and that the interest in performing arts lies partly in the fact that there will inevitably be some degree of difference (in contrast to movies) — although part of the dancer's skill will sometimes consist in concealing that fact.

Others have aimed to model that role as a kind of co-author. One such theorist, Collingwood (1938 p. 321), taken seriously, would have demeaning impact — as an idealist, Collingwood finds the musical work "... complete and perfect in the composer's mind"; not a promising position from which to do justice to the performer. Elsewhere, Nöel Carroll (2012 p. 446) apparently adopts a strategy that — applied to dance — might be thought to offer an account on which *both* choreographer and dancer are artists. But what would be his argument?

Writing about theatre, he comments that "[t]he different kinds of *artists* here signal different arts of drama: the art of composition or creation and the *art* of performance or execution". Given this claim, someone might think that if Carroll is right to identify two kinds of *artists* here, or two types of *arts*, I must be wrong. But, before jumping to that conclusion, let us consider two or three features of Carroll's discussion. First, it is an exploration of the distinctiveness of theatre (which I had contrasted with dance); and ultimately does go on to contrast performing arts with, say, film. So what is the "two-tiered structure" here? Carroll (2012 p. 448) comments: "Because of the duality of drama, plays have as tokens both objects and performances". That is to say, for typical cases of drama, we have both the *text* of the play (the object) and the *performance* of the play. Carroll regards both of these as tokens of the *type* that is the play: at the least, this is not the case for music — we do not really regard the score as *the music*, but only a recipe for it (the music at least necessarily includes tones); and, even in those cases where there *is* a score for a dance, that score is not the dance (as with *music* requiring tones, the *dance* necessarily includes human movements — or so I urge). Thus, when Carroll (2012 p. 450) writes that "[d]rama is a two-tiered artform, an artform comprised of two kinds of works: creations ... and performances ...", he is not offering a parallel for dance.

By bringing out imagined parallels and differences, this speaks to our second point. For what should one say in the dance case? Carroll (2012 p. 446) notes:

> As the choreographer is to the dance troupe, and the composer is to the conductor-cum-orchestra, so normally is the author of the play to the director, actors, designers, and so forth.

In this description, the dancers are compared directly with "the conductor-cum-orchestra": but in what role? The orchestra-members, and even the conductor, do not stand on a par with the composer, as co-authors of the work performed. Hence, in effect, Carroll here concedes that point for dancers, by drawing this comparison. However, he goes on to say that, "[i]n these cases there are two discriminable *arts*: the art of composition and the art of performance" (Carroll, 2012 p. 446: my emphasis). But now any attempt to apply the distinction to dance and music (where there is only one *concrete* art-object, the performance) seems merely verbal: the dancers and musicians have a role in bringing to fruition the artwork that is that performance. And there is no more difficulty here in calling this an *art* than, say, to calling one's book *The Womanly Art of Breastfeeding* (Best, 1992 p. 174). But nothing follows. Further, that situation is contrasted with the one Carroll (2012 p. 445) envisages for drama, when he claims that "[d]rama, *in this respect*, is a dual-tracked or two-tiered artform" (my emphasis). In *what* respect? Carroll's answer is: because *here* (and, by implication, not elsewhere) "one word applies to these two distinguishable artforms: the art of composing texts (or, broadly, performance plans) and the art of performing them" (Carroll, 2012 p. 445). That is to say, there are two *artforms* here, since the *respect* in question involves recognizing that for drama (as Carroll conceives it: contrast, Hamilton, 2007 p. 23, on the priorities) the text is also an artwork available to an audience.

What, then, should one say about the contribution of performers? Carroll (2012 p. 446) is clear that:

> Just as we expect different violinists to bring out different qualities of the musical score, so we expect actors and directors to disclose different aspects of the relevant composition. ... Different performances make different choices concerning [what exactly is to be done]. In order to produce a performance, the executors must go beyond what is given in the play text or performance plan.

We can imagine similar claims made for a dance with an adequate score, and then modified to accommodate cases where the dancers learn the constraints on adequate performance *of the work* from some other source, such as a previous dancer in the role or a stager. For, of course, there must be some such constraints, however weak, if the performance is to count as of that work and not some other. So Carroll has here described the important role of the performer, such that the performer's contribution is clear; and has done so without (yet) deploying the term "art". Further, what he says applies directly to dances: just as the contribution of the violinist does not put him on a par with, say, Beethoven in respect of the work performed (they are not co-authors), so the contribution of the dancer cannot put him on a par with Martha Graham. Of course, to the degree that the work itself — in dance as in music — is heavily circumscribed by the composer or choreographer (as in some classic music and some ballet), the scale of the variety introduced by performers in satisfactory performances may be correspondingly reduced; but not its importance!

Above, though, it seemed that Carroll wished to insist on the term "artist" for these 'executors', practitioners (it seemed) of "the art of execution". Now the force of the term "art" is clear: those people who make concrete the Shakespeare play have, for Carroll, a role very different from those who make concrete the play-text (the book, as it were). This is what the "two-tiered structure" reflects: but Shakespeare is the *artist* in both cases, if by "artist" is meant, roughly, "creator". That is why, as I urged above, when Carroll (2012 p. 450) claims that, "[d]rama is a two-tiered artform, an artform comprised of two kinds of works: creations … and performances ….", he is not offering a radical account of art-authorship that might be applied to music or dance. He is writing solely about drama — as his paper/chapter title indicates!

Still might a parallel argument be presented for dance? Clearly, it is hard to see how: even when a dance has a notated score, that score is not the dance; and it scarcely seems an artwork in its own right (however beautiful in its calligraphy). But might focus on a notated score, especially one elaborated in (say) Labanotation, offer a more limited role to dancers, whereby the dancers provide *only* the bodily movement? And might these ideas be expanded, again on a parallel with music, such that the notationality offered by a potential score (real or imagined) really constrained *only* those bodily movements?

The short answer is, "No". First, recognizing our concern as with *artworks* — with those dances that are art — grants that there can be 'confusable counterparts' (Danto, 1981 p. 138: PAD p. 17) of non-art actions. Hence more than just those movements are required to identify the dance — they must be rightly seen *as dance*. Thus, in Chapter One, Carroll & Banes (1992 quoted Banes, 1994 p. 11) rightly described Yvonne Rainer's "Room Service" (1963) as including a sequence of "… ordinary movement", a potential 'confusable counterpart' — seeing these movements aright (not misperceiving them) requires addressing these movement *as dance*; that is what transfigures them, rather than (say) how the dancers think about them, or how the audience (somehow) approaches those thoughts. So it cannot help to suggest, as Montero does, that "… the neurological activity [of a suitably qualified spectator] … will mirror the neurological activity in the dancer" (Davies, 2011 p. 196). Since the dancer's neurological activity does not make these movements *dance*, such neurological activity is shared by perceiving the artwork and its confusable-counterpart.

Then, second, the movement involved alone cannot identify performances as of a particular dancework. For confusable counterparts can misfire in other ways: for instance, by generating rehearsals of those danceworks, rather than the works themselves. Indeed, the idea of *rehearsal* of a work remains crucial to illustrating this argument (UD p. 93; PAD p. 70), by introducing art-type 'confusable counterparts': a work one can rehearse is a work (in principle) capable of being performed on more than one occasion — that is to say, a *performable*. After all, the rehearsal is not typically specific to any performance; Monday's rehearsal counts as preparation for the performances on Tuesday, Wednesday, and Thursday. Yet performances of the very same dancework will not typically be indistinguishable either from the other performances or from the rehearsal (assuming it was a dress rehearsal of one kind); and, even where *no* difference exists between that rehearsal and, say, Tuesday's performance, the rehearsal *still* would not typically instantiate the dancework; it would not be (or become) another performance. As with, say, the rehearsal for a marriage, even were the whole ceremony included, the *context* ensures that the rehearsal lacked the normative force of the *real* 'performance'.

This is another place where, to my mind, one must stick as closely as possible to danceworld practice (without giving up all hope for 'rational reconstruction"). For again, as Reid ([1815] 2002 p. 577) remarked, "[p]hilosophers should be very cautious in opposing the common sense of mankind; for, when they do, they rarely miss going wrong". Consider the suggestion, sometimes called "musical perdurantism" (Caplan & Matheson, 2006), on which musical performances are temporal or spatio-temporal parts of works: applied to dance, its most typical version would have the following characteristics:

- danceworks persist over time, but only by/when 'present' in some particular location (so that a discussion of 'them' at other times is just a reference to a past historical event — when there was an 'apparition');

- performances are constitutive of the dancework: nevertheless, they are, somehow, both artworks in their own rights and parts of the real, purduring artwork;

- that all, or anyway, most of the dancers involved are co-authors (if any are — they all have the same claim);

- there are no mistakes as such: performances lacking "structural similarity or causal connections" (Caplan & Matheson, 2006 p. 62) might not be genuine parts.

The difficulty of drawing up this list already speaks against it, when compared with that in the previous paragraph:[15] I certainly do not know how to prove which of these most dancers accept. But, from those I know, the suggestion of a variety of performances of the same work seems better to reflect their conception than the thought that all contribute to some single work, never completed while future performances could occur, of where all have equal authorial status; and where there cannot be real mistakes in performances, but only interpretations of differing plausibility. Moreover, where some classic performances (say, Martha Graham's *Lamentation* [1930]) lack properties of the *real* work, since it has 'moved on' since then. (In fact, my dating of works throughout my discussions would be misplaced.) If it is insisted that, in the end, the suggestion comes to no more than a re-description of the everyday account, it has become ontology for its own sake — a game I prefer not to play.

Further, any suggestion of difference must do more than show that a *majority* of some group adopts it: the majority can be mistaken. As a contextualist, while I do not expect an exceptionless response to the questions about the 'nature' of dance, clearly actual dancing should be prioritized. Dancers may *say* things that need not be taken seriously: not *all* remarks by the danceworld must be retained as truths, in the light of the need to make sense of what was urged ('rational reconstruction').

Of course, adherents of my view must grasp some nettles: but, as I have illustrated, most arise from a commitment to commonsense.[16] Thus, perhaps my taking dances as, minimally, an assemblage of moving bodies means (counter-intuitively) that we will discuss dances we have not seen; but, if we are scrupulous, we will do so only on some other basis — testimony, or the sorts of materials that might find a place in reconstruction of the dance at issue. Or if a type/token account of danceworks can never accommodate the creation of dances (at some time, in some place — at least roughly), it should be rejected for that reason. On this view, dances are abstract objects ('*abstracta*'). But most people have no clear view of what to say about the least contentious of abstract objects, such as numbers:[17] does *two* exist even when there are no extant instances of the numeral nor extant pairs of things? Such a question invites ontology.[18] But much higher mathematics can be conducted without answering it. Then the philosophical argument must take as basic some commitments from practice; for instance, as the cases against which putative definitions are tested or that allow putative counter-cases to be derived. And, of course, the best way to discuss these cases can be contested. At the least, there are clear roles here. (That is why the relevant section in PAD is called "The Dancer's Share" — a fact its critics seem to ignore.)

Still, at the least, *dancers* are required to generate performances, at the least in turning the choreographer's 'recipe' into a performance. But how do they do that? To see that such a question has no answer, compare seeing a particular cricketer bowl a delivery where the ball spins, and asking that bowler, "How did you do that?". And perhaps she explains that it is a *leg-break*, a right-handed delivery based on a wrist-spin technique, turning from the *leg side* to the *off side* (usually away from the batsman, for a right-handed batter). Then she demonstrates an *off-break*, depending on finger-spin technique, turning from the off side to the leg side (usually into the batter). And she explains the differences in grip and flight that each deploys. With luck, you might learn how she produced these deliveries — and perhaps, ultimately, learn how to achieve them yourself. But you have not really learned how *she* bowled the leg-break; but rather how *to* bowl a leg-break, or how one bowls a leg-break. That is to say, you might learn the skill, but not how the person achieves that skill on a particular occasion. Or, rather, you have learned what there is to learn — there is no *how* here, beyond her having the skill and actualizing it in practice: she does not do anything here, *beyond* (or different from) bowling the ball.

In the cricketing case, not only is the skill itself closely defined but it typically has both a place in a particular match, and a clear goal (through its relation to winning-and-losing at cricket). For the dance case, the selection of particular actions cannot be explained in this way. Thus, here, an additional normativity should be considered: as dancer, how do I know I did it *right*?

While a dancer might offer suggestions in the choreographic process and make decisions to deal with today's contingencies, the intelligence of the dance-maker functions to ensure that the originality of the movements is appropriate: that it *makes sense* in terms of the dance as a whole. We assume that, in part, whether it 'makes sense' is something that, say, audience-members could determine but — to do that — they must appeal (if implicitly) to the *fulfilled intentions* of the dance-maker. In this sense, then, Levinson (2015 p. 110) rightly regards the audience's part as "... more akin to finely backgrounded perceiving of a performance". Certainly that is the dance-maker's view of the candidate audience; but, as above, since this is not mere psychology, the 'fulfilled intentions' can only be gainsaid when replaced (that is, as 'failed').

A clear account of working with a director exemplifies the point. Thus, Glenda Jackson comments, of her interaction with director Peter Brook:

> He refuses absolutely to settle for boundaries in life. But he knows when to say no. *Very firmly*. So you begin again and eventually he says, "No". And it goes on like that until you call for an oxygen tent. But perhaps you do discover something. And he says, 'Yes, that's a bit more like it.' And you say, 'A bit more like *what*?' To which he smiles in his benign way, and replies: 'I don't know. Show me.' (quoted Heilpern, 1999 pp. 15-16)

If, as your choreographer or director, I told you just to 'go on' ("Do whatever you like") — as Brook (quoted above) *appeared* to, dealing with Glenda Jackson — one would lack any basis for normative decisions: that is, decisions as to the right thing to do next. In fact, Brook is drawing (if implicitly) on a shared context: on what (in our case) I called "the performance traditions" of dance. It requires, of course, both dancers able to instantiate the work — or, when it is not yet complete, able to offer continuations that make sense in the context of the rest of the dance (where, naturally, there need not be just one) — and an audience capable of recognizing the unity in the resultant work, even if they learn that (in part) *from* the work itself.

So how do you, as the dancer, know what to do (= 'how to go on') in offering dance ideas? You draw on what you already know about *this* dance — some of which the dance-maker may have provided: thus Tharp (2009 p. 15) urges, "I don't tell, I show. Then they do. Something doesn't work? We'll try again, look at it closely, make a modification. Dancers ... learn best by example". And then, what you know of dances in the style, or using this technique. Further, the dance-maker may have given hints (in the form of images: for instance, when Christopher Bruce tells a dancer, "I want your body twisted, as if drawn on a rack": Austin, 1976 p. 99; or when he offers the target that the dancer be "... almost insane, with an empty grin on your face": Austin, 1976 p. 99) — if one does not know *exactly* how to actualize such images, perhaps one knows where to start. And perhaps "empty grin" constitutes a powerful hint!

§6.   Locating responsibility

So, post-transfiguration, such movement (or such dances) can be misperformed, or performed badly, as well as not performed at all: that is, the movements in context function normatively. That returns us to normativity for the dancer, as illustrated via the fate of Archie Gemmill's goal (against the Netherlands) in the 1978 FIFA World Cup. Having been recorded using the movement notation system Labanotation, that goal was 'translated' from the score into a dance by Andy Howitt — and performed on at least three occasions, including at Sadlers Wells theatre. But how exactly does the dance relate to the goal? If successfully performing *that* dance required, say, following the Labanotation score, Gemmill's own dribbling run and goal have the wrong 'direction of fit'. Since the Labanotation score was made from what Gemmill *actually* did, any mismatch between notated score and his behaviour would be a criticism of the score, not the movement. Not so for the dance! Yet, then, the elegance of that sequence of movements — as captured through the score, perhaps, and then transfigured into art — has really nothing to do with football. Yet, at best, Gemmill's movement pattern is elegant *as a goal*, as part of the match, with concomitant connections to the aspiration to win. In abstracting from that, the dance loses any connection to football (as though, were it performed tomorrow, a new player might succeed in tackling the Gemmill figure!). Hence the dance can *go wrong* in ways that make no sense applied to Gemmill himself: he either scores the goal or fails to — the normativity of art (here, of dance) means that the dancer generates other possibilities, for misfire and such like.

Foregrounding responsibility re-introduces concerns with *normativity*. As a dancer, for what am I *responsible?* My task is to *instantiate* the work; to turn the recipe (from the notated score, say) into a performance. To approach *responsibility* here, one might ask: *Which parts of the dancer's behaviour are intentional or deliberate?* My task as dancer involves instantiating the dancework, thereby posing at least two issues: first, what are my responsibilities — what must I deliver? Second, for what may I legitimately be criticized? What, as dancer, counts as part of the dance? The slogan 'no modification without aberration'[19] encapsulates one problem here: that, whatever answer is given, it will be tempting to look for *deliberation or intention* in those actions, rather than others, in ways that would not apply to human action more generally. For most of what one does is not deliberate (if that requires explicit deliberation); or, better, only *deliberate* when the alternative would involve its being accidental. So this is quite the wrong picture. If I am sweating ... and I do not excuse it, and especially if I aim to reproduce it the next time I dance that role, presumably I regard it is part of the role. But the dance-maker decides here. The 'dancer's experience' in the process of dance-making is logically *irrelevant* — ideas (especially movement ideas) offered to the choreographer, however extensive, must be accepted by the choreographer (that is where the responsibility will reside, in the dance-making process).

Thus, faced with the question "deliberate or not?" I would say that *all* of it is deliberate, since not accidental: that is, *all* was responsibility-bearing (*pace* Carroll & Seeley, 2015 p. 180b), unless the dancer offers an excuse. And this simply tracks previous comments on meaning and intention: the normativity required for meaningful language-use is precisely that required for the possibility of morality. As Stanley Cavell (1969/2002: 29-31) rightly urges, we *must* mean what we say: this obligation has two related dimensions — that what one says *is* what one means (other things being equal) just because it is what one *says*; and that one *should* mean what one says, with the major alternatives being either lying or failing to take the interchange sufficiently seriously. Similarly, what among the things I do, as dancer, counts as part of the dance? Clearly, what is not *action* cannot count here; but what is (or is not) *action?* The best answer would stress responsibility! If I am sweating ... and I do not excuse it, I am offering it as an action. Thus:

• "I did not mean to be sweating" — this was not part of the dance;

- "Being sweaty was unavoidable" – so, a foreseeable consequence (not set aside, but not stressed).

Taking *ordinary* sweating as part of the dance will confuse the dance with some counterpart. Further, the need to exclude irrelevance here is familiar, although difficult to elaborate. Thus, in a typical painting, "... we do not notice the shadows that fall on it or, unless it is excessive, the light reflected from the varnish", as Collingwood (1938 p. 143) notes. Moreover, such things are set aside as not relevant, rather than our 'not noticing' them: at most, they might reflect badly on the *hanging* of the painting. Of course, in a particular case, these might indeed be reasons for concern: each might reflect the fulfilled intention of the artist in such a way that to fail to notice it, or to set it aside, would involve misperceiving the work. But this is not the usual situation. And, were that acknowledged, still other aspects of our engagement with the work could be set aside as irrelevant. Further, this might be expected, given the general impact of explaining behaviour as *human action*.

Thus, when Anscombe (1957 p. 80) looks for "... a device which reveals the order that there is in this chaos" of explaining one's behaviour, she starts with the offering of reasons that exhibit the action as appropriate: we ask the boy who strikes his sister, 'Why did you do it?', and he replies (say), 'Because she hit me first' — in seeing his action as retaliation, we understand both why he did it, and what kind of action it is. Thus, if the boy had replied, 'Because that loud bang made me jump', we would understand that this was not really an *action* at all: it occurred for no reason; or, at least, no reason *of the boy's*. Moreover, excuses and such like enter the picture here: the boy might now express his regret, and similar.

Some actions, though, are attained through doing something else, as Danto's initial discussion of *basic action* recognized. Suppose we understand the boy's retaliatory intent, and learn that (in response) he embarrassed his sister: now one might ask, 'How did you do that?', as a way to learn how the embarrassing was achieved — say, though displaying a childhood picture in a public place. And, importantly, this is only one set of actions (from among many) that would achieve the overall action; so he might have found another way to place her in an embarrassing situation. Moreover, the same behaviour of exhibiting the childhood picture might achieve a quite different — even directly contrastive — overall action. So the action cannot here by identified through the bodily behaviour only; and hence not via that particular causal narrative.

But similar forms of words ('How are you going to do that?') can request a breakdown of the bodily movements involved: thus, in the movie *True Lies* (1994), Harry lays out the sequence of events that will lead to his escaping from the villains, including killing the one planning to torture him (see

Chapter One §6). To achieve this, he must first do A, then B, and so on: so there is a chain of questions here, all asking, 'And how will you do that?' for each of the components — "will" because it is still a prediction — and beginning with what he will do first; namely, pick the lock on the handcuffs. And perhaps he could describe how that was managed. But, in the end, such questions come to an end: there was nothing as such that he did to achieve the manipulation that releases the handcuffs — if you still need an explanation, perhaps he could sometimes say (as in this case) how he *learned* to do it, but that is a very different question.

Such a sequence of questions is also typical of some enquiries by children: once they learn that it makes sense to ask, of some actions, 'How did you do that?', they then ask, in respect of the reply, 'And how did you do that next thing?', and so on.

Yet how many such steps should be considered? Obviously, there is no limit: occasion-sensitivity points to our mentioning such steps as we take to be informative, faced with a particular question (or questioner). Yet is there always a first step? As we saw in Chapter One, Davidson mistakenly takes reasons to operate causally, and so imagines that there must be — after all, chains of causes have a beginning, although we might not know it. Thus Davidson (1980 p. 83) imagines a kind of 'pure intention', of which the agent might not be aware; and which, since it might not issue in behaviour, cannot be inferred from what one does. But, first, such "an interior act of intention" (Anscombe, 1957 p. 47) is not necessary once one grants that *persons*, as agents, can initiate actions; second, in this case, the burden of proof would be on the person claiming (say) that he genuinely intends to build a squirrel house: perhaps the most plausible course would involve denying such an intention to this person!

Asking how one *did* such-and-such can highlight three or four features of actions that apply to dances: first, the question has value in clarifying what sub-actions were performed in the performance of the overall action; second, the chain of questions comes to an end when there are no more actions of mine, when I just did the last thing mentioned; third, that chain involves the explanation of actions, and terminates when no more action is involved. So there is nothing more that one *did*; no more *action* to describe. That is why, as Anscombe (1957 p. 80) points out, while the question, 'What is the stove doing?' is answered by replying, 'Burning well', there is no exact parallel for Smith, although we might respond that he was resting, or lying extended on this bed. For our 'Why?' questions ask for reasons for actions, rather than the causal narrative appropriate to such bodily events. Then we realize that such chains of questions come to an end: as we saw Wittgenstein (OC §471) inform us, "... the difficulty is to begin at the beginning. And not try to go further back". Yet answers to such 'back beyond the beginning' questions are regularly requested. Hence, as Wittgenstein (OC §402) was fond of quoting, "In the beginning was the deed": people are agents, and therefore there are typically answers to such, 'Why did you do that?' questions; and often to, 'How did you do that?' questions. But chains of such questions come to an end, with an action I just perform (perhaps because I learned to). And (recall) Danto postulated *basic actions* because chains of requests for explanation come to an end. Yet, in context, no particular actions need *always* be basic: that will be resolved contextually. Then one can ask, 'How are you able to do this?', with answers registering, for instance, one's abilities ('Because of my slender physique'; 'Because I am double-jointed'), or one's powers ('Because I practice regularly'). And, of course, one could perhaps explain *how one learned* to do such-and-such: this would typically be true of dance; and would be answered by looking at, say, the activities or the curriculum in any half-decent dance school (Royal Ballet, Kirov).

Indeed the causal story sketched by neuroscience does *offer* to explain how it comes about that we behave as we do: yet there, explanation is neither necessary nor possible. Rather, as above, the same causal description of bodily behaviour is consonant with the performing of a variety of actions: in context, my asking to leave the room or my buying a table in an auction. Further, I do not typically know the causal story (say, in terms of the contraction of muscles with Latinate names) for *how* I did that thing.

§7.   Pursuing philosophical aesthetics

Moreover, the differential focus of philosophy (as opposed to various causal studies in the sciences) sets different standards for proof here — for instance, our concerns are not well-expressed in probabilistic terms. Exceptions must be recognized, where appropriate. Thus philosophy begins from our acceptance that some people will act in this way and others will act differently: we are not typically looking for trends and tendencies. That is, the Iron Law of Wages is recognized as at best a useful generalization in economics; but not as a (genuine) *law*, as perhaps Ricardo thought – and certainly not as *iron*! As Nagel (1995 p. 183) puts it, the discussion is of "... human motivation in the aggregate: how the decisions ... of millions of people combine to produce large-scale results". To apply: when a causal story admits of exceptions, why should *this* be the case where it *does* hold?

Our reply necessarily addresses the detail of both data and the conclusions drawn: "... we should not avail ourselves of a particular scientific view without taking account of the critical discourse within the relevant branch of science", as David Davies (2013 p. 199b) rightly acknowledges. Then his sound methodological criticisms[20] of the tradition in neuroscience beloved by, for instance, Barbara Montero raise doubts about "... the Parma School and, by extension, to Calvo-Merino and associates' interpretation of their experiments" (Davies, 2013 p. 2000), as well as granting that, in some cases, "... the empirical evidence in no way *resolves* the philosophical issues ... [The] essentially normative question is untouched by our reconception of the empirical facts" (Davies, 2013 p. 198a). Such doubts bear on the credibility of work in neuroscience (at least, as popularly presented), as well as its application (generalized) to dance aesthetics.

But, of course, generalizations from neuroscience are especially fallible: here are just four ways. First, typically the brain is not being observed directly, but rather through some gadget (fMRI, say), its dependability itself only *statistically* reliable. And what is observed just records changes in blood supply, against a complex general background. Yet the reports seem to be presenting direct access to the brain ("... what occurs in dancers' brains when they observe kinaesthetically familiar movements": Montero, 2013 p. 170a). And this is particularly true in those studies (for instance, Calvo-Merino et al. 2005; Calvo-Merino, 2008) 'applying' such techniques to dance. Second, the brain is rarely observed (even 'indirectly') during the key activities themselves; thus, if our interest lies in responses to *watching dances* ... well, such responses will not be authentic if the subject is required to enter some machine — even depending on the observation of *images* of dance (say, on film or video) is not obviously the same as seeing the dance; another doubtful assumption is imported. Third, how confident can one be that the original subjects, those used to build up the initial 'information' base, are typical? The best reply *probably* explains that matter statistically too (say, 'random sample of a certain size').[21] So this is one case where "... statistics provide a highly convenient way for people to deceive one another" (Hurley, 2014 p. 587), whether deliberately or not. Facts like these "... explain why mathematicians choose to use the words of their calculus as they do and to count alternatives as they do", as Wisdom (1953 p. 212) puts it. For they make "probably" explicit. Yet both the second and third of these points conflict with the assumptions typically imported with, say, fMRI, where the 'data', or conclusions drawn from it, are not presented as probabilistic.

Moreover, and fourth, once grant that, in such cases, brain states cannot be aligned exceptionlessly to thoughts/feelings, and there will always be issues about finding data here; as above, when will the exceptions apply? Further, the only (relatively) uncontentious 'data' here — when the person reports truthfully what we or she thinks/feels — are nothing like as atomistic as the brain 'data' appealed to. To recognize the *dance* (or action within the dance) requires complex background considerations: indeed, the point is two-fold, as a comparison with chess brings out: first, one must (say) recognize this piece as *the King*; second, one must see the importance of the King in chess. The second of these, at least, cannot be reduced to events concerning *this person only* — the normativity of chess draws on a nexus of agents and practices, not just one.

There remains an additional issue concerning what follows for philosophical aesthetics of dance; and therefore the need to express exactly what follows from the neuroscience: it will not help to attribute to brains what are properly the properties of *persons* only. Thus, as Davies (2013 p. 201a [both quotes]) grants, "... the normative dimensions to the questions that engage us as philosophers of art", noting — as an example — that "... the Calvo-Merino et al. experiments ... do not address the question that concerns us as epistemologists of dance, namely, whether the discriminations made by the trained dancer are relevant to the proper appreciation of dance".

I would have said "cannot", rather than "do not", as this limitation is built into their methodology, arising whenever one attempts causal explanations of normative matters — since there are causal explanations of bad moves, the causal story cannot uniquely characterize good moves. So our normative process cannot be reduced to such causal explanation: just "[a]s I do not create a tree by looking at it, ...neither do I create a thought by thinking. And still less does the brain secrete thoughts, as the liver does gall" (Frege, 1979 p. 137). Moves here can be in dance as well as in chess; yet, in fact, the dancer's failure to do what he/she intended might be more easily recognized — just the sort of thing that the mirrors were in a dance studio to permit one's checking. Indeed, the very possibility of dancers being corrected by choreographers (or other dancers) recognizes the priority of that 'third-person' perspective on the position of one's own limbs that judiciously placed mirrors allow one to adopt oneself!

Equally, Davies (2013 p. 201a) joins me in requiring that "... a philosophical theory must tell us what it is to apprehend a dance performance *as art*" [my emphasis], agreeing that cognitive neuroscience "... cannot tell us what sort of regard is at issue" (Davies, 2013 p. 201b) when a dance is so regarded. In particular, my general worries concern what exactly can be extracted from fMRI data, when one's interest is in dance, or even dance appreciation (not so different from those voiced by Davies, 2013 p. 200), since that technology does not lend itself to real-world situations; but those are precisely the ones that concern us. For instance, as above, how might such research acknowledge the contrast between genuinely seeing dance and seeing film of the dance?

Further, one's attention must remain on *artworks*, especially once the possibility of 'confusable counterparts' is conceded. For example, can one assert with justice that "... motor perception is a means by which we can appreciate the aesthetic qualities of a dancer's movements" (Montero, 2013 p. 174a)? Certainly, as Reid ([1815] 2002 p. 595) noted, "... the name of beauty belongs to this excellence of the object, and not to the feelings of the spectator". But that is this *object*? If the topic were merely the line, grace, and so on (*aesthetic* properties), and the agent being a dancer is just a coincidence (so these are *not* the properties that following from art-status or from the artform), it is easier to imagine a causal story accommodating it. But recognizing those involved as persons explains the capacity for normativity (lacking in such a case), as with the capacity for language (which also embodies such normativity): any further comments merely elaborate the fact that persons, as agents, have these capacities.

Here, though, we have also stressed both the dependence of philosophical investigations on *conceptual* questions (of the kind that cannot be answered by natural science), and the dependence of our enquiries about the sublunary world on *answerability*: that is, claims about danceworks must be answerable to the features of those works.

Such answerability is, of course, problematic, not least because it is easy to mistake the relevant features of some artwork, such as a dance or a painting: as the 'confusable counterpart' cases expose, two objects readily mistaken for one another might be, say, one artwork and one un-enfranchised 'real thing' (Danto, 1981 p. 138) or two different artworks — or, of course, two Danto-esque 'real things'. Although the differences between such cases may not be wholly perceptual (unlike, say, differences in colour), they will be open to informed perception by sensitive spectators:[22] the same will hold for danceworks.

Feeling a need to offer some kind of general title here, Bob Sharp describes as "a deflationary view of music" a conception that, like ours for dance, stresses the *practice* of the artform: that is, it stresses — in ways we have — the *possibility* of performance. What more can we need? Whenever an actual performance of a dancework is encountered, the possibility inherent in regarding danceworks as *performables* has therefore been actualized. Then we can no longer persist in asking:

> ... 'Where then is the work really?' or 'What sort of existence does it have?' ... [but] simply refer the questioners back to what we have just said about the possibility of performance ... to persist in such a line of questioning shows the presence of a false picture based on misleading analogies with the visual arts. (Sharpe, 2000 p. 99)

My view, like Sharpe's, is 'deflationary' precisely in offering no wholly-general exceptionless explanations, but rather contextual ones.

Chapter Six

Welcome to the studio! — the dancer's role

§1.   Introduction

Dancers are conceptually connected to danceworks, as sketched previously (Chapters One and Five): that, in typical cases at least, performances require performers. Hence dancers are, in some sense, the 'raw material' that dance-makers work with, even if the dance-makers sometimes utilize their own bodies (as it were, temporarily adopting the other role, wearing the dancerly 'hat'). But, as Deborah Jowitt (2004 p. 117) points out, "[i]n none of the other arts does the artist have to create a work from scratch with materials that get injured, have upset stomachs, talk back, or can't learn fast". So, in this chapter, some relations of dancers to dance-making are drawn out, by presenting ideas on these topics from one major choreographer, Twyla Tharp (largely through her own words). Thus it offers one perspective on the task of choreography, from someone who was/is a distinguished dancer as well as a distinguished dance-maker.

Tharp's distinction as a choreographer has long been widely recognized. As Marcia Siegel (1977 p. 48) said, "Tharp uses the classical movement vocabulary with distortions, changes, interpolations". Or, again:

> Tharp is everything the old modern dancers were — individual, tough, far out, charismatic. Instead of allowing her work to merge and fade into some facile eclecticism, she has turned the ballet vocabulary to her own account. Tharp's steps and the virtuosity of her dancers may be balletic, but the compositional mind, the use of space and flow are hers alone.(Siegel, 1977 p. 159)

But her work was not discussed in Sally Banes magisterial *Terpsichore in Sneakers* (1987), being:

> ... excluded from this study even though many of her early interests and methods were closely intertwined with those of the postmodernists [because] Tharp's aspirations have changed, or so her recent work seems to say ... she works seriously in mainstream forms ... (Banes, 1987 p. 19)

For Tharp is hard to categorize. My project focuses on the contribution of dancers to dance-making by commenting on cases *she* mentions (in two books, plus her autobiography). Consonant with these characterizations from both Siegel and Banes, I do not suggest that Tharp is typical: nor even that the descriptions here represent what she *always* does, both because these accounts were given for specific purposes, and because these cases need not be standard. Indeed, no uncontentiously exceptionless description for all dance-making could be forthcoming. In that sense, the point is partly methodological: that we must make what we can from cases or examples. Even here, Tharp's writings offer diversity: two of her texts that provide passages here have ostensibly different targets. But, with all these qualifications, a view of choreography appears; and especially one importing a view of the nature of dancers, and of how they function.

§2.   Dance-making: a worked example (Twyla Tharp)

What is that view? Tharp (2009 p. 26) reports her first company as "... an extraordinary collective of women who were smart, talented, strong, and independent", commenting:

> We began dancing together in 1966 and stayed together the next five years. Without pay. On the rare occasions when we were paid to perform, we split the fee seven ways. (Tharp, 2009 p. 26)

This might sound like a democracy: *everything* split seven ways — but that vision cannot actually be sustained, given some of Tharp's other working practices. For the ethos is not always that suggested above.

Thus, while Tharp (2009 p. 59) claims, "I want [the dancers] to know I'll let them contribute, that they can modify my dream without offending me, because my vision is such a big target that even if they move it to the left or the right I can still see it" (a passage we will return to!), this willingness may be limited, since on one occasion at least she grants that, "I'm willing to be regarded as a tyrant to keep my vision intact" (Tharp (2003 p. 216). And, although one text here aims at building collaboration, that is not quite what one finds (for all that Tharp presents the process as collaborative). Rather, she demonstrates ("shows") and "[t]hen they do"! So, despite the alleged focus on collaboration, the identity of the dance-maker is clear here; and her responsibilities involve ultimately determining the *content* of these dances. And Tharp (2009 p. 57) outlines a similar position when describing her expectations of her assistant, Crista:

> I tell Crista right off: I am demanding; I expect you to be at least as early as I am to rehearsal (hey, if you aren't early, you're late), to know the scores and to calibrate the rehearsal audio, noting music entry points for all the dance phrases, to oversee the studio video, to work late editing the day's tape, to have prepared any phrases that will be introduced to the dancers in the next day's rehearsal. And there's more: ...

There seems little recognizable as collaborative here; and lots recognizably authoritarian.

So, without suggesting either that Twyla Tharp is typical of choreographers, or that these examples are typical of her, I shall piece together some descriptions given of her own process in making and rehearsing danceworks. For both what she does and what she complains about display some of her priorities.

Our topic chiefly turns on how the dance-maker's *responsibility* for the work is realized, which Twyla Tharp elaborates in terms of the need to develop her vision — to give the work *detail* in ways that elaborate and clarify that vision. *All* that detail will not *always* come from Tharp. Yet, if the dancers are a *resource* here, how are the powers and capabilities of those dancers to be drawn upon, so that *responsibility* is maintained? For instance, what degree of *prior planning* does the dance-maker bring to the sessions, such what occurs might be presented as following a recipe she has elaborated? (Even here, some diversity might be possible.) And are there any hints of answers *different* to the ones instantiated in Tharp's practice?

What must be done differs from case to case. Thus, one picture of the dance-maker's profession appears when she discusses a dancework she created "... more than a year ago on many of these same dancers, and ... [has] spent the past few weeks rehearsing ... with the company" (Tharp, 2003 p. 5). Notice here, especially, (i) "created on" — rather than, say, "with" or "for": it is really on their *bodies* that she has created the abstract object that is her dance (see Chapter Five §5); (ii) the place of rehearsal, rightly stressed as fundamental to the possibility of a performing art, since it suggests both training in repeating the work and the importance of the dancers as needing both to learn the dance and to rehearse it. Moreover, as Tharp (2003 p. 5); recognizes, "[t]he length of the piece will dictate how much rehearsal time I need"; no doubt doing so — in other cases — in combination with factors relating to the preparedness of the dancers: these were already taught the dance, and could be trusted to retain it.[1] But, at that time, another dancework was also required, where she faces a blank canvas, not knowing "... what music I'll be using. I don't know which dancers I'll be working with. I have no idea what the costumes will look like, or the lighting, or who will be performing the music" (Tharp, 2003 p. 5).

How much of a plan must the dance-maker have, going in; and of what kind? Tharp (2003 p. 118) grants that, "... there's a fine line between good planning and overplanning". She compares her own practice to that of photographer Richard Avedon, who "... doesn't have a preconceived notion of what he wants a photo to look like ... He plans ahead, but not too far ahead, so that he can recognize *amazing* when he sees it" (Tharp, 2003 p. 119). That is her hope too.

However, Tharp (1992 p. 18) sometimes expresses her point differently: "When I go into a studio, I know exactly what I want ...". Taken at face value, this might seem to contradict the story she tells with approval about Avedon (above). That it does not is plain when she continues, "... but never quite how I'll get it. Each dance is a mystery story" (Tharp, 1992 p. 18). Few artists can honestly *imagine* to the degree of specificity required to know *exactly* what one wants (perhaps Mozart[2]). For most of us, this says no more than that I can imagine *something*; and will (probably) recognize when I am satisfied: if one choses to call this a process of, "realizing what I imagined", that will be a very confusing way to put the point. For what exactly was *imagined*?

Those, like Collingwood (1938 p. 142), who think that "[t]he work of art proper is something not seen or heard, but something imagined" seem confronted with "[t]he familiar objection that an artist may be able to imagine but not to execute what he imagines ..." (Donagan, 1962 p. 117). Then one response, as Donagan (1962 p. 117) continues, is that:

> ... if you can imagine as magnificently as Raphael, only blindness or paralysis can prevent you from painting as he did. Genuine imagination is in terms of the medium employed ... and it is exact to the last detail.

On this (Collingwoodian?) view, then, if someone could *imagine* as well as a great painter, nothing could stop him/her *painting* as well as he did: as though, if someone could *imagine* that exactly, nothing could stop that person realizing that imagined object. But, as Wollheim (1980 p. 42) notes, "... this would involve not merely foreseeing, but also solving, all of the problems that will arise ... in the working of the medium". This counterblast renders the Collingwoodian view implausible, especially applied to dance, just because technical mastery *is* important (in many cases). And one easily thinks of distractions, defeaters, and the like. Moreover, if Collingwood insists that someone lacking the technical mastery is not actually *imagining* as well (or as fully) as the great painter, he is making true by fiat what should have been an empirical claim.

What Tharp has — as she elsewhere describes it (Tharp, 2009 p. 59) — is a *vision*, one expansive enough that she can rightly claim the whole work once it is completed, but with sufficient indeterminacy as to require elaboration and filling in. Certainly, at the beginning, one does not need to know everything. In fact, Tharp (2009 p. 107) concedes that, in one case, "... it was not until I wrote this lecture that I realized the simple fable at the heart of the story I was telling ..."; but that fable was, in fact, central to her *fulfilled intentions* (embodied in the dance) as she came to recognize them, providing its "spine", when "... for me, the spine was an essential preparatory step in the ballet's creation" (Tharp, 2003 p. 142). Another case had the corresponding element in the forefront of her mind. Thus, she claimed that a piece of hers was based on Euripides' *The Bacchae*: the audience could not see this (could the dancers?). Either way, she insisted that "*The Bacchae* had been compelling source material that I latched onto as the spine of the piece when I started choreographing" (Tharp, 2003 p. 142).[3]

In general, though, Tharp presents herself as entering the studio with at least a broadly-conceived plan. Contrasting her practice with that of Jerome Robbins, with whom she was working, Tharp reportedly said that: "I plan what I'm going to do, I do it, I'm ready to go on; he plans what he's going to do, he does it, he's ready to go back" (Jowitt, 2004 p. 473). Clearly, that was not the way she thought one *should* operate. Still, Robbins perhaps represents the other end of some spectrum here, insisting on a design he was not really following. Thus:

> ... Ann Hutchinson [Guest] noted that when asking to see a section he [Robbins] had choreographed the day before and finding it unsatisfactory, he would be far more likely to say, 'What *are* you doing? I never gave you that' than 'Was that what I did yesterday? I don't like it. I want to change it.' (Jowitt, 2004 p. 117: PAD p. 83)

Any changes were not *his* changes of mind!

Further, Tharp gives the impression of having something approaching a method in the background (at least now). She reports that:

> ... in devising *The Fugue* [1971] ... I discovered I had given myself a completely new way of handling movement. Reversal, inversion, retrograde, retrograded inversion, stuffing, canon, and so on. It was a vocabulary sufficiently rich in possibilities and variations that I would be using it and building on it for the rest of my life. (Tharp, 2003 p. 199)

But of course musicians — and especially those with a theoretical bent, such as Webern — use just these sorts of structural devices to give unity to works once some of the sonic unities no longer satisfy. Thinking of one's work this way will make it harder for others to suggest changes unless those changes are within one's framework.

Tharp's approach to dance-making apparently varies along a continuum, with one project permitting "...a midway approach between weeks of improvisation and a work completed before I have even begun rehearsals" (Tharp, 2009 p. 60) — she has obviously done both of the extreme versions, at some time! So both ends of this continuum should be recognized, as well as the intermediate position — although that 'intermediate position' does little more than combine the others. For, discussing 'the choreographer's lot', Tharp (2003 p. 217) reports that it is "... create a dance, teach it to dancers in rehearsal, watch it being performed, and ... teach it to new dancers so it can be performed again and again and again". In this case at least, the *real* difference between the versions is that, in one, she has a dance to *teach* (perhaps one made previously) while, in the other, she does not.

Throughout, she is the dance-maker, looking to almost every thing: "With lights, costumes, and injuries, I have issues enough" (Tharp, 2009 p. 67). So, in this case (for example), she effectively delegates the music. Still, she is in charge throughout. As she says:

> In my world, I see opening nights as a wrap party — that is, the ballet is finally wrapped in its costumes, its lights, its hair and makeup, and its full live orchestration. It's a momentary triumph of theatricality over 'real' life, and it is to be cherished. (Tharp, 2009 pp. 68-69)

Like those musicals that begin a run "off-Broadway" (or the equivalent) to still permit changes to be made, the finality Tharp describes here may be more imaginary than real, or more celebrated in the breaking than the observance. Or that is my experience. Certainly, Tharp (2003 p. 219) willingly acknowledges:

> ... a long tradition in the American musical theatre of trying out Broadway-bound shows in towns like Chicago, Boston, New Haven, and Philadelphia. You do this to smooth out the kinks, to let the performers find their legs, and to fix anything that doesn't work for the audience.

So this too might play a role in her thinking. She also calls the opening night, "... the celebration of a group endeavour" (Tharp 2003, p. 69); but who has contributed what, exactly? To put that in more familiar terms, who is *responsible* for what?

§3.   Place of the dancers?

As we have already seen, Tharp might arrive with the programme (or work) needing anything "... between weeks of improvisation and a work completed before I have even begun rehearsals" (Tharp, 2009 p. 60). So, under the second description, it is at least possible that the dancers contribute nothing *more* (or nothing *else*). And, even when there is more, Tharp (2003 p. 216) is willing, "... to be regarded as a tyrant to keep my vision intact". Contrast that idea with one quoted earlier, where Tharp (2009 p. 59) claimed, "I want [the dancers] to know I'll let them contribute, that they can modify my dream without offending me, because my vision is such a big target that even if they move it to the left or the right I can still see it" — a passage that now indicates how, within her vision, there may still be places for augmentation, rather as with Avedon's vision of his photography, described above.

Certainly, Tharp's characteristic ways of working can involve dancers offering movement ideas, when not everything is *set*. As she describes it:

> Late in the sixties, I acquired a third-hand video system ... in the ensuing four decades, I have documented my career in video diary form, in part

to record my evolution as a dancer and choreographer, in part to have valuable material on hand, much as composers might go to their trunk for a tune they have never used before but have not forgotten. (Tharp, 2009 p. 64)

Note the nature of the possibilities inherent in this arrangement. Of course, the dancers can contribute substantially *in the session* — elsewhere Tharp (2003 p. 213 quoted below) speaks of "... taping a three-hour long improvisation" in such a context — but once the dancers leave the studio, the decisions can only be hers. Moreover, she justifies the fact of her making the choices by stressing the nature of her *responsibility* to the audience members: they have put their *trust* in her. But, equally, she is inspired by "... the trust my dancers show in consigning their bodies to me" (Tharp, 1992 p. 225). (Of course, the dancers have no guarantee that such trust will not be abused; or, better, none but their trust *in her*.)

On one occasion, then, Tharp (209 p. 65) uses the video material to "... create a virtual dance of sorts" — "Using the phrases created in Miami ... I re-edit the dance so it's synced with the new music ...". Again, this solidifies (if only temporarily) one's work; making progress, as it were. Then, later, a more complete version of the score arrives. So:

I proceed to invent new material for the second half of the ballet while Crista [the tireless assistant above!] doubles back to rehearse the dancers with material from the spring and a mile-long list of cuts, loops, and juxtaposed phrases that I'd edited in New York. (Tharp, 2009 p. 65)

So here, too, the technique mentioned carries over material, but edited by our dance-maker. Sometimes that may not be wholly desirable. Thus, Tharp (2009 p. 66) writes:

As for using video, a good solution in one situation turned out to be not so successful in another. Watching a dance video, I miss context: I miss process. I miss the ability to ask the dancer — right now, please — to try it another way. And I resent the pressure to respond immediately — machines do not afford the time for a lot of stewing.

So we can readily imagine that Tharp would prefer a more responsive arrangement, one that imports the movement ideas of the dancers, allows them to try out the dance-maker's ideas, and keep a reliable, technological record — of the same kind as the video system described.

One such difficulty: "every technological compromise is compromise only on the human side; we adjust to the computer, never the other way round. So there are times for me when face-to-face is still required" (Tharp, 2009 p. 66). But why exactly? Certainly, Tharp's willingness to use the technology, to whatever degree she does, points again towards her central conception of the dance-making role.

This might still seem rather abstract. Can some details of working, and especially of dancer and dance-maker working together, not be provided? Tharp (2009 p. 15) highlights one reason for a "no" answer, at least as far as the written word is concerned:

> For dancers, the process of working together doesn't look like what you may think of as a collaboration – nothing's written down, and very little is spoken. If you stepped into my studio while I'm working with dancers, what you'd see is ... dance. I don't tell, I show. Then they do. Something doesn't work? We'll try again, look at it closely, make a modification. Dancers are smart, quick and practical. Like intelligent people everywhere, they learn best by example.

Almost all of this invites commentary, but at its centre is Tharp's regard for the intelligence and responsiveness of dancers — in marked contrast to, say, the view of film actors attributed to Alfred Hitchcock (Truffaut, 1985 p. 140): that they were to be treated like cattle! Nevertheless, Tharp (2003 p. 216) admits, "I've auditioned 900 dancers in order to hire 4 of them ...".

At this point, notice a slogan Tharp, (2003 p. 50) attributes to Yogi Bera: "You can observe a lot by watching". This slogan makes another point for Tharp, discussed below. But it also stresses the general idea of the central importance of what is *seen*, of our perceptiveness with its dependence on (visual) perception. Moreover, Tharp appears here as someone with discrimination, someone who can learn by *looking*.

Such discrimination is central when Tharp (2009 p. 59) says that she wants "... [the dancers] to know I'll let them contribute, that they can modify my dream without offending me, because my vision is such a big target that even if they move it to the left or the right I can still see it" (Tharp, 2009 p. 59). We have already commented on what this passage says about her vision; but what does it say about working with dancers? Well, perhaps "... I tape a three hour improvisation session with a dancer and find only thirty seconds of useful material ..." (Tharp, 2003 p. 213). Since much here is characterized as *improvisation*, we can assume these were chiefly movement ideas supplied initially by the dancer. Most find their way onto "the cutting room floor" — almost literally, given Tharp's use of video-editing. But she readily presents this as part of her task as dance-maker: "You're editing out the lame ideas that won't resonate with the public. It's not pandering. It's exercising your judgement" (Tharp, 2003 p. 213). For, in a way, the public comes to *your* dances precisely because they credit you with such judgement. Thus, one useful strategy for assessing the capabilities of dancers will be to watch the artistic director of the company:

... give a thorough barre, obviously one that his dancers have done hundreds if not thousands of times. But no one is bored — they all understand that these challenges must be readdressed every day. (Tharp, 2009 p. 58)

This both recognizes the dancers' understanding of 'what happens next', and guides to us of the importance of the discipline — not just the literal discipline of the technical prowess, but the discipline 'of mind' (really, of the whole person) that offers concentration and a readiness to work.

As the dancers come to the center, I can see they're strong from the rigor of the discipline. When I look at gorgeous women and elegant men like these, their limbs well prepared for the tasks ahead, I always feel the same emotion: enormous gratitude to the trainers, coaches, and teachers who have lovingly groomed their charges, day after day, year after year. They build my resources. Thanks to these silent and unnamed collaborators, I stand a chance of getting something done." (Tharp, 2009 p. 58)

Moreover, some of the responsibility here rests with the dancers: those with:

... great leg extensions but deficient arms ... will spend more time working on leg extension (because the effort is rewarding — it looks good and feels good) and less time on their arms. Common sense should tell them the process ought to be reversed. That's what the great ones do. (Tharp, 2003 p. 167)

So, central to the readiness of the dancers, as Tharp here recognizes, is their physical conditioning: "... conditioning ... [is] an obvious concern for the dancer, who won't return to the studio after two weeks away with the same physical condition and stamina as when he left it" (Tharp, 2003 p. 166) — although, again, the term "physical" here ideally denotes a process involving the whole person since, as Tharp (2003 p. 167) notes, "[p]ractice without purpose ... is nothing but exercise". What can motivate dancers such that "... we'll keep perfecting our craft" (Tharp, 2003 p. 173), given that the practice of this 'perfecting' often seems unrewarding? Tharp (2003 p. 173) settles on the term "passion", although it is difficult to explain clearly what exactly she means by "passion". But commitment of the kind indicated is apparent throughout Tharp's descriptions of dancers. Indeed, now we see why her first company (as described above) danced "[w]ithout pay!" (Tharp, 2009 p. 26): they were committed to an ideal of dance, to put the point somewhat grandly. And that provided the "passion". For this commitment is, for Tharp (and rightly), fundamental to the right attitude here. As she says, "[w]ithout passion, all the skill in the world won't lift you above craft. Without skill all the passion in the world will leave you eager but floundering" (Tharp, 2003 p. 173).

The term "craft" is used here in Collingwood's sense, not mine (see §6 below), where such craft "... involves a distinction between planning and execution" (Collingwood, 1938 p. 15). For, with *craft*, one could specify what one was going to do independently of the manner of doing it (not so for art: Collingwood, 1938 p. 15). Hence Collingwood's famous contrast between art and craft could be viewed as between intrinsic and extrinsic conceptions of value: craft involves "... the power to produce a preconceived result by means of a consciously controlled and directed effort" (Collingwood, 1938 p. 13). In explanation, for Collingwood (1938 p. 15), craft "... always involves a distinction between means and ends, each clearly understood as something distinct from the other ...": so there is a means to an otherwise-specifiable end — and as such ends here Collingwood cites amusement, propaganda, exhortation, instruction and a kind of practical value Collingwood calls "magic". To work towards such ends is to be producing (at best) *art so-called*. By contrast, a genuine artwork *might* be "... done without being planned in advance" (Collingwood, 1938 p. 22), as it lacks an *independently* specifiable end. Of course, the idea is not that art might never be *planned* in roughly this way, but that it *need* not. For this does not deny the importance, for art, of technique: Collingwood (1938 p. 26) is not endorsing the idea "... that works of art can be produced by anyone, however little trouble he has taken to learn his job, provided his heart is in the right place". On the contrary, as artists know, there is:

> ... a vast amount of intelligent and purposeful labour, the painful and conscientious self-discipline, that has gone to the making of a man who can write a line as Pope writes it, or knock a single chip off a single stone like Michelangelo. (Collingwood, 1938 pp. 26-27)

For Collingwood (1938 pp. 15-16) is explicit in classifying craft-based questions as technical: indeed, his discussion flows from the Greek root of the work "technical", and results in rejection of what Collingwood (1938 p. 17) rightly calls "the technical theory of art". There is a connection here to the acquisition of *know-how*: to training in dance-technique, where such methods are regularly employed. Thus Ryle (1949 p. 42) notes that, "[d]rill (or conditioning) consists in the imposition of repetitions": this might seem the way to describe the regime of bodily conditioning, and building a technique through repetition, that characterizes the life of the dancer-in-training; but that leaves out much. Thus, it is not true "... that competences and skills are *just* habits ... We build up habits by drill, but we build up intelligent capacities by training" (Ryle, 1949 p. 42: my emphasis). For this reason, "[t]raining, ... though it embodies plenty of sheer drill, does not consist [only] of drill" (Ryle, 1949 pp. 42-43).

Here, Ryle (1949 p. 41) urged that "[w]e learn *how* by practice, schooled indeed by criticism and example, but often quite unaided by any lessons in the theory". For the dancer, though, the lack is not so much 'theory' (whatever Ryle meant by that) as *context*. The best comparison might be with someone learning a number of languages, without the corresponding literatures, and then being asked to write poems in French. The training of the dancer of today does not typically support expressive performance in a particular technique; whereas, in the past, members of Graham's company learned the technique in the *context* of segments of the danceworks; and hence in a context where the expressiveness of those movement in that work was also learnable, in principle.[4]

For dance, the point here is subtle: it is more familiar in, say, the case of the pianist whose playing is described as 'merely technical', in contrast to the more expressive playing of another. It is tempting to claim that the 'merely technical' playing differs in some *imperceptible* way from the other: what is right about this is that the difference in the expressive playing may be difficult to describe (especially in words). But, first, it *is* a perceptible difference, since we perceived it in listening to the two performances; and, second, it amounts to more than just how the performer *feels* about work or performance. Similar points apply to dancers, and their performances, with the additional thought that so performing some works expressively (one thinks first of works by Martha Graham) requires *mastery* of the relevant technique. Too often, the requirements for a more generalized bodily mastery conflict with this one: hence Foster (1997 p. 255: quoted PAD p. 266) rightly characterizes the "hired body" of many modern dancers with its "... rubbery flexibility coated with impervious glossiness". Such dancers have taken the road of 'practice without purpose', so that (while they may have passion for dance in general) they cannot embody the passion required for *this* dance.

This commitment to suitable expressiveness is one of the aspects of performance that Tharp keeps under her scrutiny. Much else falls there. Indeed, in claiming, "You can observe a lot by watching", Tharp (2003 p. 50) returns us to the slogan she attributed to Yogi Bera. Now, focusing more specifically, it can be read as stressing the need to know what you are looking at, or what you are looking for. For only then can you really learn a lot by looking. This is an issue for selecting dance ideas and for training dancers but also for the audience. Tharp (2009 p. 5) recounts a story of Jerome Robbins[5] faced with the seemingly inexplicable failure to generate laughs of the play *A Funny Thing Happened on the Way to the Forum*. Robbins quickly realized that the audience did not know what to make of the work: he "... offered simple, commonsense advice: It's a comedy. Tell them that". So "... Sondheim quickly wrote an opening number called 'Comedy Tonight' ... — and once ticket buyers knew what they were supposed to do, they laughed". Robbins's story relates directly to *traditions of performance* within an artform (or some subset of it): when these are familiar, the audience knows what to expect.

To accommodate innovation, one must learn to make sense of the unfamiliar, both in practice and in theory: but knowing (or thinking you know) what to expect in a dancework (say, knowing its category or genre) gives both dancers and audience a familiar *how to go on* in making sense of the work; and when that is missing, gestures to the familiar may help (allusions, or 'quotations' for example). With artforms incorporating language — which *is* familiar — this is easier (at least if the language is familiar). As with Robbins's story above, a song could tell the audience what they were about to watch. This effect is harder to achieve for (word-free) dance than with words — you can't tell the audience as easily with a dance! (The use of titles may sometimes help, if they are constructed with this purpose.)

§4.   Demonstrating, rehearsing and preparing

As mention before, Tharp (2003 p. 217) saw the choreographer's lot as "... create a dance, teach it to dancers in rehearsal, watch it being performed, and ... teach it to new dancers so it can be performed again and again and again". Three features are emphasized here: first, the centrality of rehearsal to the performing arts — for what does one *make*, in making a performable? Seen one way, it amounts to a set of instructions that, if followed by dancers, will therefore instantiate that dancework: one way to actualize the instructions would be in a score. But, of course, if the work can still be danced, that amounts to a kind of preservation for it. And so it can be held in the memory of dancers who have been properly taught the work. Second, there is the place of rehearsal in the discipline itself: for what can be performed can also be *rehearsed*; and one rehearsal might serve a whole week's performances. (Thus, asked, 'For which performance is this the rehearsal?', one might have no good answer — it is for all and none!) Third, above, one needs *dancers*, not just bodies. Yet what makes a dancer? In part, one's answer might refer to technical mastery, such that Sylvie Guillem could be described as having "... an extension that challenged the Tour Eiffel" (Tharp, 1992 p. 320) or explaining that Baryshnikov's "... speed, maneuverability, and power were unmatched, the height of his jump breathtaking" (Tharp, 2009 p. 41). But clearly this is not enough: what are the dancer's *responsibilities*? To count as a dancer, at least four obligations might be identified:

- bodily conditioning;

- technical mastery;

- knowing the dance?;

- bringing the passion (as above).

The first and second of these are offered primarily through class, while the last lies chiefly in the ability to make sense of the dance, and then to dance it in that spirit: so what can be said about learning the dance? Of course, some of the movement ideas may be familiar to a particular dancer: perhaps he or she supplied the "... three hour improvisation session ..." from which could be extracted "... only thirty seconds of useful material ..." (Tharp, 2003 p. 213: both quotations). Although beginning from *improvisation*, the fate of the movement ideas has a predictable trajectory for, as we saw, Tharp (2003 p. 213) readily takes "... editing out the lame ideas that won't resonate with the public" as part of her task as dance-maker.

But what of those passages of improvisation that meet the challenge of Tharp's judgement or vision. As we noted, her comment on working with dancers was: "... I don't tell, I show. Then they do" (Tharp, 2009 p. 15). Here both her autocratic attitude and her emphasis on demonstrating movements to the dancers are clear. With this second thought in mind, Tharp (2009 p. 99) recognizes the need of many a dance-maker to "... demonstrate what he wants when he teaches. And that's one reason why I train so religiously". Similarly, she commiserates with those who cannot:

> Jerome Robbins told me that when he became too old to dance, he lost much of his ability to create dances. I'm not sure about that — Jerry, on a chair, was still a great choreographer — but I do think it bothered him greatly not to be able to show dancers what he wanted. (Tharp, 2009 p. 99)

For me, "show" is crucial here, because the need was for these people to *see* what he wanted; and he could not readily explain it. And it makes no sense — in the absence of their seeing the movement — either that the dancers were, somehow, kinaesthetically prepared or that this preparedness was lacking, since Robbins would certainly have told them (in no uncertain terms) if they were not performing the movements as he wanted! Indeed, this *was* what permitted his being "on a chair" but "still a great choreographer". For the judgement as to the rightness of the movement rested with the person looking at it (even if in a mirror) rather than the person somehow *feeling* its rightness. Certainly the Yogi Bera slogan above supports the thought that 'one look is not enough': as choreographer, you may change your mind (as perhaps Jerry Robbins did: quoted above) or you may not notice at one time what later strikes you as crucial. Further ideas might also suggest themselves. But his was the appropriate perspective (in informed visual perception) for the normative conclusion.

So, how to prepare? There is not one model here. For one project, they can "... afford a midway approach between weeks of improvisation and a work completed before I have even begun rehearsals" (Tharp, 2009 p. 60) — she has obviously done both of the extreme versions, at some time! However, since rehearsal is clearly important, it will be crucial to allow *sufficient* time for rehearsal: but this can be problematic. Often the time to the first performance will be set independent of such a consideration. It is all very well to say, as above, "[t]he length of the piece will dictate how much rehearsal time I need" (Tharp, 2003 p. 5). Perhaps such time is not available: indeed, as I understand it (see Rosen, 1976 p. 65), Schoenberg's Society for the Private Performance of Music was formed to give him the control he need over the timing of performances,[6] as a way to ensure adequate time for rehearsal! In the dance case, as in the musical one, the amount of time needed for rehearsal is related to the state of preparedness of performers (here, dancers). But it may also bear on their commitment, and other personal factors.

§5. Some dancers are more equal than others — star dancers!

When first commissioned to choreograph what became *Little Deuce Coupe* (1973) for New York City Ballet (NYCB), Tharp felt she had an unmissable opportunity to work with these star dancers, but was unsure quite how to harness the available resources. And, in addition, she had made a questionable choice as to the music. Thus:

> I wanted to get every dancer I'd admired at NYCB into my ballet. I pushed some very accomplished soloists to dance in ensembles, which they considered demeaning. They all wanted to be featured, but I had a large cast and not everyone could get a satisfying star turn. Too many dancers, not enough notes. I would have been better off choreographing a duet. (Tharp, 2003 p. 129)

A part of the problem was that many of the traditional ballet dancers found it hard to make sense of the project: as a result, it did not go well. For instance, Tharp's sense of the obligations of the dancer was clearly offended by one typical group, who she called "... slackers — snobs who took long breaks, marked most rehearsals, and never fully worked out" (Tharp (1992 p. 178).

Here too, "... not enough notes" refers to difficulties with the music. But Tharp, (1992 p. 136) had adopted an imaginary version of Ballachine as a kind of guide: "... I parked him in the corner of my studio, [as] ... my invisible mentor". Now he came into his own, such that Tharp (2003 p. 130) imagines Ballanchine "... up in heaven", giving her the following advice:

> "You're using Beethoven. I never used Beethoven. I was too smart to use Beethoven. He's too good and very tough to dance too. And why are you only using a piano? How many times have I told you, 'Use the damn orchestra'? The audience has paid for it. They want to hear it. And it will make everything else bigger."

Certainly, Tharp was aware of the idea that "... the music should not upstage the dance" (Banes, 1994 p. 311). Yet, of course, this is much more difficult to guarantee for the dance-maker of today, who will often rely on recorded music. For, as Sally Banes (1994 p. 311) reminds us, Tchaikovsky was surprised, when "... working on the 1877 version of *Swan Lake*, to see Julius Reisinger reverse the usual work process by choreographing to the music — rather than ordering the music by the measure to fit the dances". Here, "ordering" might mean literally asking for so many measures of music, either to be composed or to be played by the on-site orchestra. At the least, it was *not* importing established music. Such 'importing' is surely now the norm, a situation exploited by some dance-makers, who take structure (as well as inspiration) from the music. Tharp would be one such choreographer; Mark Morris another.

Famously, of course, Twyla Tharp would later manage to deal with a greater star dancer. As Judith Mackrell (1997 pp. 183-184) put it:

> When Twyla Tharp choreographed the ballet *Push Comes to Shove* (1976) for Baryshnikov it was a love letter from a modern-dance choreographer to a great classical dancer.

Tharp, (2009 p. 40) offers her own picture of this star dancer:

> Opening night of *Push Comes to Shove*. Baryshnikov entered, a dazzling rake with a hat. He danced. He circled. He ran his fingers through his hair. Then he was aloft. Talk about a high — this was a record breaker. He'd honoured his compact with the audience; they got what they came for. And he went on to give them so much more than what they had expected in the form of many surprises. ... He'd forced audiences to expand their idea of him. In a word, he'd freed himself.

It is clear, then, that she was able to make the most of his startling virtuosity; and that, unlike the NYCB dancers, he never needed to be persuaded of the judgement of his choreographer. Thus:

> ... Tharp tells how she raided Baryshnikov's technique for its virtuoso jumps and turns and then forced him to dance them in a new way, so that the moves 'twisted or lay far back from his supporting leg' .... (Mackrell, 1997 p. 184)

In her *Autobiography*, Tharp (1992 p. 220) recalls that "[h]is solutions were breathtaking. He was learning to manoeuvre round an even tighter base and the precision and audacity of his leaps and *pirouettes* astonished me". Perhaps only this great a dancer, though, could describe the intensive rehearsal process thus demanded as "... a cross between the perfect vacation and being in church" (quoted Mackrell, 1997 p. 184).

On the other hand, the dancer's recognized strengths are something that might, with justice, be brought to a role — with the star dancer, one might expect these strengths to be present to a marked degree. And therefore to be available to the dance-maker. As Tharp (2009 p. 41 explains:

> Baryshnikov was, of course, among other things, a sublimely coordinated athlete. His speed, maneuverability, and power were unmatched, the height of his jump breathtaking. So when we held this jump back in order to show another dimension of his talent, many felt we were mean-spirited.

It was as though the audience took a view of what they should see, and were disappointed when it was not offered: but, of course, this was precisely a *strategy* of Tharp's, to be applauded in realizing her fulfilled intentions.

Sometimes, inevitably, the star dancer's contribution is not wholly positive, partly because he/she simply provides 'the familiar', or what is expected. Thus, of Rudolf Nureyev dancing with the Graham Company, Arlene Croce (1978 p. 162) accurately records "... [i]t wasn't good Graham dancing, but it was good Nureyev"; for, here, one can imagine the clash between the 'vision' of the work and the virtuosity of this performer.

Moreover, the star dancer's position may be less clear than in these two cases. Hence Mackrell (1997 p. 182) compares Baryshnikov rehearsing to perform a role in Mark Morris's *Wonderland* (1989) with Morris's own dancing of it. Having described Baryshnikov as "... one of the most powerful dance intelligences of our time – a star by virtue of his instinctive grasp of whatever style he's dancing and his ability to show it beautifully plain", Mackrell (1997 p. 182) comments on Baryshnikov performing a movement that required him to tilt his head back "... as if about to have his throat slit. When Baryshnikov performed the move it seemed right – a tense nervous baring of the neck". But she recognizes that here, "... there were qualities even he [Baryshnikov] didn't naturally reproduce ... [so that] when Morris did it, it had become something more, a sensuous stretch that seemed an invitation to violence, bringing an unsettling note of depravity and complicity to the moment" (Mackrell, 1997 p. 182).

So what is the upshot of the star dancer? As Tharp describes it, based on working with Baryshnikov, the benefits are two- or three-fold: the wonderful bodily conditioning, the commitment to dance and to *this* dance (the passion), and the virtuosity that can be 'played with' (against the audience's expectations). Again, if this is what the star dancer *can* bring, we see some of what is generally to be expected of dancers.

§6.   Dancers and craft-knowledge (and reflective practice)

Much of that discussion focused on the various strategies of the dance-maker, together with their justifications. But weight must also be given to both the contribution of dancers to dance-making, and their contribution to/through performance. The second offers a useful starting place, since we have already acknowledged (Chapter Five §§3-4) that typical dancers do more than simply respond as marionettes to the choreographer's string-pulling. But how should this "more" be understood?

Here, a central question might be: to what extent should every performance be thought of as involving (a kind of) improvisation? Surely the right answer, for most dances and most performances, is: *not at all* (contrast Levinson, 2015 p. 103). For surely there is a place for simply fulfilling one's role as a dancer, which involves (say) filling-in, in appropriate ways, any 'gaps' in the score: that is, places where the score leaves it unclear or unspecified what the dancer should do. In such a case there would be no inclination to designate what occurs as "McFee's interpretation of the role" (or of any segment of it). Of course, *all* dancers *always* contribute, in the sense of their turning the choreography into a performance. But, in doing that, they are simply doing their job.

Some progress is made by contrasting 'doing one's job' in this sense with, say, the car-mechanic (of some time ago) following the manual for that make-and-model. No doubt the mechanic manifests skill: in terminology from Ryle (1949 p. 28) above, he has *know-how* — he knows how to perform such-and-such tasks. But there is a lower degree of regularity in the fine (yet crucial) details of the initial situation facing the dancer. This is the sense in which the dancer resembles other professionals. Like the architect or pianist described by Schön (1987), the doctor and the lawyer face situations that, although regularly occurring, each differ slightly but significantly from ones previously encountered, or ones from the training manual. To become *proficient* in these contexts, to become a professional, more than mere *know-how* is required: one must be able to judge reliably in these (slightly) new circumstances, where "reliably" does not mean "*always* correctly"; but, rather, "arguably", so that later one's choices might be explained and perhaps justified. Similarly, the context for each dancer performing a particular role is slightly different, to reflect the different local context (of other dancers, costumes, stages, and such like). The dancer is responsible for dancing that role (as previously set, perhaps) in this new-ish context: that grants to the dancer a set of 'decisions' approximately equivalent to those of the lawyer who, although involved in the purchase of another house, recognizes and responds to how this situation differs from all the other house purchases. Moreover, this is a practical skill: the lawyer should *act* reflectively (not just reflect), a capacity Donald Schön characterized as *reflective practice*, his version of *craft-knowledge*. Here, the term "reflective" operates attributively, so that the expression could not be *split* (as a *beautiful dancer* is one who dances beautifully, not just one beautiful and a dancer: PAD p. 203). The 'difficulty' lies both in saying more to characterize *reflective practice* and in elaborating, in the abstract, how one acquires mastery of reflective practice of this kind. But in practical terms, this second is fairly straightforward: we know, in practice, how to develop such *reflective practitioners*! Looking for an abstract description, one could turn to Schön's own book, *Educating the Reflective Practitioner* (1987), for descriptions of people acquiring the requisite craft-knowledge — especially its presentation of the pianist-in-training, Franz (Schön, 1987 pp. 182-201). Equally, this sort of thing is achieved effortlessly (?) in *good* dance training: above, Tharp describes some of its outcomes.

What does such training involve? If it could be specified exceptionlessly, that would reduce it to the training of our auto-mechanic, where (in almost all cases) the manual circumscribes the actual situations one will confront. In that sense, we require from our auto-mechanic the *know-how* to actualize what the manual prescribes. But this is the very reason we defer to the judgement of professionals such as doctors and lawyers: we recognize their relevant knowledge (which is also true of the auto-mechanic) but, additionally, their capacity to actualize it in this distinctive situation. So we must trust their judgements. Further, what they must do is *act*, not prevaricate. For the dancer, of course, that trust is implicit from the audience perspective. Yet it is precisely the kind of thing in which a choreographer like Tharp might want to be confident. That makes sense of her vetting of the dancers – she needs to be confident in their 'judgements' in this respect (turning her choreography into performance), so ideally she gives time to both teaching the choreography — or developing it, for a new work — and to rehearsing that work, so that the dancers will be *reflective practitioners* in respect of it. Thus, having noted that she " ... spent the past few weeks rehearsing ... [a work] with the company", Tharp (2003 p. 5 [both quotations]) recognizes that "[t]he length of the piece will dictate how much rehearsal time I need".

In the same way, we saw (§5 above) that *her* judgement, rather than their's, determines what to include in the choreography: for this is her *responsibility*. She must ensure that changes cohere appropriately with the rest of the dance (and with her vision). So, while it may be important to consider what dancers offer, that dance-makerly vision is typically of a more synoptic kind: in at least some cases (as we saw: §3 above), Tharp may not have each movement laid out; and so be open to ideas. But these ideas must by the end be incorporated into, or be circumscribed by, her vision because, as she noted above, "... my vision is such a big target that even if they move it to the left or the right I can still see it" (Tharp, 2009 p. 59).

For, to repeat, no question really remains (in practice) about how one learns this mastery — as Schön's discussion of the pianist shows, both the training itself and the schedule of practice resemble those of the typical dance school. Yet, if asked how to *conceptualize* such learning, here too there is really no residual question: we know what its outcome will be, in the professional whose 'in work' judgement about what to do next is generally to be trusted.[7] And we know how to train such a professional (by one of many routes); but, amongst these, there will be bodily conditioning, the training in technique, and the practice and rehearsal that individuate (for example) the concert pianist, or the dancer. Further, we can see that nothing conceptual can usefully be added to applying such a picture to dance training or the understanding of dances. So that a key question ('How does one do this?') disappears: all we can say by way of useful answer is that *one learns to do this*. Moreover, there are lots of models (with this certainly one) of how teaching and training contribute to the mastery of whatever it is: so, here, to practical judgement in dance as well as to performance. We see too the centrality of practice, both as a tool for bodily conditioning and as an opportunity to build *reflective practice* as action where (separable) thought is typically not required.

§7.   Dancing a role

One useful suggestion is that, in a typical dance work, a dancer is *portraying a role*: such a role, understood as "... impersonating the protagonist" of the song is perhaps unusual for a jazz singer (see Levinson, 2015 p. 113); yet more or less normal for a dancer — except that it is not impersonation, but rather *acting* (the dancer portrays that role). [The exception might be some star dancers (for example, Nureyev) who are offering a bigger-than-role persona; but these *are* the exceptions (see §5 above).] And here one of my favourite cases (PAD p. 111) is the performance of Mikhail Baryshnikov as Yuri Kopeikine in the movie *The Turning Point* (1977). A key question here is: 'Can Yuri be a better dancer than Mikhail?' There is clearly one sense in which the answer must be "no": any jump, say, that 'Yuri' can do must be within the performance-range of Mikhail — but there is room for various kinds of cinematic variety. At the least, Yuri might perform a whole sequence, filmed in segments, when the *whole thing* is (say) beyond Mikhail's stamina to perform continuously. But of course, this is far from being a usual case.

Again, it worth comparing the dancer with that jazz singer who, Levinson (2015 p. 103) urges, could present the song itself "... without interpreting it": that is, present the song but "... convey nothing about [the] song or one's view of [the] song". Although he regards this as unlikely, and offers comments to suggest that doing so amounts to conveying "... overwhelming admiration or respect for the original composition", Levinson (2015 p. 103) regards it as at least logically possible to present the song without interpretation. For the dance case, too, there is, as it were, a minimal 'performer's interpretation' that just consists in dancing the role, but with no particular contribution of one's own.

This will doubtless strike many dancers as impossible: surely, they will say, there is always something of oneself in any performer's interpretation, however minimal. Three factors weigh heavily with me in denying such a claim, all seeking to avoid a proliferation of 'interpretations'. First, as a matter of logic, one would prefer the possibility of an un-interpreted performance, with which to contrast the interesting ones. Second, the role might be danced by another dancer in the same company on another night, and fit seamlessly into the overall work: it seems simpler to regard both as instantiating either just *the dance*, or the view of it of the company or stager (where this is viewed as a minimal interpretation), than to proliferate 'interpretations' — given that *sometimes* the distinctive interpretation of a role, especially by a star dancer, *is* recognized. The third feature points in another direction, one relevant here. For at least sometimes the role itself draws on capacities of the dancers who dance it — or, at least, those who do so successfully. Thus, recall that when working on his ballet *Black Angels* (1976), Christopher Bruce set material for one dancer (Lucy Burge) that reflected her "... richer, more sensual way of moving", calling her "the dancer of the earth", and contrasting her in this respect with another dancer (Catherine Becque), "the dancer of the air" (Austin, 1976 p. 115). Moreover, if either dancer offered movement ideas to Bruce during the choreographic process, these ideas should be expected to reflect those movement characteristics. So that dancers may have contributed to the role in just such a way as to permit the subsequent performance to count as only minimally an interpretation because much that is characteristic of *this* dancer (the dancer needed for this successful instantiation of *this* role) is *already* in the role, perhaps reflecting that dancer's contribution to choreography, as incorporated by the choreographer.

How widespread a feature might this be? Certainly, to the extent that a choreographer works with dancers in building a work, drawing movement ideas from their improvisations, and subsequently uses those same dancers to perform the work, it may be extensive. Further, if changes to the company require another dancer for that role, selecting another with 'the same' movement characteristics will amount to reinforcing that (minimal) interpretation as *the role*. Moreover, we are familiar, from extreme cases, with the difficulty of casting thereby generated: when Martha Graham could no longer perform the lead roles in the ballets she had choreographed, the company looked for sometime for dancers who could perform these roles convincingly — ones who could, in a literal sense, fill Martha's shoes. Thus Marcia Siegel (1977 p. 214) reports that seeing Linda Hodes dancing a role taken over from Graham as "... a shock, as all Graham roles are when first done by other people", although she does applaud "...Yuriko Kimura's performance" (Siegel, 1977 p. 216) in another of them. For, having been made on a particular body, with its peculiarities (here, the choreographer's own), the expressiveness of dance requires something similar, if it is to be convincing.

At the least, this thought offers a model for what dancers do in performing: for not just anything would make sense as a continuous unity with the segments of the dance already choreographed. But how can the dancer know what it would be appropriate to offer; for example, if asked for movement ideas? As a slogan for success here, one might urge that the 'next move must make sense', where this idea of 'making sense' is familiar from at least two contexts. First, when one asks in what ways creativity goes beyond mere originality, the answer is (roughly) that mere difference to the past is not enough: rather, to count as *creative*, the actions must be original *and right*. Thus, it will not do *just* to produce an original response: perhaps there is a good reason why teddy bears typically lack sharp claws, such that adding such claws would not be a positive innovation (would not count as creative merely in being novel, original, or distinctive). To be creative is, somehow, to be 'original *plus...*': that is, it must be different *and right*. But how is such rightness to be understood? Clearly, any answer will be contextual: it is right *in this context*, not (necessarily) more globally.

Second, Walton (2015 pp. 238-244) has written of one's interpretation 'making sense' in just this way; and has aligned it specifically both with improvisation and with the activities of performers in realizing (or instantiating) works — although, of course, his primary interest is music. The root idea is of a performance as both presenting a pattern, the pattern set primarily by the fixed features of the work itself, and as portraying that pattern, "... in a certain light. It interprets, parses, organizes the pattern in some way or other, as well as individuating what it is" (Walton, 2015 p. 238). So we have, as it were, a pattern in raw material: for dance, this might be secured by notationality, as long as what resulted was a dancework (an artwork), as opposed to a mere structure of movement. Thus Walton (2015 p. 244) writes of "... the pattern indicated by its score". But then there can be, and often is, a role for dancers in providing that raw material, as well as their role in instantiating the work: that is, in portraying that pattern in performance.

Moreover, "[e]xactly what patterns are to be heard [or seen, for dance] in a given piece is a subtle and delicate question demanding the utmost in ... sensitivity" (Walton, 2015 p. 242: he writes "music sensitivity", but the same point applies for dance). For that amounts to asking how it should be appropriately made sense of. Nor can some recipe be expected: there may be useful suggestions, of the kind a class in choreography might consider;

appealing to canon, or to the retrograde, or some such. But nothing applies exceptionlessly: we only *know* for sure what works, what 'makes sense', when we see it working!

§8.   Conclusion

What has this case-study of Twyla Tharp really shown us? What does it suggest about the *responsibilities* of dancer and dance-maker? What does it tell us about 'craft-knowledge' for dancers? Overall, what have we learned? This case illustrates from a practical example how concern with the dancers' responsibility might be combined with recognition of the priorities deriving from the dance-maker's overall responsibility.

Of course, we must first reiterate our disclaimers from the beginning of the chapter: we are *not* assuming that Twyla Tharp is, somehow, a paradigmatic or exemplary choreographer in terms of her working with dancers *nor* that the examples discussed here reflect her invariable ways of working — indeed, we have highlighted enough diversity both within her claims and between her claims and her practices to undermine any sense of there being just one way in which she works.

Nevertheless, her practices as portrayed here have brought to light some features plausibly taken as broadly characteristic of a choreographer's working with the dancers, as well as offering some explanation or justifications of those practices by tracking them back to the nature of dances as performables. First, the sense in which it is the choreographer's *judgement* that guides the development of the work (and that the audience puts trust in) relates directly to Twyla Tharp's decision-making: even when she does not set *all* of the movements for a segment of a dance prior to working with the dancers, the decisions as to what goes in, and where, remains hers. In this way, the dance-maker's *responsibility* for the dance is re-affirmed. Further we saw that one's capacity for right-judgement here is what permits one to adopt the role of dance-maker — the others trust one's judgement. Of course, manifesting or demonstrating that judgement typically involves making dances!

Then, for some dances (those already made), the dancers must be *taught* the dance — and afterwards rehearsed in it. Both aspects of the practice are important if we are to make sense of the *obligations*, the *responsibilities*, of the dancers. Moreover, it must be acknowledged that, in what is taught, there is room for *difference* (as among different performances of what is, after all, broadly a *norm-kind*: Woltersdorff, 1980 pp. 54-58), with much of the difference reflecting either the different context provided by the staging (or even the brute space) or the different technical capacities of *this* group of dancers, as opposed to *that* group. This last point turns partly on the technique-training of the dancers, and partly their bodily condition. And Tharp would have liked close control of both of these, ideally by having a touring company performing established works ("...performing and generating income":Tharp, 1992 p. 169), and a 'home-based' (or, in her case, farm-based) company learning the old works as well as contributing to the choreography of the new ones; not least because "... developing dance means developing dancers — the two are inseparable ..." (Tharp, 1992 p. 85).

So, although selecting Twyla Tharp as our example has inevitably inflected the discussion towards the dance-maker's perspective, the variety of *roles* and *responsibilities* that can reasonably be assigned (in the abstract) to the dancers has also been brought to the fore. For my point, throughout, has been to characterize — via this worked example — some of the contributions to dance-making that might be offered by dancers (although without impugning the dance-makers responsibilities); and some of the importance that comes from recognizing the performance-skills of dancers — that they are not all equivalent, however much the alternative view is suggested by the tendency among today's dancers to cultivate the "hired body" with its "... rubbery flexibility coated with impervious glossiness" described by Foster (1997 p. 255: quoted PAD p. 266). Hence Twyla Tharp acknowledges at least three of the specific aspects of training required for dancers adequate to perform (in this case) *her* dances: their bodily conditioning, their having learned the dances, and their rehearsing them — although, in a typical case, all three might come together in the class for a company primarily instantiating those works, since this permits training in technical aspects also. Still, all three elements are crucial to the responsibilities of dancers: they must be willing and able to undertake this process or set of processes.

Moreover, the stress on the importance of *class* must not go unnoticed. It is true that Tharp (1992 p. 169) used classes as an additional (to performing) way to attract revenue ("The fees we received were for performances or classes ..."). For this was not just bodily preparation but often used movements from elements of the repertoire (following a model perfected by Martha Graham; and see the descriptions of Cunningham: Tharp, 1992 p. 52); and hence amounted to training in aspects of the relevant technique.

Tharp rightly stresses the role of rehearsal: that dances must be *learned*, even by skilled dancers (and even by skilled dancers with the appropriate technical mastery). The role of rehearsal is easy to underrate. Indeed, many dancers tend to forget, when reporting the transition from their trained body to the dance-role, that a great deal of rehearsal was involved, much of which was repetitive performing of the movements once they have been set — even if one's full intensity was not always required, nor delivered (compare the comments above on some of Joffrey's dancers from NYCB: "The worst of these dancers were slackers — snobs who took long breaks, marked most rehearsals, and never fully worked out": Tharp, 1992 p. 178).

Twyla Tharp's teaching of dances is certainly presented as taking place primarily through demonstration (recall "...I show. Then they do": Tharp, 2009 p. 15); but that demonstration is supported by correction — hence she grants that the choreographer who can no longer demonstrate (she cites Robbins: Tharp, 2009 p. 99) can still be "... a great choreographer". At the least, the dancers must accept that the final judgement on the movement performed is not theirs.

Although Tharp does not seem to use an 'authorized' notation (such as Labanotation) in presenting what she did last time, nor in planning where to go next, her efforts are typically presented using video. Since she edits the video (doubtless with the help of an assistant), she can get from it some of the benefits of notating a *recipe*: namely, she can bring out the relative importance of what was done. (It is no longer just a record of everything; but a selection for a *purpose*.) Moreover, since editing past video is presented as one way to plan for the future, it reflects (again) some of the advantages of working with a recipe (rather than a record): after all, this is far from being a *pure* record.

Twyla Tharp's control here is such that, as we saw, she is not averse to plotting some of the choreography whose content might be the improvisations of dancers. The key points are visible here too: first, that Tharp as dance-maker decides which segments of the improvisation – that is, the dancerly contribution of movement ideas – have a place in the ballet; doing so partly on the basis of her 'vision', or her sense of what is right for the ballet as she sees it. In this sense, the dancers' contributions are vetted or filtered. Second, there is nonetheless a role for those dancerly contributions. However, that role is not as artist, since not as the final *decider* here: any putative 'decisions' must be ratified! Precisely because Tharp has typically owned a broad vision of the prospective work, the details involved in its implementation have yet to be determined; and this is where ideas extracted from the dancers (say, during their improvisation) can be selected as appropriate to that vision.

One reason further to elaborate this example was to shed light on the work in the studio (typically, if not wholly) from which the dance appears. So what exactly is the studio-time for? This is a question besetting those who were excluded from it but condemned to wait outside — always in the cold and rain (or so it seemed). Basically then, in summary, we have seen the studio-time provide three opportunities for dancer and choreographer, as Tharp has elaborated above:

• first is *class* (thought of partly as a kind of bodily *training* [with dancers understanding "... that these challenges must be readdressed each day": Tharp, 2009 p. 59; §3 above] and partly as an opportunity to acquire the *manner* of performance characteristic of that technique and of the company's version of that technique);

- second, the *rehearsal* of the dances from the repertoire, where (of course) the possibility of such rehearsal is built into the idea of a *performable*, a work to be performed (in principle) on more than one occasion — and the primary significance of the rehearsal is to habituate, onto the dancers, the movement sequences that (partly) comprise the dance;

- third is to *make the dances*; As we have seen, while much of this activity takes place in the studio — permitting the choreographer to draw on the ideas of the dancers (one aspect of this is what Tharp (2003 p. 213) calls "improvisation") some of it may take place without the dancers: for Tharp (2009 p. 54: §3 above), this involved the use of video; but we can equally imagine, for instance, a choreographer developing a notated score. For the point is just to aid the choreographer in thinking-through the dance, given the building-blocks currently in her control. And, of course, we have recognized that different degrees of planning may all be successful.

Moreover, it stresses two other features arguably crucial in performing arts: the conceptual importance of the place (or possibility) of rehearsal in the performing arts; and our understanding that the dancer's realization of the actions comprising the dance amounts to responding appropriately to the instruction, "Now do it!", where the dancer has learned to do so; and where there may be no *way* that this is accomplished, beyond simply doing that action in the context, rooted in one's knowledge, training and understanding (see Chapter Five §§4-5).

My worry, of course, is that these descriptions of what can go on in a studio still do not reflect what some writers with a dance background have wanted to stress as the role a dancer might play in the choreography. At the least, though, the cases here demonstrate that it cannot be a role essential to being the kind of dancer who is involved in the making of top-flight dances, such as those of Twyla Tharp. And, while the detail will surely be different, the manner in which the roles and responsibilities attributed to dancers here build on the logic of the making of performables suggests for the framework offered a longevity rooted in its identifying and justifying the fulfillment of key tasks.

Chapter Seven

Persistence of dances

§1.   Introduction: numerical identity again

Reprising a contrast fundamental here (from Chapter Two §1), Stuart Hampshire (1959 pp. 36-37) urges:

> It seems ... that there must be one fundamental use of 'one and the same' which requires a persisting thing of some kind as a constant object of reference, a thing that has a constant history since it came into existence and that may have changed in the course of its history. For this use of 'the same', we require some criterion of identity which may vary with every kind of thing singled out. Certainly the distinction between the use of same that requires a criterion of identity through change, and the use of 'same' in 'same colour', cannot be made altogether sharp and precise ...

The standard philosophical tool here distinguishes *numerical identity* ('very same one') from *qualitative identity* ('same sort', 'same kind' — indistinguishable, or something similar, and exemplified for Hampshire by 'same colour'). In the first case, with numerical identity, only one object is under discussion in a favoured example; in the second case, the features or properties of one object are being compared with the features or properties of another.

So how should one describe performances of *Swan Lake* on two successive nights? I have always held (although perhaps not as explicitly as it should be in either UD or PAD) that these performances were of the *very same work of art*, the very same dance (at least in favoured circumstances) even though such performances were typically distinguishable: that is, different members of the company may be involved; at the least, dancers more or less tired or motivated on the different days. Thus, more generally, *differences* here should be expected among what, for me, are uncontentiously performances of the same artwork, the same dance. My reasoning here (explicit in PAD) turns on the need to recognize typical danceworks as performables: hence, as capable in principle of being performed on more than one occasion — thus with different casts, or in different spaces. This is surely implicit in the very idea of a *performing* art: that it permits of *re-performance*! Then these performances will instantiate the very same artwork. That means, of course, that correctly recognizing performances as of the same dancework can accommodate this degree of difference. This view of 'the very same artwork' does not align seamlessly with either of our standard philosophical accounts of identity.

Hence this case represents either a different version of identity or a realization of the possibility of diversity within (simultaneous) numerical identity. Obviously, danceworks are not *substances* in the sense in that persons are. Three features should be noticed: *first*, and unlike standard cases of numerical identity for *substances*, we can imagine having two 'objects', two performances before us at the same time (say, if the stages were adjacent) — or, at least, the possibility of John viewing one performance while Jane simultaneously views the other.[1] But, ordinarily, the possibility of two contemporaneous objects guarantees that it is, after all, (just) *qualitative* identity. For, in our imagined case, the two performances will differ qualitatively — different things will be true of each, to the point that one could be *valued* over the other (although the degree of difference tolerated with reflect the artform, and perhaps even this artwork). Indeed, we regularly do precisely this. That is, we rightly value *this* performance, or even performances of *this* company (this staging, costume, setting and so on), over *that* performance, or even the performances of that company, with its characteristic staging, and so on: and do so while conceding that they are performing *the very same artwork*. In this light, consider for instance (see §3 below) *Hamlet* from Hamilton's CLC[2] as a kind of 'confusable counterpart' (Danto, 1981 p. 139).

Then, *second*, the idea of numerical identity ('the very same one') always tolerated considerable diversity, in recognizing (for example) identity over time: thus, the boy who climbed the apple tree was tall (for his age), plump and hairy; the middle-aged man who made restitution — the man he became — was short, bald and slim. But, in favoured cases, this is clearly the very same person, such that the man should inherit the legacy his grandfather left the boy (after all, the person who enacted the will, setting up the legacy, was his grandfather too!).[3] And those who understand the case well enough, as I have stated it, will not be confused by it.

But, third, once the *dance itself* is contrasted with *performances* of it, one is tempted — since the performances are clearly concrete objects — to regard the dancework itself as an abstract object, an *abstracta* explained as:

> ... those entities that are not rigidly constantly dependent on any real entity and so lack a spatio-temporal location. This conception is close to the most common understanding of the term 'abstract' and makes *concreta* and *abstracta* mutually exclusive ... categories. (Thomasson, 1999 p. 127)

Such a description captures something about the ways in which dance performances (as *concreta*) relate to *the dance itself*: compare contrasting dances and musical works with "... easel paintings, carved sculptures and frescoes ...", each a "material *particular*": see Wiggins (1980 p. 125: quoted Chapter Two §2 note). It also accords with our treatment both of abstract nouns and of their referents ("love", "fear"). But, for artworks (such as dances), it makes sense to raise the question of whether what I am viewing now is the very same work as that I encountered yesterday: that is, to raise identity questions.

§2.   Identity-claims for dances

Why are we interested in identity statements (for dance)? In fact, we are not: or, more exactly, our interest resides in the *nature of dance*; and *identity-statements* about dances reflect at least some aspects of dance, by showing us something about the kinds of things *dances* really are.

Two comparisons may help: once we recognize that — for persons — finding that the *very same* person (a *numerical* identity judgement) may think different things on two occasions proves to us that persons cannot be *identified* with their psychological content (see Chapter Two §5). Or again: if one thought music was just organized sound, then the same organized sound would be the same music — and if this is *not* true, it follows that music is *not* just organized sound. Again, the identity-question is revealing.

So it would be interesting, if true, that dances necessarily involved bodies in motion, such that claiming to have seen such-and-such a dance (say, *Nutcracker*) required having seen bodies in motion. For then we would know exactly how to describe people who had only watched videos or films of danceworks. In that way, the issue of identity is *one part* of the question: "what sorts of things are dances?" Here, too, another kind of question appears: once we distinguish the dance itself from particular performances of that dance, we recognize that the dances we see are always *performances* — but, in seeing those performances, we (somehow) see the dance itself.

A better understanding of how performances relate to the dance *itself* might also help us recognize what *kinds* of things dances are, or the *nature* of dance. Suppose one deploys a verbal contrast (between *types* and *tokens*: see Chapter Two §10; Chapter Five §2; PAD pp. 56-65); and then asks whether the features that strategy would require then permit our description of dances to accommodate what we recognize as facts about *danceworks*. This second idea can be applied to the more specific context of aesthetics. For a significant feature there is that, whatever one says more generally (say, for persons), there is a specific reason (or set of them) for doubting that our concepts can handle the extreme problem cases in respect of artworks. For, of course, the ontology of artworks must reflect their status as human creations. As Amie Thomasson (2005 p. 228) records:

> ... since facts about the ontology of art are determined by human conceptions, the resulting facts are, as we might say, ontologically shallow — there is nothing more to discover about them than what our practices themselves determine.

For this reason, we should not assume that the concepts here can deal with all the relevant cases, as we might with natural-kind terms (say, "person"); and especially faced with problem cases generated by thought-experiments. Peter Lamarque (2010 p. 115) recognized this in urging that, for artworks:

> Work-identity, like the identity of all intentional objects, is 'soft' identity. It is dependent on what is 'thought' as well as what merely is. It rests ... not just on cultural factors but on values perceptions, meanings ... A work of art is not just a thing with intrinsic properties contingently related to its environment that can be transported 'objectively' from world to world.

For it is precisely the *meaning* of the artwork that bears (in some ways) on its continuity-conditions: in typical cases, the canvas is no longer *that painting* if the pigment on its surface is radically rearranged. Or, as David Davies (2003 p. 18) put a related point:

> Artworks must be entities that can bear the sorts of properties rightly ascribed to what are termed 'works' in our reflective and appreciative practice; that are individuated in the way that 'works' are or would be individuated, and that have the modal properties that are reasonably ascribed to 'works', in that practice.

So rational reconstruction is required to recognize "properties rightly ascribed", and so on. Moreover, I cannot understand, nor do I assume others can, what it would be for a *part* of a person to be an author, unless this meant simply a co-author or some such — with many different cases here; so that, for example, Raymond Chandler started *Poodle Springs*, but Robert B. Parker finished it. Certainly, the role here must not fall to any "backstage artiste", as Austin (1975 p. 10) put it; nothing less than a human agent counts.

§3.   Becoming?

Agency brings with it *responsibility*; and meaning (in language as in art) builds in the *intention* to mean. But these insights should not be psychologized. Applied to art, as to action, the anti-intentionalist theorist is right both that what is *done* is what matters; and that what is *done* cannot (always) depend on what the agent *explicitly* meant (UD pp. 229-232; PAD pp. 12-126). But the "explicitly" here is key — thus ordinary action is intentional *unless*, say, accidental. (We do not need to look for *explicit* planning or deliberation to decide what was intentional; but we may need to look for excuses — for instance, this may be accidental; or, like Francis Bacon approaching some of his paintings, I can be satisfied with something I did, even by accident, and hence avow it). More importantly, the agent has *responsibility* for the work; for its features.

A worked example from another preforming art is revealing. In this context, James Hamilton (2007 p. 182) imagines the "... Culturally Lethargic Company (CLC)":

> ... a group of performers [actors] who assemble for a rehearsal and select some features for display acknowledging neither that they are engaged in making selections nor that there are alternatives from which to select. The CLC fails to deliberate about its selections.

But now, by chance, the CLC:

> ... plans and executes a performance called "Hamlet" that turns out to be moment for moment consonant with the laboriously considered Freudian performance, inspired by Ernest Jones' essay, undertaken and eventually filmed by Lawrence Olivier. (Hamilton, 2007 p. 182)

The point, of course, is that (as Hamilton, 2007 p. 182 notes) even with the CLC "... there are decisions made, to be sure, and there is something like deliberation", since these are not accidental actions. And we can imagine that the actors could offer explanations of their actions, although not by reference to explicit, prior decisions.

Should reference to the Jones essay be made in discussing the CLC performance: for instance, in critical writing? It seems clear that, as set up, the answer is "yes": these ideas are in the background here, although that essay is not in the foreground. That it played no part in any prior deliberation is beside the point. Of course, any reference to Jones' essay might be withdrawn if, say, the CLC performance pre-dated it: although even then reference to "precursors" is possible (consider Hieronymous Bosch, sometime viewed as a precursor of surrealism: see AJ p. 124). We might even dispute the claims of a member of CLC who denied any connection to Jones, unless another account of the details of the performance were offered. For, although culturally lethargic, the CLC is still *part* of that theatrical culture.

As Hamilton (2007 p. 185) concludes from this example, "[t]heatrical conventions cannot be thought of as a sequence of features that are always actually selected for display *as the result of deliberation*". And the same applies for other performances; indeed, for other artworks — they are not accidents, but neither are they always the result of explicit prior planning. (In this respect, they resemble other human actions.) Yet, if the CLC did not *plan* what its members did, they nevertheless did it deliberately — it was not accidental.

So the issue really concerns what is required for deliberation or "intention". For nothing here is either accidental or (ultimately) inexplicable. What goes for the CLC goes for most/much artistic activity: it is not accidental (and hence counts as intended or deliberate); its features are (often) explicable in ways the artist might acknowledge if asked (as one might explain an action one had previously claimed to "just do"). (Comparison as above is with, say, Francis Bacon who, on occasion, *decided* to use 'accidental' techniques, and *decided* when that process is over — hence the outcome is one he chose, even though he might not have recognized it prior to starting. In that way, there is no *prior* planning.)

§4.   Preservation

These represent ways to offer something positive in justification of activity, even though we grant that the justification is contemporaneous with the work. Furthermore, we recognize the limitations of such justificatory narratives in typical cases. At any time, most dances composed and performed — like most novels, plays or poems written, or paintings and sculptures produced — are, frankly, *bad*. So much in the past of any artform is not worth the effort of 're-finding' if (when) it has been lost.

Still, for analytic purposes at least, two occasions for concerns of this sort should be distinguished. In the first, the work passed out of the repertoire some time ago, so dancers, stagers, and choreographers of today have comparatively little on which to base a performance of that past work — call that *reconstruction of the dance* in question. For the other case, imagine a choreographer hoping that his or her work will be viewed by posterity; or an audience that hopes the work will be available to later generations. Here, then, the concern is with the *preservation of danceworks*. It might seem that danceworks cannot be preserved, at least beyond the memories of those involved in creating and performing them. Minimally, their preservation seems hampered when relying simply on the memories of dancers, choreographers, and those involved. Although both positions — *reconstruction* (see PAD 216-221) and *preservation* — have been urged for danceworks, the concern of this chapter is with *preservation*.

On this conception, the task I have called the *preservation* of the dance simply involves putting that dancework back into the active repertoire. Others — such as companies, stagers, and the like — could then add that dance to their repertoires, should they want to. Here the parallel with plays is fairly exact: not all plays that could be performed at a particular time actually are. For instance, this seems a judgement on the plays of Jack B. Yeats (W. B.'s smarter brother, remembered primarily as a painter) that they have disappeared from the active dramatic repertoire; or perhaps never entered it. Indeed, while a student, I directed a performance of a play by Jack B. Yeats, "The Deathly Terrace";[4] and some of his *Collected Plays* (1971) were written to be performed in a puppet theatre (such that the stage directions are written backwards: see Yeats, 1971 p. 94), partly — no doubt — so that Jack could paint the scenery and such like. But, despite some positive criticism of the plays by Samuel Beckett ([1971] 1983 pp. 89-90; 148-149), these plays seem no longer in the dramatic repertoire. Certainly, the copy I found in the university library showed no signs of wear. Indeed, it looked pristine to my untrained eye, except for the accumulated dust. And the copy I bought later (used, of course) was also not marked by its 40-plus year journey. At the least, then, these plays might be thought to have failed a 'Test of Time'.

Such a verdict in this case reflects the current state of affairs (let us suppose); but is it inevitable? Well, that conclusion may be premature: a new director might find exciting new ways to stage one of these plays (or what he *took* to be exciting and new). Then that play would return to the repertoire, and its fate — its artistic merit, as then determined — would rest with appreciators. Surely the possibility of a renewal of interest in the plays of Jack B. Yeats cannot be set aside (see PAD pp. 210-211). And, of course, the plaudits from Beckett might partly ground one's confidence in that possibility: given that Beckett, with his immense literary prestige, thought well of some of these plays (or at least took them seriously), a revival of interest in them might be imagined, growing from a concern with (especially) Beckett's "Homage to Jack B. Yeats". As institutionalists (AJ pp. 148-150), we might imagine success in the relevant 'Republic of Art' as operating via a phase of *self-election* (in which works are put forward as art) and a phase of *other-acclamation* (where the works are acknowledged by the Republic). Then, faced with silence in place of this second phase, the artist's supporters might be imagined as mounting what is, in effect, a public relations campaign, designed to change taste.

On this model, Beckett's piece might seem the initial shot in that campaign. His "Homage to Jack B. Yeats" appears in the 'Words about Painters' section of his *Disjecta* ([1971] 1983). However, the same volume contains an appreciation of The Amaranthers (1936), a novel(?) Becket describes in dramatic terms; or at least terms applicable to his own plays (and perhaps his novels). Having urged that both the irony of the work and its discontinuity are "Ariostesque" (Beckett, 1983 p. 89), he continues:

> There is no allegory. ... There is no symbol. ... There is no satire. ... The end, the beginning, is among the hills, where imagination is not banned ....
> (Beckett, 1983 p. 90)

If this sounds like praise for things Beckettian, it will come as no surprise that the end of one of the plays has a major character wondering, "Have I done anything or nothing?" (Yeats, 1971 p. 80). Further, Robin Skelton, in his "Introduction" (Yeats, 1971 p. 8) suggests that one of Jack B.'s plays "... resembles the apparently inconsequential short late plays of Samuel Beckett where little that is dramatic occurs...": Skelton does not speculate on Yeats as an influence here (although the play referred to was first produced in 1939 — while Beckett's short stories were first collected in 1934). One can readily imagine such material deployed in the public relations exercise on behalf of the plays of Jack B. Yeats.

Very roughly (compare AJ pp. 153-156), the substance of the position derives from the thought that artists put forward *as art* only those works they consider worthy of appreciation and not time-wasting for the audience for art (of this type). Further, an audience for the artwork requires that the work is received or acknowledged as worthy of appreciation and not time-wasting. In such conditions, there will be an almost universal generalization to the effect that an artwork has a positive evaluative content: and the *onus of proof* will be on those who doubt that this is true of some particular artwork. But, since their view may carry the day *in this specific case*, it follows that the idea of a minimal evaluative content is not incompatible with the possibility of *bad art*.

Such a model provides, at best, a strategy *once* someone sees the work (or, in this case, works) positively: that is, we see how one of these works might return to the repertoire, based on someone's finding something else vivid in that work. And here one should recall the point Joan Acocella raised (in her Introduction to Sally Banes, 2007: p. xvii): that "[j]ournalism ... is the first draft of history" — well, it can be. And here we see how. For the historian must not merely "... explain things, chart trends, note developments" (Acocella, in Banes, 2007 p. xvii): there is also an imperative to direct the changes *towards the good* even in much history, but more so in critical writing such as Beckett's. Thus, in this case, it is clearly not enough that such a public relations exercise might begin: it too must be motivated in the imagination of those wishing to see the play staged. And that motivation must be passed on to those who might bring it into being.

In respect of the play ("The Deathly Terrace": hereafter DT followed by page numbers in Yeats, 1971) that will form the basis of the rest of the discussion, one difficulty to be overcome is formal: it consists of three Acts, one five pages of text, and only one scene; the second, having two scenes (the second less than a page) totals four pages; while the third, which is almost entirely composed of two characters having a conversation, is sixteen pages of a single scene — although the last two pages are preceded by "A Wait", during which the "[s]un sinks more towards the edge of the sea" (DT p. 117). Any performance answerable to the work's architecture should reflect the play's two part structure: first, based on a filming model, suggested in part by Skelton ("Introduction", Yeats, 1971 p. 5), who remarks that "[i]ts characters are all involved in a world of imaginary events, in the world of the cinema"; second, the sitting part — it couldn't be managed on the same model, so was treated as a kind of dialogic-chorus or commentary on the first part. As one character remarks, "Ah words! I often do talk about them, and with them too. It's a superstition using words for speech ..." (DT p. 114). And that, in turn, provides a key for the understanding required by (most of) this long scene: one must be given the opportunity to savour the words.

Here, then, one way to begin making sense of this work was sketched, a way that exploits the critical commentary on it provided by Beckett (and hence central to the Art World). Of course, that could only happen were the work still somehow extant. Hence a broadly reconstructive process could be justified as preserving works. And for danceworks, again on a parallel with plays, this form of reconstructive *preservation* might involve collecting scores, notes, photographs, videos and such like, so that — should anyone *want* to stage that dance — he/she would be able to do so.

Of course, that justification for retaining the works would not, of itself, justify the *performance* of the works thus preserved. For these are not being offered as *worthwhile* works of the period; but only as *works* of that period. The dance then resembles a play-script on a shelf: the possibility (but not the actuality) of a performance. That would (or certainly might) preserve a work in a performing art. Yet, then, to justify *actually* performing the dancework requires some *purpose* for that performance: and that purpose, although requiring clarity, need not always reside in the dancework's *artistic* appreciation. Thus, for visual art, and very roughly, preserving what is *live* in art (in an art gallery) is contrasted with preserving what is of merely historical importance (in a museum) — that some galleries, such as MOMA, are *called* "museums" confuses this point in practice. Relatedly, a concern with the *history* of dance — of the kind dance scholars might embrace — might also speak for the preservation of dances. Doing so, however, still requires asking exactly what dances of the past have to offer; and why the students of the present (and future) should want access to these danceworks. Further, we should reflect on the nature of that access — what will the student of the future need to be able to see and/or to do?

As with music, a notated score for a work might offer just such a way to preserve that work, although *notationality* (rather than an extant notated score) must be stressed. Or a complex video recording might offer another route to preservation. Exploring that topic requires considering precisely what such recordings of the work might offer. In particular, more must be said about the *logic of notationality* for performing arts (see Chapter Two §10; Chapter Five §§2-4). This will involve positive accounts of the value of notated scores for danceworks (were they to be got), as well as the rejection of apparent contenders for a similar role in securing the authenticity of dance performance.

The *reality* of danceworks in this sense might also be denied: a typical critic's commitment to an ontology might draw on parallels in literary theory whereby the dance exists *only* at the moment of performance to suggest that "[t]here is no original work to which subsequent instantiations ... must necessarily conform" (as Sarah Rubridge, 2000 p. 207 notes). Yet even such theorists treat danceworks as performables:[5] they compare this performance *of the work* with another performance (or one by another company); they regard rehearsals as *for* performances, and those performance as of the work at issue; further, that is what the notators are notating. All this reiterates the traditional ontology of *the performable*.

Since a dancework that *remains* in the repertoire is not a set of indistinguishable performances, it asks too much of our historical case to insist that repeating the work requires indistinguishability from some past performance. (Which?) Here, our goal in preserving a work for posterity is simply to keep that work in the repertoire. Then doing so draws on the under-determination of performance by dancework; the continuity of that very dancework allows for difference. And a notated score will be a suitable way for forward recording that dance itself (and especially what, if anything, is *crucial* to that dance). For the comparison with music suggests beginning from the score.

A key distinction here (see Chapter Five §3) is between the score *as a record* of a particular performance — which seems to follow from its being notated 'after the fact', perhaps by a notator — and the score *as a recipe*, such that one can use the score (as instantiating constraints from the type?) to differentiate appropriate from inappropriate performances, and good from less good ones too! That is, the score can function *normatively*. Of course, the second of these — score as recipe — draws on the fact that (in principle) one can make dances by writing the score; but it also recognizes how the score can be used, however it was generated.

So why is the notated score (of whatever form) for a dance *important?* Notation systems such as Labanotation are essentially movement notations (see McFee, 2004 p. 13): they can be used to record bodily movements in lots of contexts. As Blacking (1985 p. 66) accurately writes, like films and videos:

> ... various notations such as Laban and Benesh are ... useful tools for referring to the object of study [of the anthropologist], but they cannot describe or explain what is happening as human experience ...

For these notations, and so on, record *movement*, not (human) action. And, as we noted in Chapter Five, a strength of such notation systems is that (by recording movement) they allow comparison of movement patterns across different actions: thus, the dance can be compared with the ritual or with the exercise routine. But (to repeat) if scores in a notation system are used to provide the *constraints* from the *type*, those scores are treated as *normative* — as saying what one *should* do in order that one's movement instantiate the particular dancework. That, in turn, treats the score *as a recipe*, even when that score is actually made by notating what was done: that is, as a recording of a particular performance.

Moreover, having a score of this kind enables works to remain in the repertoire just as long as there were performance traditions among dancers that permitted the following of that 'recipe'. So there is a connection here with the posterity of dances; or, what may come to the same thing, with the place of the history of dance in our understanding of works of the present; or even works in the repertoire. This discussion also allows consideration of the preservation or permanence of dances. For the fragility of this connection for dances has already been noted.

§5.   Disappearance

So there is a good reason in principle why danceworks — as performables — should not simply be *dismissed* as existing only "... at a perpetual vanishing point" (Siegel, 1972 p. 1). For the possibility of an artform of performing instances or performables — that is, a performing art — necessarily has an extant past to which contemporary practitioners could refer, in one of the many ways such references occur. So that, were there reasons, in principle, for choreographers to retain their works in the repertoire, this could be achieved. Or those works that disappeared from the contemporary repertoire could be re-introduced through some history-based process collectively called "reconstructive preservation". And since danceworks from the past of dance must provide us with 'temporary paradigms' to allow us to learn to see and learn to value (art-type) dance, it seems to me there are such reasons. Further, performances too require such 'temporary paradigms' to show choreographers some of the possibilities for making dances; and dancers some of the possibilities of performing them.

Nevertheless, it is crucial to recognize a kind of canon that can function, at least for a time, as a kind of (temporary) paradigm of dance (in its various genres), to give purchase to those learning what is valuable in dance. Comparative consideration will be central here: as Hume ([1741] 1985 p. 238) puts it, "[b]y comparison alone we fix the epithets of praise and blame, and learn how to assign the due degree to each". Further, a grasp of such a canon is essential if one is to be taken seriously as a critic: list only Bach and Beethoven in one's account of the 'greats of classical music' and one's taste is too eclectic; but there is no precise list characterizing the canon. Thus, leaving out Wagner is something one might argue for; leaving out Sibelius seems to require less justification.

As we saw in Chapter Five, Banes (1998 p. 11) is rightly suspicious of any "received canon" for dance, recognizing that "... it necessarily leaves out many valuable works and authors" since (and contrary to the reality of such a canon, at least until recently) it tends to include "... only dances made by

Euro-American Choreographers" (Banes, 1998 p. 11). But she retains the notion since, as she notes, "... my purpose in analyzing the high art canon cannot be to reinscribe it" (Banes, 1998 p. 11). Still she recognizes the examining of such a canon as "an important project" since:

> The canon we have inherited — the dances that have survived for myriad reasons, including both the test of time and the fallibility of human memory as well as the distribution of cultural capital — cannot be wished away by fiat.

For there must be *a* canon, to ground critical practice and art-teaching (dance-teaching, in this case). Then the first hurdle lies in identifying the *right* or appropriate canon, or overlapping set of them, not in rejecting the whole idea; while the second lies in never rendering that canon immutable, not setting it in stone. The danceworld does not stand still: the 'moment of ballet' gives way to, say, modern ballet. At most, any canon remains a temporary paradigm, a place for arguments about the status and value of particular danceworks.

But sometimes my enthusiasm to retain dance of the past, and to find it a role in the creation and performance of dance, as well as in its criticism, has been misunderstood.[6] So here I will comment briefly on a case running in the opposite direction, on which works lose their audience but without the kind of disappearance suggested by Siegel's "vanishing point" expression. This kind of case is well exemplified in a comment by Arlene Croce (1982 pp. 28-29[7]):

> I watched Martha Graham's *Primitive Mysteries* (1931) die this season in what seemed, for the most part, scrupulous performances. The twelve girls looked carefully rehearsed. Sophie Maslow, who had supervised the previous revival, in the season of 1964-65, was again in charge. Everybody danced with devotion. Yet a piece that I would have ranked as a landmark in American dance was reduced to a tendentious outline, the power I had remembered was no longer there ... Perhaps there's a statute of limitations on how long a work can be depended upon to force itself through the bodies who dance it.

Of course, the example does not matter: but here is a description of a phenomenon all too familiar to those of us who have been watching dance for a long time — and, moreover, this description sets aside some of the explanations familiarly offered. So that it is not that the dancers lacked rehearsal, nor that those rehearsals failed to be scrupulously conducted. (After all, we can imagine that a similar pattern of rehearsal preceded that "previous revival" referred to here; and it was a success.) Moreover, as described, the problem was not strictly one of *memory* of the previously-successful sequence of movements (and so on), since this unsuccessful version shares at least the 'supervisor' — someone involved in transmission of the movement-sequences (and so on). Croce here offers only two hints in explanation: first, perhaps "devotion" is not the right attitude for performance; second, she refers to some kind of transition in "the bodies who dance it". Let us consider each in turn.

The first of these (if I read it correctly) *is* a criticism of how the dance was presented, presumably by those who supervised rehearsal: to present a dancework of the past in its artistic greatness, one must approach it as one would a current work — the term "devotion" suggests the wrong attitude to the possibility of the current performances differing from those of the past. What is required is the life and energy the work would have had in its previous performances: this might have required the rough edges that often accompany vivid performances. The reverence implicit in the term "devotion" does not suggest this, but instead points in the other direction. Since that possibility for a limited performance exists in all cases where performing arts are at issue, it must be acknowledged here — that does not mean that one lacks proper regard for the dancework itself. On the contrary, the work is respected as *in a performing art* — as a performable — precisely by thinking carefully about how much deviation from past performances can retain same-work identity.[8] (My point, then, is only that one treat works from the past like any other work — after all, the works from last year's repertoire are, in one clear sense, works from the past now: they were not choreographed specially for this season.) And, to repeat, the term "devotion" suggests to me that the dance company's attitude to the past of this work was unduly reverential. While we see how this can come about, it is clearly something we would hope to avoid. In that sense, if true, this *is* a criticism of the company's activities.

Croce's second point (as I read it) recognizes differences in "... the bodies who dance it". This criticism should separate, for analytical purposes at least, into two aspects. One is broadly technical: the typical dancer of today has been trained in a number of techniques (since 'regular' employment requires this), and probably trained to a higher pitch — thus, justifying Judith Mackrell's characterization of today's dancers as "Olympic-standard" (Mackrell, 1997 p. 7[9]): they usually have physical conditioning beyond what was common in, say, the 1930s (when *Primitive Mysteries* was choreographed). The powers and capacities of such bodies differ from those on which the choreography was initially composed: these bodies may have greater flexibility; and sometimes their movements reflect their mastery of different dance-styles; say, of Bharata Natyam. The other point, though related, is more directly aesthetic; that is, *dance techniques* (such as Graham technique) also involve the learning (or, at least, acquisition) of a 'vocabulary' of movements appropriate for dances created using those techniques: such that for (say) Graham, "...

emotion molded the whole body into a heightened gesture" (Jowitt, 2004 p. 208). This comment applies to the technique, although also the dancer's mastery of it. In this sense, then, Marcia Siegel (1972 p. 107) is right to speak of "technique-as-aesthetic". Thus, mastery of even one technical resource (such as ballet) typically involves mastery also of a 'vocabulary' of movements appropriate to the dances deploying that technique. And many techniques, originating in the requirements of specific dances for the companies concerned (UD p. 205), reflect this connection between technique and dance-character. As I put it elsewhere (McFee, 2003 p. 137):

> On this model, ... dancers undergo a kind of apprenticeship, in which they learn two (or two-and-a-half) crafts: they undergo the bodily training and are inducted into the understanding of the movements (and the dances) that result — and they may in this way gain insight into choreographic processes (although they need not [so this is the "half"]).

Further, expectations can change: thus Jowitt (2004 p. 45) claims that:

> Today's ballet dancer tries to show straight knees and pointed toes as much of the time as the choreography permits — that is, on descending from a jump, the toes stay pointed until the last second; the standing leg is arrow-straight in pirouettes.

And comments that "Ballet Theatre dancers of the 40s cared less about these issues ... the shape of a phrase seems to matter more than the pictorial beauty of each individual movement" (Jowitt, 2004 p. 45). All this I call a *performance tradition*: dancers learn to perform dances, and to understand them in a dancerly way. And, typically at least, both that learning and that understanding took place in the context of a *company* whose members were trained in that manner of delivering the choreography. That tradition, of course, allows the performances of dances of the past in what might be called a "reasoned" way: that is, in *new* performers' interpretations (UD pp. 100-101). For any changes can then be explained by reference, first, to the tradition and then, second, to the kinds of deviation that tradition licenced. For the tradition has a *normative* dimension. Without such a tradition, no one would be capable of performing certain dances; dancers would not understand how such movements should be performed. And so, even if the dances were 'preserved' (say, in notated form), they could not be danced.

So, does the performance tradition for, say, the current Royal Ballet dancers overlap sufficiently with those of (say) Paul Taylor or Fredrick Ashton to permit those dancers to perform these choreographers' works? Suppose that it does not (see Challis, 1999). In that case, perhaps the *performance tradition* required for these works either never was part of the training regime for these dancers (Taylor) or has ceased to be (Ashton) — because, say, a British style of ballet performance, with its "emotional depth", has been replaced by a Russian style, with its "formal precision" (quoted Challis, 1999 p. 147, both quotes). In the most extreme case, of course, the performances (and hence the works) would be rendered unintelligible to a knowledgeable audience: in the less extreme case, this audience would just struggle to understand. Certainly, such a possibility illustrates what it would be for *performance traditions* to cease to be available.

One thinks about this *most*, in recent times: for instance, fragility of performances of particular works that (as we have seen) depend on dancers, as well as audiences. To understand here one needs a vocabulary to deal with many cases, including a contrast between the dancers' *training in performance traditions* (as above) and the understanding of traditions of performance, typically crucial for audiences. So, first, another aspect of performance needs to be ensured (although, again, contrasted only for analytical purposes), which highlights the importance of another aspect of 'skill' here, different from that identified by Croce: there are not only *performance traditions for dancers* as sketched above, such that the dancers have a familiarity with dances of the particular style or genre. Or, if they presently lack this familiarity, they can acquire it through the rehearsals.

But also, second, there are *traditions of performance*: the audience must know what to expect, even if that expectation is sometimes deliberately frustrated or thwarted by the particular dance, as when DV8: Physical Theatre include some speech in their works — this is not what we expected of ballet! In effect, this is the requirement for an informed audience, an audience of 'competent judges' (AJ pp. 45-47) for danceworks. Without such an audience, dance performances would typically fail; or be reduced to a 'lowest common denominator' of the kind present in many a Christmas *Nutcracker*. And such an informed audience must understand these works through experience of them *as performed*, since that is how such an audience comes to understand such works[10].

These *traditions of performance* amount partly to understanding the narrative of dance history; but they also embody contemporary understanding of how these danceworks should (typically) be performed — an understanding that later stagers might contest profitably in making new versions of particular (extant) dances, and one to which choreographers could respond. (as Mats Ek does, in his comic traducings of the typical expectations of classical ballet: say, in his *Swan Lake* [1987]). It permits both the audience to distinguish interesting and valuable difference from mere mistake, and the impact of 'posterity' to lead to a revision of that judgement. For a 'knowledgeable audience' just is one that can distinguish originality from mere novelty (is Matthew Bourne's *Swan Lake* [1995] really doing anything new at the level of artistic meaning?); and can find the continuity within trivial changes. Hence the audience also needs to be able to recognize (at least) when dancers fail to instantiate a particular choreography. All-in-all, such traditions form a background here (part of what Noël Carroll [2001 p. 91] calls "the lay of the artworld") which permits the choices made to be *reasoned* choices, defensible (in principle) in discussion. Without such a tradition, "however small and special" (Cavell, 1969 p. xxvii), choices here could only be arbitrary.

With the disappearance (from the background) of these features required for intelligibility, one would expect exactly the sort of disappearance of danceworks from the realm of *understandability* by audiences that Croce describes as the 'death' of Graham's *Primitive Mysteries* (whatever one makes of the example); as well as its connection to the failure by the rest of the danceworld to grasp such works any longer. So, in this concrete case too, failure to maintain either *performance traditions* (among dancers) or *traditions of performance* (in the audience) generates one kind of failure of a dancework of the past. And this failure might well constitute the disappearance of the dancework in question from the artistic canon, since it will no longer be experienced as expressive.

The upshot here: the *experience* of dance has such traditions implicit within it. I do not mean, of course, that these traditions must be part of what the audience must know, if that means that all audience members must be able to recite the history, and so on, to us. Rather, the knowledge might well be acquired *other* than as a kind of book-learning (it almost always will be for dancers), and be manifest in action and in intelligent attention.[11]

Of course, on this picture one kind of failure of a dancework of the past — of the kind Croce assigned to *Primitive Mysteries* (above) — is a failure to maintain either *performance traditions* of the dancers or *traditions of performance* in the audience. So that the very tools which, elsewhere, explain the persistence of dance of the past and its centrality for understanding and performing dance today can also explain cases where even established works disappear from the canon.

In one sense, then, it is because the work can no longer be seen *as it was* that explains its disappearance from the possibility of appreciation. Two points should be noted, though, by way of qualification: first, this work "dies" because it loses both its audience and those able to instantiate it — in that fashion, its demise results from its losing an audience that responds to it: that we can no longer see it as it was seen. But, second, Croce describes an extreme version. For the kinds of response that would have kept the dancework alive need not be *very* positive. As we might say, one kind of 'life-support' involves simply being in the repertoire (or not far out of it, so that the work could be re-staged relatively easily). For such works might continue to be staged, but without an excess of enthusiasm. Works can remain in the canon, even functioning as temporary paradigms, even though they are now regarded as pretty *weak* — they are still clearly works of a certain kind, at least. So they might limp by, without dying but without immense enthusiasm. And, of course, as noted (again!), *most* of the works currently produced in any artform are pretty weak!

My conclusion has been that a 'live' artwork must be (a) performable, and (b) open to appreciation — these two conditions together sound *just* like a truism. But complexities within each mean that, instead, this just points to the beginning of the discussion. Thus, to be *performable* here as a particular artwork in a multiple artform requires at least meeting the constraints from *the type*; any performance must reflect those constraints to be a candidate for a performance of that work. For instance, the artwork must not be forgotten, or otherwise lost. Hence, in the simplest case, there would be an authoritative score. Further, as the discussion of Graham's *Primitive Mysteries* (1931) above shows, the capacities of the dancers must be appropriate — and these can be lost; and lost, in the contemporary danceworld, partly because today's dancers must typically have some mastery of numerous dance techniques: that can break the connection that once existed between the company and the choreographer (and especially her choreographic style as reflected in the technique used). Likewise, openness to *appreciation* too has a connection to the dancers as well as the audience. Thus, Croce's discussion seems to be highlighting simply a collapse on the part of the audience: the work was no longer available to that audience. But, in fact, the collapse in respect of that work was more total: the work *as performed* lacked something; but that reflected defects in the dancers' ability to *instantiate* that work, given both their training and their understanding. That is, this became a work that standardly-trained dancers could not perform.

Of course, the requirements for an audience able to appreciate the particular work applies in other artforms, as well as in dance. So what is the new ephemerality here? How does this case differ from (say) painting? The discussion of Arlene Croce illustrates the additional need to retain traditions of performance and performance traditions: for these are prerequisites for the training and experience of the dancers; and — since those dancers will be performing — of the audience for dance also.

§6.   Endurance?

Croce's conclusion (above) was that "[p]erhaps there's a statute of limitations on how long a work can be depended upon to force itself through the bodies who dance it" — her implication is that, at the least, there ought to be! We have seen one sense in which she is right: in practice, either or both of what I have called the *performance traditions* of dancers and *traditions of performance* in the audience (but not excluding the dancers) required for the intelligible performance of a dancework may be lost. And this is likely to happen, given the passage of time. Yet, of course, there is no real *necessity* here: we might confidently predict such changes — and we might be right — but that simply reflects the contingent history of dance. We might even highlight features of experiences common among dance audiences (the hunt for novelty, in particular) that might encourage such changes. Still, not all novelties tend in this direction. But what can be made sense of by the audience can still be cast in terms of the traditions of performance with which they are familiar. And then the dance-maker's task can be formulated in those terms. As I wrote elsewhere (McFee, 2004 pp. 271-271), my choreography might be thought *safe* if it drew extensively on the forms (and so on) of the past, *radical but intelligible* if my work is a challenge to a past aesthetic in recognizable ways, or *powerfully challenging* if, say, a whole genre is contested. Certainly the first two options would draw directly on established *performance traditions* (to permit the dancers to learn to perform my dance, and to understand it in a dancerly way) and *traditions of performance* (to permit the audience to locate this dancework of in a narrative of the history of recent dance). And, if the third option challenged some of this — as perhaps Isadora Duncan's work might be thought to — the possibility of her success (of the implicit 'argument' being accepted) requires a particular, appropriate "lay of the artworld" (Carroll, 2001 p. 91) at that time. So, while the dancers have a key role in maintaining the possibility of performance of a particular dancework, that is not their only role.

Part Three

Persons Appreciating Dance

Chapter Eight
Answerability of judgements

§1. Introduction: avoiding misperception

Addressing appreciative judgements here, the informed perception of the art critic provides a typical case: she can see cubist painting, hear atonal music ... where the alternatives would count as misperceiving these artworks. And, while such misperception of art cannot be identified exceptionlessly, in any cases where *misperception* is granted, answerability will be to the non-misperception case.

Then an initial sketch of dance-appreciation begins from a simple-enough *Principle*: namely, that *critical appreciation of a dance is answerable to features of that dance*. For, as Reid ([1815] 2002 p. 595) put it, "... the name of beauty belongs to this excellence of the object, and not to the feelings of the spectator". In part, this principle says no more than that a critic's claiming such-and-such about some dancework must depend on the features of the dancework, such that one could say, "No, you are mistaken — the dance lacks that feature"; or perhaps even "... that feature of the dance should be read differently". Moreover, critical commentary must be evaluable in this way to avoid the charge of "reading in": that one's criticism *reads into* the dancework something that is not there. So the correctness, or not, of one's criticism (and any other commentary on the dance) must depend on the way things are, where discerning 'the way things are' will be a matter of 'looking and seeing', a perceptual matter. In turn, that recognizes that:

> Seeing is a form — visual — of awareness of one's spatial surroundings. Sight affords awareness of some of what is there, or there happening. Seeing that dirty cup on the counter, just after having started the dishwasher, is enjoying some of what vision places on offer. (Travis, 2013 p. 179)

Moreover, Travis (2013 p. 189) acknowledges the connection between the conceptual and the perceptual:

> A recognitional capacity in the present sense — an ability to recognize a pig at sight,[1] say — would be a capacity to recognize the reach of the conceptual to the non-conceptual. One sees, and recognizes, the nuances of something being a pig.

Hence sufficient mastery of the concept "pig" is required to mobilize it in my perception: the same will hold for danceworks. Thus what one sees answers partly *what is there* to be seen, depending partly on the contribution of one's conceptual mastery, the array of concepts that Wollheim (1980 pp. 193-

194) calls "the cognitive stock" that one brings to bear in perception. For only someone master of the concepts of *ash, elm, oak, sycamore* can make these discriminations; and hence see *these* trees (as opposed to just *trees*). That such a person is an *informed spectator* of trees typically reflects an interest on her part — her interest leads her to this knowledge of trees (this *cognitive stock* in respect of them) that permits her to see the world of trees *differently*. But *what* she sees is still answerable to *how the world is*: that *trees* are indeed of these different kinds; and hence, in taking as an oak what was in fact an elm, one can *misperceive* trees. This point is perhaps clearest when one *learns to see*: from the X-ray plate, the radiologist can discern the condition of the internal organs, while the untrained cannot even make out the ribs[2] — although, with practice, one can learn to do so. Again, the process is familiar. Encouraged to view the characteristics of the X-ray plate in a certain fashion, one learns to see X-ray photographs appropriately: one learns to 'read' them or to understand them, although this is just a matter of *looking* at them — it is perceptual rather than inferential. Then, to repeat, the informed perception of the art critic in a typical case will avoid misperceiving these artworks, although such misperception of art cannot identified exceptionlessly in the abstract.

§2. Seeing the dance — ringers, etc.

But *what* one sees is equally important. Then central or typical cases of seeing danceworks must at least involve viewing (and attending to) an assemblage of moving bodies, human bodies in motion: as Merce Cunningham (1984 p. 27) puts is, "... the way of seeing [the dance] has everything to do with dancers". Obviously art is, roughly, *embodied meaning* (Danto, 2013 p. 48); for dance and some other arts, the embodiment contains bodies in some way — and *real* human bodies are needed, since these are what comprise a performance of the dancework, in typical cases. Lacking that, what is present to one's senses cannot be the thing itself (here, the dancework), but only something else. Missing that, perhaps one is not actually seeing the artwork — instead, for dance, one thinks first of a recording!

In the philosophy of perception, the possibility of *ringers* must be confronted head on: that is, cases so arranged that I, or anyone in that situation, might be mistaken — this is not a pig but, say, "... a stuffed mechanical pig — so cleverly done as to look like the real thing"; what Travis (2011 p. 91) calls a *ringer* for a pig. From there the *argument from illusion* may be confronted, since empiricism regularly regards "the argument from illusion ... [as] the means of locating the observable" (Travis, 2011 p. 91). Yet, in fact, the possibility addressed here must be a public one: "Locked in an inner world, whether it is a pig or a pig-ringer means nothing to me ..." (Travis, 2013 p. 235). So I am not in such a world. Further, what I know has an impact: how can I see a pig, even in a favoured case, if I know nothing about pigs? In particular, I must know what a pig looks like. Perhaps, after all, the creature in the pantry is a peccary — in the pig-family no doubt, and therefore pig-*like* to some degree (Austin, 1962 p. 74), but not a pig. My ignorance left me making the wrong claim.

For artworks such as dances, what must be made of 'confusable counterparts' (the road-sweeping that I *mistake* for a dance, because it is ... well, confusable for that dance: see Chapter One §4)? A second case raises questions of a broadly ontological character, when we ask whether we have seen 'the work of art itself'', for what is "the work of art itself"? These topics can be addressed in that order.

Faced with the demands of exploring answerability and needing to introduce the *ringer* case, John Wisdom (1953 p. 42) rightly recognizes that there is not just one problematic area, writing:

> [o]ur assertion with confidence that there is cheese on the table ... raises at least these three problems: (1) *the category problem*, which finds expression in 'We ought not to speak of a cheese ... but of bundles of sense-data'; (2) *the knowledge problem*, which finds expression in 'We ought not to say "I know there is cheese on the table" but 'Very, very probably there is cheese on the table"'; (3) *the justification problem*, which finds expression in 'Empirical conclusions are not really justified'.

All and any of these problems might beset us. Still, 'confusable counterparts' will provide the primary kind of *ringer* here, of two sorts: first, when the movement pattern is not *a* dance (it is, say, road-sweeping: Chapter One §4); and, second, when it is not *this* dance, but some other. Further, these need only be *confusable*, not (necessarily) indistinguishable: one might notice differences without regarding them as relevant or significant — as the miniscule differences between two forks in my flatware set allows me to tell them apart, if I care to. Equally, the *knowledge problem* arises when one imagines that one somehow always *builds* to certainty, approaching it by steps — but in fact, once it has been proven that I have *not* read the book, despite my previous claims to know I had, one certainty becomes another (see Stroud, 2000 pp. 48-49); while the *justification problem* seems to leave open any issue where human discussion, or human categories, are required. But this is mistaken, for (as *occasion-sensitivity* shows us) much that is human-sized is nonetheless *determinate* once the right category is identified or the right question asked. Wisdom (1953 p. 95) himself provides a clear example, when someone asks, "Could anything which is not a bridle serve the purpose which a bridle serves?":

The Red Indian [better, Native American] with his single strip of hide can stop and turn his pony with it, so the practical, debunking person will say 'Yes', may even then insist that it is a bridle, which of course is quite untrue. The instructor in equitation will say 'No' because he cannot obtain with it the balance and 'collection' he obtains with a bridle. ... Shall we say 'It serves the same purpose' or shall we not?

There is no single answer here, but we recognize why the question that concerns the "instructor in equitation" is rightly answered "No"; *and* that this answer is not thereby rendered vague (say) by recognizing that there are *other* questions, other occasions. Hence questions demanding answers of other kinds.

For dances, the conceptual element might be thought stronger: the temptation to distinguish two apparently 'confusable' performances — to regard them either as performances of different works, or to view only one of them as a dancework (an artwork) — may perhaps employ our category-noting powers to a greater degree than determining whether there is cheese on the table, just because there are more ways to fail; and some of those require informed perception. That might be just what is missing. Thus, to mobilize Wisdom's framework, the primary *categorial* question is whether this is a dance: the answer depends on features of the dance; and hence on perception of those features ('across the footlights'). And, since even the fullest notated score can only ensure the movement patterns (as we saw: Chapter Two §10), ruling out confusable counterparts requires special vigilance! Here too the kinds of informed perception potentially taught by dance criticism have their place. Then the *knowledge* question asks whether are we *sure* of the features claimed for the dance. In favoured cases, our answer is, 'As sure as we can be!". An issue of fallibility is raised, with a practical dimension we will come to. Finally, the *justificational* question is comparatively easily answered for artforms, since artforms have (are made to have: see §8 below) an audience. This logical point requires that the features of artworks be so designed that relevant aspects show (or can be seen), at least in principle.

A realistic account of perception (and, especially, of objects of perception) must be added to this picture: that is, the connection of perception to our conceptual mastery must be recognized, accepting that what can be seen should also be described in human-sized terms, not in the reduced terms of empiricism. Thus we could concede that, say, a Breugel painting might depict peasants dancing; and hence that we might see peasants dancing in it! Similarly, Wisdom (1953 p. 107) writes of the dancer's grace that "[h]er grace *is* a matter of the patterns she gives to our eyes and the lift she gives to our hearts. So there is no problem of how we know she is graceful". And if, more exactly, we wonder how one learns to recognize "... the lift she gives to our hearts", that too should be open to perception — visible to those suitably sensitive, suitably informed and (as we shall see) also suitably *placed*.

If that discussion deals in general terms with our ability to see (or to recognize) dances, it poses once again the other question raised above: the broadly ontological question raised when we ask whether we have seen 'the work of art itself'.

§3.   Limitations on perceiving artworks

What are the limitations here? In fact, there are many ways to be unable to see a particular dance. Four seem especially relevant. No doubt one such involves having a poor seat.[3] Then one is, as it were, in the presence of the dance but cannot see it. (The most extreme version here might be to wear a blindfold to the performance. But, even in this case, light reflected from the dance strikes us. So that the contrast is just with the having of better sight-lines — where one can therefore try to improve those.) Then, as John Wisdom (1991 p. 80) recognized, while you can recognize such-and-such as a dance, "... parrots may not know it, yet perhaps they have even better eyesight than yours". The visual acuity thereby granted to the parrot does not allow her to see *dance*: or, better, to recognize dance when she sees it. Parrots with superb visual acuity instantiate other ways to fail here, for the parrots cannot see dances (whatever is in front of them). Yet this is not a failure to encounter the dance but, as it were, a failure to make anything of that encounter. Your capacities exceeding those of parrots might be explained by (i) your mastery of concepts (and of the relevant concepts) and (ii) your sensitivity to differences between what is dance and what just resembles it; between *good* and *better* dances; and so on — differences we recognize as cultural, and evaluative, and beyond the scope of the parrot. Contrast dance-critic Lewis Segal (2008 p. F9[4]) claiming that:

> My parrot, Steve, lives in a cage near the TV set and so has seen more dance than many Southlands balletomanes — although he much prefers car chases, parades, game shows, hurricanes ...

A parrot that stares at the television is not seeing (televised) dance, and nor really seeing televised versions of these other things. Moreover, genuinely seeing the dance requires recognizing the dance as of this or that *kind* (or category) because different criteria of success follow from differences of kind. Thus an audience in 1800 — even an audience for advanced music — would find Schoenberg's *Six Little Piano Pieces* Opus 19 unintelligible. Even later, critical discussion may be needed to build an informed audience, the only kind that could make sense of such a work.[5]

Further, another, simpler way to not see a particular dancework is, surely, to fail to be *in the presence* of the dance — and, for me at least, encountering the work typically requires being in the presence of a performance: dance is a performing art; and therefore danceworks are encountered only through, or in, performances. The contrast, here is, say, with both *just* seeing the score and *just* hearing a report, where the second (hearing the report) also fails the condition above: that the aesthetic (likewise the artistic) is perceptual, requiring one's own sensory, and hence potentially sensuous, engagement with the work. So four overlapping explanations of failing to see the dance have been briefly noted:

1. *Poor views of the performance*: bad sight-lines, say, may offer a very skewed view of this performance, and hence of the dance; perhaps (to anticipate) one not adequate for analysis of that dance. Then you are, as it were, in the presence of the dance without seeing it;

2. *Failure of seeing dance*: despite greater visual acuity than yours, parrots cannot really see human actions or events at all;

3. *Failure of concepts*: lacking the concepts to recognize dance of this kind, one cannot make sense of it. To *see* the dance, one must see it *as dance*, and not merely human movement; and as *this* dance;

4. *Not being in the right 'room'*: one is not confronting a performance *of that work*, because some other work (or no dance-work) is being performed (but see Chapter Eleven §5 for a complication: the 'revised situation').

More positively, one's ability to recognize, as well as value, has a conceptual dimension reflecting both what one knows and what one can make sense of ("mobilize in one's experience"). As with one's capacity to make sense of (say) X-ray images, one can learn from radiographers to see the condition of the body, by having those conditions pointed out. Further, the radiographers are also drawing attention to the *relevant* features.

This is broadly the situation when one learns to understand artworks: one learns to see their characteristics — and certain ways are appropriate to doing so (not only one, but not 'anything goes'). For, as Wittgenstein (PO p. 106[6]) reportedly urged:

> *Reasons* ... in Aesthetics are 'of the nature of further descriptions' ... all that Aesthetics does is 'to draw your attention to a thing', to 'place things side by side'. ... in giving 'reasons' of this sort, you make another person 'see what you see' ...

So the idea of *learning to see* identifies the perceptual base of artistic understanding, recognizing the possibility of misperception. It highlights the fact that, try as I might, I may be unable to see a certain artwork in the appropriate way — just as I may be unable to see the young woman depicted in the multiple-figure or unable to see such-and-such in the X-ray plate. Still, once both are well-versed in the appropriate concepts (perhaps we are even Hume's *ideal critics*: Hume [1741], 1985 p. 241), these concerns disappear, since each has the requisite conceptual mastery. Then, ultimately, our concern will reside with the answerability of what one sees or does to the state of the world:

> To take Sid's face to be smeared with food is to see oneself as purely registering how things are; as doing what proper sensitivity, and suitable exposure, to the world makes compulsory ... it is the world that does the forcing ... my attitude would be forced on anyone suitably exposed to, and discerning of, things being the way they are. (Travis, 2011 p. 89: my order)

Not so my disgust at Sid's face: still, that "[d]isgust is not optional *for me*. I am saddled with it by the way *I* am" (Travis, 2011 p. 89). But the difference here is that, in the first case, were my stance correct, "... it is the world that would have to be different for it not to be ..." (Travis, 2011 p. 90). This, in turn, shows the interlock between perception and answerability:

> Perception's *essential* role in the life of a *thinker* is to allow the world to bear, for him, on what he is to think according to what bearing that thinker is aware of on what is so. It thus does such things as allowing the presence of a pig before me to bear, for me, on whether there is a pig there. For it to serve this role requires nothing less than for it to bring the non-conceptual — that which the world provides — within our recognitional (so conceptual) capacities. (Travis, 2013 p. 189)

Moreover, answerability of this sort is fundamental to artistic appreciation.

Further, this perceptualist account locates our *learning to value* in the right place: that too we can be taught, and in more-or-less the same manner — seeing the artworks in their appropriate categories, or genres, cannot be fully separated from valuing those works, for (in understanding the work in its narrative) I will come to see what is valuable about it. So students are being taught how to (appropriately) value; that is, *one learns to value*. All this might be summarized, building on an assumption made explicit above, by saying that I learn to be a competent judge.

The perceptual nature of artistic judgement can be brought out by contrasting this position with that of theorists who appeal to the *imagination* here, appeals usefully seen in relation to the bigger question. My claim to have been looking at some soldiers, rifles, and such like, when I have been looking at Manet's *Execution of Maximillian*, must be distinguished from that made by a time-traveller (or perhaps someone from a museum) who really had *seen* these things — have I only seen them 'in my imagination', or 'imaginatively', or some such? Or I claim I saw Othello murder Desdemona: certainly we do not want to say that I saw one actor murder another. Yet what can we usefully say here? What question would we be addressing? Contrast the view of Frank Palmer (1992 p. 114): "In imagination, I engage with the fictional world of *Othello* of which the murder is only a part". As he goes on to note, the engagement is not a voluntary activity[7] — except insofar as I choose to go to the play. But this "in imagination" is just a place-holder for "we humans do it, I know not how" (plus some remarks about mobilizing concepts in our experience, having learned them, and so on); and this is precisely my point about the lack of a gap between seeing and judging (at least for artistic judgement). Here, Collingwood (1938 p. 147) explains the art critic's use of tactile values as referring "... not of touch sensations, but of motor sensations such as we experience by using our muscles and moving our limbs. But these are not actual motor sensations, they are imaginary motor sensations ...". Later, he applies the idea to painting, such that:

> ... what we get from looking at a picture is not merely the experience of seeing ... certain visible objects; it is also ... the imaginary experience of certain complicated muscular movements. (Collingwood, 1938 p. 147)

Yet such claims precisely concede the issue here, by conceding the point about perceptual answerability: something I *imagine* is precisely not something I see or hear. Hence, not something answerable. Again, the force of the word "imaginatively" when Palmer (1992 p. 219) speaks of artistic judgement as involving "imaginatively projecting" is just to deny certain inferences. As, perhaps, saying that I climbed Mount Everest *in my dream* means both that I did not climb it and that *therefore* there is little point in your asking me about the equipment used or the view from the top. So the appeal here is not to some *faculty* ("imagination") through which (or with which) I engage with artworks but to a *capacity* humans can have (with the right training etc.), the capacity to engage with artworks!

For such reasons, Peter Kivy (1990 p. 42 ff) is rightly critical of "Helen's way", named for the second sister in E. M. Forster's *Howards End*, "... who can see heroes and shipwreck in the music's flood" when listening to Beethoven: as Kivy (1990 p. 53) sees it, this is an attempt "... to 'representationalize' pure instrumental music", although "... there is no end of objects for the fertile imagination to conjure up for music to present" (Kivy, 1990 p. 56). But doing so fails to recognize the music as "... an object of perceptual consciousness" (Kivy, 1990 p. 42). However one takes such cases, an emphasis on one's response to artworks as *imaginative*[8] certainly *seems* to locate the answerability of one's response to that artwork in the wrong place: that one should be attending to the features of the artwork (here, the dance), to what it is like, rather than to one's own thoughts or imaginings about it.[9]

Moreover, it will not be helpful to use the term "imagination" or "imaginative" in some special sense here[10] since what is or is not a product of *imagination* seems shared (and fairly well-understood). If by "imagination" or "imaginative" you do *not* mean imagination or imaginative in some perfectly ordinary sense, your coining (in addition to needing explanation) seems uninformative. And if you use the term as normally, then you owe an explanation of why your responses to an artwork would not be more appropriately based on — and hence answerable to — the features of that artwork, rather than to some imaginative project of yours.

But, first, none of this requires a single response; and, second, one must grant at least three different cases here, previously mentioned:

- because of the differences between "disgusting" and "smeared with food" (see Travis, 2011 pp. 88-89), as above — the first requires more for the perceiver than the second;

- because of contextual factors — what we say when, in responding to what particular problem or perplexity (what question is at issue?);

- because of perceptual factors (what concepts can you bring to bear?).

Thus, when thinking about the accountability that answerability provides, a crucial contrast (as above) is with 'reading something in' to the work, where one's responses would not be accountable. Hence claims about what one *imagines* when faced with a dancework will lack the appropriate answerability. Further, our comments above on 'learning to see' illustrate how, to make more of accountability, one must think about the *cognitive stock* appropriate to one's answerable responses, since perception is concept-mediated. Moreover, how does the causal story for perception acknowledge concepts? As Wollheim (1980 pp. 193-194) recognized, "... what is perceptible is always dependent not only upon such physical factors as the nature of the stimulus, the state of the organism, and the prevailing local conditions, but also on cognitive factors". It is easy to imagine the causal story, once elaborated, dealing with these "physical factors", but much harder to conceptualize its treating the cognitive ones.

Of course, much here remains unclear. Yet having learned to *see* art of a certain type, I may not be inclined to revise my judgement of a particular artwork of that type in the light of later information about that work. And this might be put as my already having a *clear view* of that work. In a language Stanley Cavell (1981 p. 37) prefers, "[c]ompleteness is not a matter of providing *all* interpretations but a matter of seeing one of them *through*". This refers centrally to my explaining my artistic judgement, typically after the fact, in the face of a questioner. As with answering any question, the reply is *complete* when it deals with that precise question, in that context — it does not have to deal with *all* possible questions; not even all that might be asked with that form of words.

§4.   Against psychologism (Frege-plus)

Standardly, Wittgensteinians write against psychologism by referring to Wittgenstein's so-called "Private Language Argument"; but, first, I have reservations about the unity sometimes supposed to produce a single argument (McFee, 2015a pp. 217-270); second, a central argument (there called 'the Popeye-the-Sailor Argument') could arrive at a limited conclusion very quickly, by recognizing the absurdity inherent in Popeye's claim that he can read reading but cannot read writing (what is reading for him must necessarily be writing for someone else!); third, much of the content one needs here is also found in Frege — and, as Frege's supporters are often not co-extensive with Wittgenstein's, this may attract an alternative audience, if by a complex scholarly route.

Today, rejection of psychologism in logic — of the kind that addresses what the utterer intended or meant to characterize a concern with the truth of what is said through some utterance — might first be associated with other thinkers; here it is revealingly located in Frege's work, by sketching his arguments. In rejecting the kinds of psychologism (exemplified by John Stuart Mill) on which logic reflects psychological 'laws' in accordance with which thinking takes place, Frege was by no means unique. But Frege also wished to reject idealism. And, by 1918, earlier strategies in this direction had crystalized into the clarification of the insight that "[a]n utterance is meaningful just in case it can be understood, which means: understood as *saying* something. ... Frege called what is expressed by a sentence a 'thought' ..." (Dummett, 1993 p. 59). Then "thoughts" (*gedanke*) in a non-psychological sense were described as "... something for which the question of truth can arise ... [although] without offering this as a definition" (Frege, 1984 p. 353 [my order]: see Chapter One §7). In elaboration, Frege first sets out the properties of what he calls "ideas" (*vorstellung*), which *are* the proper concern of the psychological, since they are:

> ... part of someone's consciousness: an idea needs an owner (for it to be a particular part of someone's consciousness); no idea can be part of two different thinker's consciousness. (Travis, 2011 pp. 93-94)

Then *ideas* (in this sense):

> ... cannot be seen, or touched or smelled, or tasted, or heard. [Moreover,

when] I go for a walk with a companion ... [and] I see a green field, I thus have a vivid impression of the green. (Frege, 1984 p. 360)

Hence such ideas "... cannot be an object of judgement" (Travis, 2013 p. 226). Thus, as Travis (2011 p. 94) puts it:

Properties of ideas cannot have the sort of systematic, or extensive, import for their behaviour that properties of environmental objects do for theirs, for ideas exist only as a content of consciousness.

Then, for such ideas:

When the word 'red' is meant not to state a property of things but to characterize sense-impressions belonging to my consciousness, it is only applicable within the realm of my consciousness. (Frege, 1984 p. 361)

Further, no amount of *evidence* can reach that conclusion about the state of the world when/if that 'evidence' is regarded as composed of (private) 'ideas' of mine. Hence these cannot generate the kinds of 'ringers' for real cases that seem to generate the argument from illusion: "Locked in an inner world, whether it is a pig or a pig-ringer means nothing to me ..." (Travis, 2013 p. 235).

By contrast, what Frege calls "thoughts" (*gedanke*) have a connection to truth, not least because, in logic, it is *truth* that is distributed by argument. And, for sublunary truths at least, those truths must by answerable to the ways the world is. Thus, "[a] thought always contains something which reaches beyond the particular case ..." (Frege, 1979 p. 174), towards a generality. Hence we can understand the properties of thoughts (really, these are non-psychological) by contrast with those of ideas. (Such *answerability* will be fundamental throughout this work: see below.) And then, when:

I say that the word 'red' was applicable only in the sphere of my consciousness if it was not meant to state a property of things but to characterize some of my own sense-impressions. Therefore [were this true of thoughts, as it is of ideas] the words 'true' and 'false' ... might also be applicable only in the realm of my consciousness, if they were not meant to apply to something of which I was not the owner, but to characterize in some way the content of my consciousness. Truth would then be confined to this content and it would remain doubtful whether anything at all similar occurred in the consciousness of others. (Frege, 1984 p. 362)

Frege (1984 p. 360) is rightly very clear that, for this vivid impression, "... I *have* it, but I do not see it ... ideas are something we *have*" (my emphasis). Again, "[t]hat the sun has risen is not an object emitting rays that reach my eyes" although a claim that the sun had risen is "... recognized to be true on the basis of sense-impressions" (Frege, 1984 p. 354). Although not widely regarded as a *linguistic* philosopher, Frege in fact offers here a clear exemplification in broadly linguistic terms of a fundamental point made later, and adequately (if in linguistic terms), by a philosopher who concerned himself more substantially with language; namely J. L. Austin. In elaborating the visual, Frege contrasted two available objects of perception to demonstrate that laws of thought cannot be "... psychological laws" (Frege, 1984 p. 351): as he put it, one can see *that* the sun has risen (see Frege, 1984 p. 354) — there is a candidate *truth* or *fact* here (namely, *that* the sun is risen). This is what we can *judge*. Then, by contrast, in seeing the sun rising, there is (as yet) no *fact* that one sees:

> That the sun has risen is recognized to be true on the basis of sense-impressions. But being true is not a sensible, perceptible, property. (Frege, 1984 p. 354)

At best, one watches the sun's rising, in ways one cannot watch '*that* the sun has risen': I see *that* the sun has risen only in the sense in which I recognize the truth of the claim. And, notice, just as one cannot watch *that the sun has risen* (but only its rising), neither is '*that the sun has risen*' brief, nor does it go on for a long time. *That* it is rising (unlike its rising) does not form images on our retinas nor look peculiar ways. Of the two forms of words, it is clear which identifies the truth (or falsity): one can judge *that the sun has risen*. So no plausible view could take '*that the sun has risen*' as a possible visual experience; say, a possible object of our perception. For "[t]ruth is not a quality that answers to a particular kind of sense-impression" (Frege, 1984 p. 354).

Moreover, thoughts (as something non-psychological) are independent of us: "... a thought is something impersonal" (Frege, 1979 p. 134). So that:

> The metaphors[11] that underlie the expressions we use when we speak of grasping a thought, of conceiving, laying hold of, seizing, understanding ... put the matter in essentially the right perspective. What is grasped, taken hold of, is already there and does not come into existence as a result of these activities. (Frege, 1979 p. 137)

One danger here arises, for Frege (1984 p. 363), because, if thoughts are "... neither things in the external world nor ideas", this seems to lead directly to the postulation of some third Realm[12] (see Dummett, 1993 pp. 99-109[13]). For, one might think, where else can thoughts reside? Frege's 'myth' of the third Realm here may treat 'the thought' as though it were an independent entity, in the idea of grasping *the thought*; thereby reifying the thought, and leading to the Platonism of this third-Realm-type idea, which I shall reject.

It might seem that one could move forward by defining "truth". But, as Frege (1979 p. 128) notes, such a strategy cannot be usefully employed here — as he says:

If, for example, we wished to say 'an idea is true if it agrees with reality' nothing would be achieved since, in order to apply this definition, we should have to decide whether some idea or other did agree with reality. Thus we should have to presuppose the very thing that is being defined.

Rather, "[t]he meaning of the word 'true' is spelled out in the laws of truth" (Frege, 1984 p. 352) — but how are these discerned? Again, the 'third-realm' Platonism beckons.

But one need not go so far: one might consider first the contrasts Frege applies negatively, to show what thoughts are *not*. That might be adopted independently of the Platonism. And *here* Frege recognizes that, unlike ideas, thoughts must be public. Thus he dismisses as "ludicrous" the suggestion of two people disputing the genuineness of 100-mark note, "where each meant the one he himself had in his pocket and understood the word 'genuine' in his own particular sense" (Frege, 1984 p. 363). Here Frege in effect embraces directly what, above, I called the "Popeye-the-Sailor Argument" (McFee, 2015a p. 220-221), for Popeye urges on one occasion: "I can read reading but I can't read writing" — an obvious self-contradiction since what is *writing* for someone must be *reading* for someone else! No, what is available to any must be available to more than just that one, at least in principle. For, again, "[t]ruth is not a quality that answers to a particular kind of sense-impression" (Frege, 1984 p. 354).

What here is *visual*? What did I see? As Travis (2013 p. 241) notes, Frege rightly takes "[p]erception's role ... [as] to provide awareness of particular cases". For some of the truths are not *seen*. Austin (1962 pp. 98-99), recognizing a similar point, draws a contrast here:

> Suppose you ask me 'What did you see this morning?'. I might answer, 'I saw a man shaved in Oxford.' Or again I might say, no less correctly and referring to the same occasion, 'I saw a man born in Jerusalem'. Does it follow that I must be using 'see' in different senses? Of course not ... two things are true of the man I saw — (a) that he was being shaved in Oxford, and (b) that he had been born some years earlier in Jerusalem. And I can certainly allude to either of these facts about him by saying — in *no* way ambiguously — that I saw him. Or, if there *is* ambiguity here, it is not the word 'saw' that is ambiguous.

Saying "I saw him" can refer to either fact: I saw the man being shaved; so I saw *that* he was shaved in Oxford, because I saw his being shaved. But, while I saw a man born in Jerusalem, I did not see him *being* born: hence, while I did not see that he was born in Jerusalem, in seeing him, I did see a man born in Jerusalem! As Austin (1962 p. 99) continues:

> Which way of saying what I see I actually choose will depend on the

particular circumstances of the case — for instance, on what sort of answer I expect you to be interested in, on how much I know, or on how far I am prepared to stick my neck out.

For the point, of course, is that many ways of describing what I see "... may all be correct and therefore compatible" (Austin, 1962 pp. 97-98); moreover, sometimes:

> When something is seen, there may not only be different ways of *saying* what is seen; it may also be seen *in different ways*, seen *differently*. (Austin, 1962 p. 100)

As we saw (§1 above), we require someone able to make such discriminations: hence, for instance, an *informed spectator* of trees, able to see *these* trees (as opposed to just *trees*), where that typically reflects an interest on his part — his interest leads him to this knowledge of trees (this "cognitive stock" [Wollheim, 1980 p. 173] in respect of them) that permits him to see the world of trees *differently*. But *what* he sees is still answerable to how the world is: that there are indeed *trees* of these different kinds; and here one can *misperceive* a tree by taking to be an oak what is in fact an elm.

Here, we saw previously that typical cases exploit the informed perception of the art critic, where the alternatives would count as misperceiving the artworks in question by not recognizing their atonal or cubist character. And, while such misperception of art cannot be distinguished exceptionlessly, answerability will involve human capacities; and be to the non-misperception case in any cases where *misperception* is granted.

§5.   Respect for answerability

Some recent philosophers have tried to undermine the 'personal' character of *answerability*, by undermining the boundary between philosophy and science. For instance, Quine (1960 p. 235) certainly aimed to blur that boundary,[14] declaring that the:

> ... relevance of sensory stimulation to sentences about physical objects can as well (and better) be explored and explained in terms directly of the conditioning of such sentences and their parts to physical irritations of the subject's surfaces.

For, as he put it later:

> Why all this creative reconstruction, all this make-believe? The stimulation of his sensory receptors is all the evidence anyone has to go on, ultimately, in arriving at his picture of the world. Why not just see how this construction really proceeds? (Quine, 1969 p. 75)

And how would it proceed? In summary, and showing where it would end, Quine (1969 p. 75) asks: "Why not settle for psychology?". For Quine (1987 p. 5):

> In psychology, one may or may not be a behaviourist, but in linguistics one has no choice. Each of us learns his language by observing other people's verbal behaviour and by having his own faltering verbal behaviour observed and reinforced or corrected by others. We depend strictly on overt behaviour in observable situations.

Here, this 'settling for psychology' raises two fundamental questions: first, would such a strategy leave anything left *as philosophy?* The answer is "no": that thought is behind our rejection of 'empirical philosophy' (see "Preamble" §5). Second, can such a strategy succeed in giving us truths? Travis (2011 p. 92) rightly questions Quine's claim that "[o]bserving speakers of an unlearned language, ... [one could] not observe, say, that someone is complaining over spilled beer, or asking someone to leave"; concluding that, when asked, 'Why?', "Quine does not say" (Travis, 2011 p. 92). But Quine is clear that such concepts apply to more than he counts as *his* stopping point: that is, as what he calls *behaviour* — "roughly, bodily movements and emissions" (Travis, 2011 p. 92). Quine here appeals to the familiar empiricist doctrine that no data could rule-out all *mis-readings* of such cases. As with the argument from illusion, "... whatever evidence there *is* for science *is* sensory evidence" (Quine, 1969 p. 75[15]); and all that 'evidence' might be compatible, on some occasion, with something else (other than, say, beer spilling) taking place. So the dispute cannot be recognized as over *spilled beer*; or anything comparably sublunary.

Hence (to revert to Travis's example), "[f]or Quine, it is not a fact that 'renarde' means vixen" (Travis, 2011 p. 93)), since there are no such *facts* here. Then, if Quine begins to insist that we humans prefer some 'translation manuals' to others, he in effect concedes that point: for these are "... mere facts about human predilections and preferences" (Travis, 2011 p. 93), the kinds of purely causal stories set aside above. What was required here was *correctness*; that in turn requires the answerability of our claims to the sublunary world. Austin (1962 p. 130 note), recognizing this point, applied it directly to sense-data:

> To stipulate that a sense-datum just is whatever the speaker takes it to be ... is to make non-mendacious sense-datum statements true by *fiat*; and if so, how could sense-data be, as they are supposed to be, non-linguistic entities, *of* which we are aware, *to* which we refer, that against which the factual truth of all empirical statements is to be tested?

So that a coherent account of knowledge requires that our stances to sublunary facts be answerable in ways that claims about ideas or sense-data could not be. And Quine (1953 p. 43) at least recognized this as an issue: thus he writes:

> Any statement can be held true come what may, if we make enough adjustments elsewhere in the system. Every statement very close to the periphery can be held true in the face of recalcitrant experience by pleading hallucination or by amending certain statements of the kind called logical laws.

Hence, as far as experience goes, any claim might be true, depending on what one supposes of other claims. But, were that the case, what could our experiences be *of*? How could there be any answerability, if any claim can bear on the truth of *anything*? Indeed, how could it so *bear*, unless it is secure (at least temporarily)? And how could any such claim be "recalcitrant"? For to accept that such claims might be true no matter what, since other claims can always be modified, is to have "... already stripped experience of any substance" (Travis, 2011 p. 103). So something in this picture is clearly mistaken or misleading.

§6.   Answerability of bodily position

One potential 'power' of dancers, as well as observers of dance, can become contentious when turning to dance aesthetics: that concerning a so-called "kinaesthetic sense", offering knowledge of the position of one's body-parts. Here again the primary issue concerns answerability: to what are claims to know the position of dancers' limbs (and so on) *answerable*? This issue arises both applied to the audience and the dancers (and see Chapters Nine & Ten). For both, a distinctive mode of access, or sensory modality, has been postulated; but I shall urge that both postulations must be rejected.

To acknowledge my debt to Anscombe here, while making this powerful point relatively succinctly, consider again (UD pp. 264-273) her compelling demonstration that our knowing the position of our limbs (to the degree that we do) neither involves nor requires a sensory modality. As Anscombe (1981b p. 71) urged:

> ... if ever one did have to use the feelings of resistance on the upper leg and pressure on the lower leg as clues going by which one judged that one's legs were crossed, one would also need assurance that the sensations of pressure, weight, and the resistance were produced in one leg by the other, and not by some quite different bodies. *Ex hypothesi*, knowledge of the position of one's legs could not itself supply that assurance.

For clearly, *were* such an assurance required, it could never be provided in this way. Hence one should conclude both that such a model of 'assurance' is misconceived, and so that the corresponding picture of one's knowledge of one's own body was mistaken.[16]

Of course, that argument does not imply that, somehow, the positions of our limbs *escape* us. In a related discussion, Hanna Pickard (2004 p. 228) reports the case of Ian Waterman, who:

> ... suffers from a unique form of neuropathy: ... a virus briefly damaged most of his sensory fibres but none of his motor nerves. As a result, he lacks virtually all feeling in, and awareness from the inside of, his body: he is 'body blind'. [At first] Waterman ... was effectively paralyzed despite the continued functioning of his motor nerves. But ... he has managed to learn to control his movements using vision. If he looks down at his body, constantly and assiduously monitoring it through vision, he can guide his movements in this way.

In the case as described, the expression "virtually all feeling in, and awareness from the inside of, his body" is ambiguous between a reading simply noting that he lacks a power or capacity the rest of us have (so treating his description metaphorically), and one that ascribes to the rest of us this very specific "feeling & awareness" package — that is, which imagines that something more could be said in elaboration. But one need not take that further step. Further, the term "body-blind" (apparently) begs the question, by comparing that set of powers and capacities with sight (and hence with its lack, blindness); here too the term "body-blind" might simply characterize the condition, without making the further step involved in trying to cash out the trope.

Pickard (2004 p. 228) describes Waterman as "... a living counter-example to the claim that bodily awareness is what sustains one's knowledge of what one is doing over time". Certainly, on *one* reading, this case supports my view that, typically, one just knows where the parts of one's body are (with some of the prerequisites, or mechanisms, for this knowledge depending on what Waterman damaged). Then this 'knowledge' could be augmented, should it need to become very precise (as in a dancer's leg position), in exactly the way it is augmented in the dance studio — through the mirrors! And the movement itself can be trained; so, although dancers speak of the leg's position *feeling* right, that just offers a characterization of the result of such training. For, however the position of the leg *feels*, its actual position determines whether the dancer correctly performs that movement.

This should be recognized here as something we humans can typically do, by noting the case where it fails: if we then ask, 'How do we do it?", there is no answer at the level of human agency – this is something we agents can typically do! Then pressing for some explanation of *how* we do it is attempting to go "further back" (OC §471) than the beginning of the story. Of course, questions remain here: an important one will be how we *learn* to do this, both at a minimal level (shared by most humans) and at a high level achieved by, among others, dancers and sportsplayers. Here, the answer reflects familiar learning-occasions. A different question might ask for the causal story: how does our body function when we do these things? But, again, that is not strictly a question for the agent — to develop our capacities here makes us revisit the question of learning (and the importance of *practice*: see Syed, 2010). Rather, I do not typically know the causal story for how I did that thing; that is the sort of thing that might be discovered by observation, either of me or of various bodily features or characteristics of mine — with the emphasis on the 'bodily'.

Anscombe's arguments here derive from Wittgenstein. Thus, as Malcolm (1984 p. 42 [four following quotations][17]) records, Wittgenstein urged that:

> In order to move my arm voluntarily I must know what position it is in and whether I have moved it. Now how do I know what the position of my hand is, when I am not looking at it or feeling it with the other hand? How do I know, e.g., that my fingers are bent? There is a temptation to say 'I feel they are bent.' This is a peculiar reply. For do you always have a certain feeling when your fingers are bent in that way; have you always noticed that feeling; and what feeling it is?

Wittgenstein's point is precisely that there is no single and distinctive (much less unique) feeling here: after all, do I *always* pay attention to the feeling in the hand? Obviously not. And yet that does not hinder my ability to act. We see the point more sharply if we try to be more precise about this supposed feeling:

> The feeling that my fingers are bent: is it subject to more and less, to degrees, as are feelings of temperature and pressure? No. This may [NB "may"] show that 'I feel that my fingers are bent' means nothing different from 'I know that they are bent.' If we try to say what feelings of temperature, pressure, etc. go to make up this feeling that my fingers are bent, we shall see that it is not easy to say what they are, and furthermore we see that we rarely have them. [NB "we" here is typical people – dancers may be different.]

Wittgenstein also recognizes the impact of imagining the case where I cannot feel my hand — where my hand is anaesthetized, say: then, at least typically, I would not be able to move it nor to locate it in space. That the *absence* of feeling has this result, might tempt someone to conclude that therefore it was the *feeling* that provided this 'information'.

> There could be cases in which I knew the position of my hand by a certain feeling. It may also be true that if my hand were anaesthetized I should *not*

know its position. But from this it does not follow that I normally know the position of my hand by certain sensations.

Why is that? Wittgenstein's answer is clear:

> The question, "How do I know my fingers are bent?" is just like the question, "How do I know where my pain is?" I do not need to be shown where my pain is. My pointing gesture and verbal description *locates* the pain. Likewise I do not need to find out the posture of my body.

Moreover, whatever one thinks of the general cases, the danceworld surely cannot take the view that one can reliably locate one's bodily positions through how it feels to one, since dance studios are filled with (expensive) mirrors precisely to allow the dancers to adjust where, say, the leg is in arabesque by looking in the mirror! The aim, of course, is to train oneself to act in certain ways: to build up that 'muscle-memory' (PAD pp. 200-204) that means one can strike certain positions or do certain actions without having to think about them. But even experienced dancers know that the final arbiter of whether the leg is in the correct position is *how it looks*, where that means "looks to an observer", even when that observer is the dancer herself! The perception here is fundamentally visual.

So, for me, no *additional* sensory modality is required: instead, the mechanisms of 'ordinary' perception are sufficient here, once properly understood. This requires a richer reading of the objects of perception than is sometimes adopted. So my interest in, say, perception here lies in the human capacity to recognize and enjoy dances. Nothing more is needed, especially once the point is expressed as concerning powers and capacities rather than *senses*. Thus, appeals to the sense of direction or the sense of humour are just familiar invocations of human powers and capacities, rather than sensory modalities. Such cases involve the senses, but invoke no *distinctive* sensory modality: talk of "a sense of X" lacks that implication — thus, we *see* the amusing slapstick; we *hear* the one-liner; we *read* the comic novel [a special case]; just as we *notice*, however subliminally, whatever landmarks permit the sense of direction. Further, in each case, appeal is to a complex package of powers and capacities of humans. But there is no *sense*, no sensory modality. Then, in invoking a sense to explain the location of bodily motion, we depend here heavily on *seeing* the position (in space) of our bodies, both to correct ourselves and to receive correction from others — hence the mirrors in typical dance studios! When they conflict, this takes precedence over any (supposed) kinaesthetic evidence.

In fact, my argument is directed not only against the idea of a kinaesthetic sense in terms of which one knows the position of the parts of one's body but also, more importantly, against the possible *use* of such a sense (were there one) in the appreciation of artworks. Negatively, the upshot of our insight-bearing slogan from Frege ([1918] 1984 p. 351) is exactly that the same causal mechanisms and the same sensory modality must apply to someone (say, some critic) *misunderstanding* the dancework under consideration as when that critic *understands* it. Therefore, insofar as what *is* at issue is whether our critic's judgement is correct, disputes over the sensory modality at work are beside the point — both claims must be *answerable* to the details of the dancework; and justifiably offer the audience a way to make sense of that dancework (and hence a way to *see* it). Positively, we recognize that the capacity to make, and to make sense of, dances is something to be learned; that the passage of time, as well as cultural changes, mean that different features are recognized by informed perception at different times, and valued differentially. It is this aspect that permits us to see criticism as a *rational* process, whatever its causal story. Hence even if a *kinaesthetic sense* were granted, it could not bear on the artistic appreciation of either audience or dancers.

§7.   Conclusion

This chapter has explored some features of the answerability of our judgements of artworks concluding with a discussion of arguments fundamental to a realistic analysis of the answerability of some judgements claimed in the philosophical aesthetics of dance: namely, those claiming to deploy a *kinaesthetic* sense, or something similar. Such judgements recur, in concrete form, in Chapter Ten. Here, some more general and abstract considerations have been raised: the public character of the judgements of sense has been stressed by deploying some arguments from Frege. Then judgements of art (such as those made for danceworks) might *seem* subjective in a dismissive way. But we have seen that this is not so: while there are differences here, many judgements where diversity of view is possible are nevertheless answerable to the sublunary world. In recognizing this, we are locating a general account of perception as concept-mediated within a distinction between those cases where agreement among perceivers is typically possible (say, colour-judgements), despite the acknowledged fact of colour-blindness — such cases can be resolved; and *misperception* thereby avoided. At the least, "it looked green to me" is no defence, when charged with 'running a red traffic-signal'! Again, the reality of taste does deny that there are real disputes about, say, whether the state of Sid's face — acknowledged as smeared with food — is thereby disgusting. So such differences will be enduring; but a place must be found for disagreements resolved:

(a) by closer attention, when I point out features you have missed, or seen another way;

(b) by 'learning to see', as one might learn to master certain concepts that permit one to make sense of X-ray photographs;

(c) by 'learning to value', where one comes to see certain features as valuable, perhaps under the influence of a perceptive critic (see also Chapter Nine §§4-7);

(d) by becoming able to mobilize (in one's experience of the artwork) the critical concepts learned.

Throughout, the need for human powers and capacities was stressed: *misperception* of artworks remains a live possibility just because the artworks are meaning-bearing objects; hence normatively-structured. And so, as elsewhere, we are true to our slogan from Frege ([1918] 1984 p. 351): that "[e]rror and superstition have causes just as much as correct cognition". Or, as we expressed it above, in context, that the same causal mechanisms and the same sensory modality must apply to someone (say, some critic) *misunderstanding* the dancework under consideration as when that critic *understands* it.

In particular, the possibility of 'ringers' — objects mistakeable for, say, a pig — recognizes a contextual element in perceptual claims: but such cases can typically be resolved by closer attention, or by distinguishing actually seeing/ hearing something from mere *evidence* of doing so. Moreover, the similarity of such cases to 'confusable counterpart' objects in aesthetics warns us against treating perception in too narrow a fashion, as many empiricists have.

Chapter Nine
Crossing the footlights (1):
defusing dualism and the 'dancer's aesthetic'

§1. Introduction

This chapter and the next concern, roughly, the contribution of empirical studies in neuroscience to our understanding of dance: in particular, responding to criticisms of my account. Can *anything* acknowledged as relatively uncontentious be sketched here? All sides agree that care is needed. Thus, Carroll & Seeley (2013 p. 184b note) extract from David Davies the "sage advice" that:

> ... philosophers of art [should] be circumspect in their search for support from behavioral sciences – to pay careful attention to the scope of experimental studies, to be wary of reckless generalizations, and to tread gingerly in domains where the interpretation of experimental results is itself controversial.

Davies (2013 p. 199a) himself comments that:

> As long as philosophical reflection on the arts [or elsewhere] requires some empirical foundation, it should be furnished by the best available theories in relevant branches of empirical enquiry.

From this he draws a sensible conclusion:

> ... this means we should not avail ourselves of a particular scientific view without taking account of the critical discourse within the relevant branch of science. (Davies, 2013 p. 199a)

[Some material regularly deployed may not meet these standards; Davies sometimes seems to share these worries: see Chapter Ten §8.]

However, philosophical criticisms of the assumptions of some neuro-scientists and/or the expression of their conclusions rightly emphasize the need to ensure that the language used by neuroscience is *neuroscience* language, and not 'human being' language. For example, the 'merelogical fallacy' (see Chapter Four §9), whereby properties of persons are ascribed to brains (and parts of brains, such as neurons), must be avoided. Equally, much neuroscience retains the dualistic picture of the mind that was widespread when cognitive neuroscience was galvanized by comparatively recent studies of brain activity; or, if such a picture is replaced, the replacement is some identity theory. Both these views, having been refuted as philosophical positions, must not be re-introduced via this 'back door'. So mistaken accounts of what is *said* in applying the neuroscience to dance must be avoided. As Austin (1962 p. 91) points out, it will be permissible "... to cut down verbiage ... [to] use in one situation words appropriate to another; and no problem arises provided the circumstances are known". The dangers arise when the different circumstances are not recognized; or, more likely, where the impact of those differences is not acknowledged. There will always be a causal story, as our slogan from Frege reminds us. Hence, in context, not all such stories are equally helpful. For instance, loose talk permits what is *said* as neuroscience to become more dubious when applied to, say, philosophy of mind, leading some to embrace (if somewhat subliminally) various destructive kinds of dualism. But what is wrong with urging, say, *muscular sympathy* to explain the 'dancers' appreciation of an observed dancework? Offering "... a condensed and simplified outline" of an answer, Best (1999 p. 133) notes that, on dualistic conceptions:

> ... just as, for example, fear-behaviour is supposed to be the external manifestation of the 'inner' mental/emotional feeling of fear, so language is supposed to be an external symbol of the 'inner' mental thoughts, ideas, conceptions which give linguistic terms their meaning.

Similar points apply for the meaning of dance. Like the traditional 'Other Minds' problem, the issues involve making sense of the psychological by referring to our physical structures — building up correlations between this and that: say, 'mind states' and brain states; or meanings and dance movements; or symbols and what is symbolized (see Best, 1978 pp. 124-142).

Instead, remarks reflecting choreographer's *intentions* (or something similar) must be recognized as referring to human intentions as *embodied-in-the-performed-works*: contemporary theorists have set aside the conception of intention as prior planning, 'in the head' of the artist, at best causally connected to the artwork itself (PAD pp. 125-126; UD pp. 230-231). One does not interrogate the choreographer's psyche, but rather looks to the dance itself, properly understood. For only a misconceived account of the relation of intention to art separates that intention from the artwork.

Such misconceptions readily generate dualism of (roughly) mind and body. Thus, Collingwood (1938 p. 147) attempts to explain the art critic's use of tactile values as references "... not of touch sensations, but of motor sensations such as we experience by using our muscles and moving our limbs". But, as he continues:

> ... these are not actual motor sensations, they are imaginary motor sensations ... what we get from looking at a picture is not merely the experience of seeing ... certain visible objects; it is also ... the imaginary

experience of certain complicated muscular movements. (Collingwood, 1938 p. 147)

Such a characterization, applied to dance appreciation, raises three issues. First, are we confident in the move here from "... the experience [had] by using our muscles and moving our limbs", to our somehow getting those experiences from observing, say, a painting? As Collingwood at least saw, deploying such an idea literally makes no sense: instead, these are just "imaginary motor sensations". Still, for our art appreciator, that again raises the issue of *answerability* — when is this *imaginary* motor sensation actually the appropriate one? To put that in another way (see §2 below), to what in the sublunary world is our claim here *answerable*? (Roughly, what makes it true, when it is?) Again, appeal cannot be to what the artist *actually did* to create that texture — his causal story is certainly not available to us directly. Or, rather, the relevant causal story is available to us only *through* the artwork! Then talk of "imagining" here must be confusing: we *see* the marks on the canvas, and seeing them permits recognition of just those tactile properties to which Collingwood's critic refers.

Second, the situation might be different if, in general, our awareness of our own bodily movements (say, the position of our limbs) involved this experience of 'motor sensation'. Having recycled Anscombe's argument against *that* possibility (see Chapter Eight §6), I regard the capacity to know the position of one's limbs as a typical power or capacity of typical persons. Granting agents such powers concedes that people typically do not do these things *by* doing anything else. There need be nothing I *do* to give me knowledge of the position my limbs, as this is not typically evidential (from my point of view). In particular, acknowledging Anscombe's conclusion should lead to our rejecting the suggestion that a *sensory modality* grounds our capacity to recognize or to understand our bodily posture (to the degree that we do).

Yet, third, suppose I were mistaken about this, as applied to the position of *my* limbs. Even its advocates recognize that such a 'kinaesthetic sense' is not a *projective* sensory modality like sight or hearing (UD p. 267). Then one reaches my conclusion by granting that only projective sensory modalities could provide audience-style access to typical artworks. And standard dances (ballets, modern dances, etc.) count as typical artworks for these purposes. As above, Collingwood (1938 p. 147) takes the process he describes to involve *imagination* rather than perception: "the *imaginary* experience of certain complicated muscular movements" [my emphasis]. So, while I differ with him about one's *own* case, that dispute need not carry over to audience perspectives: he recruits imagination rather than perception. Hence no 'sixth sense' is postulated.

Why might one insist that projective sensory modalities are required here?

The reply lies in *answerablity* to the artwork: our critic's claims, say, must be true of the artwork — as Beardsley (1970 p. 33) remarked, one must be "a poem-reader, not a mind-reader". Thomas Reid ([1815] 2002 pp. 573-574) put the point eloquently (for music):

> When a beautiful object is before us, we may distinguish the agreeable emotion it produces in us, from the quality of the object that causes the emotion. When I hear an air in music that pleases me, I say, it is fine, it is excellent. This excellence is not in me; it is in the music.

And later "... the name of beauty belongs to this excellence of the object, and not to the feelings of the spectator" (Reid [1815] 2002 p. 595). For whatever is claimed about the poem or the music, or equally the dance, must be true *of that artwork*. Thus critical commentary must be answerable to the *features* of the dance. That, of course, contrasts with any features I *imagine* of the dance (or the poem): critics are prohibited from 'reading in' to the dance (or poem) something that is not *there*. That would not be criticism *of the dance*.

Further, as above, only a misconceived account of the relation of intention to art separates that intention from the artwork: instead, one needs an account "... not stopping short of, but terminating on, the work of art itself" (Wollheim, 1980 p. 185). For example, Carroll (2001 p. 91) urges that Isadora Duncan "... was able to solve the problem of the stagnation of theatrical dance by repudiating the central features of the dominant ballet and by reimagining an earlier ideal of dance" (also quoted PAD p. 19). This could only happen both at a particular moment, and with dance in a particular state ("stagnation"). But what was possible when? In particular, what can be intended at a particular time?

To approach such questions, consider briefly Danto (1987) discussion of the art-status (or otherwise) a three-hole 'outdoor' toilet-seat decorated by de Kooning in a style "... reminiscent of the style used by Jackson Pollock" (quoted Danto, 1987 p. 59). In 1947, the visual effect of thrown and dripped paint might have seemed controversial: Danto (1987 p. 59) recalls Jackson Pollock demanding that Lee Krasner confirm that his works were indeed *paintings*. But that was no longer an issue by 1954, when the three-seater was painted; the techniques Pollock used were recognizably ways to make art. So the look of the three-seater *resembled* that of paintings.

Yet this alone is insufficient to guarantee its art-status. For what could, or could not, be intended *as art* in a particular period is circumscribed: as Wölfflin (1950 p. ix) acknowledged, "[n]ot everything is possible at every time". Further, as Danto (1987 p. 60) recognizes, the question *But is it art?* "... cannot be asked of isolated objects". Rather, there is "... an implicit generalisation in the question" (Danto, 1987 p. 60). Of course, by then the Duchamp *Fountain* was recognized as a Ready-made, one of the class of "...

commonplace objects transfigured into works of art" (Danto, 1987 p. 60). And, as Danto notes, getting *one* work of a *kind* (such as this) into the artistic canon in effect licences the production of that kind (here, Ready-mades) as a legitimate way to intend to make artworks — although (of course) many will be *unpromising* artworks! In thus preparing the *place* for (further) Ready-mades, Duchamp established the power of the argument-form, "It is art *because* it is a Ready-made". By that time, the *kinds* of reasons potentially deployed there were recognized as *candidate* reasons for art-status. Such reasons offer features to which critical claims would be *answerable* — whether they were *good* reasons in any particular example could then be explored case-by-case.

But, in this case, Danto (1987 p. 61) rightly concludes (a) that "... this particular object can be a work of art only if it is a de Kooning"; but (b) "... there is no way it can be that" (Danto, 1987 p. 61). For, to reiterate, "[n]ot everything is possible at every time" (Wölfflin, 1950 p. ix). And, at that time, "... there is no space in his [de Kooning's] corpus for an object of 1954 like this" (Danto, 1987 p. 61): this was not *an art-making process* that *de Kooning* could have used then. Hence it cannot be a de Kooning, and therefore is not an artwork.

Acceptance of the three-seater as art would require substantial re-writing of de Kooning's corpus, and the trajectory of his art. The sorts of *huge* changes in the future of art required to permit de Kooning, in 1954, to create something *precursive* of, say, Jasper Johns (or whomsoever) are not *unimaginable* — although we think these changes in our understanding unlikely. Either way, we see how the state of the art world at the time may constrain critical commentary, and one's possible fulfilled intentions, thereby reinstating our view of the place of intention in art appreciation: the artist's fulfilled intentions connect with what suitably positioned, suitably informed, and suitably sensitive spectators see in the work, with the "suitably" locating the critical moment in its history. For, in a painting:

> ... if we take any particular painted surface, it is always possible that suitably sensitive, although insufficiently informed, spectators will be able to see different things in it. (Wollheim, 1995 p. 34)

But such disagreements must be resolvable (at least in principle) for the ascription of meaning to the painting to make sense: that is, the bulwark of answerability is deployed against this incipient subjectivism. For, "... of those things which the spectator can see in the painting, it is correct for him to see only ... those things which the artist intended" (Wollheim, 1995 p. 34[1]), as long as one focuses on *fulfilled intentions*. After all, the artist *is* (sometimes) rightly seen as a spectator of his own work.[2] So, as Wollheim summarizes a key thesis from his *Painting as an Art*,[3] "... the meaning of a painting combines what a sensitive spectator can see in it and what the artist intended it to convey" (Wollheim, 1995 p. 36). And, of course, the same would be true *mutatis mutandis* for the meaning-bearing aspect of other artforms. Moreover, both elements — artist's intention and suitable spectator — involve, in different ways, "the artist's perspective".[4] In the case of intention, it is explicit; for the spectator, it involves being *suitably* informed: for instance, as to the narrative of art history.

§2.　Answerability again (for art)

Artistic judgement — that is, judgement appropriate to the appreciation of artworks *as artworks* — has, at least, a perceptual *base* (as we recognized: Chapter Eight §§2-3): critical remarks about a painting or dance would rightly be dismissed if not based on seeing that painting or dance (at best, this would just be my repeating someone else's judgement). First, taking the object to be *a work of art* requires *artistic* judgement *rather than* (mere) aesthetic judgement, in terms of the distinction drawn previously (PAD pp. 12-20) — this possibility involves, at the least, both the object's having been intended as art and its meaning-bearing character. Second, and relatedly, artistic judgement involves seeing works in the appropriate *category of art* (Walton, 2008); categories both supplying the concepts through which the perception is mediated, and importing the contrast between standard, non-standard and irrelevant properties for artworks of that kind. Third, reference to *categories of art* implies that, in artistic judgement, the artwork in question is located in its appropriate history or tradition: what Carroll (2001 pp. 83-95) calls a "narrative", since there might be competing ones. Fourth, as just noticed, the judgements one can make centrally depend on what one can *see* in the work — as we might say, what one has learned to see. Fifth, there is an essentially affective element in artistic judgement:

> To describe something in artistic terms *is to describe it*; but it is to savour it at the same time: to run it over your tongue and lick your lips; to 'investigate' its pleasurable possibilities. (Kivy, 1975 p. 210[5])

So we need not deny the essential sensuousness of artistic appreciation.

　　Then sketching dance-appreciation can begin by reiterating our simple *Principle* (Chapter Eight §1): namely, that *critical appreciation of a dance is answerable to features of that dance*. Then, if a critic wants to claim such-and-such about some dancework, that claim must depend on the features of the dancework. So that one's criticism (and any other commentary on the dance) will be correct or nor according to *the way things are*. In particular, one's critical commentary must be evaluable in this way to avoid the charge of 'reading into' the dancework something not there. And discerning 'the way things are' will be a perceptual matter — here, a matter of 'looking and seeing'. For "[s]ight affords awareness of some of what is there, or there happening" (Travis, 2013 p. 179). Moreover, Travis (2013 p. 189) acknowledges the connection between the conceptual and the perceptual, such that with "... an ability to recognize a pig at sight, say ... One sees, and recognizes, the nuances of something being a pig". Thus sufficient mastery of the concept "pig" is required to mobilize it in my perception. Hence the contribution from one's conceptual mastery can often be developed: one can *learn to see*, just as the radiologist, having learned to discern in the X-ray the condition of the internal organs, can sometimes train others to do so, by encouraging them to view the characteristics of the X-ray plate in a certain fashion. Here, learning to 'read' the X-ray plates appropriately, or to understand them, becomes just a matter of *looking* at them — a perceptual matter rather than an inferential one (see also Chapter Five §7).

This repeats fairly exactly the situation of one's learning to understand artworks: one learns to *recognize* their characteristics — and certain ways of doing so are appropriate (not only one, but not 'anything goes'). Moreover, noting the possibility of misperception makes answerability of this sort fundamental to artistic appreciation. And highlights the fact that, despite my best efforts, I may be unable to see a certain artwork in the appropriate way — just as I may be unable to see the young woman depicted in the multiple-figure or unable to see such-and-such in the X-ray plate. Further, Wollheim (1993a p. 142) rightly urges, "... perception of the arts *is* ... the process of understanding the work of art". In addition, this perceptualist account finds the right place for our *learning to value* (see Chapter Eight §3): in understanding the artwork in its narrative, one comes to see what is valuable about it. So, through art criticism, students are taught how to (appropriately) value such works.

Moreover, as we saw, the accountability provided by answerability contrasts crucially with 'reading something into' the work, where one's responses would not be accountable. Since perception is concept-mediated, making more of accountability requires thinking again about the *cognitive stock* appropriate to one's answerable responses. For "... what is perceptible is always dependent not only upon such physical factors as the nature of the stimulus, the state of the organism, and the prevailing local conditions, but also on cognitive factors" (Wollheim, 1980 pp. 193-194). Then the causal story for perception must acknowledge the role of such *conceptual stock*. As noted before, it is unclear how the elaborated causal story that seems so suitable to explain these "physical factors" will treat cognitive ones satisfactorily (although perhaps some of the enthusiasm for neuroscientific explanation comes — mistakenly — from here).

So emphasizing answerability here means that we are appealing not to some *faculty* ("imagination") through which (or with which) I engage with artworks but to a *capacity* humans can have (with the right training, etc.), the capacity to engage with artworks! The misplaced appeal to the *imagination* brings out, through the contrast, the *perceptual* nature of artistic judgement: as in Chapter Eight §3, what I have only seen 'in my imagination', or 'imaginatively', or some such, I have not actually *seen*. Thus, when Palmer (1992 p. 219) speaks of artistic judgement as involving "imaginatively projecting", the force of the word "imaginatively" here is just to deny certain inferences: to imagine climbing Mount Everest, or to say that I climbed Mount Everest *in my imagination*, means both that I did *not* climb it and that *therefore* there is little point in your asking me about the equipment used or the view from the top. Hence claims to *imagine* such-and-such (compare Carroll & Seeley, 2013: Chapter Ten §2) must lack the appropriate answerability.

§3.   What crosses the footlights?

Asking 'what crosses the footlights?' is a figurative way to introduce the encounter between the audience and the dancework: obviously, there are not always actual footlights at dance performances. As a sketch, consider three or four candidate answers, in terms of increasing complexity.

My preferred answer to the question 'what crosses the footlights?' is the simplest: only light and sound — projective sensory modalities = light and hearing (setting aside smell = sweating, and such like). As we will see (Chapter Ten §2), this answer sometimes seems endorsed by Carroll & Seeley (2013), in their role as representatives of "neuroscience" — they *seem* to agree that blindfolding audience-members leaves them without access to the dance, while disputing what this shows or permits. Now, there *will* be a causal story for any interaction, whatever answer is offered to our key question; so, by itself, locating that causal story is of limited utility. Hence the right reply cannot stress *a matter of complexity* or *levels of response* — what is answerable will be answerable to all.

Of course, since no "complete description" of the dance performance can capture all its features (or all those relevant to its appreciation) — as such features do not constitute a finite totality — more may always be said; although, in the absence of a specific motive to expand my comments, I may have no reason to say more. But the possibilities for a criticism suitably informed (mastering and mobilizing the appropriate concepts), suitably sensitive, and suitably positioned are open to us all. Hence, critics are rightly seen as *shapers of taste*, for one can be brought or taught to see the artwork in an appropriate way, as John Martin recognized (see below §5).

In particular, despite the "... wealth of propositional knowledge about their artform that bears productively on the conceptual lens through which they view dance" (Conroy, 2013 p. 203b), professional dancers are not automatically "... better equipped than non-dancers to apprehend aesthetic features of a work of art *as* it is being performed" (Conroy, 2013 p. 203b). So it makes no sense to *require*, say, dance-training of any suitable critic or appreciator of dance. When dancers turn out to be closer observers in practice, this can be explained as drawing on a richer view of visual or auditory perception than the empiricist allows; one recognizing again the "interlock between perception and cognition" (Wollheim, 1993a p. 134). For, as traditionally understood, a 'scrutiny thesis' was assumed to ground critical practice, insisting that:

> ... the critic who is concerned to grasp the meaning of the work of art should utilise only what he has come to know through scrutinising the work ... [but] omits to say anything about what cognitive stock the critic may draw upon when he scrutinized the work. (Wollheim 1993a p. 135)

Rectifying that omission in turn acknowledges again the place of one's "cognitive stock" in what one can see: as Wollheim (1993a p. 135) remarks, "I shall be able to perceive that there is a row of elms in front of me only if I perceive the concept 'elm' in addition to the concept 'tree'". So the dancer's experience might be brought to bear through this cognitive stock, and its mobilization (AJ pp. 113), conceptualized as a capacity to *notice*, or to pay attention to, what others fail to attend to — one way to keep our claims within the bounds of reason, and hence answerability!

Thus, when Collingwood (1938 p. 147: §1 above) explains the art critic's use of tactile-value terms as referring to "... the imaginary experience of certain complicated muscular movements", the emphasis on the *imaginary* raises again the issue of *answerability* to features of the artwork. For one worry for dance appreciation involves the postulation of a 'sixth sense'. What alternatives might there be? Four related possibilities might involve postulating:

- A 'Sixth Sense'; but, if not projective, it could only operate in respect of one's own body, for one's own bodily position; and that would precisely not 'cross the footlights', in our sense.

- Next, a 'Sixth Sense' but somehow projective: such an answer might be suggested in writings of Barbara Montero;[6] and sometimes John Martin is read in this way (mistakenly, to my view). For how can there be such a modality? (Our response, for Martin, involved a reconsideration of his position: see §§ 4-7 below.)

- Some "mirror-neurons version": there seem two possibilities — (a) if triggered by what we *see*, then (as above) this might be accommodated through a richer version of visual perception, with the brain-studies offering (at best) some aspects of the mechanism of that perception;

- The other version takes this structure to operate projectively ("cross-modally"?), with mirror-neurons describing the mechanism: but of what? (b) if triggered by what we *do*, the issue lies in 'getting it right': that is, in its answerability. Further, an answer is still needed to the question of how the response 'reaches' its audience.

However, here, we recall that "[e]rror and superstition have causes just as much as correct cognition" (Frege, [1918] 1984 p. 351): so that the same causal mechanisms and the same sensory modality as applies when someone (say, some critic) *understands* the dancework under consideration must also apply when that critic *misunderstands* it. Insofar as the correctness of our critic's judgement *is* at issue, disputes over the detail of the sensory modality at work are therefore beside the point: whatever response is supplied must be *answerable* to the details of the dancework and justifiably offer the audience a way to make sense of that dancework (and hence a way to *see* it).

To defend my view, then, I shall suggest that the resources required for dance criticism (of the kind Martin did) are explicable without appeal to any 'sixth sense'. This strategy involves exemplifying treatment suitable to someone apparently urging the "sixth sense" route: here, John Martin's discussion of *metakinesis* was selected since (as we will see) a number of claims, seemingly supported by talk of *metakinesis* or "inner mimicry", can be sustained without that theoretical structure; moreover, Martin might embrace this redrafting of his claims.

§4.   John Martin, dance critic: a worked example

While many key authors from the early days of dance studies (for instance, Humphrey, 1959; Laban, 1966) had choreographic credentials, John Martin was a *theorist* of dance (especially his *Invitation to the Dance* [1939], 1965 — cited throughout as "M"); and perhaps primarily a dance critic. Texts from dance studies at that time were rife with dualism of a destructive kind, as Best (1999 p. 133) rightly noted. And certainly Martin sometimes wrote as though understanding dance should be modeled on a broadly perceptual process, distinctive of dance, reflecting the causality characteristic of natural science. Would such an attitude make Martin a dualist? His writing sometimes seems committed to dualism; for instance, in understanding the dancer as aiming to "... direct his emotional reactions so that even his most subjective experiences become visibly externalized" (M p. 232); or seeing "... all dance [as] ... the externalization of inner, emotional force of some kind in terms of bodily movement" (M p. 26), with references to *the inner* — implicitly contrasted to *the outer* — or of being *externalized*, in contrast to *internalized*. He emphasizes the "inner man" (M p. 37), "movement sense" (M pp. 42-47), and "inner mimicry" (M pp. 47-52). Each expression permits a dualist reading; hence Best might identify dualism here, not without reason. However, Best sometimes seemed to write as though the merest whiff of dualism was damning — as though any form of words that *could* be read dualistically (as when committing myself 'body and soul' to a project), *should* be read that way: it *could* mislead; and therefore it was *misleading* (even though no one was actually misled).

So, need (say) Martin's reference to "muscular sympathy" (M p. 53) be read dualistically? The term "sympathy" here need have no specific implications, just as talk of "an objective *correlative*"[7] (my emphasis) is not *necessarily* dualistic. In part, the issue ultimately concerns the relationship of what one *says* to what one *means*, or is thereby committed to. As Wittgenstein (PI §79) urged, one should *say* what one liked — with the proviso that there are various things one will *not* say, once paying attention to the consequences or implications of what one says. This point is complex: to what does saying *such-and-such* commit one? And, with those commitments made explicit, does one still want to say that thing? Even then, "saying that thing" might be contrasted with *retaining that form of words*. Fearing that others will conclude, from my talk of *sunrise*, that my cosmology is Pre-Copernican, I might reject talk of "sunrise". But the inference such people would be drawing does not *follow* from that talk; so I need not forego it — no one (attentive) is being confused! Sorting wheat from chaff here may clarify some projects in today's philosophical aesthetics of dance.

§5.   Gathering some evidence: "... the underbrush of erroneous theory" (M p. 14)

When first discussing the transmission of "the movement sense" from body to body, in *The Modern Dance* (1933), Martin urged that this "sixth sense" derived from the fact that "[m]ovement ... in and of itself is a medium for the transference of an aesthetic and emotional concept from the consciousness of one individual to that of another" (C&C p. 23[8]). Initially Martin called the phenomenon *metakinesis*. He saw "[i]ts externalisation in some form which can be comprehended by others ... by 'feeling through' with a sensitive body" (C&C p. 24). In *Introduction to the Dance* ([1939] 1965), the emphasis remains on the "movement sense", with the mechanism characterized as "muscular sympathy" (M p. 53); and inner mimicry, where "... a sympathetic awareness of our own bodies ... [means that] ... all types of gesture and facial expression convey meaning to us automatically" (M p. 48: although "inner mimicry" occurs in scare quotes on M p. 55). Martin grants the artist — here, the choreographer — "... a special gift ... recognized as having meaning for the whole group" (M p. 16), such that "[g]ood art speaks *directly* from its creator's emotions to our own" (M p. 14: my emphasis).

Our project is not Martin's biography. But, given what was important to him, was dualism inevitable? Or was it just a consequence of the period in which Martin lived and the circles in which he moved? If so, we (from a different period, moving in different circles) might identify insights here. And, as we will see, Martin tended to re-write his balder claims. So a degree of 'rational reconstruction' should leave Martin with the claims (and the insights) he was entitled to, without committing him to those he was not.

Of course, making sense of dance requires a person-based normative story, as reflected in Martin's focus as dance critic — a requirement Martin regularly set aside when writing about inner mimicry, or metakinesis. In part, he seems mesmerized by his felt need to *explain* the process of understanding dance, thinking (mistakenly) that such an explanation must draw on a distinctive mechanism. Urging that "... we have grown insensible to the medium in which dance operates" (M p. 22), Martin believed that filling the gap required a "source ... [of] ... sensorimotor experiences ... a sixth sense which concerns ... that elaborate and intricate world which is comprised in the body itself" (M p. 43). Hence Martin seems to stress *metakinesis* (or its later incarnation) as such a "sixth sense" (M p. 43), a distinct sensory modality.

That position is problematic, in three ways. First, the kind of causal answer invoked here is neither required nor possible. Like Martin, I begin from the fact of people appreciating dances. He asks how this was possible, sometimes acting as though this "how?" question required a *causal* answer describing the mechanism. When I recognize my leg's position by seeing it in a mirror, a sensory modality (sight) is deployed in knowing that position. That might tempt someone, as it tempted Martin, to urge that — when no mirror is used — some *sixth sense* explains the mechanism of (generally) knowing the positions (and so on) our limbs; and allows us *sympathy* for the movement and position of others. But the causal story is not relevant to our understanding even where we *know* the sensory modality (say, as vision). For, having conceded *that* causal story, one still cannot guarantee that the person in fact knows, say, the position of her leg — that is Frege's criticism of reliance on the causal: her 'getting it wrong' has a causal story too. And the issue is further complicated because the 'accuracy' of the *sympathy* also needs some guarantee — ideally, some criterion of 'appropriate' sympathy, reflecting the other's position. Those rightly critical of dualism must accept the quite general irrelevance of explanatory structures of this sort.

Could our bodily reactions — our toe-tappings, and sitting up straighter, and holding our breaths, and tensing our legs, and so on — somehow (in some small way) play into our appreciation of dance[9]? This is precisely what makes no sense; what Best's prohibition on dualism proscribes. Of course, as Wittgenstein (CV §389[a]) noted, an outsider might (in certain contexts) take my tapping my toe, and so on, as *evidence* that I understood the dance. In context, that behaviour might justly be taken to indicate understanding; but only because the *understanding* itself is independent of these responses. And, of course, it would not be *how* I understood the dance, as though I might conclude, from studying my behaviour, that (since I am doing these things) I *must* understand the dance.

Indeed, there is no *how* here. One neither has (nor needs) criteria for one's understanding in such cases: this is just a capacity people have, often improved by practice. So that artistic value can sometimes just be recognized, although with no specific exceptionless causal story for doing so; no single "how" here. Addressing that causal "how?" question seemed to require a mechanism such as inner mimicry, or *metakinesis*, or a sixth sense. But, with Putnam (1999 p. 132), when doing philosophy, one must sometimes reject "*... the idea that the question makes sense*" (his italics). Then one's attention turns to the training and practice that develop this capacity. In this respect, it resembles our capacity to know where (in space) our own limbs are: to the degree that we can do this, there is no *manner* in which we do it.

Second, Martin's taking the phenomenon as central to appreciating modern dance but not ballet is inconsistent with this view: after all, a sensory modality cannot differentiate among its objects. Now, if my eyes are open, and in good working order, I *automatically* see the world around me; I do not choose to do so. Training can improve my grasp of *what* I see, but cannot change that fact. Thus, characterizing inner mimicry, Martin writes that, "... a sympathetic awareness of our own bodies ... [means that] ... all types of gesture and facial expression convey meaning to us *automatically*" (M p. 48 [my emphasis]). But what is *automatic* here either operates or does not: a mechanism just causal or perceptual cannot be exploited *here* yet not *there*. Hence claiming the priority of some dance in those terms, as when Martin writes: "... no conscious artistic use was made of metakinesis until modern dance arose" (C&C p. 24[10]), makes no sense. Watching different danceforms cannot, of itself, involve different sensory modalities. So, if some writers[11] urge that, say, Graham's dances are more visceral than their predecessors, this should be read as a comment on *what* one sees, not on *how* one recognizes it!

Third, Martin's perspective as dance critic is in tension with such a view. To explain one's *understanding* dance, Martin should focus on humanistic explanation that takes *dance* as its object. But he often wrote as though the capacity originally identified as *metakinesis* applied equally to aspects of the non-human world; or, at least, as though a perfectly general human power (or sense), unrelated to dance, were operative here. He takes for granted that

"... we respond muscularly to the strains in architectural masses [human, and arguably art-based] and the attitudes of rocks [obviously non-human]" (M p. 53 [my inserts]). So the scope of Martin's "sixth sense" picture is unclear. But, as such, it lacks any special connection to dance. One only needs a "... perfectly functioning neuromuscular system and an equally healthy general physical organism" (M p. 54).

Yet artistic appreciation requires more: one must see the red patch in the painting (depicting the cottage roof, say) but one must also see the cottage, and recognize that painting as balanced — where the balance is achieved by the red patch. That is, one must recognize the artistic properties of the artwork. And the same must be true for dances. Indeed, Martin makes this point in urging that, for dance appreciation:

...it is necessary to appreciate the stuff of which dance is made, namely the movements of the human body ... [but also to appreciate] form, or the arrangement of this essential material of movement into such sequences and relationships that it assumes significance for the onlooker. (M p. 26)

And he also mentions *style*. Clearly such features cannot be transferred by "inner mimicry'. So, doing justice to Martin's insights here requires stressing additional (and more traditional) concepts from aesthetics. That, in turn, puts pressure on the importance his account gives to "inner mimicry" or other mechanisms of perception of dance, running together two themes that dance critics should keep apart: *first*, the concern with explaining how one appreciates dance (that mechanism must, in the end, reflect a *projective* sensory modality) and, *second*, intentional (or non-causal) questions about the understanding of dance. In recognizing the force of the movement in this particular *dance*, one *really* recognizes the complex intentions involved in dance-making, reflecting the *normativity* of judging dances. Hence, it respects Frege's dictum: it is intentional rather than causal, having fundamental cultural elements, of a kind Martin recognized explicitly for music (M p. 23). Moreover, the issue is not simply perceptual, although one element is still visual since, "[w]e have forgotten how to *look at* movement and how to respond to it" (M p. 22; my emphasis). Martin's use of "look at" here is revealing, for — in the end — even he recognizes the visual as ultimately the key perceptual mode here: we *look at* dances, responding to them on that basis. These last points, while music to the ears of John Martin *dance critic*, might appeal less to John Martin, theorist (or metaphysician) of dance.

One then confronts a difficulty Martin had, in writing as a dance critic: that one requires *training* to appreciate the movement in dance. Someone whose perceptual apparatus functions correctly may still fail to *see* the dance *as dance*, still less to *appreciate* it *as dance*. You can know that such-and-such is a dance but, as Wisdom (1991 p. 80) remarked, "... parrots may not know it, yet perhaps they have even better eyesight than yours". The visual acuity thereby granted to the parrot does not allow her to see *dance*: or, better, to recognize dance when she sees it. Your capacities exceeding those of parrots might be explained by:

- your mastery of concepts (and of the relevant concepts);

- your sensitivity to differences between what is dance and what just resembles it; between good and better dances; and so on — differences we recognize as cultural, and evaluative, and beyond the scope of the parrot.

Moreover, Martin was typically well aware of this: indeed, his criticism functions as a *maker of taste* (see below: Carroll, 2008 pp. 192-193) precisely because one can learn to *see the dance as dance*; and hence *learn* to appreciate it as dance.

Of course, that does not deny the biological substrate. No doubt eyes are a prerequisite of vision but the eyes do not see; and neither does the brain: vision is a property of the person. Similarly, some of the structures beloved of my critics *might* play a role — perhaps, as a prerequisite for our building up (or otherwise developing) the causal powers that many humans typically have, although I would want better evidence.[12] This exemplifies clearly the danger of insisting that such processes *must be* at work here (PI §308), while setting aside their detail *sine die*. For, in the absence of a view of those processes, we cannot really decide, one way or another — despite granting that typically explaining the mechanism of the causal sub-strate for our perceptual powers draws on contemporary science. (In PAD, I mention mirror reflexes and mirror neurons.)

§6.   Martin's dualism

A first step in dealing with Martin's own account returns us to the philosophical problem of 'Other Minds', on which there is no *independent* access to, say, the other's psychological state. So any correlation can only be built up by assuming what is at issue: namely, that there *is* such a correlation in contentious cases. Progress involves realizing that there is no *logical* bar to knowing the thoughts and feelings of other people: instead, that knowledge operates defeasibly, reflecting how well we know the person in question. In particular, this is a capacity people possess: no specific mechanism is deployed here — not (typically) *sympathy* or *empathy*, although these might be grounded in this human power or capacity; and not involving some distinctive sensory modality. Further, Martin sometimes wrote as though his model was the Central Nervous System narrowly conceived: he grants that the "postural change" involving this "movement sense ... [includes] ... the movement of the eyeballs in following an object, ... the periodic contractions of the stomach" (M p. 44). Yet these are precisely *not* objects of perception; we are typically unaware of them.

Sometimes, Martin's claims may be read, for instance, so that remarks reflecting choreographer's *intentions* (or something similar) refer to human intentions as *embodied-in-the-performed-works*: as Beardsley (1970 p. 33) put it, one is "a poem-reader, not a mind-reader" — one does not interrogate the choreographer's psyche, but looks instead to the dance itself, properly understood. This is consistent with our having set aside the conception of intention as prior planning, 'in the head' of the artist, at best causally connected to the artwork itself (PAD pp. 125-126; UD pp. 230-231). Such a misconceived account of the relation of intention to art separates that intention from the artwork: instead, as earlier, one needs an account "... not stopping short of, but terminating on, the work of art itself" (Wollheim, 1980 p. 185) — that is how reference to intention is read by contemporary theorists, as represented, say, by Noel Carroll (2009 pp. 134-15) and by me (PAD pp. 135-146).

Thus, when Martin claims that the artist's purpose is "... to arouse us to feel a certain emotion about a particular object or situation" (M p. 53), is that "emotion" (on his account) at best *causally* related to the artwork itself? If so, the account is dualist in the ways criticized above. Yet such an account might instead just reflect the artist's intention as embodied in the dancework. In such a world, how have we access to what might seem like the choreographer's psychological state? Rejecting dualist pictures of intention will be one precondition. Martin simply recognizes this human power: in the artistic case, the force of a person behind artistic creation (AJ p. 85-91), as well as the dancer's role in making (some) choices and decisions. Since the dancer "... is himself the instrument" (M p. 62), one might hope to give the dancer due weight as *human agent*.

Martin must also explain how what he claimed was *there* could be recognized in the dance (and in this performance of it, and valuable in those circumstances) — recognized, first, by him; and, later, by a suitably informed and suitably sensitive audience. He was keen to deny that appreciation of this dancework requires of audience members sophisticated knowledge of the history of dance (the sort of thing dance history classes offer): such knowledge alone cannot generate artistic understanding. Rather the audience's appreciation of the bodily movement must be manifest (even if that appreciation drew on seeing the dance). So Martin adopted a line from New Criticism for literature (compare also Franko, 1996 p. 28): that one need only scrutinize the dance itself to understand it, although that may involve recognizing it as dance (and of a certain kind). Further, dance understanding could not be forever unavailable to an audience willing to make appropriate efforts: for instance, one educated through attention to Martin's reviews. Martin recognized that possibility, not least from his own case. For, with a few other pioneers (such as Mary Watkins), Martin was literally inventing the role of dance critic as we know it.

Doing so implicitly stressed two roles central to art criticism — first, as *consumer guide*, with the audience advised of the value (and otherwise) of particular performances currently on offer, to generating attendance *here* rather than *there*; and, second, as *maker of taste* (Carroll, 2008 pp. 192-193). Here, Martin sought to lead that audience to value what he saw as valuable in much modern dance; in particular, in the dances of Martha Graham. For Martin, this task was indeed partly educational: as Selma Jean Cohen (1998 p. 273) noted, the audience was required to widen its perceptions, away from the familiar from ballet. Martin's main target was to show that *critic* represented a role to be fulfilled. That capacity is more easily located in our conceptual mastery and in our cultural assimilations. Hence Martin discusses the interchange between artist and layman (M pp. 16-17), or compares dance to music as "a recognized part of our cultural life" (M p. 23).

No doubt, for instance, Twyla Tharp (2003 p. 156) was exaggerating in suggesting that, "[s]omeone in the audience could write ten thousand words about this single movement in a three hour ballet. That's how right movement can be". But her comment highlights something of the complex relations of description, evaluation, and 'taste-making' that can occur, while granting the impossibility of a *complete* description even of a small piece of a dance, let alone a *complete* account of its meaning. As an example, consider one from Tharp (2003 pp. 155-156) herself:

> Take the White Swan's last exit in Act II of *Swan Lake*. The ballerina turns her back to the audience, facing Albrecht, her prince, and bourrées across the stage with her arms extended at her sides. As she executes her delicate journey on the points of her toes, a ripple of movement begins at her left hand's fingertips and continues through all the joints of her left arm, her shoulders and back, through all the joints of her right arm to her right hand's fingertips. The ripple then returns from right to left, again and again, until the undulating gesture accumulates power and creates a burning image of a wave.

This fine description results from developed powers of *observation* of dances, and especially of this dance (and perhaps this moment). Tharp (2003 p. 156) continues with commentary:

> It is one of the most marvelous moments of beauty and heartbreak in the entire ballet canon. It never fails to elicit a gasp from the audience. It is a gasp of wonder and sorrow. We immediately sense that this ripple is a metaphor

for the fluttering of the bird's wings. The ballerina is, after all, portraying a swan. But the exquisite movement across the stage also reminds us of the wavelike motion of the water supporting this ballerina-swan. And her gesture suggests so much more. Is the swan waving good-bye to her prince? Or is she beckoning him? 'Come with me.' Or is the ripple a gesture of resignation, her final spasm of life? Or is it all of the above.

I would certainly speak for "all of the above": one cannot typically paraphrase (without leaving anything out) even a gesture or movement in a dance — more might always be said, at least in usual cases. But here we note both what is going on and some of why it is effective. Moreover, if it did not yet strike me as "...one of the most marvelous moments of beauty and heartbreak in the entire ballet canon", that thought — and some of the material needed to see the moment that way — has been provided to me.

By contrast, here is Joan Acocella (1993 pp. 186-7) writing about Mark Morris's *The Hard Nut* (1991):

> Throughout, Old World quaintness and Old World assumptions are replaced by the things of the New World: the pushy, the democratic, the cheerfully crass. Eyes bug out; things go pow. The tone is something like Mad magazine. To a certain extent, *The Hard Nut*, like so much other art in our time, seems to be saying that the Old World is dead. ...

> And, to a large extent, it is saying the opposite: that the ideal meanings of old art ... are still very much alive – indeed, the centre of our existence. ...

> So *The Hard Nut* sets two emotional currents, joy and sincerity, against each other, and this is typical of Morris. Of the leading qualities of his work — its musicality, its structural clarity, its danciness, its mixture of story-telling and abstraction — none is more constant than his use of divided emotions: nastiness and cheerfulness, pathos and dryness, horror and hilarity....

These passages, too, offer ways to make sense of our experience of danceworks, as well as ways to describe them for ourselves. Of course, eventually we must come to see the work that way *for ourselves*; or fail to, and then repudiate it. Here, we confront the plausibility of that 'take' on the dancework, determining its plausibility (and especially implausibility) by reference to the fulfilled intentions of the artist, as embodied in the work. So we might begin assembling criteria for the accuracy of critical comments for dance (where the point is to avoid 'reading in'), drawing on:

- the fulfilled intention of artist;

- the bodily movements comprising the dancework, under a suitable interpretation (such that this is dance — and, especially, not a confusable counterpart).

Moreover, Martin rightly grants the logical importance of an *audience* by stressing the centrality, for art, of communication: "[w]ith the desire for communication, then, there comes ... the beginning of art" (M p. 54); and in writing of "... communication ... which [art] demands" (M p. 41). So Martin's project, unlike (say) Montero's "aesthetics for dancers" (Montero, 2006 p. 236a; see PAD p. 188), has the audience for dance (roughly the audience for his reviews) coming to understand dances seen in performance. Since Martin's target is an account of the *audience* for dance, *metakinesis* cannot be a property of dancers (only) but must operate in *general* audiences for danceworks. Yet any specificity to danceworks speaks against treating it as a sensory modality, a "sixth sense".

This offers a *rational reconstruction* of Martin's position, given his other commitments. For example, he later comments that "[i]t is useless to approach any work of art with the notion that it must be understood before it can be responded to" (M p. 51). But one must grasp that *this* is a cubist painting or a piece of atonal music to avoid misperceiving it: in both cases, some understanding is a pre-requisite for (appropriate) response, as Martin's own comments on the dances of Martha Graham and Mary Wigman illustrate. One should look to what Martin meant — to the contrasts that were important to him — rather than what he actually said, where these conflict; that licenses our reconstructing such passages. Moreover, Martin occasionally seems aware of this: for instance, writing that sense receptors "give a signal, *as it were*" (M p. 44 [my emphasis]) registers that this talk of sense *receptors* and of *signals* is metaphorical.

§7.   Appreciating dances: a human task?

So, is *metakinesis* (or inner mimicry) a normative *human* property, associated with the actions of persons? One might think so. As dance critic, Martin seems never to have imagined responding *metakinetically* to, say, the behaviour of stilt-birds (as described by Kurt Sachs, 1937 p. 9): and rightly so, were metakinesis a response to *dance* — that is (roughly) to culturally inflected, normatively-positioned *action*; and, moreover, action comprising an *art-form*. These conditions are the province of persons only. Certainly, Martin recognized the distinctiveness of our perception of art: "... if a man made no more active response to art than the table to sunlight he would experience no more reaction" (M p. 33). And, of course, the table responds to the sunlight *automatically* here (see above).

No doubt some artistic properties are response-reliant (AJ pp. 103-106):

the lemon really is yellow (its yellowness is a property of the lemon) even though recognition of that property requires specific capacities. But the property itself is a property of, in this case, the dance. Then the worry is clear: talk of "muscular sympathy" (M p. 53) will be dualist precisely to the degree that a property of the dancework is located on/in the audience.

Despite occasional problem cases, constituting an audience to make sense of the resultant dancework typically requires more than the "contiguous" sensory modalities (UD p. 266). Standard examples of dance appreciation require that, as it were, the dancework reaches 'over the footlights' to the audience, who then recognize its features. Roughly, one only appreciates (as audience) danceworks one has seen; and on the basis of one's seeing them. Hence, even leaving open *which* sensory modalities there are, the operation of an audience for dance requires (at least) that only what I call "projective" sensory modalities (UD p. 266) be involved in dance appreciation.

Moreover, Martin sometimes writes as if this 'movement sense' were projective, but offers no explanation of how it might be. Thus, he discusses knowing how heavy a log is (M p. 45). But the log's weight is not typically *perceived* at all, but rather inferred; and were it perceived, the sensory modality would be visual — we *see* the log. Certainly, humans can often prepare to lift the log: again, nothing in that process seems essentially perceptual or sensory. And reference to the "sensorimotor" here cannot concede what has been denied. For that just *names* the set of human powers and capacities.

Of course, my objection was never to the *words* here, but to the implications others sought to draw from them. Thus, I no more aimed to deny others the use of the expression "kinaesthetic sense" than I denied *sense of direction*, *sense of humour*, or even moral sense. But I did dispute that they were *senses* in the ways that sight and hearing were. Hence, noting the distinctiveness of sight and hearing as projective stresses their connections to the requirement for an *audience* for dance.

Such a focus on the audience is easily misunderstood. Thus Barbara Montero (2012 p. 66) quotes UD p. 273: "... the focus on the performer is not appropriate to an artform such as dance". She reads this as my repudiating *any* mention of the dancer (for example, in dance criticism). But *of course* dance criticism can invoke the dancer: just as criticism concerning painting might mention the quality of brush strokes. These are a part of this artwork: and hence a part of the artform. But to think *only* about brush strokes is not really to discuss the painting itself. The line quoted is from my summary of a section entering two important qualifications. First, as I put it slightly later, "[i]f one had to choose a viewpoint for aesthetic appreciation, it would necessarily be the viewpoint of the spectator ... [since] artistic appreciation is first and foremost of the creations of others" (UD p. 273) — but perhaps *both* perspectives could be accommodated. Second (as here), the centrality of the audience was being recorded: artworks necessarily have audiences (Cavell, 1969/2002 p. xxvii; see Chapter Two §11; PAD p. 186). That was the context for my putting aside attention to the performer's perspective. The "focus on the performer" here means *this* focus, treating the dancework from the perspective of dancer *rather than* of audience, not just *any* mention of performer or performance. The context for these comments was my rejection of appeals to a kinaesthetic sense: that is, to claims for dancers while performing the dance. Thus I doubt that the dancer is typically well-placed to judge the dance she *presently* performs; and certainly "... kinaesthesis plays no part in our audience-style understanding of the dance" (UD p. 270). Further, judgements from the dancer's perspective cannot replace that understanding. Hence this criticism involves a misreading.

Montero uses these ideas to suggest that (say) ex-dancers might have an insight into dances. Like Montero (2012 p. 67), I accept that practice in judging dances is likely to be advantageous (see PAD pp. 244-246 on "learning to see"). For surely 'practice makes perfect': but what is thereby perfected is what is being practiced, not some *other* activity. So her experience here (hence what she has practiced) involves her watching sequences of the dance: therefore the relevant practice lies in watching dances, not in performing them.[13] Whatever is said at the practical level, such roles can be distinguished in theory.

Granting this point opens up two broad strategies. First, someone can assert that there is a distinctive kind of *projective* sensory modality here, explaining both the nature of the modality and its relation to dance appreciation — does it relate to other kinds of appreciation also, or only to dance? — as well as its origins: is this modality the province of trained dancers only, as Montero (2006 p. 236a) seems to think, or can be it mobilized by others of us? Either answer must then be explained or justified.

As I urged in the past (UD p. 266; and see Chapter Eight §6 above), a sensory modality of the kind suggested by such a line of thought *cannot* explain our capacity to know the location of, for instance, our limbs; but that argument does not imply that, somehow, the positions of our limbs *escape* us. In a related discussion, quoted there, Pickard (2004 p. 228) reported the case of Ian Waterman, who:

> ... lacks virtually all feeling in, and awareness from the inside of, his body: he is 'body blind'. ... But ... has managed to learn to control his movements using vision. If he looks down at his body, constantly and assiduously monitoring it through vision, he can guide his movements in this way.

Hence, for Pickard (2004 p. 228), Waterman is "... a living counter-example to the claim that bodily awareness is what sustains one's knowledge of what one is doing over time".

On my view, then, there is no *additional* sensory modality; instead, I urge that the mechanisms of 'ordinary' perception are sufficient here, once properly understood. This requires a richer reading of the objects of perception than is sometimes adopted. Thus my interest in, say, perception here lies in the human capacity to recognize and enjoy dances. This accords with Martin's account when reconstructed, for his emphasis too is really on the human powers and capacities. In its most full-bodied version, *metakinesis* is clearly a complicated name for the capacity that humans have (once they have learned to do it) to recognize the bodily or embodied character of the movement of (pre-eminently) early modern dances. It need be nothing more, especially once the point is expressed as about powers and capacities rather than senses. Martin sometimes writes as though a modality of *sense* was involved, but appeals to a sense of direction or a sense of humour are familiar invocations of human powers and capacities (see Chapter Eight §6). Such cases involve the senses, of course; but, despite the forms of words used, no *distinctive* sensory modality is involved — to repeat, we *see* the amusing slapstick; we *hear* the one-liner; we *read* the comic novel (a special case); just as we *notice*, however subliminally, whatever landmarks permit the sense of direction. Further, appeal is to a complex package of powers and capacities of humans. So, as with these cases, no *sense* (no sensory modality) is required for the location of bodily motion. And certainly such powers do not have priority: instead, we look at the position of the leg (in arabesque, say) — hence the mirrors in typical dance studios! And, if corrected by the choreographer, we do not insist that we *must* be right ("*metakinesis* is always correct"). Rather, we recognize the heavy dependence here on *seeing* the position (in space) of our bodies, because that is both the authoritative position, and typically the one for the audience-appreciation of our dancing (and of the dance).

§8.   Four supportive criticisms?

Given this general account of Martin's work, and in particular the insights it offers both into the nature of dance-criticism and the explanation of the possibilities of audience, we can turn to a broadly supportive set of four criticisms from Renee Conroy (2013 p. 207b). These were presented as ways to resist my "... assertion that bodily reactions are *irrelevant* to the appreciation of dance". First, and perhaps following Montero, one could urge "... that our kinaesthetic responses constitute a discrete aesthetic object to be relished for its own sake" (Conroy, 2013 p. 207b). I have problems with this, which Conroy too classifies as a "side effect" of the dance: where I differ from Montero is in denying that appreciation *of the dance* could take this form. Second, one might find a "... use of the word 'appreciation' wider than McFee's, ... [a use] closely aligned with our sense of what is special about interactions with art objects" (Conroy, 2013 p. 207b). My difficulty here is that I can discern no such use; and indeed took my own discussion for a naturalistic presentation of what can actually be "special about interactions with art objects". Conroy (2013 p. 208a) points out that there need be no single "correct" understanding of a poem, making her point eloquently with the example of a poem by Wallace Stevens (one of my favourites). She claims to "... *appreciate* Stevens's poetry and its complexity precisely because it defies my (full, apt, or even minimally correct) comprehension" (Conroy, 2013 p. 208a). Here, the bracketed modifier provides the problem. I agree that no one's understanding of a poem or dance could ever be *complete* — that there are no finite totalities here is more or less a mantra of mine. But surely "apt" is required to meet the charge for answerability: her understanding must be *of the poem*! As for the idea that it might not be "even minimally correct", I know her too well to think she could believe this: one cannot admire a poem one does not understand to at least some degree; just as one cannot *admire* a poem in French without some mastery of that language, for (without that mastery) whatever I admire cannot be words! What may have gone wrong here is that I sometimes write as though there were only one way to understand a dance or a poem. That is not my view. But I do, of course, think that there are minimal conditions for seeing a dance or reading a poem; and both require access to the art object via appropriate sensory modalities.

For Conroy (2013 p. 208b), perhaps — and in agreement with me — "the observed work of dance art ... [is not] ... the object that is more aptly or fully comprehended by means of 'kinaesthetic resonance'" (my order). Rather, such resonances (whatever they are) are part of "... the broader artistic practices of dance ... by affording us greater insight into the embodied character of the art form ... while also underwriting a limited set of artistic judgements that reflect the degree to which a given performance enhances this kind of understanding" (Conroy, 2013 p. 2008b). My claim had been that, for example, my tapping my toe could not be *evidence* that I understand the dance: it could not be evidence *for me*, since I neither need nor use evidence for my own understanding; and it could not be evidence *for you* unless you build in the idea that someone who did understand would behave in this way. But, for that, independent evidence is needed that, in the past, *other* toe-tappers understood the dance: were such evidence available for them, it would be better to use it for me too, rather than taking this roundabout route. If the point here is that people do such things, I agree (unsurprising, given my naturalism). But that does not show that there is any "kinaesthetic resonance" at work in such appreciation.

Fourthly, and finally, Conroy (2013 p. 208b) urges that "some choreographic creations ... in virtue of the way they are crafted, *demand* of the viewers that they attend to their bodily responses", citing Laura Dean's

Skylight (1982) and offering a vivid description of that work. Conroy (2013 p. 2009a) claims that Dean "... invites us into the world of the dancers and encourages us to attend to the most basic features of our embodied selves by choreographically compelling us to be gripped viscerally by what we see and hear". The descriptions both of the work and of our responses strike me as exact: a response to what we attend to, to what we *see and hear*. Can one be compelled in this way to visceral reactions? Of course! That is the stock-in-trade of the horror movie, amongst others. But there is a huge difference between being 'corporeally engaged' in that way, as a result of what one sees and hears, and imagining some sixth sense or "kinaesthetic resonance" is at work. In respect of "the experience of being bodily involved", Conroy (2013 p. 208a) says, "... I can attest ..." — but we should not take her word for it without having an answer to our primary question: 'What gets over the footlights?'. Then I will first remind Conroy that horror movies typically produce a proscribed bodily response without kinaesthesis, and second reserve the right to recast her remarks, in line with my recasting of Martin (see above §§4-7).

If Conroy's account (with such modifications) is accepted, answerability is to features of the dance, flowing from the fulfilled intentions of the choreographer: we are *compelled* or *instructed* to see the work that way, where — from a first-person perspective — "that way" seems visceral. And I have tried to give that substance by referring to a more familiar, less contentious, case. But notice that, on such a conception (a) this is something everyone could do, in principle — no doubt there is a need for training: 'learning to see' and 'learning to value' remain tasks for, say, the dance critic to develop in the audience members: compare Martin; and (b) this could be accommodated by me — I do not deny it, but I re-interpret it (in line with my 'reading' of Martin).

§9.   'Dancers aesthetic' — not a route to audience?

One problem is that, although a dancer's knowledge of bodily position, and such like, is extensive (let it be granted), saying this might in the first instance just be thought a way to recognize the impact of the training. But if someone wanted to assert a specific sensitivity here, I need not deny it: as I have suggested elsewhere (PAD p. 201), this might even explain why that person entered the training in the first place. Hence I agree entirely with the claim that "... dance training does, or should, make an aesthetic difference to one's ability to appreciate dance" Davies (2011 p. 198). My concern, though, is simply with the appreciation of a dancework *as an artwork*: here, I want to insist that such a dancerly perspective is not really artistically relevant, since danceworks (like other artworks) are created *for an audience*. And this is true, as Cavell (1969 p. xxvii/2002 p. xxxviii) noted, "... however small and special" that audience: moreover, as he continues, "[t]he ways in which it sometimes hides from its audience, or baffles it, only confirms this". In part, Cavell is acknowledging the logical point that artworks are, as it were, *aimed at* an audience — that they are for appreciation by that audience, even if (in practice) the audience consists of no one but the artist (as certainly happened for some works by Francis Bacon: PAD p. 187). This just reaffirms that, in most cases, art must be viewable as such from the perspective of the audience. But, as Cavell also recognizes, works must ultimately find an audience: a work forever without an audience will not be an artwork. In a different terminology (AJ pp. 149-150), being an artwork requires 'other-acclamation' by the relevant segment of the artworld. Of course, one might wait for posterity, or engage in a public relations exercise on one's own behalf (or someone else's), to achieve such artworld acceptance.

These points count against one version of the suggestion, by Montero (2006a p. 236a), of "... an aesthetics from the point of view of ... the dancer", an aesthetic apparently motivated because "... proprioception can allow one to perceive aesthetic qualities of one's movement and positions" (Montero, 2006a p. 236a). Put like that, the suggestion seems to require a distinctive modality, *proprioception*, as well as an acknowledgement of the relevance to artistic appreciation of the performer's perspective. As Conroy (2013 p. 204a) rightly notes, Montero's own account draws directly on evidence she finds in neuroscience. But Montero's "dancer's aesthetic" gets no evidential support from the mirror-neuron discussion mentioned, as Davies (2013 p. 205a-b) points out (and see Chapter Five §7), since that discussion is:

> ... focused on the perception of *aesthetic properties* that, in the case of a dance performance, must be closely aligned with the apprehension of movement qualities and cannot depend only on the recognition of various spatial configurations.

Or, in my language, it cannot align with the apprehension of those movements *as art*. Indeed, a positive reading of one of the studies Montero deploys would yield the conclusion that "... female dancers were significantly more adept than male dancers at noticing slight differences between qualitatively similar performances" (Conroy, 2013 p. 204a-b) — nothing as yet to contribute to 'an aesthetic for dancers'. Further, we must be sure that the results are at an appropriate scale: if the choreographer would be equally happy with either of two performances of a sequence in her ballet, despite "slight differences between qualitatively similar performances", those performances count as *indistinguishable* from the artistic perspective. Or, better, they are simply *confusable* from this perspective: as I have elaborated the case, those differences need not matter.

Perhaps Montero admits that her theses "... are speculative extensions of the relevant current literature in neuroscience" (Davies, 2011 p. 196). But could they ever offer insight into the appreciation of art? Montero (2006 p. 236) offers two possibilities for the relation of our judgements of visual beauty and of proprioceptive beauty:

> In some cases, one might proprioceptively judge that a movement, if seen, would look beautiful. But in other cases one would visually judge that a movement is beautiful because one knows that, if proprioceived, this movement would feel beautiful.

This is a difficult passage even if one sets aside the concept of *proproceptively judging:*[14] as I read it, in the first set of cases, one is aware of a movement that "... if seen, would look beautiful": that is, one is *aware* of a beautiful movement. But, since its beauty requires that one *see* it, one is not actually *aware* of the beauty — one *knows* about it but does not *experience* it. This seems a good description of a failure of appreciation: however much I know about the work's beauty, I am not engaging with that beauty. But, in the second set of cases, too, I *know* (or, anyway, *claim* to know) that the movement "... would feel beautiful": yet, although I am seeing *the movement*, I am not seeing its *beauty* since that beauty resides (somehow) in what is proprioceived — I *judge* it to be beautiful, but do not feel or experience it *as beautiful*. This account, if correct, would seem to preclude *appreciation* of the beauty of the movement — it is a little more as though one took the movement to be beautiful because one had been told! And notice that this is not, or not necessarily, about movement in a dance.

But do movements really *feel* beautiful? Montero uses two different locutions here: in one case, seeing the movement, I know that it would feel beautiful. This seems problematic in two ways: first, there seems nothing that it would be to *feel beautiful*, no particular way to capture that in the ganglia, say; second, the beauty or otherwise of the dancer's movement (when beauty is required) is determined by the choreographer — the dancer may claim that it feels beautiful, only to be told it was wrong in some way — or, of course, the dancer may see its wrongness for himself in one of the many mirrors located in the studio for just that purpose. The dancer thinks it looks a certain way; and will usually be right, based on practice, training, and experience. But that feeling cannot *determine* the rightness of the movement. The other locution requires knowing through proprioception: or, more exactly, judging that way. Yet, in addition to the difficulty (above) in finding *aesthetic* judgement in such judging, one must be aware of the limitations of one's claim to *know*: that one might well be wrong (with phantom limb cases providing the extreme example). Further, the real difficulty here is that, when one knows the position of one's own limbs, this does not (in the same way) offer a means of knowing

— in the last analysis, one just knows. There seems little likelihood that a similar analysis will apply to others 'proprioceptively knowing' things about someone else.

Yet that is just what is needed. To claim that spectators of a dance "... can share a proprioceptive awareness of what it is to perform that sequence of movements, and thus a proprioceptive awareness of its aesthetic properties" (Davies, 2011 p. 196) involves at least the speculations about the dancer's own appreciation of an artwork she performs (the kind the 'dancer's aesthetic' might seem to licence) as well as the claims about the access *of spectators* to the dancer's bodily understanding.

Neither of these claims is appealing: first, we will come to the difficulties in saying *how* the dancers know what they know about their own bodies (compare §1, §7 above) — the thesis here requires a proprioceptive 'sense', when in fact nothing is needed; or so I urge. Yet, if the dancers do not have such a proprioceptive basis for their claims, they cannot be *sharing* such a basis with spectators.

Now, I happily grant that (in certain favoured circumstances) *some* spectators — and perhaps led by those with most experience of dance — might be at least as good at making sense of the danceworks as art as the dancers: further, if we think about the great critics who had limited experience in dance performance, that point is obvious. Certainly training for critics here would be training in observation, not in kinaethesis. So one may grant the audience, say, knowledge of bodily position of dancers: but I see no evidence that it is either proprioceptive or kinaesthetic. Indeed, prior to this discussion, the explanation offered of the proprioceptive and the kinaesthetic (in terms of knowing the positions of one's own limbs) would have counted against such an account.

Three main issues remain: first, how does the 'information' get to the spectators? I remain convinced that the only genuinely *projective* sensory modalities are sight and hearing: moreover, they seem to me sufficient to offer the full explanation here, once the thin, empiricist account of perception is set aside, such that space is given to the interlock between perception and one's concepts, as above. But suppose I am mistaken about that. Then, second, what kind of engagement with the spectator is offered? If the answer is a causal one (say, in terms of the functioning of so-called 'mirror neurons'), one must recognize the limitation of causal explanation and its extension: insofar as the audience simply *receives* something from the performer, as the causal model implies, that does not yet imply that this is something true of the performer, a point made sharply by McTaggart ([1906] 1968 §73 p. 72):

> A man who boils a lobster red may have a red face — there is nothing to prevent it. But his action in causing the redness of the lobster gives us no

reason to suppose that his face is red.

If our knowledge is of his action, that only tells us something about him if the knowledge flows from a projective sensory modality. That is needed is to *understand* his behaviour. And we are looking to the normativity of judgements of dance: is it a good dance or not? But, of course, bad artworks have causal stories just as much as good ones. Yet then, third, the requirement is now for understanding *normative* with respect to judgement of *artistic value*: that is not so easily gained.

Thus, faced with a genuinely *confusable counterpart* for a dancework, and adopting Montero's idea, the spectator would have some kind of access to the *movements* performed. But what is needed is that understanding that permits appreciation of the movements *as comprising an artwork*. To distinguish appreciation of art from appreciation of graceful movement, David Best (1978 p. 115) raises fundamental considerations in a Danto-esque vein. While watching Ram Gopal perform a dance in an Indian dance-form (Bharata Natyam) of which he was ignorant, Best recognized that his enjoyment as just of the quality of the *movement* that comprises the dance, reporting himself "... enthralled by the exhilarating quality of his movements" (Best, 1978 p. 115). But, as he acknowledged in the case as described, Best is not really confronting the *dance*, since his confrontation lacks the understanding appropriate to dance of that kind — not recognizing what it is *about*, as Danto might put it (although, since the dance is an artwork, it *is* about something): it has a meaning that, as he imagines the case, Best misses. And one of the indicators of his failure here is that a slightly different sequence of movement, although in reality *about* something different (it could, say, have a different subject), could have the same "exhilarating quality" (Best, 1978 p. 115).

Making sense of this case *as art* requires bringing to bear on it the battery of concepts appropriate to danceworks, and danceworks of that *category of art*. As an audience member, I must do more than simply grasp what the dancers are doing at the level of movements of their bodies: I must recognize the steps and gestures in the context of *this* dance, as *art*. For artworks today can involve *the transfiguration of the commonplace* (Danto, 1981) partly as a way of offering a commentary on other elements of the human world: this was both the sense in which they (but not their confusable counterparts) were *about* something, thereby reiterating his conception of art as *embodied meaning* (Danto, 2013 p. 37) — and hence as embodying its *aboutness*. For artworks bring with them "... an atmosphere of theory the eye cannot descry" (Danto [1964], 1989 p. 177) that must be acknowledged in recognizing them *as art*. Moreover, and especially given the possibility of such 'confusable counterparts', contemporary artworks can have a kind of visual irrelevance: in recognizing this, Danto (2013 p. 25) was effectively following Duchamp's dismissal of "... what he called 'retinal art' — art that gratified the eye". Moreover, as Danto (2013 p. 37) noted, "... if there were no visible differences [between some artworks and some 'real things'], there must have been *invisible* differences" — the sorts of differences perhaps explained by reference to the narrative of art history, since it is "... quite out of the question that one identify the content of works of art on the basis of their visual properties" (Danto, 2000 p. 134). But such cultural matters can only be explained by drawing on human normativity; again, not the province of causal explanation.

Montero's final suggestion for a "dancer's aesthetic" might focus instead on dance making. Yet what of discussion of the *experience* of making the dance: is that just part of its causal story? Or it has a bearing on the work, such that — seeing the dance — one is seeing this 'activity'? Yes, insofar as one is looking at the artist's (here, the choreographer's) fulfilled intentions; if he failed to do something, or changed his mind, that is irrelevant to what finally ended up in the dance. Since our interest is in the artwork, that is where such interest should be directed.

§10.   Conclusion

Our central idea has been that judgements about dances must be answerable to what occurs, identified in sublunary descriptions of danceworks. Then our concern with the audience for danceworks draws our attention to the sensory modalities potentially involved here, understood metaphorically as the question: 'what crosses the footlights to the audience?'. For answers clarify what can be used appropriately to make sense of danceworks. Thus central questions concern (first) whether the idea of a kinaesthetic sensory modality makes any sense in explanation of dancers knowing their own bodily positions; (second) whether the idea of a kinaesthetic sensory modality makes any sense for the claims of audience members to know the bodily positions of dancers; (third) whether the appreciative understanding of the audience could be explained via a kinaesthetic sensory modality for dancers. Moreover, a receptive audience is not, say, one with powerful proprioceptive receptors (on a parallel with enhanced visual acuity): as above, what one needs is not those parrots with greater visual acuity than people, but people who can recognize and respond to *danceworks*.

Setting aside as misconceived those places where John Martin seems to appeal to *metakinesis*, and rewriting and up-dating his view in this respect, we have seen that reliable criticism requires our attention to the fulfilled intentions of artists; and that observers should be suitably informed, suitably sensitive, and suitably positioned. Of course, an idealized critic might represent all these dimensions to the highest degree. Still, a John Martin-type project is validated by the fact that we can learn to see artworks appropriately, and learn to value them, where that involves both learning the concepts and learning to mobilize those concepts in our appreciation of the dancework. For we can be taught to be *better* appreciators (see also Chapter Ten §§6-7).

Of course, such appreciation, and one's education into it, are normative, human procedures: we need to improve our *perceptiveness*, and not just (say) our visual acuity. And such improvement is possible, through practice. So there is a limit to what the empirical investigations can tell us while they do not focus at this human level. The interface between dancers and audience (through performance) must offer just that accountability for artistic judgements of danceworks. That will speak against the relevance, if not the possibility, of a "dancer's aesthetic" (PAD pp. 188-189); and focus attention away from the claims of the audience to kinaesthetic appreciation.

Chapter Ten
Crossing the footlights (2):
meeting neuroscience

§1. Introduction

Reservations concerning the appropriateness of the neuroscientific investigations of dancers to our discussions in philosophical aesthetics really amount to difficulties in determining the compass of neurobiology; as such, they raise doubts whether what is *taken* from neurobiology and cognitive science is what it really says. Such issues remain in the background of any such attempt to apply 'knowledge' within philosophy; my discussions addressed two or three central questions (see Chapter Nine §9-10):

- Did the idea of a kinaesthetic sensory modality make any sense applied to dancers knowing their own bodily positions?

- Did the idea of a kinaesthetic sensory modality make any sense applied to audience members knowing the bodily positions of dancers?

- Could a kinaesthetic sensory modality for dancers have a bearing on the appreciative understanding of the audience?

I took (and take) arguments from Elizabeth Anscombe to demonstrate the "no" answer to the first question (see Chapter Eight §6): such a sensory modality is not needed to know where our bodily parts are. Knowing this is just something we humans can typically do, although more and less well. Hence, if asked, '*How* do we do it?', no answer at the level of human agency is forthcoming. So, pressing for some explanation of *how* we do it attempts to go "further back" (OC §471) than the beginning of the story.[1] And we know how one learns to actualize the capacity. Further, kinaesthesis cannot offer the kind of projective sensory modality required to reach 'across the footlights', as it were. Finally, knowing the causal history of movements could never be decisive here, since artistic appreciation depends on those (cultural) features of the dancework recognizable only after the 'transfiguration' of these movements into dance.

§2. Just what is my view?

Carroll & Seeley (2013 p. 180b) report that "[t]he key to McFee's position is a set of claims about the nature of kinaesthetic exchange in perceptual contexts". But I am at a loss to recognize myself in their description, partly because I cannot grasp some of their uses of terms (for instance, "kinaesthetic" in the passage quoted, not "kinetic" — which appears later with no explanation that I can discern), but chiefly because their expositions of 'my' points differ very radically from any I would use: thus I took myself to be arguing against the possibility of "kinaesthetic exchange".

Apparently I urge "... that the expressive bodily movements of an agent are involuntary and so do not embody any intention to communicate anything" (Carroll & Seeley, 2013 p. 180b). But "involuntary" here subverts my commitment to 'no modification without aberration' (Austin, 1979 p. 189; see Chapter One §6). Instead I acknowledged, as fundamental, the contrast between so-called "lingcomm" and "percomm" (see Best, 1978 pp. 138-162): the first involved action embodying the intention to communicate, the second merely behaviour from which an observer could learn facts about me. Thus the yawn at the meeting (Best's *percomm*), from which my boss learns that such meetings bore me (the very last thing I wanted her to discover), contrasts with my catching your eye and yawning extravagantly (Best's *lingcomm*: see PAD p. 190; compare the different use in UD pp. 243-244, relating specifically to intention). Then bodily movements not embodying the intention to communicate could not be *communicative* in the sense in which the actions of the dancer, actions for which he/she is *responsible*, clearly were. Yet, for Carroll & Seeley (2013 p. 180b), my view was "... that even if such an intention were present, automatic sensorimotor responses do not constitute knowledge of any intention to communicate something in moving that way". Here, one must be careful: genuine *meaning* requires the intention to mean; thus, the cracks in the wall, resulting from the earthquake damage, not only *do* not spell my loved one's name, they *could* not. And that intention is absent in *percomm* cases. Further, I am unsure what is meant by "automatic" above: but, on our primary question about 'what crosses the footlights', I take it that any such responses derive from what is *seen*! That has been my view throughout. Further, I allegedly have some problem with 'levels' here, reputedly arguing that:

> ... although motor perception may operate at a subpersonal level to convey subliminal information involved in the social coordination of action, it cannot constitute an explicit channel of communication. (Carroll & Seeley, 2013 p. 180b). [Citation to PAD p. 190]

Again, this contravenes my Austinian principle: "explicit" here is hopelessly misleading as to my view, in implying that there is indeed *communication* here — that is what I deny! Further, Hornsby (1997 p. 164) rightly raises an objection to sub-personal Psychology in general: that its purpose is "... to explain over again the things commonsense psychology can be used to explain", but this will not be its outcome. Hence:

We can understand how a person is able to catch balls by supposing that certain calculations are carried out. But they are carried out inside her; and not *by* her. (Hornsby, 1997 p. 165)

And so that task is misconceived, precisely in failing to address what *the person* does (the behaviour understood as human action), rather than the causal story underpinning it, or something like it.[2] Similarly, Anscombe (1957 § 23 [p. 38]) rightly notes that:

> ... the description in 'Why are you contracting those muscles?' is ruled out if the only sort of answer to the question 'Why?' displays that the man's knowledge, if any, that he was contracting those muscles is an inference from his knowledge of anatomy.

So that he did not, say, *try* to do this! Further, as she continues:

> ... the description in the question 'Why are you generating those substances in your nerve fibres?' will in fact always be ruled out along these lines unless we suppose that the man has a plan of producing these substances (if it were possible, we might suppose he wanted to collect some). (Anscombe, 1957 § 23 [p. 38])

Or, like a character in Iain M. Banks's 'Culture' novels, that he had the power to 'gland' certain desirable substances — an alternative to drug-taking! But this is something we can neither *do* nor aim to do.[3]

Moreover, I appear the one not giving due weight to the potential for action of *persons*. Apparently my "... central assumption is that kinaesthesis lacks the structure necessary to explain artistic communication ... [because that] ... requires a higher-order capacity to recognize how a movement, an action or a gesture is being used as a communicative device" (Carroll & Seeley, 2013 p. 180b). But I would never assert this. For me, speaking indifferently of "... a movement, an action or a gesture" (quoted above) is a huge give-away: *movements*, *actions* and *gestures* must be sharply distinguished precisely to recognize the possibilities of actions. That is, my response emphasizes the need for wariness of, say, 'confusable counterpart' cases (in the manner of Danto): a *movement* (perhaps even an 'automatic' one, as with the yawn) may be mistaken for an *action* — and then the (lack of) communicative possibilities will be missed.

But, in focusing on our human capacity for actions, has insufficient weight been given to the explanation of the bodily movement that 'underlies' it? And so on, for other biological underpinnings? Against me, Carroll & Seeley (2013 note p. 185b) urge that:

> ... it is hard to see how facts about the biological substrate for the higher capacity for communication could fail to be relevant to a *complete*

explanation of dance communication. (my emphasis)

Three issues arise here: (a) about "higher capacity" — I distinguished the kind of communication involving the intention to communicate from cases where, despite the absence of such an intention, there were inferences to be drawn (say, about thoughts or feelings). Where is the 'higher-and-lower' here, unless language (obviously involving intentional meaning) is regarded as somehow the 'top of the tree'? As repeated below (§4), the differences here have nothing to do with levels: rather they relate to the difference between what is meaning-bearing and what is not; or, if this is different, what is deliberate and what is not. The preferred language of Carroll & Seeley here, of *cues* and such like, makes the difference between a sound and a word seem, roughly, what can be *inferred* from each. But I do not *infer* the meaning of words in a language I know, except in some very unusual cases. Since I can *read* and *understand* the word, no cues are necessary for my making sense of it. Then (b) the explanation should be "complete": for what purposes? Given my occasion-sensitive account of understanding, asking for *completeness* will always be relevant to some purpose. Likening the problem to a jigsaw puzzle, Austin (1962 p. 120 note) says, "... since the number of pieces in a puzzle [of *that* sort] is not finite, we can never know that any puzzle is perfect, there may be pieces missing or pieces that won't fit". So such *completeness* is an unattainable ideal. Finally (c) "relevant" to what? No one would deny the tongue being a 'biological substrate' normally necessary for speech; but neither is that relevant to most discussions of what is said!

Then how are dances to be understood? I certainly stressed the connection of answerability to the sensory modalities involved. To characterize my emphasis here on the relevant sensory modalities of perception, Carroll & Seeley (2013 p. 178a) offer:

> Blindfold audience members and they miss the dance. Therefore dance appreciation cannot be a matter of kinetic transfer [whatever that is] – rather, we see the dance. Of course, this may be correct as far as it goes – our primary perceptual engagement with dance in ordinary contexts is visual. But this does not go very far.

Have I been negligent in failing to mention sound (that is, hearing) in my account of dance appreciation? No: for, summarizing my position, I urged that "... the artistic appreciation of dance ... must draw on *projective* sensory modalities (sight, hearing) rather than the contiguous ones (taste, touch)" (PAD p. 186), explicitly mentioning hearing. Likewise, I urged that, whatever the detail of the mechanism of perception, "... the mechanism must, in the end, reflect a projective sensory modality" (McFee, 2013 p. 189). Again, I said "... even leaving aside *which* sensory modalities there are, the operation of an audience for dance requires (at least) that only what I have called 'projective' sensory modalities be involved in dance appreciation" (McFee, 2013 p. 191b). Certainly I join commonsense in thinking that recognizing or appreciating dances was, or involved, a modality of sense: but what sensory modalities are there? Again, I have stressed 'the five senses' here. Of course, appeals to the sense of direction or sense of humour are familiar invocations of human powers and capacities but no *distinctive* sensory modality is involved in such cases (we *see* the amusing slapstick; we *hear* the one-liner; we *read* the comic novel [a special case]; just as we *notice*, however subliminally, whatever landmarks permit the sense of direction). No distinctive modalities are invoked here, although such cases involve the senses: appeal is to a complex package of powers and capacities of humans. Similarly, for invoking a sense to explain the location of bodily motion (but whose? That will be key) when, as here, there is no *sense*, no sensory modality: we depend here heavily on *seeing* the position (in space) of our bodies — hence the mirrors in typical dance studios!

Carroll & Seeley urge that my account lacks something perceptual: but what? Not some sixth sense, surely? On the contrary, as quoted above, their claims about a blindfolded audience seem to grant the dependence on the visual: vision typically is a necessary condition for reading, and hence for appreciating, the poem *and* (something like that) for appreciating the dance. So no sixth sense seems postulated. I certainly stressed auditory impact, but this is not where Carroll & Seeley go: instead, they move from perception to imagination!!

> It is not absurd to suggest that appreciating written poetry may sometimes involve seeing and aurally *imagining* listening to ourselves or others speaking. Analogously, there should be no problem in asserting that dance appreciation can involve (at least at times) the interplay of both vision and kinaesthetic apprehension. (Carroll & Seeley, 2013 p. 178a: my emphasis)

[But what is "kinaesthetic apprehension"; and how do we do it? Presumably it differs from "kinetic transfer", but in what ways?]

Of course, a few poems ("Easter Wings") require both looking at and reading; and with others, perhaps Manley Hopkins, we might try to insist on reading aloud (you need to read and hear: but then that seems the right thing to say about the sensory modalities involved). And, in typical cases, opera and dance require both seeing and hearing — we might urge that opera was more directly aural, dance more directly visual. While nothing much turns on this, it offers two thoughts: first, this does not seem to be "crossmodal" in any way; second, this discussion is still about perception, unlike the example above. Imagining listening is precisely *not* listening (it is not perceptual): faced with a poem in French, sometimes I must know what, for example, French *sounds* like; and, if that is required, I do not have to *imagine* what it sounds like, but rather find out — perhaps my mastery of reading allows me to make sense of the French poem sonically as well as for its (other) cognitive content. [If reading is imagined, in what accent?] Moreover, the audience at the performance of a dancework should certainly be *watching* the dance; and not imagining *for themselves* features that dance lacks (or may lack). For how can *imagination* be answerable? Any answerability can only be to what audience see or hears — via projective sensory modalities (my point throughout); but what cognitive stock constrains answerability? We must return to these issues (see §5 below).

§3.   What sensory modalities?

> The general literature in neuroscience and psychology does not support the strong division between vision and kinaesthesis that underwrites this objection. (Carroll & Seeley, 2013 p. 178b)

Has neuroscience found another route? Seemingly not since, above, Carroll & Seeley — here as representatives of such neuroscience — accept that blindfolding the audience would limit access. Still, such an emphasis on the commonsense of perception seems outmoded:

> Rather, current research paints a picture of an integrated, crossmodal, *projective kinaesthetic perceptual capacity* that engages embodied motoric, skeletomuscular, somosensory, visual and auditory processes. (Carroll & Seeley, 2013 p. 178b)

The emphasis is on (or anyway suggested thereby) "... an integrated system of crossmodal network [that] biases perception to *diagnostic cues* in the local environment" (Carroll & Seeley, 2013 p. 178b: how exactly does it merely *bias* perception ...?[4]). Here, "[d]iagnostic cues" are explained as "... minimal sets of perceptual features sufficient to enable an organism to categorize, and thereby to recognize the shapes, identities, and affordances of objects, agents and events in a given context" (Carroll & Seeley, 2013 p. 178b) — such an appeal to "cues" should be contrasted with just seeing, hearing, etc.; yet even here it is (and is portrayed as) *perceptual*. Is the "crossmodal" perhaps no more than a combination of modalities? Again, this will not do, since such a combination would only be projective through the projective sensory modalities.

So, on this view, how do I acquire/notice the cues? (I'd say, "visually".) To what is one's appreciation *answerable*? Obviously, to the features of the dance. Then, how do I gain access to those features? I'd say, "through perception". But clearly this is not supposed to be the right kind of answer: what is? This talk of the "crossmodal" suggests I should "... deny the yet uncomprehended process in the yet unexplored medium" (PI §308: See PAD p. 195). Any more charitable response, then, requires explaining how others activate it. Carroll & Seeley, 2013 (p. 181a) take themselves to be agreeing (with me!) that "... a perceiver involuntarily discriminates subconscious bodily cues diagnostic for the kinematics and dynamics of bodily movement", while disputing my claim that such "... automatic causal-perceptual processes ... do not track these kinds of cognitive variables" (Carroll & Seeley, 2013 p. 181a).

§4.   Issue of cues/evidence

Two points must be made here, for later elaboration. First, of course, achieving all this through perception requires a rich account of perception, and especially of visual perception (McFee, 2013 p. 192a-b; PAD p. 188): certainly richer than the minimalist one's offered in some psychology – what does one see (or hear)?[5]

But, second, the account offered by Carroll & Seeley seems flawed, running together the *understanding* of the meaning-bearing and the causal *response* to signals. So, as above, this 'evidential' language (especially talk of "cues") raises problems for me in the context of our seeing and understanding; especially in respect of our grasp on meaning in respect of artworks such as dances. That worry is compounded to the degree that the so-called "cues" are treated as evidence of what is seen. For, as Austin (1962 p. 116) pointed out, my witnessing the murder is not, strictly, *evidence*: "I don't *have* evidence for my own statement that the shooting took place, I actually *saw* it". Perhaps, initially, one has evidence (say) of a pig: "... plenty of pig-like marks on the ground, ... a few buckets of pig-food ... the noises and the smell may provide better evidence still" (Austin, 1962 p. 115). But Austin was rightly insistent that I am not drawing on mere *evidence* of a pig when the pig is before me, in plain sight: my previous worries whether the creature was a pig have disappeared, "... I can now *see* that it is, the question is settled" (my emphasis). Moreover, Austin (1962 pp. 115-116 note) rightly acknowledges the special case where one speaks of the "evidence of one's eyes": "... the point of this trope is exactly that it does *not* illustrate the ordinary use of 'evidence' — I *don't* have evidence in the ordinary sense".

Similarly, neither saying nor reading is well-understood as just encountering evidence for some view: that I *say* such-and-such means, in typical cases and other things being equal, that I am asserting whatever — this is a consequence of my meaning what I say (see Chapter One §2), where what I say is typically something meaning-bearing. Similarly, reading the assertions of another (or my own from another occasion) is engaging with the meaning-bearing: that is what is simulated by children playing at reading, who pretend that squiggles on a page are actually words and sentences.

Taking one's engagement with meaning-bearing texts (or objects) as simply causal interaction misses much that is crucial. For the idea of the *meaning-bearing* makes sense only against the contrast with the causally-efficacious but *not* (genuinely) meaning-bearing. Someone's saying, "Argh!" may be sufficient to warn one of an approaching car or an angry bull. But if one fails to distinguish such a case from one where there is a genuine warning uttered — even if it takes the form of just shouting "Bull!" or "Watch out!" — one has lost the sense in which these later sounds instantiate *words* (and words in a language), such that one can understand them or fail to understand them. For instance, if I say, "Bull", intending only to contribute to your quadruped-identification skills, and you take it (as above) as a warning, you have mistaken it — that is not what I said! And, of course, that point becomes *more* profound the more that is actually said; for that leaves more to misunderstand and, correspondingly, more ways of misunderstanding it. The words themselves must be appropriately understood *in this context*: thus, in "Mary had a little lamb", Charles Travis (2006 p. 127; 2008 p. 84; 2013 p. 83) rightly recognized the possibilities of Mary as pet-owner, as meat-eater, and as unfortunate cross-species birth-mother. Once the context of utterance is clear, what is said is typically also clear, although the words *alone* do not always or even usually resolve the matter. So, again, Travis (2011 pp. 243-244) recognized some cases when the instruction, "Bring me the meat!" would be satisfied by bringing offal (say, kidneys), so that offal counts as meat; and those where it would not. (Similarly, "blue" still means "blue" in the case of occasion-sensitivity in Chapter One §7.)

Thus, when confronting a particular sequence of *words*, one must recognize what those words amount to then (that utterance) in this context; and that may further require my recognizing both formal features — for example, that it is a poem; and a poem of a certain kind — and other contextual contributions. Many examples here would, in effect, draw on confusable counterparts. If I mistake "Herr" for "hair", I have misunderstood — it has a meaning I have missed: taking the sound for just an inchoate grunt would be a different mistake. Again, in a well-used example, if I read Swift's *Modest Proposal* missing its irony, such that I take it as seriously suggesting cannibalism, I have drastically misunderstood it: it was not the document I took it for. Moreover, I might have been mistaken because I mis-valued Swift, in spite of everything. For the task involves correctly identifying what Swift said, in presenting those words in that order; and hence what these words mean as 'uttered' in this context.

Of course, the term "meaning" is used in a number of ways: for instance, to identify what is important to me (perhaps through some association to another, unrelated event). Then its *meaning for me* is not, after all, meaning! But, with genuine meaning, there is an implicit contrast of *understanding what*

is meant not only with *failure* to understand but also with *misunderstanding* —
only the first of these could be causal. For, of course, only what is rightly
understood — even if in a variety of ways — can also be misunderstood; and
that in turn must be contrasted with its lacking *causal* efficacy. The shout that
warns me, but in a language I do not know, succeeds as a warning, although
failing as a (meaning-bearing) word. If one does not differentiate one's
encounters with the meaning-bearing from those lacking (strict) meaning,
one cannot give a good account of either: that, of course, remains the point in
drawing the *lingcomm/percomm* distinction (Best, 1978 pp. 138-162). Again,
our general discussion of meaning (in earlier Chapters) factors in here: in
particular, the idea that *responsibility* for what we mean/say follows from its
normativity.

These insights bear directly on the explanatory force of the claims of
neuroscience in respect of danceworks: what is needed, as a parallel, is not
the recognition of various *cues* or *indicators*, but the *understanding* of various
meaning-bearing signs — and even the term "sign" makes the process
sound too reductively causal. For words are ... well, *words*: that is, roughly,[6]
meaning-bearing units in the context of utterances. Further, the impact of
those words changes to some degree when they are found in the artwork:
that is, (especially) the poem and the novel. But critical commentary on
other artworks will recognize the formal impact from those artforms. So here
again (see Chapter One §3) understanding language, as meaning-bearing,
is acknowledged to offer a model for understanding both action and the
arts — and hence understanding dance. For the *intentional* differs from that
merely involved in the working out of causal forces: what is intentional is
thereby *normative* — we can fail to understand it, despite responding to it:
our responses can be inappropriate. Moreover, the meaning of danceworks
is *embodied* meaning; that guarantees the answerability of its meaning to
the embodied object or event. (Again, the simplest version of the idea here
is visible in reading language: what these words amount to in this context
depends, roughly, on the words and their order, plus the punctuation — with
perhaps certain occasion-based features to add.)

Drawing their discussion together, Carroll & Seeley (2013 p. 182b) offer
a "... take-home point [they urge] is threefold". (I will comment on each
element in turn):

> First, the formal-compositional practices of choreographers (and dancers)
> are explicitly and intentionally directed at the production of sensorimotor
> cues diagnostic for the content of their work.

No: although unsure just at what *all* the "formal-compositional practices"
of choreographers are directed, nor that there is one target at which they
are *all* directed, I am sure it is not this. Why? Because choreographers, like

other artists, are engaged in making *meaning*: artworks are *embodied meanings* (Danto, 2013 p. 48). My conclusion follows from Danto's insight, although accepting that insight need not commit us to everything he said. Further, just as understanding meaning is not a matter of grasping cues, so making meaning also does not amount to making "cues diagnostic" of that meaning — since we do not offer *evidence* of its meaning when we compose a poem. Rather, the words *comprise* the poem: they are not *evidence* for it, or *cues* to its understanding. And the same goes for dance, once the complexity of its meaning is acknowledged.

> Second, crossmodal sensorimotor processes are critical to the role these diagnostic cues play in our capacity to perceive, recognize and understand these works. (Carroll & Seeley, 2013 p. 182b)

Again, not hardly: even without doubting the 'crossmodal' as a category, or the sleight-of-hand that permits processes to be "sensorimotor" when the 'sensori'-part refers to my perception and the 'motor'-part to the dancer's movement, we know that the *understanding* of the works cannot be reduced to a causal story about them, no matter how complicated, until such a story can address the normativity of misunderstanding, thereby precluding misunderstanding. But this cannot be available to such causal stories because, as Frege pointed out, there will be causal stories for the good and the bad, for understanding and misunderstanding — while I might not believe it, some might even be *crossmodal sensorimotor* stories: still, all the complexity is wasted!

> Finally, we can intend to communicate things without knowing what makes the communication possible. (Carroll & Seeley, 2013 p. 182b)

This is both true and important; but if our concern is with dance *the artform*, first, genuine communication (Best's *lingcomm*) must be at issue; second, 'not knowing what makes the communication possible' is consistent with knowing *for sure* what would preclude it: for dance, Carroll & Seeley agree with me that a blindfold and earplugs (that is, excluding the projective sensory modalities) would achieve this; and, third, the training needed to become a better observer of dance, a closer critic of what happens in danceworks, begins from watching and discussing dances, embodied cultural meanings — merely improving one's eyesight alone will not achieve this. Given the grounding these three points provide, perhaps we know rather more about what makes communication in dance possible (and especially *impossible*) than we thought.

§5.   The need for naturalism

Carroll & Seeley (2013 p. 183) refer to the roots of my position by calling it a "Wittgensteinian objection": they suggest preferring the naturalism of Aristotle. And apparently Conroy (2013 p. 2007) accepts both the description of me they offer and the preference for Aristotle they urge. But Aristotle was a careful drawer of distinctions, especially in respect of *agency*. As Austin (1979 p. 273) points out, Aristotle is alive to just the distinction here, dismissing the causal story in favour of that normative one that permits excuses and the like; and thereby stresses intention. As I have made clear (McFee, 2015a pp. 341-342), I admire this Aristotle. So my view here is strongly motivated by the naturalism that begins from what people can do; and hence takes as its starting point the view of persons as agents, typically able to use language (with its associated normativity). This naturalism imports the idea that typical people can just *do* certain things, where typically no answer is possible as to how they do them (see §6 below): there is no *way* that the people do it, or nothing to say about why, beyond, "Well, they are people ...". And that in turn implies a class of things that *one knows without observation*. Giving the example of knowing the position of one's limbs without observation, Anscombe (1957 p. 13) rightly infers that "[i]t is without observation, because nothing *shews* him the position of his limbs; it is not as if he were going by a tingle in his knee, which is a sign that it is bent and not straight". And given that this is what one can (typically) do, it is easy to recognize how that fact came about: one *learned* to do the thing — and, for dancers, dance-training with that as its aim can be identified in practice.

Moreover, there was nothing especially Wittgensteinian about the arguments here, although (of course) both Anscombe and I are Wittgensteinians. But, with that suggestion made, one might appeal to Wittgenstein's insight that, in philosophy, the difficulty is often "... to begin at the beginning. And not try to go further back" (OC §471). For often that makes the mischief: a further layer, or level, of question to be asked is imagined, especially when a causal description (not explanation, note) seems to be available. But that is to fall into the pit that, throughout, I have diagnosed by quoting Frege.

§6.   Thinking about perception

When one has a response to seeing a dance, that response could be given a causal description (like any bodily response, but also any human response). But is one's response appropriate, given the kind of dance this is?

(a) that it is a dance may be contentious: consider confusable counterparts, where the 'bodily movements' are the same in both cases — where does that leave the "... sensorimotor diagnostic cues" (Carroll & Seeley, 2013 p. 178b)?;

(b) that it is a modern dance, and therefore appropriately judged as such, may be contentious;

(c) that it is a Cunningham-technique-style modern dance might escape notice, although that would be appropriate.

Like many accounts of perception, one failing to address at least the second and third questions (or their parallels) is flawed in that it "... ignores the interlock between perception and cognition" (Wollheim, 1993a p. 134).

There are (or might be) three causal stories in these cases. Since their contours are necessarily similar, the same causal mechanisms and the same sensory modality must apply when someone (say, some critic) *misunderstands* the dancework under consideration as when that critic *understands* it. That is the upshot of our insight-bearing slogan from Frege. So, despite our previous discussions, there is therefore no benefit to disputing the sensory modalities relevant to dance appreciation: disputes over what sensory modality is involved must be beside the point, insofar as what *is* at issue is whether our critic's *judgement* of the dancework is correct, since both aim at *answerability* to the details of the dancework and at justifiably offering the audience a way to make sense of that dancework (and hence a way to *see* it). Hence Frege correctly identifies that some stories are, others are not, normatively correct: to understand the differences in responsibility for actions that are 'confusable counterparts', think about naming ships — the difference does not lie in, say, the changes in musculature; but the Queen can name ships, and I cannot (even if I say the right words); and we can imagine a case where the Queen, saying the wrong words, mis-names the ship — that is, gives it a name other than that intended.

The *real* history of the philosophy of perception (the one flowing through Austin) distinguishes seeing a person from seeing a depiction of a person, on the assumption that (at least usually — and hence defeasibly) these can actually be distinguished in practice. For I see myself "... as purely registering how things are; as doing what proper sensitivity, and suitable exposure, to the world makes compulsory" (Travis, 2011 p. 89). Indeed, the standard response to the starting point of much philosophy of perception, in the argument from illusion,[7] falls down here: as though, when looking at a straight stick immersed in water, we do not *notice* the water! And, even in more artificial cases,[8] any mistakes as to what we are perceiving can often be pointed out and typically rectified.

Further, and crucially, perception is a property of *persons*,[9] not of eyes, brains, and so on, even if eyes seem a precondition for *seeing*. So there is a limit to what a story about eyes, or brains, can really tell us here. No doubt that causal substrate is important; but it will not help us distinguish seeing the *ringer* (as Travis, 2011 p. 91 calls it: Chapter Eight §2) from veridical perception. But that does not mean that we cannot do it.

What can one really learn about our perception of, for instance, dances from our perception of *depictions* of dance? Only a special (very strong) view of the transparency of the photographic process seems to make even vaguely plausible the suggestion that one should learn that much by comparing those cases. And, certainly, such a view of transparency for photography does not seem defensible across the board. The confusion comes, of course, because advocates of research protocols of the sort that depend on *depictions* of dance (say, on film) imagine that at some brute, empirical level there is no difference: that (say) the very same light rays strike the retina of subjects in both the case of *real* perception and the perception of depictions. So there is no room for such differences in *what is seen*. But, at best, this is simply an assumption — and one that conflicts with our commonsense recognition that we can typically tell one from the other.

Moreover, the *passivity* of perception in this way is another key — and contestable — assumption of the kind of experimentation discussed earlier. The assumption seems to be that watching a real action and watching a depiction of that action (say, on film) are equivalent. Yet we know that is false, in at least two cases. First, as earlier, the depiction is not typically mistaken for the event — the murder depicted on television is not typically confused with one some unfortunate might see ("witness") on a closed-circuit television camera. Indeed, context plays in more crucially: the murder depicted in a play in a theatre is not typically confused with the real murder; and here there is no mediating technology. Further, experimenters here do not attempt to trick their subjects as to what is occurring; nor express the desire to do this, were it practically feasible. They seem content to ignore what their subjects *know* to be taking place, as though that were irrelevant.

Yet, second, (human) perception is typically concept-involving (and hence regularly concept-mediated): seeing a tree involves the capacity to recognize trees; and hence mastery (to some degree) of the concept *tree*. Then our perceptual range can be modified by acquiring a more refined conceptual repertoire: say, mastery of the concepts *ash, elm, oak*, such that I can see elms and oaks, when you only see trees, more generically. Such concerns are excluded from the picture — common in psychology — that reduces perception to what the case where I can distinguish elms from oaks *shares* with one where I have only mastered the concept *tree*. And, again, patterns of light and shade on the retina need not be important here, since they need not differ relevantly. In thus reflecting our concepts and their contexts of application, human perception is not entirely passive.

Dustin Stokes (2014 p. 1) asked whether perception, especially artistic perception, "... is *cognitively penetrable*", such that "... there [are] instances where two perceivers, by virtue of distinct background beliefs, visually perceive the same object as distinct, say, in size or colour". Here, Stokes (2004 p. 2) remarked on:

> A commonsense intuition ... that how one sees or hears or otherwise perceives artworks is pervasively affected by what one knows, believes or values about artworks.

But we *know* that 'confusable counterparts' objects can be seen differently: *this* one as an artwork, *that* as something else. It follows that persons with a different understanding, and so on, may see paintings differently, or hear musical works differently, for this reason: so it *seems* that, at least, *artistic perception* (the perception of artworks as artworks) will be cognitively penetrable.[10]

Certainly, artistic perception is intentional. Thus, when our person looks at the cubist painting, or listens to the atonal music, if he/she fails to recognize them as, respectively, cubist and atonal, he/she misperceives — he/she sees them as they are *not*. So perhaps this situation is not well captured by thinking about *cognitive penetration*, since only one of the 'views' is ultimately sustainable (the other being false). This fact returns us to the need for a person-centred approach to making sense of (in our case) dance.

Further, since much writing in psychology refers to *processing* (say, in the context of information processing in perception), comment on the language of 'processing' is worthwhile: my body is certainly capable of processing a fair amount of beer, turning it into urine (perhaps some gases) as well as its contribution to my 'middle-aged spread'. But the very *automatic* quality of this automatic *process* (or set of them) questions its relation to the decisions and choices of appreciation: it could have little or nothing to do with my ability to *understand* or *make sense of* dance. The first is bodily in a way that the second is not — even though I am just this body (this anatomy and physiology). And John Martin (1965 p. 33) too was keen to identify the irrelevance to his interpretative project of what is automatic in this way, commenting that "... if a man made no more active response to art than the table to sunlight he would experience no more reaction" — for the table's 'response' is passive and automatic!

Of course, I am not claiming that in every case, for all purposes, looking at the film differs from looking at the dance. Still, there is room for discussion here — especially once one recognizes sets of cases where *whether this is so* seems a reasonable question to ask, but where that question of whether there is a justifiable difference *in this context* fails to be asked, despite some obvious differences, of the kind identified here.

To repeat, my point here is not subtle: it says only that moves typical of the psychology of perception ignore facts from which such an investigation should really begin. With perception not recognized as a human power, one simply begins from the causal substrate which (as a materialist) I accept underlies such human processes. But saying *that* is precisely not granting that causal perspective as required for philosophically-revealing investigations of the perceptual faculties of humans. And, of course, once this assumption is removed, it becomes very hard to *set up* the fMRI studies required (or imagined): at their heart, the assumption concerned what was involved in studying cases of (say) my seeing X; but it turns out that, in none of the cases, is *that* actually investigated, since all the experimentation concerns depictions of events. [So, it is scientistic in not studying what is claimed ...]

§7.   Applied to art?

How should these general concerns with perception be applied to the (perceptually-rooted) appreciation of art? Well, in part such an application comes first: our interest was never in the causal substrate of artistic appreciation, shared (if/when it is) with other aesthetic interest. But, of course, one might imagine that, now, a greater emphasis could be given to the relation of artist to audience:

> As a general rule, artists develop formal and compositional strategies because ... they enable audience members, viewers, listeners, spectators and readers to recover the content of works in a range of different media. (Carroll & Seeley, 2013 p. 181a)

This claim seems to import a dualism between the "content of works" and the "strategies" of artists to permit the audience access to that content: the artwork is taken as a *means* to generate that content in ways that the audience might access. By contrast, we have seen Danto (2013 p. 37) rightly calling artworks *"embodied meanings"*: that is, for Danto, the artworks are the meanings, as the poem *just is* those words in that order — the words are not mere 'cues' to either the poem or its meaning.

By contrast, Carroll & Seeley (2013 p. 181a) write of the "[c]ues diagnostic for the category of art ...". But in what sense are these (just) "cues"? And in what sense are they "diagnostic"? Can one learn from them that one is seeing an artwork? That seems wrong both given the possibility of non-art 'confusable counterparts', and because a work in a new art-genre might lack whatever features were stressed.

We are told that such 'cues' "... instruct audience members how to engage the work — what to look for and where to look for it" (Carroll & Seeley, 2013 p. 181a). Clearly, it will be important to recognize *this* as a cubist painting, *that* as a Graham-technique dance, *the other* as atonal music — otherwise we will misperceive the works. So there is something to do here. Moreover, the broad patterns associated with such *categories of art* allows Walton (2008 p. 199) to recognize some features as *standard* for a particular category, others as contra-standard, and yet others as *variable* for that category. In effect, these terms simply offer a vocabulary for discussing the different practical examples case-by-case. For a major cubist painting can have features typically contra-standard but that, here, seem essential to its cubist character — in reality, one cannot draw exceptionless classes here; nor imagine exceptionless 'cues', even though one might begin to teach appreciation by highlighting typically-recurring features. One might even think of Aristotle's discussion of *tragedy* (Aristotle, 1984 pp. 2321-2322): while that description sits moderately well on the tragedies of Sophocles, and hence might be used to teach beginners something about the structure of tragedies, it sits rather ill on the tragedies of Euripides — works that Aristotle, like us, justifiably preferred. Perhaps the point is to offer the beginner a framework sufficient to permit an understanding of the deviations from that framework instantiated by many masterpieces.

Such a model of learning-through-experience does not readily accommodate the conception on which the learner is provided with 'cues'. As our discussion of John Martin (Chapter Nine §§ 4-7) illustrated, the possibility of acquiring *discernment* here is crucial to any conceptualization of appreciation of art (and especially learning such appreciation). And, of course, the situation is further complicated for dance by the need to accommodate, as understanders, both dancers and audience-members/critics. As suggested (Chapter Nine §3), if the powers and capacities of dancers here were contrasted with those of 'Everyperson', and especially if one focused on the epistemological stance of each (or what each could know), then Conroy (2013 p. 203b) was right to emphasize the second of these, insofar as our interest was in artistic appreciation.

But, for analytic purposes, one might sketch instead a three-part contrast, between the dancers, the 'general public', and the dance-critics (perhaps drawing, for our model, on John Martin: Chapter Nine §5). And, as Wollheim (1993a p. 133) begins:

> I shall assume what I in fact take to be beyond question: that the aim of criticism of the arts is, in a broad sense of those terms, to understand, or to grasp the meaning of, the work of art.

Answerability must embrace this meaning: how is it open to perception? For it is clear that knowledgeable observers, and perhaps sensitive ones, should rightly be accorded a special place here; for the critic requires:

> ... [s]trong sense, united to delicate sentiment, improved by practice, and cleared of all prejudice, can alone entitle critics to this valuable character;

and the joint verdict of such, wherever they are to be found, is the true standard of taste and beauty. (Hume [1741] 1985 p. 241)

This will allow works to pass the Test of Time. For instance, it might seem reasonable to support the judgement that Shakespeare's plays are great art by pointing out how many centuries they have been acclaimed. Moreover, as Levinson (2006 p. 382) noted, "[i]deal critics are best suited to judging the potential of new works because their artistic tastes and appreciative habits have been honed on and formed by uncontested masterpieces ...".

This suggestion, though, stresses again one point from the previous discussion: the differences here reside in the knowledge and sensitivity of the stance of what we are calling "the critic" — in particular, not in any epistemological advantage. So, again, appropriate visual acuity is at best presupposed; enhancing it is not automatically advantageous. For, as Wollheim (1980 pp. 193-194) expresses it:

> ... what is perceptible is always dependent not only upon such physical factors as the nature of the stimulus, the state of the organism, and the prevailing local conditions, but also upon cognitive factors ... to be filled out in terms of a person whose scrutiny is authoritative, or 'the ideal critic' ...

Moreover, this conception permits us to locate the idealization of this 'ideal critic' through the cognitive and sensitive powers thereby ascribed. Moreover, as Wollheim (1995 p. 36) summarizes a key thesis from his *Painting as an Art*, "... the meaning of a painting combines what a sensitive spectator can see in it and what the artist intended it to convey". The same could, of course, be said *mutatis mutandis* for the meaning-bearing aspect of other artforms. As we saw (Chapter Nine §1), and drawing on his specific interests in that work, Wollheim (1987 p. 36) comments, "... if we are to understand when and why painting is an art, we must consider it from the perspective of the artist". Even though, in practice: "... the spectator will always understand more than the artist intended, and the artist will always have intended more than any single spectator understands" (Wollheim, 1980 §51 [p. 119]). Of course, as Wollheim (1987 p. 39) recognizes, "... although adopting the perspective of the artist requires us to give pride of place to what the agent does, ... it does not require us to ignore or reject the point of view of the spectator". For the artist's *fulfilled* intentions are connected with what a suitably positioned, suitably informed, and suitable sensitive spectator sees in the work (Wollheim, 1987 p. 357).

Moreover, both elements — artist's intention and suitable spectator — involve, in different ways, "the artist's perspective". For, in context, this perspective on his art connects the artist's view of his own work with his view of the artform into which it is a contribution (and his conception both of the historical narrative and the current state of that artform). For intention, the connection to the artist's perspective is explicit; for the spectator, it involves being suitably informed (for instance, as to the narrative of art history) so as to bring to bear on this work the *appropriate* cognitive stock.

Of course (and retaining the example of painting, for the moment), "... if we take any particular painted surface, it is always possible that suitably sensitive, although insufficiently informed, spectators will be able to see different things in it" (Wollheim, 1995 p. 34). But such disagreements must be resolvable (at least in principle) if the ascription of meaning to the painting is to make sense: that is, as a bulwark of answerability against subjectivism:

> ... at this stage ... the intention of the artist has a role to play. For, of those things which the spectator can see in the painting, it is correct for him to see only ... those things which the artist intended. (Wollheim, 1995 p. 34)

Yet such a claim (especially applied *mutatis mutandis* to dance) must begin from our revised view of 'artist's intention' (see Chapter One §8). Then the force of the idea of *fulfilled* intentions must be stressed, since this is what permits the previous claim. As Wollheim (1993a pp. 139-140) commented, in respect of *fulfilled* intentions:

> ... to the extent to which they are fulfilled, they can be recovered from the work of art by scrutiny, and the only circumstances in which they aren't recoverable from the work of art is when they are unfulfilled and hence critically irrelevant.

For any critical commentary not answerable to the work, properly understood, is irrelevant: it will be 'reading into' the work claims not true of it. In this way, first, any *unfulfilled* intentions (or failed plans of the artists) are set aside; and, second, the cognitive stock appropriate to that critic is specified: it should be such as to permit the recognition of those fulfilled intentions. For reference to the artists' intention here just has the role "... of selecting between things that are visible in the picture" (Wollheim, 1995 p. 35). Then the net effect is that this account:

> ... leaves the meaning of the painting where we want it to be: neither in the head of the artist nor in the head of the spectator, but firmly on the surface of the painting. (Wollheim, 1995 p. 36)

And, *mutatis mutandis*, for the other arts. For it acknowledges *answerability*.

This in turn shows how the art critic can function as *maker of taste*, since these critics "... hope to shape the taste of their readers" (Carroll, 2008 p. 193[11]), by pointing out what they see as valuable in the artworks they discuss. The audience can then learn to see these things as valuable (to see value in them). In elaboration, Carroll (2009, p. 47) quotes Dryden:

They wholly mistake the notion of criticism who think its primary business is to find fault. Criticism as it was first instituted by Aristotle was meant as a standard for judging well, the chiefest part of which is to observe those excellences which should delight a reasonable reader.

For here attention is to the "excellences" that audience-members can then learn to value (that is, to see value in them); where thesevare what "should delight" them, not what will — again, there is room for learning: they can *come to* that delight when guided by our critic. (Again, the idealization of the role permits a succinct exposition of it. It also offers a reason why, in contrast to Conroy noted above (Chapter Nine §3), Montero (2013 pp. 172-173) is right here to stress the role of *critics* — who one might hope were careful in what they asserted; but, as this case would show, only some are! Yet we should not automatically accept that, because a critic speaks of, say, "kinaesthetic resonance", such a concept is philosophically respectable: indeed, the reason to worry about dualism in John Martin was precisely that even good critics can absorb some bad philosophy.

Moreover, it is important, too, that our arguments should be sound. Thus, Montero (2013 p. 174a) offers an apparently methodological point:

> ... if art critics generally accept something as a work of art, such as a Marcel Duchamp readymade, it is reasonable to accept it as such unless one has good arguments to the contrary. Correlatively, if dance critics generally accept the aesthetic relevance of kinaesthetic sympathy, it is reasonable to accept that it is [relevant?] unless there are good arguments to the contrary.

The procedure is sound as far as it goes: we should accept what (say) critics say until we have good reason not to. But there is a good argument here! If the critic imports, say, dualism in the philosophy of mind, or the identity theory, that critic's comments must be redrafted, given that those pictures embody the philosophically unsound. Also, we have seen Martin's criticism as amenable to just such alternative reading (see Chapter Nine §§ 4-7). Moreover, there is as well as an *argument* for readymades, extant in art history — we are not (or anyway need not be) simply taking them as art on Duchamp's say-so: see Danto, 1987. Moreover, that argument recognizes the need to locate artworks in their history, a process rendered impossible if one's primary explanatory tool is causal — as with neuroscience. For we acknowledge, with Frege, that bad and good artworks both have causal stories; and then the normativity must be explained.

§8. Appropriate pessimism: responding to Davies

To my way of thinking, David Davies and I broadly agree on the fruitfulness of attempting to understand dance by reference to empirical work in neuroscience, to judge by his contribution to the JAAC symposium. At the least, David there classifies us both as pessimists. However, I am accused of "extreme pessimism" (Davies, 2013p. 199b), while he, only a moderate pessimist (Davies, 2013 p. 197a), concludes "... as ever, the moderate pessimist will counsel modesty when the philosopher of art elects to dance with neuroscience" (Davies, 2013 p. 201b). I hear the rebuke implicit in this remark: it is positively immodest of me to behave as I do, voicing my extreme pessimism. Now I agree that there is an element of outrage in my pronouncements, perhaps disproportionate to the evils perpetrated. But I am frankly jealous when I see the vast amounts of money (in the UK, chiefly government money) that such neuroscience-based research attracts.

Still, Davies (2013 p. 199b) grounds his position in a justifiable scepticism here, claiming, as we saw:

> ... the moderate pessimist agrees with the moderate optimist that philosophical work on dance should take account of the best current work in cognitive science that has a bearing on the kinds of capacities exercised by practitioners and receivers.

Moreover, he grants that:

> ... this means we should not avail ourselves of a particular scientific view without taking account of the critical discourse within the relevant branch of science. (Davies, 2013 p. 199a)

Here Davies (2013 p. 200b) exemplifies this point concerning the credibility of work in neuroscience with sound methodological criticisms,[12] or at least doubts, about "... the Parma School and, by extension, to Calvo-Merino and associates' interpretation of their experiments", a tradition is neuroscience beloved by, for instance, Barbara Montero.

Whatever the outcome, there remain issues concerning what follows for philosophy; for, in some cases, "... the empirical evidence in no way *resolves* the philosophical issues ... [The] essentially normative question is untouched by our reconception of the empirical facts" (Davies, 2013 p. 198a). And that is in line with our slogan from Frege. Therefore care must be taken to express exactly what follows from the neuroscience: it will not help to attribute to brains what are properly the properties of persons only. Or to fail to retain one's attention to *artworks*, especially having conceded the possibility of 'confusable counterparts'. Once grant that the topic is merely the line, grace, and so on (*aesthetic* properties), with the agent's status as a dancer just coincidental (so these are not the properties following from the *artform*), and normativity disappears: then it is easier to imagine its accommodation by a causal story; or that "... motor perception is a means by which we can appreciate the aesthetic qualities of a dancer's movements" (Montero, 2013 p. 174a). For the concern with appreciating the artwork (the dance) has a normative dimension ill-served by attending to those causal explanations of, say, confusable counterpart non-dances (or non-artworks). Where can the theorist deploying appeal to motor perception (for instance, Montero) stand on that question?

Of course, sometimes a certain looseness in one's writing creates no big problem: as Austin (1962 p. 91) put it, "[i]n order (in this case) to cut down on the verbiage, I may use in one situation words primarily appropriate to ... [an]other; and no problem arises provided the circumstances are known". For then one circumstance will not be mistaken for the other. Or, at least, mistakes can be remedied. But here, the circumstances *are* hidden.

Davies (2013 p. 199a) mentions critically that my strategy of 'partitioning science' would bring me into conflict with central ideas from Quine, such that "... philosophical reflection is grounded in the best empirical theories available" where, in practice, such 'grounding' amounts to the kind of reductivist empiricism (with its attendant scientism) that Quine stands for, and I reject. My defence of answerability (in particular, the ideas from Travis through which I develop it) is aimed directly at this Quinean idea, and the thin account of perception that it both requires and defends — an account that resolves what is observable in terms of the argument from illusion. I have made explicit my rejection (see Chapter Eight §2; §5).

Perhaps Davies took his fundamental objection to my view to be that I denied that empirical material could *ever* be relevant to discussion in dance aesthetics. But I only deny that *certain kinds* of empirical material (roughly, causal descriptions of how X came about) can be relevant to *certain kinds* of discussion of dance-as-art (namely, the normative ones typical of artistic interest/appreciation); and then only on some occasions or in some contexts. And, above, these seem points he would share. Moreover, they reflect another criticism from the previous chapter; that most of dance history is person-sized — rooted in the embodied intentional meaning of the dancework, which in turn is answerable to the dancer-maker's fulfilled intentions in that context, where what can be intended is partially circumscribed by cultural factors (just the ones often used in distinguishing 'confusable-counterpart' actions).

Perhaps I conclude too much from my critique concerning the changeability of science: that (for example) it would apply equally to history. In this, Davies is right that I perhaps overstated the changeability of science although, especially given the propensity of some scientists to stress falsifiability of claims, I wonder if the local claims of the scientist are more regularly subjected to the kinds of tests that should lead to their rejection than are those of the historian. Equally, there is surely a 'test of time' here in humanities disciplines, which offers some guarantee for the durability of historical claims. At the least, they seem less prone to the dictates of intellectual fashion. But perhaps I am just wrong about this.

Now, there are sound reasons for hesitancy faced with claims drawing on neuroscience here, so that the default position should therefore be a more extreme pessimism than perhaps Davies suggests. The first concerns the nature of the neuroscience — or, better, its assumptions: are they really treated with the appropriate amount of scepticism? We have agreed (above) that they should be. But, for me, this does not occur: to give just one example, although almost all writers acknowledge neural plasticity, they nevertheless write as though the cognitive 'architecture' of the brain always matched its actual structure — as though the brain-functions taken to instantiate processes of thought or feeling had unique locations; and were therefore the same in all humans. But, two pages previously, they have told us this is not true. No doubt there *are* trends and tendencies here, but typical writers do not pay careful enough attention to the impact of this lack of exceptionlessness. (Tallis, 2011 highlights some useful examples.[13]) So I am sceptical about the reliability of the research: of course, the best is very good. Yet one must be wary of the tendency to "experimental methods and conceptual confusion" (PPF §371; PI part two section xiv), especially since causal explanation (primarily in science) was often a model here (PO p. 431[14]). As Wittgenstein (BB p. 18) emphasized:

> Philosophers constantly see the method of science before their eyes, and are irresistibly tempted to ask and answer questions in the way science does. This tendency is the real source of metaphysics, and leads the philosopher into complete darkness.

Frege's response was the more specific in concerning with appeals to brain activity of precisely the kind now being suggested. For as he comments:

> We believe that the thing independent of us stimulates a nerve and by this means produces a sense-impression; but strictly we experience only the end of this process which impinges on our consciousness. (Frege, 1984 p. 365)

Indeed, even Descartes (6th Med: CSM II p. 60 also 'Treatise on Man', CSM I p. 108[15]) recognized this difficulty concerning "... the mystery of nervous tissue", as Danto (2013 p. 95) points out: "Why the perturbations of nerves should be perceived as pain or tickling by the person whose nerves they are is a mystery". But once a *general* answerability of perception to the sublunary world is conceded, one can look to explaining (away/) the exceptions.

Two further features of his moderate pessimism, as Davies offers them, should (I feel) drive him to my view, especially bearing in mind his critique of Parma school neuroscience. First, with me, he grants "... the normative dimensions to the questions that engage us as philosophers of art", noting — as an example — that "... the Calvo-Merino et al. experiments ... do not address the question that concerns us as epistemologists of dance, namely, whether the discriminations made by the trained dancer are relevant to the proper appreciation of dance" (Davies, 2013 p. 201a [both quotes]).

I would have said "cannot", rather than "do not", since this limitation is built into their methodology, arising whenever one attempts causal explanations of normative matters — since there are causal explanations of bad moves, the causal story cannot be used to uniquely characterize good moves. So our normative process cannot be reduced to such causal explanation: just "[a]s I do not create a tree by looking at it, ... neither do I create a thought by thinking. And still less does the brain secrete thoughts, as the liver does gall" (Frege, 1979 p. 137). And the moves here can be in dance as well as in chess, although in fact we might better recognize the dancer's failure to do what he/she intended – as we have seen, just the sort of checking that the mirrors in a dance studio are there to permit. Indeed, the very possibility of dancers being corrected by choreographers (or other dancers) recognizes the priority of that 'third-person' perspective on the position of one's own limbs, a perspective that judiciously-placed mirrors allow one to adopt to oneself!

A similar point appears when one looks, instead, to a creator's perspective — and, indeed, a point familiar from early attempts to reduce artistic production to its sociological roots. No doubt two sculptors working on, say, the Doorway of the Maidens, on the Acropolis should be seen as operating "... under *identical* ideological, social and cultural conditions" (Fuller, 1980 p. 236); and have brains (and so on) in suitably similar states of 'readiness'. Now, grant for the sake of argument that the resulting sculpture is an artwork, and we notice that its artistic characteristics cannot be explained by what these sculptors *share* — for some:

> ... depicted folds in robes or drapery through rigid slots, dug into the marble like someone furrowing the surface of a cheese with a teaspoon. Others worked their material in such a way that their representations seemed to have lightness, movement, and translucence: the stone breathes and floats for them. (Fuller, 1980 p. 236)

As his second point, Davies (2013 p. 201a) in effect embraces this idea; and joins me in requiring that "... a philosophical theory must tell us what it is to apprehend a dance performance *as art*" [my emphasis], agreeing that cognitive neuroscience "cannot tell us what sort of regard is at issue" (Davies, 2013 p. 201b) when we so regard a dance. So what occurs is still some way from the sort of applications envisioned (or even perpetrated) in respect of dance: in particular, general worries about what exactly can be extracted from fMRI data should be voiced, when one's interest is in dance, or even dance appreciation (not so different from those voiced by Davies, 2013 p. 200). Raymond Tallis (2008 p. 19) summarises these points cogently: that such 'neuroaesthetics':

> ... casts no light on the specific nature of the objects and experiences of art or the distinctive contribution of individual artists. Nor does it offer any basis for the evaluation of art as good, great or bad. In short, neuroaesthetics bypasses everything that art criticism is about.

At the least, the technology does not lend itself to real-world situations; but those are precisely the ones that interest us. For instance, there is a clear difference between genuinely seeing dance and seeing dance on film: how might such a contrast be acknowledged in such research? Further, the standards of philosophy are the ones that should speak to relevance here; and that is not what I see. Moreover, the difficulty does not seem the kind potentially remedied by improvements in technology. Wittgenstein deplored the tendency in this way to put off *sine die* the detail of matters while simply assuming its broad contours; that is, as:

> ... the conception that there are questions the answers to which will be found at a later date. It is held that, although a result is not known, there is a way of finding it. (WWK p. 182 [December, 1931])

Later (PI §308) he elaborated the basis of the problem as he saw it:

> ...[t]he first step is the one that altogether escapes notice. We talk of processes and states and leave their nature undecided. Sometime perhaps we'll know more about them — we think. But that's just what commits us to a particular way of looking at the matter. For we have a certain conception of what it means to know a process better ...

So we seem to know the *form* of the answer: and that form typically comes from natural science. Moreover, Wittgenstein (PI §308 contd.) is clear that the move here is damaging:

> The decisive movement in the conjuring trick has been made, and it was the very one that seemed to us quite innocent.

For surely there are brain-states: our brains, being physical organs, are in a certain biochemical and biological state at a particular moment. And surely denying that would indeed be to deny mental processes (see PI §306; §308).

But, while assuring us that he is not denying mental processes, Wittgenstein (PI §308) recognizes that we must instead "... deny the yet uncomprehended process in the yet unexplored medium" — not least because this is another place where we are in danger of not beginning at the beginning; that one must not "try to go further back" (OC §471). For, as Wittgenstein (PI § 363) noticed, "[m]ental processes just are strange". So we should not rush to any particular comparison as just obvious; and especially a comparison with physical or biological processes. In explanation, Wittgenstein (PI §363) imagines someone saying:

> "The clock shows us the time. *What* time is, is not yet settled. And, as regards the point of telling the time — that doesn't come in here."

So the comparison with our knowledge of human psychological processes acknowledges their diversity: for example, how sometimes what one says expresses a desire ("I want a glass of beer", said to a bartender, is not a description of my state of mind); or a belief ("I think John is in LA" is not mere autobiography); or a feeling ("My leg hurts" is sometimes informational, but sometimes simply an expression of the pain). To assume that a single model *must* do here, since all are in some sense psychological processes, involves giving in to what Wittgenstein (PI §593) diagnoses as "[a] main cause of philosophical diseases — [namely] a one-sided diet: one nourishes one's thinking with only one kind of example".

Further, if we are told that, while not the whole story, this account of brain causality is *part* of the relevant explanation of human mental processes, we should respond as Wittgenstein (VoW p. 325) did, faced with such an enumerative conception: that "then the question would arise: Is that *all*?". For, faced with the claim to have explained *some* part, one is surely owed both an explanation of the parts currently unexplained, and a way to recognize when the enumerative exercise is complete. Neither is forthcoming; and, to me, could never be provided in principle, since these 'parts' do not form a finite totality. Yet this will be fundamental to all those who wonder whether they have, or have not, characterized *all* that is relevant in the brain in relation to particular judgements of art. Such a question becomes unanswerable in principle in a world where there is no finite totality of such features, even in principle; no *all* here.

But then one cannot have addressed *all* the issues, or elements, considered. Yet, when understanding is modelled on considerations from natural science, gaps in causal sequences are not acceptable. I take David Davies's moderate pessimism to mean that he agrees at least to some degree with some such points. Why is my pessimism more marked? I can only conclude, despite all the evidence to the contrary, that I am more dithyrambic than David.

§9.   Conclusion

By way of conclusion for this chapter and the previous one, I can do no better than repeat six general comments, offered elsewhere (McFee, 2013 pp. 192b-193a):

- *We typically know where (in space) the parts of our bodies are* — of course, this is what some unfortunates lack. (Compare the Ian Waterman case elaborated in Chapter Eight §6.) Certainly, this case could support my view that, typically, one just *knows* where the parts of one's body are (and some of the prerequisites, or mechanisms, for this knowledge will depend on what, say, Waterman damaged). Then, should one require such 'knowledge' to become very precise (as in a dancer's leg position), it could be augmented in exactly the way, recalled above, that it is augmented in the dance studio — through the mirrors! Of course, the movement itself can be trained; so, when dancers speak of the leg's position feeling right, that should be read as just offering a characterization of the result of such training. For the actual position of the leg (say) determines whether the dancer correctly performs that movement, however the position of the leg *feels*. Moreover, no sensory modality need be invoked to achieve that: it simply reflects a capacity most humans have.

- *Dancers respond to seeing dance (and perhaps some other movement) in ways they might regard as **bodily**:* of course, the dancers are trained to recognize and to discriminate movement — like the rest of us, they must usually depend on sight: but typically they are at the better trained and more sensitive end of the spectrum for that. Equally, with no 'aesthetic for dancers', this capacity is not crucial to *all* dance appreciation — even if some dancers sometimes speak of it in this way.

- *The rest of us may well think we can respond viscerally (also roughly **bodily**) to some dance*: indeed, this is a regular description here. Thus Martin is right that appreciating dances mobilizes a capacity here, ascribable to us all (see Chapter Nine §5). Yet that response is based on what we *see*, in the context of what we have learned to see. John Martin *thought* a sensory modality operative here, but no sensory modality could achieve what he wanted of it since, were it regularly deployed in other human activity, it would lack the required connection to dance to permit our appreciation *of dance*; or, if this were not needed (as, say, with vision), that point would be integrated in another way — as, with vision, when we recognize that we are *looking* at dance.

- *Sensitivity here is partly a human capacity, and partly a reflection of training within the culture.* As a result, dance appreciation is typically open in principle to anyone who gives it time and energy, possibly with a teacher (like John Martin: see Chapter Nine §6). This requirement is the flip-side of one Roger Scruton (1998 p. 20) makes (for literary discussions, but the point holds):

> ... in the nature of things, the arguments of a critic are addressed only to those who have sufficient reverence for literature; for only they will see the point of detailed study and moral investigation.

But, having seen that point, no in-principle reason precludes appreciation.

- *Appreciation of dances is (appropriate) appreciation of bodily movement:* yet the movement must be recognized as *transfigured* (PAD pp. 14-20) into dance — it is, as it were, the 'confusable counterpart' of mere bodily movement.

- *The project of a 'dancer's aesthetic' (adopted by Montero) must be sharply contrasted with a (real) aesthetics of dance,* which involves the appeal of the artwork to its audience. This is contentious only from the perspective of a putative 'dancer's aesthetic': no one gives credence to a similar conception for any *other* artform. It would be preposterous to suggest that, say, opera-singers had a distinctive (and crucial) view of opera.

The possibility of accommodating these ideas within a sophisticated aesthetic of dance may remove the tendency to think of these as claims of a sort *only* dancers want to make; but which I would deny. In fact, a proper understanding of dances requires recognizing the *distinctive* role dancers have in making concrete the dancework (see PAD pp. 167-205). These thoughts tend against a trend to explain human behaviour, and hence both dance practice and dance appreciation, by appeal to neuroscience. For answering 'back beyond the beginning' questions is regularly requested, although we recognize that chains of questions come to an end: so that, as Wittgenstein (OC §471) saw, "... the difficulty is to begin at the beginning. And not try to go further back".

Chapter Eleven

Seeing dance and seeing films of dance

§1.   Introduction

Although I have repeatedly said that, "my head does not lie with ontology" (as Hobbes reportedly claimed of Descartes: PAD p. 289), and hence that one should not begin there (Chapter Five §6), commonsense recognition of the variety of kinds of fine art locates dance among the performing arts (see Chapter One §3). Yet what does it mean to recognize dance as a *performing art*: that is, typical dances as *performed*? Briefly, that *performing arts* maintain the distinction between performer and work, even if performed by the maker.

So, throughout this work, a broad sketch of kinds of art — even if not exhaustive — indicated two points crucial for dance: first, typical performing arts enshrine the contrast between artwork, as *performable*, and the particular performance (say, last night, by such-and-such a company). Then obviously, in typical cases, saying that a particular dance is a *performable* is recognizing that *it* (that very same dance) could be performed on another occasion and by another company — even when this does not happen in practice. (Works not, in this way, performable on another occasion [not *re*-performable], I have called "happenings": PAD p. 160.[1])

So for a performing art, in typical cases, the work itself (the dance) contrasts with its various performances. Then granting that a particular dance could typically be performed with a different cast is recognizing that performances of the very same dance can differ on these occasions. There can be differences *just* between performances of same work (tired performers, different performers) — indeed, contingently, there *will* be such differences, since performables are necessarily re-performable; therefore, in principle, with a different cast. Further, some differences will be explicable by something else — staging, 'version', and so on (even for 'So-and-so's version'). Yet both performances are of the same work, despite such differences. Hence, across the performing arts, encountering the same work twice involves encountering two performances (although, of course, not necessarily performances having the same artistic *value* — one version can be preferable to another!).

Thus, it follows from the distinction between work and performance that, to see the particular dancework, one must see a *performance* of it.[2] And such performances require performers. Hence, as Williams (2004 p. 73) puts it:

> ... dancers are logically prior to dances — to the act of dancing or the notion of the dance —just as speakers are logically prior to speeches — to the act of speaking or the notion of language.

At the least, they cannot be logically secondary, since there would be no dances without dancers[3]. [Of course, *this* does not distinguish performing arts from, say, 'happenings', for seeing the 'happening' too requires watching the moving bodies — although, now, since this is a 'one-off' event, they are not rightly called *performers*.] So this answer relates to one of the harder tasks in the philosophical aesthetics of dance: that of giving *due* weight to the role of the dancer. Here, as elsewhere, stressing the centrality of the *performers* in the performing arts reflects my intention to appropriately *value* dancers, not to slight them.

So what does *seeing a performance* involve? Now identifying performing arts (such a dance) contrasts such artforms with film since (to state the point bluntly) although film is a multiple-art, it is not a *performing* art: film lacks the contrast between performance and artwork. And, throughout, the term "film" indicates all those familiar graphic representations of movements, whether stored on celluloid, video, DVD, or digital 'memories' from computers: beginning from our everyday experience, I follow common sense in not distinguishing how they are stored or projected.

Then here (and now) comparison with recorded music is set aside for, at least arguably, music is composed of (performed) *tones*; exactly what the recording[4] might be thought to preserve! For music, sounds are typically reified: we speak of clatters, bangings, murmurs, echoes, creaks, rustles, gurgles. That is, as Cavell (1979 p. 19; see Walton, 2015 p. 169) reminds us, sounds are treated as entities separate from their sources, such that one hears the *sound* of the English horn, rather than hearing the English horn. At its most extreme version, this idea reflects "timbral sonicism" (Dodd, 2007 p. 1) in identifying the music with the sound sequence, however produced. At the least the performer in music is typically contrasted with his/her instrument, such that the performer *uses* the instrument to makes the sounds. Certainly, such a general distinction has no place in dance, where uncontentiously the dancer's 'instrument' is her body. This produces a major disanalogy, insofar as recorded dances cannot involve the *bodies* necessary in performance.

So what follows from the crucial difference between dances (as performances) and films (as not)? My position is that, *because* dance is a performing art, what we can learn about a dancework by considering a film of a performance of that work is limited, since seeing a film of a performance is, in an important way, *not* seeing the dance at all: what is viewed is not itself a current performance.[5]

§2.   Contrasting film and dance

To elaborate this important contrast with film, by noting the *fixity* of the action on film, consider the Donald Sutherland movie, *The Eye of the Needle*

(1981, directed by Richard Marquand), where Donald plays a German agent during World War Two. As my wife and I agreed, Donald's character would have fared better if, at a certain moment, he had stabbed the heroine, played by Kate Nelligan. Hence, a slogan for this particular feature of films became, "He should have stabbed her when he had the chance!": that if one saw *The Eye of the Needle* again (not something I recommend), one would, again, require that he stab her when the chance arose! And again be disappointed. For the nature of the medium precludes this: insofar as we have a film (such as a Hollywood movie, but equally a *recording* of a particular performance), the outcome is necessarily unchanged. For movies, every event to be screened is fixed when one enters the cinema or movie theatre. In dances, "... everything is not present all at once" (Levinson, 2015 p. 158, quoting Sontag[6]). For this reason, movies — where exactly the same events occur — are not *performances* in the sense in which dances are: film is not "... merely photographed dramatic performance" (Sharpe, 1983 p. 26),[7] *mutatis mutandis*.

Of course, some films exist in more than one version: for instance, Sam Peckinpah's *Pat Garrett and Billy the Kid* (1973/1988), where the film was changed radically by a contextualization that casts the major story into a bleaker light, re-introducing the original 'topping-and-tailing' black-and-white sequence to show its outcome. But this is really another film, the director's cut; and now much applauded, in contrast to the panning critics gave to the studio version. For, although the *making* of the film does involve performances (despite those actors who urge that film is simply rehearsing over and over[8]), there has been selection among those performances by the time the film is completed. Indeed, this is what it means to have completed it. Equally, if a particular dramatic performance, or dance performance, were recorded, the fact that one now encounters the recording means that those performances too have become fixed.

For films in general, the 'disappearance' of the moment when "He should have stabbed her when he had the chance" poses problems for using the filming of a performance in dance-teaching, or in dance-ontology: one cannot return to such a change as a live option in the film one views. Elsewhere (PAD pp. 76-77), I took the *normativity* of notation to give one reason to prefer locating identity-conditions for works in performing arts via notationality: there, functioning as a recipe is preferable to any method (such as a film) just recording one particular performance. For which features of that *particular* performance are key for work-identity or apprecation, and which irrelevant? Glen Gould notoriously hummed while playing: so one must learn what to exclude. Collingwood (1938 p. 143) rightly points out that we learn to exclude as irrelevant some features of the experience of artworks:

We disimagine ... a great deal which we actually see and hear. The street noises at a concert, the noises made by our breathing and shuffling neighbours, and even some of the noises made by the performers, are thus shut out of the picture unless by their loudness or in some other way they are too obtrusive to be ignored. At the theatre, we are strangely able to ignore the silhouettes of the people sitting in front of us, and a good many things that happen on the stage. Looking at a picture, we do not notice the shadows that fall on it or, unless it is excessive, the light reflected from its varnish.

But how exactly is this 'decision' reached? We cannot easily say *in the abstract* what counts and what does not — these might change on another occasion. Then *what* features from such a recording of a particular performance have a place in our recipe? Again, no wholly general and exceptionless answer is possible.

Yet, as with musical works, the need to *appreciate* that dancework brings with it, not only the need for *informed* perception, but also the need, more basically, to engage perceptually with the work: that is, for that artwork to be present to one's senses.[9] So that genuine encounters with artworks may require an answerability to the work achieved through perceptual engagement of sorts appropriate to those works — seeing for painting, hearing for music, and so on.[10] Hence, say, a report by another is insufficient; thus giving the lie to the generality claimed by Collingwood (1938 p. 139) that "... the work of art is not the collection of noises, it is the tune in the composer's head". Despite some plausibility for short poems or music works, artworks *merely imagined* seem doubtful candidates here; and especially in a performing art like dance where, as Merce Cunningham (1984 p. 27) put it, "... the way of seeing ... [the dance] has everything to do with dancers": roughly, they provide what one sees. For surely the central or typical case of seeing danceworks requires at least viewing (and attending to) an assemblage of moving bodies, human bodies in motion. Missing that, one is not actually seeing the *artwork*. Then lacking direct answerability (rooted in the observer's experience) means losing any basis for critical commentary of one's own — for instance, if one's engagement were *intellectual* in an inappropriate way, as when (say) one had only heard *about* the music or dance.

§3.   Limitations on perceiving art

What are the limitations on one's viewing here? As we saw John Wisdom (1991 p. 80) note, while you can recognize such-and-such as a dance, "... parrots may not know it, yet perhaps they have even better eyesight than yours" (see Chapter Nine §5). The visual acuity thereby granted to the parrot does not allow her to see *dance*: or, better, to recognize dance when she sees it. Your capacities exceeding those of parrots might be explained by (i) your mastery of concepts (and of the relevant concepts) and (ii) your sensitivity to differences between what is dance and what just resembles it; between *good* and *better* dances; and so on — differences we recognize as cultural, and evaluative, and beyond the scope of even the parrot that stares at the television:[11] that bird is not seeing (televised) dance, and not really seeing televised versions of these other things. Moreover, as we saw, genuinely seeing the dance requires recognizing the dance as of this or that *kind* (or category) because different criteria of success follow from differences of kind. Thus, critical discussion may be needed to build an informed audience, the only kind that could make sense of such a work.[12] So, four overlapping explanations of failing to see the dance (from Chapter Eight §3) were:

1. *Poor views of the performance*: bad sight-lines, say, may offer a very skewed view of this performance, and hence of the dance; perhaps (to anticipate) one not adequate for analysis of that dance. Then you are, as it were, in the presence of the dance without seeing it;

2. *Failure of seeing dance*: despite greater visual acuity than yours, parrots cannot really see human actions or events at all;

3. *Failure of concepts*: lacking the concepts to recognize dance of this kind, one cannot make sense of it. To *see* the dance, one must see it *as dance*, and not merely human movement; and as *this* dance;

4. *Not being in the right 'room'*: one is not confronting a performance *of that work*, because some other work (or no dance-work) is being performed.

These might seem failures of answerability. But I have also stressed that seeing the dance requires seeing *bodies*: are opera and theatre *exactly* as embodied as dance (in this respect)? Comparison is difficult; typically opera and theatre involve words — that is, linguistic meaning — in a way *most* dance does not. Yet the critique that Beckett's *Breath* was not a *play* typically amounts to noting that "... there are no people doing stuff" — as though Aristotle (1984 pp. 2322-2323) was right that (some) drama necessarily depicts *action*. Then drama too can seem just as centrally to involve human bodies.

§4. Alternative encounters?

How might alternative 'encounters' with the dance be conceptualized? The resources provided by our occasion-sensitivity allow distinguishing watching a *recording* from watching the dance; hence permit one's confronting only a *recording* of the dance to *count* as seeing the dance (on some occasion, or in certain circumstances). Certainly, that explanation could apply if one's claim to watching a particular dance on Saturday afternoon were challenged: well, I was not doing *something else* — not playing bridge, nor roller-skating. Of course, exactness is my best strategy: that I was watching a *recording* of the dance — then one knows exactly what occurred.

Suppose, though, someone then points out that this dance had not been performed for twenty years — so how can I have seen it? How can I be discussing the dance *as though* I have seen it? Here, as above, I concede to having seen, *not* the dance, but only a recording of a performance. And it is of importance for aesthetics to recognize that, if pressed, I *have not* seen the dance. Hence, when discussing what *did* occur, to keep that fact in mind; therefore to *avoid* saying (for instance) that I *saw* the dance, *but on video*. For this seems, mistakenly, to imply what we recognize is false — my having actually *seen* it. And might lead others to imagine (confusingly) new ways of *seeing* things; namely, *seeing them on video*, to compete with, say, seeing the dance through opera-glasses or with the naked eye.

But, further, seeing a *recording* of the dance often involves seeing features causally connected to the occurrences in the dance: insofar as the recording is a *transparent* medium,[13] watching the recording permits us to recognize *some* features of the dance, especially when it is in a dance-style (or constructed in a technique) — and, of course, to become better at such observation with practice. So the use of recording can have an obvious place in dance-study: the parallel with looking at slides for paintings is fairly exact. Someone never in Paris cannot have seen the *Mona Lisa*.[14] Yet, for some purposes, the numerous slides, prints and the like, that he *had* seen might be enough. In practice, *all* the paintings for discussion cannot be brought into the class-room but, with slides or pdfs of them, one's students can see something (*not* the artwork) with features that might usefully be discussed, as a way to discuss the painting; say, in terms of that painting's composition. Indeed, Wollheim (1987 p. 11) rightly criticizes art-historical practice by noting that too many art historians "... have tended to *identify* the object of their enquiry with those properties of a painting which a good slide preserves" (my emphasis). For this is transparently *making do*, because key properties of the artwork, properties relevant to its artistic meaning, will typically be unavailable through such a process (see also PAD p. 102). Then if, speaking loosely, I claim to have seen such-and-such a dance (having only seen a recording of it), or to have seen the *Mona Lisa* having only seen a slide, well ... no harm need be done, and hence no correction required, if no one draws the inappropriate conclusion that these ('seeing the dance on video', 'seeing the *Mona Lisa* by seeing the slide') were legitimate ways of actually *seeing* those artworks.

But surely, say, newsreels on television allow us to see events in other places. Then seeing the recording might *seem* like accessing the event recorded. Yet this is just a casual, loose description. Further, those finding fault with television newsreels do so precisely by pointing out that they can be *managed*; and hence, by contrast with actually seeing an event, are not reliable. Moreover, the art-case is special just because the artwork is an *embodied meaning* (Danto, 2013 p. 48), so that viewing *just* the recording fails to engage with the specific embodiment. Thus, the fine details of the human movements involved, typically important for artistic meaning of dances, often disappear in the recording: one cannot recognize which are crucial.

Of course, any ways of *encountering the dance* for the purposes of analysis may involve *less* than seeing the dance. Thus, someone seeing only the dance's notated score might agree that he had not encountered the dance itself, with someone seeing only the score of music perhaps making the same concession — although, of course, musical scores are more widely grasped than dance scores. Collingwood (1938 p. 139) may be wrong to think that the score does no *more* than permit the composer to "... arrange for the tune to be played before an audience", but it does *at least* that: and only *then* can one encounter the work itself.[15]

Perhaps a hybrid form might combine dancers with filmed or digitized images of dancers, as though these dance together. But, of course, the reproductions will 'do' the same thing each evening — they will not be *performing!* And even were the dancers to produce visually identical perform-ances on each occasion, this would be a contingency, not something built into the nature of such artworks (as the image-part was). Of course, as another set of cases, especially in today's increasingly digitalized age, one can mix the moving bodies with images of a (broadly) CGI kind, where it still makes sense to regard what we see as a performance. The contrast is again with movies, where exactly the same events occur: where every event to be screened is fixed when one enters the cinema or movie theatre. For typical movies are not *performances* in the sense in which dances are. To preserve the integrity of the artform, dances — as instantiating a *performing* art (in ways necessitating the potential variability of performance) — contrast with movies in just these ways. And that limits the degree to which one can study dances *via* film.

§5.   A 'revised situation'

When remarking (above) that most art historians attended only to the properties of paintings that a good slide preserves, Wollheim (1987 p. 11) was taking such a practice to be justified — if at all — only as second-best to seeing the painting: the painting had artistically-relevant properties that a slide-projection (or a print) lacked. Thus, if one's interest genuinely resided in seeing the painting, or all its artistically-relevant properties, the art historians' practice was inadequate.

Might one argue — in a parallel way — that the experience of viewing a film of a dance performance lacked certain key features (ideally, *necessarily* lacked such features) that were artistically relevant? And then, in the same way, conclude that one had not genuinely seen *the dance* if one had only seen a film of a performance of it? I have answered, "yes". If so, what might such features be?

Once any so-called *kinetic* or *kinaesthetic* properties are put aside (either as not relevant, if tied to dancers, or not 'crossing the footlights'), those remaining might include the limited focus of a fixed camera position; the scale of things on stage — distorted by close-up perhaps; the acoustic difference, partly related to any music associated with the work, but partly to the sounds of dancers' feet and breath; the fragility of live performance of dance — roughly, how will tonight's dancers cope with the contingencies that arise in this performance, as such contingencies will typically arise. As above, these relate both to the difference between tonight's performance and yesterday's and the differences between this dancer's interpretation of a role and that one, as well as difference between this company's interpretation of the work and that company's.

Moreover, even in the most tightly circumscribed of choreographic structures, dancers on occasion will be called on to make modifications (literally) 'on the hoof' — the reason I have heard deployed most often is that musicians were playing too fast, and hence have got ahead of the dancers (an excuse I have encountered even when the music was from a tape!). Here, dancers may be called on to 'augment' what was set, in a coherent fashion; but this is *always* a possibility in live performance.

There are a number of considerations here: none is really decisive. But I have stressed the issue of immediacy or danger as crucial for performances: what, writing of music, Lee Brown (2011 p. 184) called the "in-the-moment character of live performance": will the dance as this set of dancers interprets it ultimately make sense? Will the specific choices of the performer tonight, to deal with *tonight's* contingencies (the musicians adopting too fast a tempo *again!*) fit together with the rest of the performance? So we might view the dancework *today* for *today's* answer to such questions! (To see how the contingencies are resolved for *this* performance.)

Could these considerations show conclusively that (typical) dances can *only* be seen when one shares the space, such as an auditorium, with them? No, both because our contextualism baulks at such exceptionless claims and because it may be possible, in extreme or unusual circumstances, to meet the two constraints we have implicitly set: first, the possibility of seeing the dance again must be acknowledged; and, second, that possibility is motivated here by the possibility of being surprised this time through — unlike films, this is a case where one might realize the possibility of 'He should have stabbed her when he had the chance'. Further, we should hope to avoid the 'bad seats' problem, in respect of sightlines and such like, and the possibility of appropriate close-up. So imagine a watching of the dance through a medium (say, television) that is both contemporaneous with a live performance, and more flexible in these ways.

To deal with these considerations, then, one might imagine what I shall call *the revised situation*. If the images guarantee we are looking at a dance, from multiple perspectives, with appropriately high-quality images, and with appropriate variety of close-up and long-shot and appropriately varied seating positions, in a simultaneous broadcast (so that any 'danger' is accommodated — there is no 'He should have stabbed her when he has the chance') ... it is difficult to see how to sustain the parallel for dance of Wollheim's point (above) for paintings: nothing seems missing. But two important features of this revised situation must be noted: first, much of the slack is taken up by the modifications introduced through the use of "appropriately", and similar. Thus, for music, it might be urged that no recording, in virtue of being played through speakers, can capture all of the sonic richness of a live performance: for example, the overtones from the piano interacting with cello. Still, the difficulty seems merely technical. And such a point has anyway less weight for dance, where much that one wants to see is displayed at the scale of human action, recognized in informed perception. Yet it *does* import the idea of some finite totality of features here to be considered, each neatly 'ticked off'. But I reject that assumption in principle, at least as it applies to any human action (such as a dance) in which various interests might be taken.

Then, second, constructing this 'revised situation' has, in effect, idealized each of the difficulties from actual cases of watching a dance, either 'live' or via a film: so that (a) the fixed-ness of the camera, in contrast with the potential for motion (for changes in position, even while in one's seat), and (b) the possibility of better and (especially) worse seating, are both accommodated by the various perspectives offered in the revised situation; (c) the need to sometimes see the dance close-up (or to wish one could) yet sometimes to see its patterns from a distance is again accommodated in that way; further, (d) that these images are available in the same time-scheme as the actual performance (that they are simultaneous) means that any appeal to the fragility of *this* performance, or the 'dangers' thereby embraced, is also accommodated. [Although, notice, this is so *only* when one's watching is simultaneous with the performance: otherwise, even this account cannot defend seeing the images as really 'seeing the dance at a distance'.] Through its idealization of the experience of watching, the 'revised situation' precludes any features of the experience of the dancework being less than optimal. Then, if we ask what features of our experience of that dance performance were thereby missed, the example is constructed so that the mediation is "transparent" (as Ted Gracyk said about some musical recording[16]): nothing in the optimal experience of a particular dance performance could be missing from that provided by the revised situation. Except, of course, the experience of the artwork!

The 'revised situation' offers a *confusable-counterpart* (see Danto, 1981 p. 1) of the dance-performance: something that might be mistaken for the experience of such a performance; and, as such, something from which one might learn a great deal as long as one remains confused — just as, in the original Danto example (see AJ pp. 13-15), I can 'learn' about *one* (art-type) confusable counterpart by confusing it with another. Of course, what one apparently learns is not true of the object *experienced*, but it *is* true of the object with which it is being confused. Despite her reservations about the concept of a 'work', we might even urge, with Lydia Goehr (1989 p. 55) that:

> ... the concept of a musical work is intimately tied to a conception of a complex relationship between the composer, the score, and the performance.

And *mutatis mutandis* for danceworks. For the performance itself is stressed here. Hence, despite my protestation, a kind of ontological commitment is involved, one to "the artist's fulfilled intentions" ("those that are realized or fulfilled in the work": Wollheim, 1987 p. 19): as Wollheim (1978 p. 37[17]) remarked, the novelist thinks that what she had made is hers, and that it is a novel (compare McFee, 2010a). In a similar vein, the dance-maker's fulfilled intention determines the sort of thing he had made: and, for dances, the typical cases — those most readily instantiating a *performing* art — were created for performance; hence that is how *they* can be experienced.

Of course, there remains variety among cases: if the particular dance must be performed in (and hence seen through) a proscenium arch, so be it! But, in any case where that feature is neither specified nor implicit, it is left open. We can bow to the dance-maker's fulfilled intentions; although that 'reading' might be revised in the face of another equally compelling in *any particular* case.[18] Hence, no doubt, some dances are made to be seen on film — but I cannot regard such cases as central: for me, the central case today for performing arts requires that they be seen *in performances*. Perhaps my 'revised situation' is attempts to mirror that. If so, we recognize why it might idealize a situation that could be modified for dance education, by making these simultaneous-to-performance images (when created) available for later study. But that fact cannot determine what is required to genuinely see the dance.

Four quick points in conclusion: first, both maintaining my own view and advocacy of the 'revised situation' still requires that there be dance performances: hence, that there be schools, and such like, to prepare those dancers. Second, adherence to the 'revised situation' would only permit one to view *dance* by watching dance on film when that dance was simultaneously being performed — not a position that aids the couch-potato viewing. Third, in aiming to idealize the perception of dances (thereby generating the constraints for the 'revised situation' to meet), this case ignores that, in most cases, actually viewing the dance itself is less than ideal; but is still seeing the dancework. Fourth, the upshot here is a defence of live performance only insofar as the artworks in question are *performing* artworks: a different strategy would be required to think-through cases of mixed or hybrid works.

§6.   Conclusion: what are the performing arts?

We have seen that typical performing arts embody the *work/performance* contrast; and are re-performables having a place in the performance for *action* or *agency*. Contrasting dances with other candidate 'performing arts' involves drawing not only the obvious contrasts from Chapter One §3 (with literature, sculpture, and movies as multiple arts, but not performing arts[19]) but also, at least, with the following:

(a) one-off 'happenings' (see PAD p. 182);

(b) works incorporating images from CGI, and such like, in various ways (Blades, 2015): does it succeed in "... incorporating the bodies into digital spaces" (Blades, 2013 p. 1)? What should be made of the use of a digital score from Deborah Hay's "No Time to Fly" (2010), as part of William Forsythe's *Motion Bank* project, as the basis, first, of three solos by other choreographer/dancers, and then into a trio, "As Holy Sites Go" (2012) — is it just a kind of archive? Or a special kind of notation of the work (see Jennett, 2015)? Insofar as one is addressing a new kind of artwork here, as opposed to a new way of accessing works for standard performance, these seem rightly regarded as kinds of hybrid between dance and some digital/film medium;

(c) the issue of wholly improvised works (see PAD p. 163);

(d) perhaps a dance parallel of extreme cases for music; for example, Keith Jarrett at the piano in the Kohn Opera House, in 1975, who:

... played four single notes that mimicked the house intermission bell, and then performed uninterrupted for just over 26 minutes. After a pause, he again performed uninterrupted for over 33 minutes, and then, at the urging of the audience, performed for a further seven minutes. He did this without a score and without any prior planning or rehearsal relating to the form this specific performance would take. (Davies, 2011 p. 135)

What should one make of this? Unfortunately, memorable cases are typically impure: in this one, with the performance recorded, and the recording subsequently sold as a CD, *The Köhn Concert* begins to resemble a traditional 'work performed' in ways clearly not intended. Yet how can any performance preclude re-performance? Equally, it is obviously not enough that a performer used a performance (of a given work) to make his statement (see Davies, 2011 p. 145).

There may be nothing general to say, even about this abbreviated list: still, first, we can remind ourselves that, for me, encountering "the very same dance" implies identity-conditions constituted partly through notationality (which helps to identify the actions involved, via the bodily movements that partially comprise this dance); but the work must also be a *dance*, not some confusable counterpart: that involves not just the history of dance, but also the fulfilled intentions of the dance-maker (the choreographer). For doubts about the legitimacy of some performance can be raised here by questioning whether that performance does reflect the 'history of artistic production' appropriate to artworks of that kind: the defeasible condition here (PAD pp. 150-152) is that, in the absence of direct evidence to the contrary, when the choreographer disavows a performance as of a particular work, the performance *is not* of that work — this condition operates roughly as the 'artist's hand' for painting and sculpture: its lacking the appropriate relationship to Picasso precludes its being a Picasso.[20] For dance, we will typically hope that performers were appropriately taught to perform the work (see Chapter Seven §5). But all such conditions apply *defeasibly*: in typical cases, one must demonstrate that they do *not* hold, rather than that they do. Then, second, we can apply these ideas case-by-case to any examples. But that, too, will leave us no exceptionless principles on which to draw. Further, the elaborate contrivances required to overcome the problems for genuinely seeing the dance by seeing 'appropriately' transmitted images of the dance ('the revised situation') really shows the power of the constraints to be met: even a scarcely-credible idealization of this sort provides, at best, insight into what the usual situation (seeing the dance itself) delivers.

Chapter Twelve

Conclusion

Despite the continuing debate over the precise lyrics of the Killer's 2009 song "Human", there is reason to hear its chorus as asking:

Are we humans? Or are we dancers?

Why exactly might that be the choice? Here, we have defended the commonsense conception on which only humans could count as (art-type) dancers, responsible instantiators of danceworks.

§1.   Envoi: the project

As explained initially, this text aimed to introduce philosophy, especially to those with an interest in (art-type) dance, such as ballet. Its early chapters sketch a set of concerns for our understanding of persons fundamental to the possibility of philosophical enquiry: *agency, meaning, normativity*. We begin from these whenever conceptual questions are raised about ourselves. Later chapters exemplify, and thereby elaborate, these concerns as they arise when *agents* (such as dancers, choreographers, dance audiences) generate *meanings* (in the artform of dance), where such meanings function *normatively* — where there can, in principle, be better or worse.

Here, our simplest model came from chess: there is not only the question of whether such-and-such is a move in chess, but further the question of better or worse moves; moves more or less likely to lead to victory. Moreover, one can be wrong about whether a particular move in chess is indeed good. The game of chess provides a context for chess moves, a nexus of rules that are followed by chess players. And discussing the intentions of a particular chess player (the intentions 'behind' a particular move) is typically a way to discuss the place of that move in the game; only for unsuccessful moves would reference by made to what the player was *trying* to do (his or her intention in that move), for usually one can comment on what was achieved — the move, or its contribution.

Considerations such as these ground our concern with human agency: people are agents — but this is not incompatible with the causal explanation of human behaviour (of the kind practiced by science). Indeed, one consequence of our position is precisely to give due weight to humanistic, intentional explanation of what people do, while granting the power of the explanations provided by, say, physics and physiology. But, as we have reminded ourselves throughout this text, causal explanations have an in-built limitation: since "[e]rror and superstition have causes just as much as correct cognition" (Frege, [1918] 1984 p. 351), there will be causal explanation of both the good move and the bad one — crucial for thinking normatively! And the possibility of causal explanation (or even its detail) cannot alone separate one from the other. Yet this point will be crucial for our discussion of an artform — dance — in which the meaning-bearing objects (the *dances* themselves) are instantiated in the *actions* of the dancers.

Perhaps the point most easily missed here is that we begin from what (I would argue) one must take for granted if one is to concern oneself with conceptual questions about the powers and capacities of people. Hence we generally begin from the extant practices of such people, in deciding, judging, perceiving, appreciating and the like. Of course, such notions must be interrogated; commonsense pictures of them may be misleading, on investigation. Dancers, dance-makers, and dance critics cannot, of course, always be taken at their word. But, to decide, one must do the investigation: that requires philosophy, with the human practices providing a default position here. And that seems a strength of the project. Certainly, one should stay close to danceworld practices, rather than (say) importing philosophical ontology that (whatever its metaphysical merits) ignores such practices entirely. For at least some of the examples for philosophical scrutiny arise from the practices of the danceworld; or, more loosely, to what dancers, choreographers, and such like might say.

§2.   Connections in philosophy

Two further, related, comments on the use of this text as an introduction to philosophy: first, it does not generally offer the 'Views of the Great Dead Philosophers of the Past' — but it should give resources to deal, in a perfectly general way, with important points or controversies, while insisting that one be sure in one's identification of issue or controversy. (Too often different issues are raised in the same words.) Second, it deals primarily with those philosophical issues that derive from our being *persons*: it says nothing directly about political philosophy or (philosophical) ethics — although it does bear directly on *why* we must mean what we say! For it shows how what we say *is* what we mean, unless there is reason to dispute the claim. In both these points, it follows our commitment to the *occasion-sensitivity* of meaning and understanding.

The importance assigned here to ideas of Wittgenstein and especially Austin, with both writers offered here as though transparent, may seem odd; but neither of them is much read in contemporary philosophy (especially in the USA). Obviously, it is not easy to select which philosophers from one century will be the major figures in the next. Thus Nagel (1995 p. 9) suggests the following as a list of the philosophers of the nineteenth century most-read in the twentieth: "Peirce and Frege, Mill, Bentham, and Sidgwick, Hegel, Neitzsche, and perhaps Schopenhauer"; and then asks "What will a comparable list look like next time around?" (Nagel, 1995 p. 9). As he goes on to note, this list highlights the difficulty: "... who would have bet on Peirce, Frege or Neitzsche in 1894?" His own answer, with which I concur, is that "[t]he strongest recent candidate for immortality is Wittgenstein; he certainly identified a new set of problems, although his response to them is still poorly understood and difficult to evaluate" (Nagel, 1995 p. 9 [both passages]). But, elsewhere (McFee, 2015a pp. 5-9), I have offered reasons why even this may be less obvious in 2016 than it was to Nagel in 1994. With Michael Dummett (1993 p. 166), I accept that:

> No one capable of recognizing profound philosophy can open the *Philosophical Investigations* without perceiving that it is a work of genius.

But too few people do open Wittgenstein's masterpiece, at least in the appropriate spirit. The dominant tradition in contemporary Anglo-American analytic philosophy is one growing primarily from Quine (and Carnap) — that is, a tradition in place prior to Wittgenstein's later writings (such as the *Philosophical Investigations*). As a result, many writers for whom this is not true are no longer seen as central: those with a Wittgensteinian pedigree, like Wisdom or Waismann, are the obvious cases but the same is arguably true of, say, Peter Strawson or even Dummett — their stars no longer seem in the ascendant. Perhaps the strangest example for a philosopher in the background of this text is Austin — one who, in practice, seems to have had little time for Wittgenstein. I hope the use to which such authors (especially Wittgenstein and Austin) are put in the text both explains the importance I thereby assign to them, and directs readers towards their own writing (if sometimes via secondary sources).

These features are important because it might seem that any text aiming to introduce its readers to philosophy should offer them insight into its history. But I have preferred to draw on those writers who seem to me to offer the most insight into *philosophy*: Wittgenstein, Austin, Wisdom ... and, more recently, Charles Travis, along with work of my own. The reader is recommended to follow up these authors to see what philosophy could offer.

Nagel (1995 p. 10) also raises two other key questions for writing philosophy, especially as it applies to texts with an introductory purpose. For how does one teach the sorts of recognitional ability mentioned by Dummett above? And "[w]hat is the point of doing philosophy if you are not extraordinarily good at it?" — one that cannot be expected of those newly introduced! Nagel (1995 p. 10) explains the second problem as follows:

If you are not extraordinary, what you do in philosophy will be either unoriginal (and therefore unnecessary) or inadequately supported (and therefore useless). More likely, it will be both unoriginal and wrong.

To respond, one must recognize that there are virtues in thinking about topics *for oneself* even if others have already thought about them; and even if your thinking follows broadly the same lines. Indeed, for me (though it is contentious), a major insight of Descartes' own account of his project makes it an individual or personal achievement. By contrast with the modern accounts of him (or what others take from him), Descartes implies in the *Meditations* (and states in the *Principles*) that the enquiry *he* is engaged in is something *each* of us should undertake at least once in his/her life: "... it was necessary, once in my life ..." (CSM II p. 12); and again, "... to make the effort, once in the course of our lives ..." (CSM I p. 193). If there were, say, some textbook that reported the results of such an enquiry, it would be possible (as Nagel hopes) to build up larger 'results' from the views of the past. And then the dilemma Nagel poses would be powerful.

But were the point to learn a kind of critical process *for oneself*, the ways one acquires it might necessarily reflect that fact. Seen one way, a book called "How to do philosophy" is like a book call "How to read" — if you can't read it, you can't get anything from it; and if you can read it, you do not need it. But, of course, we do learn to read primarily through texts where *others* (parents, teachers, peers) show us how to read, by reading with us — and occasionally stepping aside to explain what they have been doing. Philosophy must, in part, be taught this way: by showing philosophical insight in practice, and by finding ways to encourage others to search for similar insights. Further, the nuances provided by the different contexts in which we find one another *might* make it hard to simply adopt 'results' from the past without comment. If the term "state" amounts to something different in the twenty-first century than it did in the eighteenth, some 'translation' may be needed to apply the writers from one time to another. When a translation from Classical Greek uses the term "car" (roughly, for a chariot), we know that what might follow about modern cars does not apply — we need not ask if it has SatNav, or how long it goes between services. But what should be made of those cases where the 'nuance' is less obvious? Does it matter, when we come to apply his views to the senses, that Descartes accepted unquestioningly that there were seven senses (the five we discuss plus two 'internal' senses); and that he was part of a long tradition that did so? My point is only that such an application *might* prove problematic for that reason: and one might fail to notice *that* reason.

The strategy here has been to set aside the historical questions (perhaps for another day). If we find our philosophical questions in what vexes *our* lives, we can always ask whether similar issues vexed lives at other times;

and, if so, how similar the issues were.

Finally, I am unsure whether this work contains *theses* different from those in my other works, partly because — in line with my Wittgensteinianism — I remain unsure that it contains theses at all; but it certainly attempts to present the *redeeming word* (BT p. 300; McFee, 2015a pp. 48-49) for an overlapping set of philosophical perplexities; thereby to remove the perplexities of those not similarly treated therapeutically by my previous examples or discussions.

Notes

Chapter One

1 Some passages from PAD are recycled here. Having written them as well as I could, I felt no need to change these passages here.

2 See, for instance, Wollheim, 1993b [PAD p. 15].

3 Similarly, just attending to the elegant movements of Gemmill's goal is not really to watch the dance either — one is not recognizing the transfiguration into dance (art).

4 Note: if I write a song called, "The greatest song of all time", no one expects it *therefore* to *be* the greatest song — similarly, calling something a *happening* doesn't make it one.

5 As Austin (1979 p. 237) notes, "[p]hilosophers ... are too apt to assume that an action is always in the last resort the making of a physical movement ...".

6 My preferred example: Elaine Summers *Instant Chance* (mis-named as *Instant Choice* in PAD p. 79, and passim).

7 We should not forget "... that 'doing an action', as used in philosophy, is a highly abstract expression ..."; nor forget beginning to plot this technical/abstract use by asking, "Is to sneeze an action?" (Austin, 1979 p. 179).

8 Wittgenstein saw the connection of normativity to *human* action: hence (in PI §282) he highlights how cartoon teapots become candidate agents only when anthropomorphized; that is why (PI §281):

> Only of a human being, and what resembles (behaves like) a human being can one say: it has sensations; it sees, is blind, is deaf; is conscious or unconscious.

9 Thus, research showing a high-class batsman in cricket paying attention to the bowler's hand as he releases the ball is not relevant to the *coaching* of the game: that is not how one should *train* batters. [Better practical advice would be of the order of trying to get one's foot to the pitch of the ball.]

10 "Although a sentence can be perceived by the senses, we use it to communicate what cannot be perceived by the senses" (Frege, 1979 p. 197).

11 For elaboration, see Travis, 2008 pp. 150-160.

12 In other places, Frege deviates radically from this position (compare Travis, 2011 pp. 105-106); but at least acknowledges it sometimes. Here, I imagine him adopting it.

13 So claims that *seem* exceptionless (even speaking of "all", "never", and so on) should be read in this light: that granting their truth does not preclude contexts being found where there were exceptions. Thus, the claim that snow geese migrate to Labrador is true (if it is) even though some (the injured, the hunted) do not "... get quite the whole way" (Austin, 1975 p. 144): see EKT pp. 177-193.

Chapter Two

1 Throughout, I have stressed the concept *person* as the crucial one here: more strictly, if our concern was only with personal identity, we might follow Wiggins (2016 p. 96) in "... referring identity-questions about persons to identity-questions about human beings [since] ... [i]t is *human being* that is the plenary substance concept", and thereby avoid "... the temptation to antedate the death of a person to a time before their biological death" (Wiggins, 2016 p. 96 note 9).

2 Easy examples will be familiar material objects: tables, chairs, and the like. Aristotle (1984 p. 1624 [1028b10]) seems to suggest plants and animals as especially good examples.

3   Compare Wiggins (1980 p. 5) on Phaedrus (265e) on carving, or "dividing where the joints are".

4   Beginning from a claim by Hume ([1751] 1975 p. 307 note 2) that "... natural may be opposed either to what is *unusual, miraculous* or *artificial*" (original italics), and concentrating on the artificial, Wiggins (2016 p. 90) contrasts artefacts — such as artworks — with natural kinds by acknowledging (among other things) that for artefacts, typically, "... there are few if any lawlike tendencies that are specifically required of stoves as such (or clocks or pens or mils or ...) over and above their fulfillment of their particular function." But artworks are peculiar here; for instance in the problems typically generated for the identity-conditions of an artwork by the prospect of exchanging "... most or all of its bodily constituents for others" (Wiggins, 2016 p. 90). And, of course, dances are peculiar artefacts, both in being abstract objects and in their realizations typically being constituted of persons (substances) in action (contrast Wiggins, 1980 pp. 125-126).

5   Wiggins (1980 p. 125) addresses "... easel paintings, carved sculptures and frescoes ...", each a "material *particular*".

6   *Perdurantism*, discussed Chapter Five §5 (and note 7) offers another way to elaborate the "yes" answer.

7   I take this from correspondence; but see Wisdom, 1991 p. 40.

8   Feyerabend (1987 p. 272) provides this contrast between the practitioner's view of the matter and the philosopher's: see UD p. 307.

9   Wiggins (1980 pp. 72-73) discusses the counting principle, concluding that, "[i]t is one thing to be able to say how many fs there are in a determinate context. But it is another thing to have ... a perfectly general method of enumerating fs".

10   This point applies to ontological investigations generally: see Chapter Five § 2.

11   Here, *supervenience* is 'not arcane or theory-laden', but just one of what Anscombe ([1983] 2005 p. 103) describes as "*supervenient descriptions* ... a highly convenient *façon de parler*".

12   The long-awaited publication of Kripke's John Locke Lectures (Kripke, 2013 p. 90ff.) might re-awaken interest in Austin's claim.

13   That "Ateb" and "Aphla" are names, rather than descriptions, illustrates occasions when these too have primarily an *identifying-use*.

14   See the "man with a glass of champagne" (or martini) discussion in Donellan ([1966] 1971) esp. p. 103: and Kripke, 2013 p. 104 ff.

15   Wiggins, 1980 p. 36:

> Suppose official *a* is succeeded by official *b*. The petitioner therefore sees *b* on her second visit. She does not see the same office-holder but the holder of the same office, *whoever he is*. '*a* is the same official as *b*' doesn't ascribe numerical identity to *a* and *b* at all. It *predicates* something of them in common, holding a certain office.

As Wiggins wryly continues, "In the *sames's* extensive repertoire this is one of the better known roles". See also Wiggins, 1967 p. 18.

16   But, as with music, one can deviate from a score in an authentic performance (*pace* Goodman).

17   On this contextualist reading, determinacy only operates *in the context*, and not absolutely — a view Wiggins rejects, commenting that failure to recognize the need for absolute determinacy ignores the contribution of (especially) Frege and Lesnieskwi on "... the subject of soundness of concepts" (Wiggins, 1967 p. 43). See Wiggins, 2001 pp. xiii:

> ... to see that the principle of individuation for a buzzard is not the same principle as for a bat, to see that the principle of individuation for a teapot is not the same as for a

housefly — there is no more to this (and no less) than there is to seeing what a difference there is between *these things from a practical view of singling them out, of keeping track of them and of chronicling what they do.* (original italics)

18   Such a conception will be elaborated, and its suitability to deal with these issues defended in a projected book of mine, provisionally entitled *Philosophy and the 'Dazzling Image' of Science.*

Chapter Three

1   "... panpsychism should be added to the list of mutually incompatible and hopelessly unacceptable solutions to the mind-body problem". For his more recent view, see Nagel (2012 p. 12), where he confesses to looking for "... an alternative to physics as a theory of everything".

2   See also Williams, 2004 pp. 135-136, discussing Powers, 1983.

3   I have written in a number of places on the general philosophical issues concerning the possibility of genuine action or of free will: all contribute something here, since there are numerous overlaps amongst them. In particular, a number of passages here are drawn from McFee, 2015a pp. 311-342 (especially pp. 311-332), as my best formulation of each point.

4   To some, modern developments in science offer a different view. For a demonstration that this is false of Chaos Theory, see FW pp. 151-158: the Chaos Theorist's research tool is the computer!

5   An alternative: tendential theories urging only trends and tendencies: see Mumford & Anjum, 2014 p. 402:

Striking a match does not necessitate that it will light ... the flammable object tends — but no more than tends — to burn in certain circumstances. The match disposes towards burning when struck where such a disposition is short of necessity.

6   Consider two ideas (both from Anscombe & Geach, 1961 p. 102):

(a) ... if an expectation of the type 'it happens this way unless something interferes' is disappointed, this leads to another — often successful — attempt to find the interfering agent.

(b) ... inference cannot just be logically brought into a uniformity doctrine of causality ...

7   In alchemy, the luck of the alchemist might play a role.

8   Compare also Mumford & Anjum, 2014a p. 51.

9   For this reason, stochastic causation ("smoking cigarettes causes cancer") is often treated as incompletely-expressed causation (really, smoking plus X causes cancer), or second-class in some other away. At least, the *goal* is exceptionlessness.

10   By contrast, J. B. S. Haldane (quoted Flew, 1973 p. 97) urged:

Taking the record of any criminal, we could predict the behaviour of a monozygotic twin placed in the same environment.

This claim, while arguably false (since even monozygotic twins develop differently, both in the womb and later), catches the spirit of the determinist's assumptions.

11   Compare Davidson (1980 p. 241) where biology is contrasted with psychology.

12   See also Davidson (2005 p. 191) contrasting "... the 'strict' laws I think exist covering singular causal relations ... [with] ... the less than strict laws that can be couched in mental terms". [Why does only the first "strict" deserve the scare-quotes?]

13   From Geach's discussion of Aquinas (in Anscombe & Geach, 1961); quoted in note to McFee, 2015a p. 323.

14   Davidson (2001 p. 144) seems to exclude perception, writing that "... we can't get outside of our skins to find out what is causing the internal happenings of which we are aware"; and again: "The relation between a sensation and a belief cannot be logical, since sensations are not beliefs or other propositional attitudes. What then is the relation? The answer is, I think, obvious: the relation is causal" (Davidson, 2001 p. 143).

15   As Ryle (1954 p. 27) goes on to explain:

> ... a statement to the effect that something will exist or happen is, in *so far*, a general statement. When I predict the next eclipse of the moon, I have indeed got the moon to make statements about, but I have not got her next eclipse to make statements about.

Chapter Four

1   A fact partially recognized when the determinist treats causes as, say, "antecedent states *of the world*" (FW p. 21: my emphasis).

2   Note my account of determinism (Chapter Three §2), which requires that the conclusion be reached.

3   Of course, this is an illusion *only* for philosophy! Nothing here criticizes common-sense talk of one thing being the *cause* of another, although it might put pressure on the attempt to draw certain inferences from that talk.

4   See also WWK p. 182 [December, 1931]: Wittgenstein identifies, as a mistake typical in psychology "... the conception that there are questions the answers to which will be found at a later date. It is held that, although a result is not known, there is a way of finding it". [More explicitly, PI §308 identifies "processes and states" as seemingly requiring explanation.]

5   Contrast Anscombe (1957 §47 [p. 86] & [1983] 2005 pp. 100-101) on what counts as causal: see Chapter Three §4.

6   Searle (2008 p. 13) — where the NCC is "neurobiological" — imagines this being done in one of two ways; and, because the question is "How does the brain produce the unified, subjective consciousness field?" and "[t[he subjectivity of consciousness implies a unity", it makes sense to adopt "the unified field approach" (Searle, 2008 p. 144) — here the NNC is "Neuronal".

7   Note that for Searle (2008 p. 141) "... dreams are a form of consciousness that occur to us during sleep".

8   As above, Searle (2008 p. 13) has "neurobiological"; and later "neuronal" (Searle, 2008 p. 143).

9   For exposition, see Place ([1956] 1962); Smart ([1959] 1962). For critique, see Putnam, 1981 pp. 78-82.

10   Further, how does the physical event (say, the brain-state) come to also be a pain- or taste-sensation? Compare Nagel, 2012 pp. 38-43.

11   See, for example, Jeans (1930); and Jeans (1943 p. 216) writing, from the perspective of science, of "... the ghastly remains of matter ...".

12   That picture is further confused when causality is treated as having the kind of *forward*-looking necessity deployed by the determinist.

13   This remark is a fragment of one discussing what counts as "pain-behaviour" (or perception); specifically, Wittgenstein's point is that we can have no conception of what, say, a sea-squirt being blind or sighted would involve. Moving to the mereological fallacy involves another step. (A slightly different step yields my "Aphrodite Argument": see UD

pp. 256-266).

14   Notice here that Dennett (2007 p. 75) comments on the "crippling Cartesianism in Benjamin Libet's view of intentional action".

15   Notice that nothing here turns on my use of the term "state".

16   As my "Aphrodite Argument" (UD pp. 265-266) makes plain, with no finite totality of factors or properties appropriate to behaving *like a person*, the task of determining *success* in the project of androidology was necessarily unattainable; and the project with it!

17   At least for the sake of argument, I happily accept these claims about dreaming — since they are presented by my opponents.

Chapter Five

1   Originally called "The Pierrot Players".

2   Louther died tragically young in 1998.

3   Of course, some works may require a particular performer, not merely someone able to perform the dance (arguably, this is true of Jérome Bel's "Véronique Doisneau", 2004), or only one location might be permissible for performances of a particular work. But such works will certainly not be the *typical* cases to which a non-exceptionless characterization refers (compare "Snow geese migrate to Labrador" — true, even though some do not make it: see Austin, 1975 p. 143); here, Bel's self-definition of his choreographic style as "non-dance" surely speaks in that direction, since I take it to clarify a *kind* of dance-making, with connections to the traditions and history of such practices. Further, such works would not constitute counter-examples to my claims about the character of performables, not least because the claims were not presented as exceptionless. Moreover, even in this case, might no other account of the work be possible? Just as Michael Sheen could play the *role* of David Frost in *Frost/ Nixon* (2008), might some other dancer *play* the role of Véronique, at least in principle? What might preclude this? For one cannot automatically take the choreographer's word here: thus, although Martha Graham famously claimed that her roles would die with her, and performances by some later members of the company may have seemed to suggest she was correct, with the right dancer those roles could be danced again. Indeed, toward the end of her life, she did give some dancers the right to perform her roles: see de Mille, 1992 p. 276. [I owe much here to Anna Pakes, who kindly discussed these examples with me: I assume her rather different view of them will appear in her forthcoming monograph on dance ontology.]

4   Carroll (2001 p. 91) calls this a 'narrative', because there might be competing ones.

5   As mentioned in "Preamble" above, Peirce only gives a very thin account of this contrast (see PAD p. 309 note 11).

6   But who? Perhaps Goodman, 1969 p. 131 note. Levinson (2015 p. 45) recognizes this as a motivation only to deny that musical works were "... *pure abstract structures*, like geometrical forms"; as does Sharpe, 1983 p. 15. Applied to fictional characters, Lamarque (2010 p. 188) calls it "an eliminativist view". Perhaps it motivates *musical perdurantists* like Caplan & Matheson, 2006: see note 8 below, and §4.

7   An additional idea clarified through this example: the Stepanov-notated score fits Drigo's interpretation, but none of the others — hence, performing it generates *Swan Lake*, but it is not an adequate notation for that work.

8   Two key points here: first, my concern differs from those interested simply in elaborating a metaphysical scheme (say, the *perdurantism* introduced by Caplan & Matheson, 2006 as an alternative to *abstractionism*: discussed below §5) — having self-expressedly no interest in whether that scheme fits (for instance) music, and hence no connection to artworld

discussion, Caplan & Matheson give us no reason to adopt it. Second, locating danceworld practice may require a rational reconstruction of some claims by (say) dancers: misplaced dualism in the philosophy of mind provides the easiest example (compare McFee, 2013). But, while it is possible that (for example) large numbers of dancers just *fail to discuss* their perdurantist commitments — sitting like the felines in Eliot's "The Naming of Cats", each contemplating "his deep and inscrutable singular name" — their silence here, at least amongst those I know best, speaks against the suggestion that *most* dancers really regard dance performances as slices through a four-dimensional 'salami' that is the dancework.

9   The problem here is partly conceptual: they embody ways of looking at human movement; and must be learned as such.

10   Compare Mackrell, 1997 p. 74:

> The language that Graham invented was ... forged out of her own body. It was shaped by her own strong legs, wide pelvis and long, lean torso; it took its dramatic effect from her own darkly eloquent eyes and pale, haunting face.

11   See Levinson, 1996 p. 218 (PAD p. 136): what would most justifiably be ascribed to the artist "... on the basis of the perceptible features of the ... [artwork], a complete grasp of its context of production, and a full knowledge of the artist's intention as to how the work was to be taken, approached or viewed". Note (a) "full", "complete" represent finite totalities where there is none; (b) the artist's intention and the work's history of production can play into identification of that work.

12   Previously (PAD p. 175), my efforts were directed at explaining the real *responsibilities* of the dancer, as opposed to some he/she might mistakenly assume (see Chapter Six §§4-5).

13   Any who see the *craft* aspect of the term "craft mastery" (applied to reflective practitioners) as demeaning should recall that it is applied to, say, doctors — for instance, the eponymous hero of the television show *House*. At the least, this is not Collingwood's art/craft distinction.

14   To illustrate, Challis (1999 pp. 148-149) highlights the expressive resources of Russian vs. English ballet, noting "Ashton's choreography is not amenable to Russian interpretation ... [since it grows from] a different cultural tradition and a different historical context"; equally, for Paul Taylor, "[t]he contraction and spiral are fundamental to Taylor's style, and together with a sense of weight and undercurve [these] are the least understood movements in the restaging of his work" — not least because his version does not come naturally to dancers not trained in the technique he deploys!

15   This is true of many attempts to treat the everyday four-dimensionally: as we saw (Chapter Two §2), Wiggins (1980 p. 196) recognizes " ... some of the introductory explanations needing to lean on the crutch of the three-dimensional language ...", commenting that "... it is simply a mistake to suppose that we *must* ... identify the persisting entities articulated by the three-dimensional world view with those articulated by the four-dimensional".

16   One important reservation: if the concept of a dance-maker in my sense is a more recent innovation than I acknowledge, some of my examples (such as *Swan Lake*) will be misplaced (see PAD pp. 20-27). But the points could still be defended by more recent, if less familiar, works.

17   That there are abstract objects, or that these are examples of them, may be philosophically contentious; but it is so widely taught in schools as to offer a usual first step.

18   As Thomasson (1999 p. xii) notes, postulating *abstracta* "... lands them in the same waters as such diverse entities as numbers, universals, laws, theories, and stories".

19   For *thoughtlessly* betraying your secrets is not the same as doing so *inadvertently*. And shooting your donkey *by mistake* is not the same as shooting that donkey *accidentally*: see

Austin, 1979 p. 185 note.

20   These include: (a) "challenges to the interpretation of the work on macaques"; (b) challenges to "the supposed evidence of a mirror neuron system ... in humans analogous to the one identified for macaques"; (c) questioning "whether, if there are indeed neurons in humans with mirror properties [whatever *those* are], they are properly viewed as part of a system whose function is to facilitate action understanding or imitation" (Davies, 2013 p. 200b); and see PAD pp. 192-196. Here, I am with Tallis (2011 p. 109) that, first, the evidence from macaques is less clear than is sometimes claimed: thus, " ... mirror neurons could just be neurons that have been trained to associate with the movement of the monkey's own hand with the sight of this movement in any hand: in the first instance its own"; then, second, the scope of the connection to appreciation is easily exaggerated: "macaques who *do* have them [mirror neurons] don't seem to major in anything corresponding to human language, learned culture, art, empathy and morality".

21   Actually, many people who were studied initially were self-selected because of some possible medical condition.

22   Here, the connection of the conceptual to the perceptual must be acknowledged (see Chapter Eight §1): what one sees answers partly *what is there* to be seen, partly to the *cognitive stock* (Wollheim, 1980 pp. 193-195) that one brings to bear in perception.

Chapter Six

1   Of course, one cannot be expected to retain works permanently, thus generating problems in the reconstruction of dances lost through the memories of dancers: see UD p. 96: "What they could remember, they remembered ..." (Siegel, 1979 p. 81, discussing Charles Weidman's 1972 attempt to revive Doris Humphrey's *New Dance* [1935]).

2   See Mozart's letter of 20th April, 1782 to his sister Konstance: "... I had already composed the fugue and was writing it down while I worked out the prelude in my head" (Spaethling, 2000 p. 308).

3   She might not always be willing to report this, but ...

4   In UD (p. 204; p. 321 note 4), I reported my experience of watching a group of gifted young dancers: their technical virtuosity was sufficient for the works, but the movements were unsuited (and therefore unconvincing) on their young bodies.

5   Tharp, 2003 p. 195: "He'd sit there, viewing the catastrophe onstage, and imagine how he would have done it differently. ... It's one way he honed the skills that made him one of the greatest show doctors of all time".

Tharp, 2003 p. 233: Faced with someone who seemed to be enjoying the piece, "'Oh no,' said the woman, 'I like it. I just don't know where to get my information'".

6   Stravinsky apparently thought dance a place to appreciate his music: writing for dance "... provided him with a venue to have his music heard by people who could appreciate it" (Tharp, 2003 p. 138). But, as Eliot (1921) noted, of an early performance of *The Rite of Spring* — they do not always appreciate Stravinsky's ability:

> ... to transform the rhythm of the steppes into the scream of the motor horn, the rattle of machinery, the grind of wheels, the beating of iron and steel, the roar of the underground railway, and other barbaric cries of modern life; and to transform these despairing noises into music.

[Eliot seems right in stressing *two* transformations here.]

7   They have also acquired a sense of the *performance traditions* for works of this sort: see Chapter Seven §§5-6.

Chapter Seven

1   This is not just Ateb and Aphla (one 'object' seen from two perspectives): compare Frege, 1980 p. 80.

2   And many more. In locating an author, or an artist, in his/her period, we are typically trying to highlight the perplexities to which that work gave outlet. Sometimes, the facts will be local to this artist (say, John Donne's marriage); sometimes, they will be far more global — the preoccupations of the time, for instance.

3   Here, persons should be contrasted with, say, personalities: we do not expect man and boy to agree in politics, nor (always) even to shared memories.

4   *The Collected Plays of Jack B. Yeats* (London: Secker & Warburg, 1971) lists no "first performance" for this play: my student production was in 1973. The argument here would gain an additional poignancy were this its first (and so perhaps only) performance.

5   For instance, for Franko (1989 p. 58), the reconstructors are aiming "... to evoke what no longer is, with the means of what is present": this does not seem to reject, to the same degree, the ontology of danceworks as existent at a particular time.

6   I would insist that this is said clearly in McFee, 2003; and in PAD Chapter Ten.

7   My thanks to Renee Conroy for reminding me of this passage.

8   And, of course, I would urge that a notated score, *adequate* in my sense (PAD Chapter Three), might be an asset here.

9   Although Mackrell was writing specifically about male dancers, the point still holds for today's female dancers.

10   So these difficulties have a direct bearing on dance experience, for identifying *dance meaning* through such experience remains problematic.

11   Still, similar difficulties might arise outside of the understanding of *performing* arts.

Chapter Eight

1   "When I can tell at sight a Mauser rifle from a javelin...".

2   A personal experience of mine, although shared (or at least described) by Michael Polanyi, 1973 p. 101.

3   As Julie Van Camp noted, in comments at the ASA Pacific Division meeting, Asilomar, 2015.

4   To repeat an example (PAD p. 113-114).

5   Moreover, the dance critic can function as a *maker of taste* (see below: Carroll, 2008 pp. 192-193) precisely because one can learn to *see the dance as dance*; and hence *learn* to appreciate it as dance.

6   Moore here reports himself trying, where possible, to give Wittgenstein's own words. Compare also Moore (2016 p. 351): "All that Aesthetics does is to draw your attention to things: e.g. 'This is the climax'. It places things side by side: e.g. this prepares the way for that".

7   On the related notion of *the imaginal*, with similar points made, see UD p. 222.

8   Is this in Walton? Certainly, he sometimes writes in this vein: for instance, on painting: "The viewer imagines seeing a fire engine as she looks at a fire engine, imagining her actual experience to be of a fire engine" (Walton, 2008a p. 143). And similarly, perhaps, for dance.

9   Literature presents a problem for my view — perhaps one suiting Walton? — since there is no straightforward verb of perception here (compare Diffey, 1991 pp. 125-138); and there seems a stronger role for the reader's imagination. But Walton's own account does not seem helpful: thus, discussing Wallace Stevens, Walton (2015 p. 168) wants to see the Stevens' poem as a prop for his imagining; but that does not give the poem itself a

sufficient role — and it cannot help to make that role causal! And Stevens is not imagining, is he?

10   As, for instance, Walton (1990 p. 15) seems to, in trying to capture someone's having "bearish thoughts" as part of imagining "... coming across a bear in the forest".

11   See Frege, 1984 p. 368 note: "grasp" as metaphorical.

12   Equally, are these all the options?

13   See, especially Dummett (1993 pp. 104-105) commenting on two different pictures of *sense* [as borne by *thoughts*]: "... one when he was concerned with the relation between sense and reference; and one when he was striving to elaborate the ontological status of senses, involving the mythology of the third realm". For him, "[g]rasping a sense is immediate. An object cannot be given to us save in a particular way, the particular way in which it is given constituting a sense to which the object appears as referent" (Dummett, 1993 p. 105). Thus, although "[t]he sense may be expressed in different words ... it is not given to us at all, but simply grasped" (Dummett, 1993 p. 105).

14   Note that Quine (1974 p. 79) offered an account of analytic truths, as those truths everyone learns in learning to understand them.

15   Here, Quine also clearly applies the point through language-learning to meaning.

16   Montero (2013 p. 175 note 19), citing Anscombe's view, writes "Graham McFee seems to argue along these lines in *Understanding Dance*" — she offers no page-citation. What is the force of "seems" here? While Montero refers only to Anscombe's book *Intention* (1957) [again, without page-citation], the context there has Anscombe plotting the role of intentions in one's non-observational knowledge.

17   I ascribe the ideas to Wittgenstein, given that the notes were taken immediately after discussions with him: as Malcolm (1984 p. 40) records, "[t]hese notes were not intended to be verbatim, although sometimes they may have been partly so".

Chapter Nine

1   Wollheim, 1995 p. 35: "This point about correct and incorrect perception of a painting and the role of the artist's intention in deciding between them is most readily, most effectively, made in the case of figurative painting. But it applies no less cogently to abstract painting".

2   See Wollheim (1987 p. 43): "An artist must fill the role of agent ... but he must also fill the role of spectator" — more bluntly, "The artist is essentially a spectator of his work" (Wollheim, 1987 p. 39).

3   Wollheim, 1995 p. 34: "... recapitulating, but in a highly compressed fashion, and therefore without benefit of argument, what I have set out at greater length, and, I hope, more persuasively, in *Painting as an Art*".

4   Thus, Wollheim (1987 p. 36) "... if we are to understand when and why painting is an art, we must consider it from the perspective of the artist". This means, in context, from the perspective of that connects the artist's view of his work with his view of the artform into which it contributes (and his conception both of the historical narrative and the current state of that artform).

5   Rectified for the artistic/aesthetic contrast.

6   As Davies (2011 p. 196) rightly notes, "Montero argues ... that proprioception, insofar as it can misrepresent the disposition of my body – as, for example, in the case of 'phantom limb' experiences – has the power to represent its object as being a certain way ...". But the possibility of being *misled* here provides no basis for the general claim: it is not that I have some misleading *evidence* for the disposition of my hand, but that I am temporarily unaware of its absence.

7   T. S. Eliot "Hamlet" in his *Selected Essays* (London: Faber & Faber, 1951), pp. 141-146: quote p. 145.

8   Copeland & Cohen (eds), 1983, referred to throughout as "C&C", includes passages from John Martin, especially his *The Modern Dance* (1933).

9   I owe this formulation, and the insistence on the point, to Renee Conroy.

10   Martin famously modified this, at the end of his career, in turning to ballet criticism.

11   Compare Mackrell, 1997 p. 75: "... Graham's dance was rooted in the gut"; or urging that, by contrast with Graham's, "... Cunningham's movement is light" (Banes, 1994 p. 110).

12   Perhaps reflecting a concern with voxels, not neurons!

13   One might even question research that investigates seeing dances (and our responses to it) through watching *videos* of dances.

14   Montero thinks one can *judge* proprioceptively because one can be wrong (say, via phantom limbs: see Davies, 2011 p. 196). This account of experience is often dualist, although not in Descartes himself (CSM II p. 53), for whom amputees erroneously judging that they have pains in their missing limbs are deceived by their first internal sense: they come to the erroneous judgement *that the limb hurts*. An (Aristotelian) doctrine of internal senses cannot aid Montero; and, while the possibility of error here supports the idea of this being *judgement*, it militates against its reliability. And hence (as in the main text) reflects the gap between one's *knowledge* and what one claims.

Chapter Ten

1   Of course, we know how one *learns* to do this, at both at a minimal level (shared by most humans) and a high level achieved by, among others, dancers and sportsplayers.

2   Thus, according to Tallis (2011 p. 285), for Zeki, "Mondrian ... speaks preferentially to cells in regions V1 and V4, while Fauves stimulate V4 plus the middle frontal convolutions": see Zeki, 2000 p. 63; Kawabata & Zeki, 2004.

3   As Hornsby (1997 p. 240 note 16) recognized, "[w]hat cannot be guaranteed ... is that, having assembled a notion of behaviour by reference to two explanatory schemes, one has then accorded some stable sense to 'explanation of behaviour' or 'behavioural disposition'." Or, more forcefully, that "[n]othing in the argument holds these two conceptions of behavioural disposition together" (Hornsby, 1997 p. 124).

4   Learning that these are "bias competition models of selective attention" (Carroll & Seeley, 2013 p. 178b) has not alleviated my concerns.

5   Crucial here will be the answerability discussion: see note 7 + Chapter Eight §2

6   The units here are really at least based around the making of statements; and hence more closely resemble sentences.

7   Compare Travis (2011 p. 91) on empiricists using "the argument from illusion ... [as] the means of locating the observable".

8   Consider here Cioffi's rebuttal: as reported in Anscombe (1981a p. 12), when Frank Cioffi asked his students what they saw, presenting them with an object, they routinely reported seeing a straight stick in a glass of water; but it was a trick glass — with a straight stick *not* in the water.

9   Again the right place to begin is with actual human perception (in contrast to the study in the UK: Reason & Reynolds, 2010).

10   To motivate the question, Stokes considers a stylized experiment, imagining "[a] subject primed with either an image of a toy pony or a toy gun ... After the prime is removed, [the subject] ... views an ambiguous inkblot" and is forced to choose whether the image was

of "… something girls like or something boys like". No doubt some children, well-primed by life, will regard guns as things that girls like, and ponies as things that boys like. But suppose each was asked what he/she *saw*: I would certainly reward those who replied, correctly, that they *saw* an inkblot. And, if they are *then* asked what was depicted in/by what they saw, my vote would go to those who responded that, since this was an inkblot and *depiction* was an intentional concept, it necessarily depicted nothing.

11   Carroll acknowledges many other roles for critics (for instance, elucidation, interpretation) as well as consumer guide; but most are performed to explain this one.

12   See Chapter Five note 13.

13   Tallis (2011 p. 77) gives an example where "… all that can be observed is the additional activity associated with the stimulus …"; and such additional activity "… can be identified only by a process of averaging the results of subsections after the stimulus has been given repeatedly; variations in successive stimuli are ironed out". He comments, "[t]he raw data tell a very different story from the cooked" (Tallis, 2011 p. 77). So we are not addressing *obviously* absolute data, but rather 'trends and tendencies' across cases — there is no single uniform effect. And typically, "… experiments looked at the response to very simple stimuli …" (Tallis, 2011 p. 77) — since "… it is easier to examine the flexing of a wrist to activity recorded using electromyography than to interpret a performance of *Giselle* in this way" (Tallis, 2011 p. 282). Compare Libet (2005), discussed in Chapter Three §9; Soon et al. (2013).

14   Wittgenstein (PO p. 421) is reported as urging:

> We would never have said 'If only we knew the laws, then …' if we hadn't got science; and science could only start with obvious regularities, going on to less obvious regularities.

15   "Treatise on Man": CSM I p. 108:

> I should like you to consider that these functions follow from the mere arrangements of the machine's organs every bit as naturally as the movements of a clock or any other automaton follow from the movements of its counter-weights and wheels. In order to explain these functions, then, it is not necessary to conceive of this machine as having any vegetative or sensitive soul or other principle of movement and life, apart from its blood and its spirits, which are agitated by the heat of the fire burning continuously in its heart – a fire which has the same nature as all the fires that occur in inanimate bodies.

To the question from Danto (2013 p. 95), Descartes' answer (6th Med CSM II p. 61 [end of para 22]) is that:

> … nothing else [other than the present arrangement] which would have been so conducive to the continued well-being of the body. In the same way, when we need a drink, there arises a certain dryness in the throat, which in turn moves the inner parts of the brain. This motion produces in the mind a sensation of thirst, because the most useful thing for us to know about the whole business is that we need to drink in order to stay healthy.

So, for Descartes, my nature as a union of mind and body has been instituted by God in such a way as to promote the welfare of this mind-body union — even though God could not have made our nature as a union of mind and body such that it never misled us. This consideration helps me both to notice and to correct my errors.

Why is 'our nature' such that it is bound to mislead us from time to time? Descartes' point is that it is better that dryness in the throat should occasionally have some other cause than "… that it should always mislead us when the body is in good health" [p. 61: para 23].

Chapter Eleven

1   As we noted (Chapter One note 4), merely calling something a *happening* doesn't make it one, just as my writing a song called "The greatest song of all time" cannot alone lead us to expect it to *be* the greatest song.

2   One might worry whether dances themselves are abstract objects: but, in any case, the only concrete (therefore visible and answerable) objects here are *performances*.

3   To count as speech, sounds must have 'understanders'.

4   Interestingly, as profound a theorist (and appreciator) of music as Bob Sharpe does not seem to distinguish the hearing of the musical work from hearing a recording of that work (see, for instance, Sharpe, 1983 p. 18).

5   Here, one might usefully note the relation of features of the dance (as captured by description of it) and critical interpretations of that dance: since the interpretation must be *answerable* (with answerability in part to 'what the artist intended': PAD pp. 130-140), the difference need not be so great.

6   Sontag & I differ on movies here!

7   In a passage I remembered long after writing most of the above, Bob Sharpe (1983 p. 26) remarks:

> It seems to me that the considerations of the critic, the range of techniques available, and their peculiarity to film, make an unanswerable case for regarding film neither as a mixed art nor as a filmed dramatic performance but as an art *per se*.

I agree entirely. (See also Sharpe, 1983 pp. 71-72.)

8   This view is apocryphally attributed to many great stage actors who subsequently work on the screen: certainly, it captures aspects of Laurence Olivier's criticism of method-acting for the screen, as undermining the contrast with rehearsing or 'walking through' — that, in reality, one needed to be clear when one was *acting*.

9   As suggested by the ancestry of the term "aesthetic", in the Greek word for sense-perception.

10   NB issue of "reading" for novels (as not a verb of perception) is set aside: compare Diffey, 1991 pp. 125-138.

11   Contrast dance-critic Lewis Segal (2008 p. F9) claiming that:

> My parrot, Steve, lives in a cage near the TV set and so has seen more dance than many Southlands balletomanes — although he much prefers car chases, parades, game shows, hurricanes ...

[To repeat an example: PAD p. 113-114 + See Chapter Seven.]

12   Moreover, the dance critic can function as a *maker of taste* (see below: Carroll, 2008 pp. 192-193) precisely because one can learn to *see the dance as dance*; and hence *learn* to appreciate it as dance.

13   Contrast Scruton, 1983, who suggests that if my photograph of the goddess Aphrodite is of a woman in costume (or out of it), the transformation takes place 'in the real world', and is then photographed. It is in this sense that photography is transparent.

14   Assuming it was never part of a travelling exhibition, a facile counter-case.

15   And here the recording of music can be set aside. For music is at least arguably composed of (performed) *tones*; exactly what the recording might be thought to preserve! And hence a major disanalogy, insofar as recorded dances cannot involve the *bodies* necessarily in performance.

16   I owe the attribution to Lee Brown (2011 p. 181), who urges that, for Gracyk (1997), a recording "stands between the audience and the music 'like the sheet of glass that protects the painting from the audience in the art museum'". Brown discusses the view in his own

voice in "Phonography" (Brown, 2005; see especially p. 212).

17   For (a) "... what he has made is *his*": so he is responsible for it, both as author and as receiving any praise or blame. So, from the artist's perspective:

> [h]e made it; he is responsible for it; if it expresses anything, it expresses him; it can be properly understood and appreciated only in the light of his having made it.

For only in that light can the novel be located in its precise place in the narrative of art history in that artform (which might, say, recognize the language as English of a certain period, or as archaic, or ...). But also (b) that "... what he has made is a *novel*": that is what he is responsible for (Wollheim, 1978 p. 37: all quotes).

18   When Levinson (1996 p. 218) urges (for a painting) that understanding an artwork, or grasping its embodied meaning, is conceived in terms of what can most justifiably be ascribed to the artist:

> ... on the basis of the perceptible features of the painting, a complete grasp of its knowledge of production, and a full knowledge of the artist's intentions as to how the work was to be taken, approached or viewed ...

Of course, those committed to occasion-sensitivity would certainly want to comment on the "complete", and "full", here — seeing each as indicating potential defeating conditions. But, with that in place, this account applies directly to poems: "the perceptible features of the paining" then become the material condition of the poem: certainly the words on the page, but also (perhaps) the state of the page — paper or vellum, typed printed or autograph, and so on. For, in the right cases, any such features might with justice bear on how the poem was to be correctly read; or, perhaps better (since we do not necessarily subscribe to a single 'correct' reading), how to rule out certain mis-readings. [Compare PAD pp. 150-152]

19   Contrast various view of literature as performance: for instance, Kivy, 2008.

20   This too is complex: some painters have studio-artists who do much of the painting.

Bibliography

Acocella, Joan *Mark Morris*. New York: Farrar, Straus & Giroux, 1993.

Anscombe, G. E. M. *Intention*. Oxford: Blackwell, 1957.

———— [1958] "Modern Moral Philosophy", reprinted in M. Geach and L. Gormally (eds) *Human Life, Action and Ethics: Essays by G. E. M. Anscombe*. Exeter, UK: Imprint Academic, 2005 pp. 169-194.

———— "The Intentionality of Sensation: A Grammatical Feature", in her *Metaphysics and The Philosophy of Mind (Collected Papers Vol. Two)* Oxford: Blackwell, 1981a pp. 3-20.

———— "On Sensations of Position" in her *Metaphysics and The Philosophy of Mind (Collected Papers Vol. Two)* Oxford: Blackwell, 1981b pp. 71-74.

———— [1983] "The Causation of Action", reprinted in Mary Geach & Luke Gormally eds *Human Life, Action and Ethics: Essays by G. E. M. Anscombe*. Exeter: Imprint Academic, 2005 pp. 89-108.

Anscombe, G. E. M. & Geach, P. T. *Three Philosophers: Aristotle, Aquinas, Frege*. Oxford: Blackwell, 1961.

Aristotle *Metaphysics*, in *The Complete Works of Aristotle*. (Volume Two) Princeton, NJ: Princeton University Press, 1984 pp. 1552-1728.

———— *Poetics*, in *The Complete Works of Aristotle*. (Volume Two) Princeton, NJ: Princeton University Press, 1984 pp. 2316-2340.

Austin, Richard *Birth of a Ballet*. London: Vision Press, 1976.

Austin, J. L. *Sense and Sensibilia*. Oxford: Clarendon Press, 1962.

———— *How to Do Things with Words*. Oxford: Clarendon Press, 1975.

———— *Philosophical Papers* (3rd Edition). Oxford: Clarendon Press, 1979.

Baker, Gordon *Wittgenstein's Method: Neglected Aspects*. Oxford: Blackwell, 2004.

Baldwin, Thomas *Contemporary Philosophy (Philosophy in English Since 1945)*. Oxford: Oxford University Press, 2001.

Bambrough, Renford *Reason, Truth and God*. London: Methuen, 1969.

Banes, Sally *Terpsichore in Sneakers: Post-Modern Dance*. Hanover, NH: Wesleyan, 1987.

———— *Watching Dancing in the Age of Postmodernism*. Hanover, NH: Wesleyan, 1994.

———— *Dancing Women: Female Bodies on Stage*. London: Routledge, 1998.

———— *Before, Between, and Beyond: Three Decades of Dance Writing*. Madison, WI: University of Wisconsin Press, 2007.

Baumeister, R. F., Masciampo, E. J., & Vohs, K. D. "Can Conscious Thoughts Cause Behaviour?", *Annual Review of Psychology*. Vol. 62, January, 2011 pp. 331-361.

Beardsley, Monroe *The Possibility of Criticism*. Detroit: Wayne State University Press, 1970.

Beckett, Samuel [1971] *Disjecta: Miscellaneous Writings with a Dramatic Fragment*. London: John Calder, 1983.

Bennett, M. R. "Neuroscience and Philosophy", in Daniel Robinson (ed.) *Neuroscience and Philosophy: Brain, Mind, and Language*. New York: Columbia University Press, 2007 pp. 49-69.

————— & Hacker, P. M. S. *Philosophical Foundations of Neuroscience*. Oxford: Blackwell, 2003.

————— "The Conceptual Presuppositions of Cognitive Neuroscience: A Reply to Critics", in Daniel Robinson (ed.) *Neuroscience and Philosophy: Brain, Mind, and Language*. New York: Columbia University Press, 2007 pp. 127-162.

Best, David *Expression in Movement and the Arts*. London: Lepus, 1974.

————— *Philosophy and Human Movement*. London: George Allen & Unwin, 1978.

————— *The Rationality of Feeling*. London: Falmer Press, 1992.

————— "Dance Before You Think" in G. McFee (ed.) *Dance, Education and Philosophy*. Aachen: Meyer & Meyer, 1999, pp. 99-121.

Blacking, J. "Movement, Dance, Music and Venda Girl's Initiation" in P. Spencer (ed.) *Society and the Dance*. Cambridge: Cambridge University Press, 1985 pp. 64-91.

Blades, Hetty "Scoring Choreography: Process and Bodies in Digital Forms", *Motio: Post Graduate Journal of Dance Research and Practice*. No. 1, 2013 pp. 1-15 [on-line].

————— "Affective Traces in Virtual Spaces", *Performance Research: A Journal of the Performing Arts*. Vol. 20, No 6, 2015 pp. 26-34.

Blakemore, Colin *The Mind Machine*. London: BBC Books, 1999.

Brown, Lee "Phonography", in David Goldblatt & Lee B. Brown (eds) *Aesthetics: A Reader in the Philosophy of the Arts*. (Second Edition) Upper Saddle River, NJ: Pearson, 2005 pp. 212-218.

————— "Is Live Music Dead?" in David Goldblatt & Lee B. Brown (eds) *Aesthetics: A Reader in the Philosophy of the Arts*. (Third Edition) Upper Saddle River, NJ: Pearson, 2011 pp. 180-185.

Calvo-Merino, Beatriz "Towards a Sensorimotor Aesthetics of Performing Art", *Consciousness & Cognition*, Vol. 17, 2008 pp. 911-922.

—————, Glaser, D. E., Grezes, J., Passingham, R. E. & Haggard, P. "Action Observation and Acquired Motor Skill: An fMRI Study with Expert Dancers", *Cerebral Cortex*, Vol. 15, 2005 pp. 1243-1249.

Caplan, Ben & Matheson, Karl "Defending Musical Perdurantism", *British Journal of Aesthetics*, Vol. 46, No. 1 2006 pp. 59-69.

Carnap, Rudolf *Logical Foundations of Probability*. London: Routledge & Kegan

Paul, 1950.

Carroll, Nöel *Beyond Aesthetics*. Cambridge: Cambridge University Press, 2001.

———— *The Philosophy of Motion Pictures*. Oxford: Blackwell, 2008.

———— *On Criticism*. London: Routledge, 2009.

———— *Art in the Third Dimension*. Oxford: Oxford University Press, 2012.

Carroll, Nöel & Seeley, William P. "Kinesthetic Understanding and Appreciation in Dance", *Journal of Aesthetics and Art Criticism*, Vol. 71, No 2 Spring, 2013 pp. 177-186.

Cavell, Stanley *Must We Mean What We Say?* New York: Scribners, 1969/2002 [Updated Edition — Cambridge: Cambridge University Press, 2002].

———— *The World Viewed (Expanded Edition)*. Cambridge, MA: Harvard University Press, 1979.

———— *Pursuits of Happiness*. Cambridge, MA: Harvard University Press, 1981.

———— *Little Did I Know: Excerpts from Memory*. Stanford CA: Stanford University Press, 2010.

Challis, Chris "Dancing Bodies: Can the Art of Dance be Restored to Dance Studies?", in G. McFee (ed.) *Dance, Education and Philosophy*. Aachen: Meyer and Meyer, 1999 pp. 143-153.

Churchland, Patricia S. *Neuro-Philosophy: Towards a Unified Science of Mind-Brain*. Cambridge, MA: MIT/Bradford, 1986.

Cioffi, Frank "Intention and Interpretation in Criticism", in Cyril Barrett (ed.) *Collected Papers on Aesthetics*. Oxford: Blackwell, 1965 pp. 161-183.

Cohen, Selma Jean "John Martin", in *International Encyclopedia of Dance* Vol. 4. Oxford: Oxford University Press, 1998.

Collingwood, R. G. *The Principles of Art*. Oxford: Clarendon Press, 1938.

Conroy, Renee "Dance" in Anna C. Ribiero (ed.) *Continuum Companion to Aesthetics*. London: Continuum, 2011 pp. 156-170.

———— "Responding Bodily" *Journal of Aesthetics and Art Criticism*, Vol. 71, No 2 Spring, 2013 pp. 203-210.

Coplan, Amy & Davies, David (eds) *Blade Runner*. Abingdon: Routledge, 2015.

Copeland, Roger & Cohen, Marshall (eds) *What is Dance?* Oxford: Oxford University Press, 1983.

Croce, Arlene *Afterimages*. London: A&C Black, 1978.

———— *Going to the Dance*. New York: Alfred Knopf, 1982.

Culbertson, Leon & McFee, Graham "'The Best Way to Locate a Purpose in Sport: In Defence of a Distinction in Aesthetics", *Aesthetic Investigations*, Vol. 1, No. 2, 2015 pp. 191-213.

Cunningham, Merce *The Dancer and the Dance: Merce Cunningham in Conversation with Jacqueline Lesschaeve*. New York: Scribners, 1984.

Danto, Arthur [1964] "The Artworld", *Journal of Philosophy*, reprinted in G.

Dickie, R. Sclafani & R. Roblin (ed.) *Aesthetics: A Critical Anthology*. (3rd Edition) St. Martins Press, 1989 pp. 171-182.

———— [1965] "Basic Actions", reprinted Alan R White (ed.) *The Philosophy of Action*. Oxford: Oxford University Press, 1968 pp. 43-58.

———— *The Transfiguration of the Commonplace*. Cambridge, MA: Harvard University Press, 1981.

———— "The De Kooning Three-Seater", reprinted in his *The State of the Art*. New York: Prentice Hall, 1987 pp. 58-61.

———— *Connections to the World: The Basic Concepts of Philosophy*. New York: Harper Row, 1989.

———— *After the End of Art: Contemporary Art and the Pale of History*. Princeton, NJ: Princeton University Press, 1997.

———— "Art and Meaning" in Carroll, Noël (ed.) *Theories of Art Today*. University of Wisconsin, 2000 p. 130-140.

———— *What Art Is*. New Haven: Yale University Press, 2013.

Davidson, Donald *Essays on Actions and Events*. Oxford: Clarendon Press, 1980.

———— *Subjective, Intersubjective, Objective*. Oxford: Clarendon Press, 2001.

———— *Truth, Language and History*. Oxford: Clarendon Press, 2005.

Davies, David *Art as Performance*, Oxford: Blackwell, 2003.

———— *Philosophy of the Performing Arts*. Oxford: Wiley-Blackwell, 2011.

———— "Dancing Around the Issues: Prospects for an Empirically Grounded Philosophy of Dance", *Journal of Aesthetics and Art Criticism*, Vol. 71, No 2 Spring, 2013 pp. 195-202.

Dennett, Dan "Philosophy as Naive Anthropology" in Daniel Robinson (ed.) *Neuroscience and Philosophy: Brain, Mind and Language*. New York: Columbia, 2007 pp. 73-95.

Descartes, Rene *The Philosophical Writings of Descartes* (Three Volumes). Cambridge: Cambridge University Press, 1984 — cited as "CSM" + vol. number.

Diffey, T. J. *The Republic of Art*. New York: Peter Lang, 1991.

Dodd, Julian *Works of Music: An Essay in Ontology*. Oxford: Oxford University Press, 2007.

Donagan, Alan *The Late Philosophy of R.G. Collingwood*. Oxford: Clarendon, 1962.

Donellan, Keith "Reference and Definite Descriptions" (1966), reprinted in Danny D. Steinberg & Leon A. Jakobovits (eds) *Semantics: An Interdisciplinary Reader*. Cambridge: Cambridge University Press, 1971 pp. 100-114.

Dummett, Michael *Origins of Analytic Philosophy*. Cambridge, MA: Harvard University Press, 1993.

———— *Thought and Reality*. Oxford: Oxford University Press, 2006.

———— *The Nature and Future of Philosophy*. New York: Columbia University

Press, 2010.

Eliot, T. S. "London Letter", *The Dial*, Issue 71, October, 1921 pp. 452-455.

Feyerabend, Paul K. *Farewell to Reason*. London: New Left Books, 1987.

Flew, Antony *Crime or Disease?* London: Macmillan, 1973.

———— *Darwinian Evolution*. London: Grafton, 1984.

Foot, Philippa *Natural Goodness*. Oxford: Clarendon Press, 2001.

Foster, Susan Leigh "Dancing Bodies" in Jane C. Desmond (ed.) *Meaning in Motion: New Cultural Studies of Dance*. Durham: Duke University Press, 1997 pp. 235-257.

Franko, Mark "History/theory — criticism/practice" in Susan Leigh Foster (ed.) *Corporealities*. London: Routledge, 1996, pp. 25-52

Frege, Gottlob *Posthumous Writings*. Oxford: Blackwell, 1979.

———— *Philosophical and Mathematical Correspondence*. Chicago: University of Chicago Press, 1980.

———— [1918] "Thoughts", in his *Collected Papers on Mathematics, Logic and Philosophy*. Oxford: Blackwell, 1984 pp. 351-372.

Freud, Sigmund [1905] "On Psychotherapy" in *The Standard Edition of the Complete Psychological Works of Sigmund Freud*. Volume 7, London: Vintage Classics, 1966 pp. 257-270.

———— [1940] *The Outline of Psychoanalysis*. in *The Standard Edition of the Complete Psychological Works of Sigmund Freud*. Volume 23, London: Vintage Classics, 1966 pp. 141-207.

Fuller, Fuller *Beyond the Crisis in Art*. London: Writers & Readers, 1980.

Goehr, Lydia "Being True to The Work" *Journal of Aesthetics and Art Criticism*, Winter, 1989 pp. 55-67.

Goodwin, Geoffrey P. & Darley, John M. "The Psychology of Meta-ethics: Exploring Objectivism", *Cognition* Vol. 106, 2008 pp. 1339-1366.

Goodman, Nelson *Languages of Art*. Indianapolis: Bobbs-Merrill, 1968.

Gracyk, Theodore "Listening to Music: Performances and Recordings", *Journal of Aesthetics and Art Criticism*, Vol. 55, No 2, 1997 pp. 139-150.

Grice, Paul *Studies in the Ways of Words*. Cambridge, MA: Harvard University Press, 1989.

Ground, Ian *Art or Bunk?*, Bristol: Bristol Classical Press, 1989.

Hacker, P. M. S. "Locke and the Meaning of Colour Words", in G. Vesey (ed.) *Impressions of Empiricism*. London: Macmillan, 1976 pp. 23-46.

———— *Human Nature: The Categorial Framework*. Oxford: Blackwell, 2007.

———— *The Intellectual Powers: A Study of Human Nature*. Oxford: Wiley/Blackwell, 2013.

Hamilton, James R. *The Art of Theater*. London: Blackwell, 2007.

Hampshire, Stuart *Thought and Action*. New York: Viking Press, 1959.

Hanfling, Oswald *Philosophy and Ordinary Language: The Bent and Genius of Our Tongue*. London: Routledge, 2000.

Harris, Sam *Free Will*. New York: Free Press, 2012.

H'Doubler, Margaret *Dance: A Creative Art Experience*. Madison: University of Wisconsin Press, 1940.

Heilpern, John *Conference of the Birds: The Story of Peter Brook in Africa*. London: Routledge, 1999.

Hornsby, Jennifer *Simple Mindedness: In Defence of Naïve Naturalism in the Philosophy of Mind*. Cambridge, MA: Harvard University Press, 1997.

Hume, David [1741] "Of the Standard of Taste", in his *Essays, Moral, Political, and Literary*. New York: Liberty Fund, 1985 pp. 231-257.

———— [1751] *Enquiry Concerning the Principles of Morals*. Oxford: Clarendon Press, 1975.

Humphrey, Doris *The Art of Making Dances*. New York: Grove Press, 1959.

Jabr, Ferris "Cache Cab: Taxi Drivers' Brains Grow to Navigate London's Streets", *Scientific American*. December 8th, 2011.

James, William [1890] *The Principles of Psychology*. New York: Henry Holt/Dover, 1950.

Jeans, James *The Mysterious Universe*. New York: Dover, 1930.

———— *Physics and Philosophy*. New York: Dover, 1943.

Jenett, Lorian "Notes on Annotation", *Performance Research: A Journal of the Performing Arts*. Vol. 20, No 6, 2015 pp. 24-25.

Jowitt, Deborah *Jerome Robbins: His Life, His Theatre, His Dance*. New York: Simon & Schuster, 2004.

Kaeppler, Adrienne "Structured Movement Systems in Tonga", in P. Spencer (ed.) *Society and the Dance*. Cambridge: Cambridge University Press, 1985 pp. 92-118.

Kant, Immanuel [1787] *Critique of Pure Reason*. (trans. P. Guyer & D. Wood) Cambridge: Cambridge University Press, 1996.

———— [1788] *Critique of Practical Reason*. (trans. Lewis White Beck) Indianapolis: Liberal Arts Press/Bobbs-Merrill, 1956.

Kawabata, Hideaki & Zeki, Semir "Neural Correlates of Beauty", *Journal of Neurophysiology*, Vol. 91, 2004 pp. 1699-1705.

Kivy, Peter "What Makes Aesthetic Terms *Aesthetic?*", *Philosophy and Phenomenological Research*, Vol. 36, 1975 pp. 197-211.

———— *Music Alone: Philosophical Reflections on the Purely Musical Experience*. Ithaca: Cornell University Press.

———— *The Performance of Reading: An Essay in the Philosophy of Literature*. London: Wiley-Blackwell, 2008.

Kripke, Saul *Philosophical Troubles: Collected Papers Volume 1*. Oxford: Oxford University Press, 2011.

———— *Reference and Identity*, Oxford: Clarendon, 2013.

Kuhn, T. S. *The Structure of Scientific Revolutions (2nd Edition)*. Chicago: University of Chicago Press, 1970.

Laban, Rudolf *Choreutics*. London: Macdonald & Evans, 1966.

Lamarque, Peter *Work and Object: Explorations in the Metaphysics of Art*. Oxford: Clarendon Press, 2010.

Jerrold Levinson "Extending Art Historically" in his *The Pleasures of Aesthetics: Philosophical Essays*, Ithaca, NY: Cornell University Press, 1996.

———— *Contemplating Art*. Oxford: Clarendon, 2006.

———— *Musical Concerns: Essays in the Philosophy of Music*. Oxford: Clarendon Press, 2015.

Libet, Benjamin *Mind Time: The Temporal Factor in Consciousness*. Cambridge, MA: Harvard University Press, 2005.

Locke, John [1689] *An Essay Concerning Human Understanding*. (ed. P. H. Nidditch) Oxford: Clarendon Press, 1975.

Lucas, J. R. *The Freedom of the Will*. Oxford: Clarendon Press, 1970.

McDowell, John *The Engaged Intellect: Philosophical Essays*. Cambridge, MA: Harvard University Press, 2009.

McFee, Graham *Understanding Dance*. London: Routledge, 1992.

———— *Free Will*. Teddington: Acumen, 2000.

———— "Cognitivism and the Experience of Dance" in A. C. Sukla (ed.) *Art and Experience*. Westport, CT: Praeger, 2003 pp. 121-143.

———— *The Concept of Dance Education (Revised Edition)*. Eastbourne: Pageantry Press, 2004.

———— "Defending the Artist's Theory: Wollheim's Lost Idea Regained?" *Estetika*, Vol XLVII/III No. 1, 2010a pp. 3-26.

———— *Ethics, Knowledge and Truth in Sports Research: An Epistemology of Sport*. London: Routledge, 2010b.

———— *The Philosophical Aesthetics of Dance: Identity, Performance, and Understanding*. Alton, Hants: Dance Books, 2011a.

———— *Artistic Judgement: A Framework for Philosophical Aesthetics*. Dordrecht: Springer Verlag, 2011b.

———— "In Remembrance of Dance Lost", *Choros: International Journal of Dance*. XXX, 2012.

———— "Defusing Dualism: John Martin on Dance Appreciation", *Journal of Aesthetics and Art Criticism* Vol. 71 No 2 Spring, 2013 pp. 187-194.

———— *How To Do Philosophy: A Wittgensteinian Reading of Wittgenstein*. Newcastle-upon-Tyne: Cambridge Scholars Press, 2015a.

———— *On Sport and the Philosophy of Sport*. London: Routledge, 2015b.

———— *Philosophy and the 'Dazzling Image' of Science*. (forthcoming)

McTaggart, John McTaggart Ellis [1906] *Some Dogmas of Religion*. New York: Greenwood, 1968.

Mackrell, Judith *Reading Dance*. London: Michael Joseph, 1997.

Malcolm, Norman *Ludwig Wittgenstein: A Memoir (New Edition)*. Oxford: Oxford University Press, 1984.

Martin, John *The Modern Dance*, 1933 — cited from Copeland & Cohen, 1983 as "C&C".

————— [1939] *Invitation to the Dance*. Brooklyn, NY: Dance Horizons, 1965 — cited as "M".

Meisner, Nadine "Obituary: William Louther", *The Independent*, Monday, 3rd August, 1998.

Mellor, Hugh *The Facts of Causation*. London: Routledge, 1995.

Metheny, Eleanor *Movement and Meaning*. New York: McGraw-Hill, 1968.

Mille, Agness de *Martha: The Life and Work of Martha Graham*. New York: Random House, 1992.

Montero, Barbara "Proprioception as an Aesthetic Sense" *Journal of Aesthetics and Art Criticism*, Vol. 62, 2006 pp. 231-242.

————— "Practice Makes Perfect: The Effect of Dance Training on the Aesthetic Judge" *Phenomenology and the Cognitive Sciences*, Vol. 11, 2012 pp. 58-68.

————— "The Artist as Critic: Dance Training, Neuroscience, and Aesthetic Evaluation", *Journal of Aesthetics and Art Criticism*, Vol. 71 No 2 Spring, 2013 pp. 169-175.

Moore, G. E. *Wittgenstein: Lectures, Cambridge 1930-1933*. [eds D. Stern, B. Rogers & G. Citron] Cambridge: Cambridge University Press, 2016.

Mumford, Stephen *Watching Sport: Aesthetics, Ethics and Emotion*. Abingdon: Routledge, 2012.

————— & R. L. Anjum *Getting Causes from Powers*. Oxford: Oxford University Press, 2011.

————— & R. L. Anjum "The Tendential Theory of Sporting Prowess", *Journal of Philosophy of Sport*. Vol. 41, No. 3. 2014 pp. 399-412.

Nagel, Thomas *Other Minds: Critical Essays 1968-1994*. Oxford: Oxford University Press, 1995.

————— *Mind and Cosmos: Why the Materialist Neo-Darwinian Conception of Nature is Almost Certainly False*. Oxford: Oxford University Press, 2012.

O'Connor, D. J. *Free Will*. London: Macmillan, 1971.

Pakes, Anna *Choreography Invisible: The Disappearing Work of Dance*. New York: Oxford University Press (forthcoming).

Palmer, Frank *Literature and Moral Understanding*. Oxford: Clarendon, 1992.

Parfit, Derek *Reasons and Persons*. Oxford: Clarendon, 1984.

Parry, Jan "Let Them Eat Doughnuts", *The Observer Review*, 13th January, 2002 p. 14.

Pasles, Chris "Getting to the Root of Dance Rights", *LA Times Calendar*, 6th August, 2006 p. E35.

Perry, John *Identity, Personal Identity and the Self*. Indianapolis: Hackett, 2002.

Pickard, Hanna "Knowledge of Action Without Observation", *Proceedings of the Aristotelian Society*, Vol. 104, 2004 pp. 206-230.

Place, U. T. [1956] "Is Consciousness a Brain Process?" in V. C. Chappell (ed.) *The Philosophy of Mind*. Englewood Cliffs, NJ: Prentice Hall, 1962 pp. 101-109.

Polanyi, Michael *Personal Knowledge*. London: Routledge & Kegan Paul, 1973.

Powers, Willliam Review of Judith Hanna *To Dance is Human* for *Journal of Anthropological Studies of Human Movement*, Vol. 3 No. 1, 1983 pp. 49-51.

Putnam, Hilary *Reason, Truth and History*. Cambridge: Cambridge University Press, 1981.

———— *The Three-Fold Cord: Mind, Body and World*. New York: Columbia University Press, 1999.

Quine, Willard Van Orman "Two Dogmas of Empiricism", in his *From a Logical Point of View*. New York: Harper & Row, 1953 pp. 20-46.

———— [1956] "Quantifiers and Propositional Attitudes", reprinted in his *The Ways of Paradox, and Other Essays*. New York: Random House, 1966 pp. 183-194.

———— *Word and Object*. Cambridge, MA: MIT Press, 1960.

———— *Ontological Relativity, and Other Essays*. New York: Columbia University Press, 1969.

———— *The Roots of Reference*. Illinois: La Salle, 1974.

———— "Indeterminacy of Translation Again", *Journal of Philosophy* Vol. 84, No. 1, 1987 pp. 5-10.

Reason, Matthew & Reynolds, Dee "Kinaesathesia, Empathy and Related Pleasures: An Inquiry into Audience Experiences of Watching Dance", *Dance Research Journal*, Vol. 42, No. 2, 2010 pp. 48-75).

Reid, Thomas [1815] *Essays on the Intellectual Powers of Man*. (ed. Derek R. Brookes) Edinburgh: Edinburgh University Press, 2002.

Robinson, Daniel (ed.) *Neuroscience and Philosophy: Brain, Mind, and Language*. New York: Columbia University Press, 2007.

Rosen, Charles *Schoenberg*. London: Fontana, 1976.

Rubridge, Sarah "Identity and the Open Work", in Stephanie Jordan (ed.) *Preservation Politics: Dance Revived Reconstructed Remade*. London: Dance Books, 2007 pp. 205-211.

Ryle, Gilbert *The Concept of Mind*. London: Hutchinson, 1949.

———— *Dilemmas*. Cambridge: Cambridge University Press, 1954.

Sachs, Kurt *World History of the Dance*. (trans. B. Schönberg) London: George Allen & Unwin, 1937.

Schön, Donald *Educating the Reflective Practitioner*. San Francisco: Jossey-Bass, 1987.

Schreiber, F. R. *Sybil*. New York: Henry Regnery, 1973.

Scruton, Roger "Photography and Representation", in his *Aesthetic Understanding*. Manchester: Carcanet Press, 1983 pp. 119-148.

———— *An Intelligent Person's Guide to Modern Culture*. South Bend, IN: St.

Augustine's Press, 1998.

Searle, John *Speech Acts*. Cambridge: Cambridge University Press, 1969.

———— "Putting the Brain Back into Consciousness" in Daniel Robinson (ed.) *Neuroscience and Philosophy: Brain, Mind and Language*. New York: Columbia University Press, 2007 pp. 97-124.

———— *Philosophy in a New Century: Selected Essays*. Cambridge: Cambridge University Press, 2008.

Segal, Lewis "An Art of Stolen Glances", *Los Angeles Times Calendar*, Sunday, January 6th 2008 p. F9.

Sharpe, R. A. *Contemporary Aesthetics: A Philosophical Analysis*. New York: St. Martin's Press, 1983.

———— *Music and Humanism: An Essay in the Aesthetics of Music*. Oxford: Oxford University Press, 2000.

Shoemaker, Sidney *Self-Knowledge and Self-Identity*. Ithaca, NY: Cornell University Press, 1963.

Siegel, Marcia *At The Vanishing Point*. New York: Saturday Review Press, 1972.

———— *Watching the Dance Go By*. New York: Houghton Mifflin, 1977.

———— *The Shapes of Change*. Boston: Houghton Mifflin, 1979.

Skinner, B. F. *Science and Human Behaviour*. New York: Macmillan, 1953.

———— *Beyond Freedom and Dignity*. Harmondsworth: Penguin, 1979.

Smart, J. C. C. [1959] "Sensations & Brain Processes" in V. C. Chappell (ed.) *The Philosophy of Mind*. Englewood Cliffs, NJ: Prentice Hall, 1962 pp. 160-172.

Soon, Chun Siong, et al. "Predicting Free Choices from Abstract Inventions" in *Proceedings of the National Academy of Sciences USA* Vol. 110, No 15, April 9th 2013 pp. 6217-6222.

Spaethling, Robert (ed.) *Mozart's Life, Mozart's Letters: Selected Letters*. New York: Norton, 2000.

Spinoza, B. [1677] *Ethics*. (Ed. & Trans. G. H. R. Parkinson) Oxford: Clarendon, 2001.

Stebbing, Susan *Philosophy and the Physicists*. Harmondsworth: Penguin, 1937.

Stokes, Dustin "Cognitive Penetration and the Perception of Art", *Dialectica*. Vol. 68, No. 1, 2014 pp. 1-34.

Strawson, Peter F. *Introduction to Logical Theory*. London: Methuen, 1952.

Stroud, Barry "Taking Scepticism Seriously", in his *Understanding Human Knowledge*. Oxford: Oxford University Press, 2000 pp. 38-50.

Syed, Matthew *Bounce: The Myth of Talent and the Power of Practice*. London: Fourth Estate, 2010.

Tallis, Raymond "The Limitations of a Neurological Approach to Art", *The Lancet*, Vol. 372, No. 9632, 2008 pp. 19-20.

———— *Aping Mankind: Neuromania, Darwinitis and the Misrepresentation of*

Humanity. Durham, UK: Acumen, 2011.

Tharp, Twyla *Push Comes To Shove: An Autobiography*. New York: Bantam Books, 1992.

———— *The Creative Habit: Learn It and Use It for Life*. New York: Simon & Schuster, 2003.

———— *The Collaborative Habit: Life Lessons for Working Together*. New York: Simon & Schuster, 2009.

Thigpen, C. H. & Cleckley, H. M. *Three Faces of Eve*. New York: McGraw-Hill, 1957.

Thomasson, Amie L. *Fiction and Metaphysics*. Cambridge: Cambridge University Press, 1999.

———— "The Ontology of Art and Knowledge in Aesthetics", *Journal of Aesthetics and Art Criticism*, Vol. 63, 2005 pp. 221-229.

Toulmin, Stephen *Human Understanding (Volume One)*. Oxford: Clarendon, 1972.

Travis, Charles *Thought's Footing*. Oxford: Clarendon, 2006.

———— *Occasion-Sensitivity: Selected Essays*. Oxford: Clarendon Press, 2008.

———— *Objectivity and the Parochial*. Oxford: Clarendon Press, 2011.

———— *Perception: Essays After Frege*. Oxford: Clarendon Press, 2013.

Truffaut, François *Hitchcock: A Definitive Study* (Revised Edition). New York: Simon & Schuster, 1985.

Urmson, J. O. "The Performing Arts" in H. D. Lewis (ed.) *Contemporary British Philosophy (4th Series)*. London: George Allen & Unwin, 1976 pp. 239-252.

Von Wright, G. H. *Causality and Determinism*. New York: Columbia University Press, 1974.

Waismann, Friedrich "Verifiability" in his *How I See Philosophy*. London: Macmillan, 1968 pp. 39-66.

Walton, Kendall *Mimesis as Make-Believe*. Cambridge, MA: Harvard Umiversity Press, 1990.

———— "Categories of Art", reprinted in his *Marvelous Images: On Values and the Arts*. Oxford: Oxford University Press, 2008 pp. 195-219.

———— "Depiction, Perception and Imagination", reprinted in his *Marvelous Images: On Values and the Arts*. Oxford: Oxford University Press, 2008a pp. 143-155.

———— *In Others Shoes: Music, Metaphor, Empathy, Existence*. Oxford: Oxford University Press, 2015.

Warnock, G. J. "On What Is Seen" in F. N. Sibley (ed.) *Perception: A Philosophical Symposium*. London, Methuen, 1971 pp. 1-12.

Wiggins, David *Identity and Spatio-Temporal Continuity*. Oxford: Blackwell, 1967.

———— "On being in the same place at the same time", *Philosophical Review*, 1968 pp. 90-95; reprinted in Wiggins, 2016 pp. 33-38.

———— *Sameness and Substance*. Oxford: Blackwell, 1980.

———— *Sameness and Substance Renewed*. Cambridge: Cambridge University Press, 2001.

———— *Continuants: Their Activity, Their Being and Their Identity: Twelve Essays*. Oxford: Oxford University Press, 2016.

Wilkes, Kathleen *Real People: Personal Identity without Thought Experiments*. Oxford: Clarendon Press, 1988.

Williams, Bernard *Descartes: The Project of a Pure Enquiry*. Harmondsworth: Penguin, 1978.

———— *Essays and Reviews 1959-2002*. Princeton, NJ: Princeton University Press, 2014.

Williams, Drid *Anthropology and the Dance: Ten Lectures*. Urbana: University of Illinois Press, 2004.

Wimsatt, W. K. & Beardsley, Monroe "The Intentional Fallacy" in J. Margolis (ed.) *Philosophy Looks at the Arts*. (2nd ed.) New York: Scribners, 1978 pp. 293-306.

Wisdom, John *Philosophy and Psycho-Analysis*. Oxford: Blackwell, 1953.

———— *Paradox and Discovery*. Oxford: Blackwell, 1965.

———— *Proof and Explanation: The Virginia Lectures*. Lanham, MA: University Press of America, 1991.

Wittgenstein, Ludwig *Philosophical Investigations*. (trans. G. E. M. Anscombe). Oxford: Basil Blackwell, 1953. [50th Anniversary Edition, 2001; 4th Revised Edition, edited by P.M.S. Hacker & Joachim Schulte. Oxford: Blackwell, 2009.].

———— *The Blue and Brown Books*. Oxford: Blackwell, 1958.

———— *Zettel*. Oxford: Blackwell, 1967.

———— *On Certainty*. (trans. D. Paul & G. E. M. Anscombe) Oxford: Blackwell, 1969.

———— *Philosophical Grammar*. (trans. A. Kenny) Oxford: Basil Blackwell, 1974.

———— *Philosophical Remarks*. (trans. R. Hargreaves & R. White) Oxford: Blackwell, 1975.

———— *Wittgenstein and the Vienna Circle*. Oxford: Blackwell, 1979.

———— *Culture and Value*. (trans. Peter Winch) [2nd Edition: 1998] Oxford: Basil Blackwell, 1980.

———— *Philosophical Occasions 1912-1951*. edited J. Klagge & A. Nordmann. Indianapolis: Hackett Publishing Company, 1993.

———— *The Big Typescript: Ts 213*. (trans. C. G. Luckhardt & M. A. E. Aue) Oxford: Blackwell, 2005.

———— & Waismann, Friedrich *The Voices of Wittgenstein*. (ed. Gordon Baker) London: Routledge, 2003.

Wölfflin, Heinrich *Principles of Art History*. New York: Dover, 1950.

Wollheim, Richard *On Art and the Mind*. Harmondsworth: Allen Lane, 1973.

———— "Are the Criteria of Identity that Hold for a Work of Art in the Different Arts Aesthetically Relevant?" *Ratio* Vol. 20 No. 1 (June) 1978 pp. 29-48.

———— *Art and Its Objects* (Second Edition). Cambridge: Cambridge University Press, 1980.

———— *Painting as an Art*. London: Thames & Hudson, 1987.

———— "Art, Interpretation and Perception", in his *The Mind and Its Depths*. Cambridge, MA: Harvard University Press, 1993a pp. 132-143.

———— "Danto's Gallery of Indiscernibles" in M. Rollins (ed.) *Danto and His Critics*. Oxford: Blackwell, 1993b pp. 28-38.

———— *On Formalism and its Kinds*. Barcelona: Fundacio Antoni Tapies, 1995.

Woltersdorff, Nicholas *Works and Worlds of Art*. Oxford: Clarendon, 1980.

Yeats, Jack B. *The Collected Plays of Jack B. Yeats*. (ed. R. Skelton) London: Secker & Warburg, 1971.

Young, Liane & Durwin, A. J. "Moral Realism as Moral Motivation: The Impact of Meta-ethics on Everyday Decision Making", *Journal of Experimental Social Psychology*, Vol. 49, 2013 pp. 302-306.

Zeki, Semir *Inner Vision: An Exploration of Art and the Brain*. Oxford: Oxford University Press, 2000.

Index

Lightning Source UK Ltd.
Milton Keynes UK
UKHW011251110621
385340UK00002B/70